Ada
for Experienced Programmers

A. Nico Habermann
Carnegie-Mellon University

Dewayne E. Perry
Pegasus Systems and Carnegie-Mellon University

ADDISON-WESLEY PUBLISHING COMPANY

Reading, Massachusetts · Menlo Park, California
London · Amsterdam · Don Mills, Ontario · Sydney

This book is in the Addison-Wesley Series in Computer Science

Consulting Editor
Michael A. Harrison

Library of Congress Cataloging in Publication Data

Habermann, A, Nico, 1932–
    Ada for Experienced Programmers

    1. Ada (Computer program language) 2. PASCAL (Com-
puter program language) I. Perry, Dewayne E. II. Title.
QA76.73.A35H3 1982   001.64'24   82-20757
ISBN 0-201-11481-X

Scope ® Registered trademark of Control Data Corporation
VMS ™ Trademark of Digital Equipment Corporation
CP/M ® Registered trademark of Digital Research Incorporated
UNIX ™ Trademark of Bell Laboratories

Reproduced by Addison-Wesley from camera-ready copy prepared
by the authors.

ISBN 0-201-11481-X
ABCDEFGHIJ-AL-89876543

Preface

The goal of this book is a presentation of the major features of the Ada programming language and their relevance to software engineering. Since concepts such as data abstraction, exception handling and concurrency are of fundamental importance to the design and maintenance of software systems, we will explain in detail how Ada's facilities support such concepts. We do this by discussing a series of non-trivial example programs that exhibit the typical use of the relevant language constructs. The examples are chosen on the basis of their suitability in illustrating specific language features. Software engineering issues are taken into account, but are not the primary motivation for selecting the particular examples. Our goal is achieved if the examples demonstrate to what extent the Ada language supports good programming style in software engineering.

This book is written for experienced programmers who, when learning a new language, must often choose between using an introductory text and using a reference manual. Either choice is unsuitable, because an introductory text contains too much explanation, ignoring a programmer's knowledge and experience, whereas a reference manual contains too little explanation, aiming at a complete and concise description of the language syntax and semantics. This book supplies a need between these two extremes. On the one hand, unlike an introductory text, it exploits the reader's general knowledge of programming languages and standard programming techniques. On the other hand, unlike a reference manual, it explains the significance of the language features by detailed discussions and apt examples.

There are several ways in which this book can be used. The most obvious use is for Pascal programmers who want to learn Ada, because we have chosen the Pascal language to establish the level of experience we expect of the reader. An equally valid use is for programmers who want to learn Ada, but have experience with languages other than Pascal. These programmers can restrict their reading to the Ada sections, because the Ada sections are not dependent on the Pascal sections. A further use is as a handbook on Ada for software engineers. If a programmer wants to refresh his memory regarding a particular Ada feature, he will find, in many cases, a concise discussion of that feature and an illustration of its use. Finally, the Pacal discussions by themselves constitute an adequate introduction to Pascal for programmers who are familiar with other languages.

Certain language constructs receive more emphasis than others. We believe, for instance, that the control structures for conditional and repeated execution are well understood. We also believe that the concept of subtypes is more important than that of derived types and that the notion of model numbers is of only minor importance. Thus, instead of containing an exhaustive list of every Ada feature, the book presents the facilities that every programmer should use.

We use Pascal as a convenient stepping stone towards Ada for two reasons: First, Ada is a new language in the tradition of Pascal and hence, there is a close similarity between the two languages with respect to the control constructs, the concepts of user-defined types, and the functions and recursive procedures. Second, a demonstration of the serious deficiencies of Pascal yields a better appreciation for the importance of many design decisions in Ada.

All chapters, except the introductory chapter, have the same format. Each chapter begins with a problem statement and a discussion of an algorithm independent of programming language considerations. To provide a basis for the comparison between Ada and Pascal, the problem discussion is followed by the development of a complete Pascal solution in which we comment on the suitability and limitations of Pascal. Subsequently, we present a solution in Ada, introducing suitable language features and discussing important language issues as they arise. We begin the discussion of the Ada solution with a version that closely resembles the preceding Pascal solution. We then refine the Ada solution into one that exploits more fully the richness of the Ada language.

The discussions of a solution in both programming languages are followed by a presentation of a complete program in each language. This enables the reader to compare the programs as a whole, which is difficult to do solely on the basis of the detailed discussions. Each chapter concludes with a set of reminders and a number of programming problems. The reminders are a summary of the particular features that were applied and of the language issues that arose in the development of the programs. In addition to the obvious purpose, the problems also serve to elaborate the language issues and sometimes to extend the discussion to related issues that were ommitted. Hints to the solutions of these problems are collected at the end of the book.

The book consists of three parts: an introductory chapter, nine chapters dealing with sequential language features and six chapters and an appendix dealing with concurrent language features. In the introductory chapter we present a brief look at the development of programming languages, discuss the similarities and major differences between Pascal and Ada, and cover the traditional language constructs of declarations, control statements and expressions.

In the sequential part, the central themes of our discussions are the concepts of data types in Pascal and of data abstraction in Ada. Starting with the open types and the limited abstraction in Pascal, the discussion proceeds to the various degrees of information hiding and abstraction available in Ada. In addition, we show the generalization of the static objects in Pascal into the flexible, dynamic objects in Ada.

In the third part, we discuss the traditional problems of concurrent processes such as synchronization, mutual exclusion and communication. First, we solve a number of classical problems that naturally require concurrent solutions. We then consider some typical systems programming problems that require the use of Ada's low level language features in addition to the concurrent features. Since

Pascal has neither facilities for concurrency nor low level features, it is difficult to maintain the comparison between the two languages in the third part of the book. However, there is some merit in solving the classical problems in Pascal and in comparing the result with a solution in Ada because the original solutions to these problems were described in the literature in languages like Pascal. The difficulty is partly resolved by extending Pascal to include semaphores with P and V operations and the notion of a process. For the remainder of the third part, we drop Pascal because too many additional features would be needed.

Earlier, we remarked that the examples were chosen for their suitability in demonstrating specific language issues. Likewise, a particular approach to a solution is chosen primarily for pedagogical reasons rather than for reasons of efficiency or elegance. For example, extraneous variables may be introduced for clarity, subprograms that are called only once may be used for partitioning a program into subproblems, or language constructs may be applied just for the sake of illustration and comparison. In those cases in which we do pay attention to efficiency or elegance, the purpose is to demonstrate the capabilities of the Ada language rather than the existence of an efficient or elegant algortihm.

Discussions of major language issues are complete and self-contained, and do not require the availability of the reference manuals. However, we provide extensive citations to the reference manuals in order to correlate our presentations with the relevant sections in the manuals and we encourage the reader to consult the language manuals frequently. The abbreviation for the Pascal reference manual is PRM and that for the Ada reference manual is ARM. The editions we used are:

Pascal	Pascal User Manual and Report
	Lecture Notes in Computer Science, 18
	Springer-Verlag, Berlin, Heidelberg, New York (1974)
Ada	Reference Manual for the Ada Programming Language[1]
	United States Department of Defence (July 1982)
	Draft Revised MIL-STD 1815
	Order Number l008-000-00354-8
	U.S. Government Printing Office, Washington DC 20402

---

[1]Ada is a registered trademark of the U.S. Government, Ada Joint Program Office

Acknowledgement

Many people have made valuable contributions during the writing and production of this book. We are very grateful to Dorothy Josephson for typing the manuscript and to Cynthia Hibbard for carefully reading the text and correcting our writing style. We also wish to mention Ed Frank for showing us how to handle the Omnitech printer and Suzanna Garreau for her assistance with the editing. Both our families were very helpful in proofreading and correcting the text. Finally, a number of reviewers made useful suggestions for improvements in the presentation of the material and the organization of the book.

Pittsburgh, Pa
Summit, NJ
February 1983

Table of Contents

One

Ada Compared to Pascal

In this chapter we first characterize the major ideas that underlie the programming languages Pascal and Ada, then we compare the two languages with respect to the traditional programming language constructs and finally we survey the Ada language features that support software engineering. The discussion of the traditional language constructs shows that the control structures, the expression syntax and the subprogram constructs are very similar in the two languages. However, the survey of Ada's support for software engineering shows that Ada has many important facilities that are lacking in Pascal.

The introduction gives the reader a first impression of the Ada language, its special features and its relationship to Pascal. The examples presented in this chapter are brief and do not deal with the issues in detail. This is done in order to avoid duplication between this chapter and subsequent chapters in which the language constructs and their variations are discussed in detail and are applied to realistic problems.

1.1 The Basic Ideas Underlying Pascal and Ada

The history of symbolic programming languages begins with the design of FORTRAN in 1957. FORTRAN is the first language that liberates the programmer from having to name registers and memory locations and that allows the programmer to write expressions in the common mathematical notation instead of as sequences of machine instructions. Among the important contributions of FORTRAN are the introduction of control structures for iteration (the DO loop) and conditional execution (the IF statement), and the concept of subprograms that allows for parts of a program to be defined separately from the main program (computational abstraction).

The next important step is the design of Algol60 which strongly influenced programming language design during the sixties. This language introduced a number of fundamental concepts that are still of great significance in modern programming languages. The major concepts introduced in Algol60 are dynamic arrays (the size of such arrays is computed when the declaration is processed), recursive procedures (procedures that can call themselves), value and name parameters (cf. Chapter 6), and scope rules (which limit the existence of named objects to parts of a program).

The development of programming language design during this period was strongly dominated by concerns for the definition and processing of language constructs. Research focused on programming language syntax, formal grammars, parsing and compiling techniques. Simula67 and Algol68 are the culmination of this development. Pascal, which was published in 1970, represents a simplification of the results of this period.

Many of the ideas of Algol60, such as recursive procedures, scope rules and control structures, are retained in Pascal. Some important simplifications are static instead of dynamic arrays, reference instead of name parameters and the removal of block structure. The major extensions of Pascal compared to Algol60 are the inclusion of type *character*, of record structures and of user defined types. These ideas are not unique to Pascal, but have their analogues in languages such as Simula67 and Algol68. Programming languages of this period provide mechanisms for computational abstraction (provided by their function and procedure mechanisms) and for structuring of data (through their user-defined data types).

The emphasis of language research in the 1970's shifted considerably from that of the 1960's. Researchers and practitioners alike realized that there were more important issues than just language constructs, namely programming methodology and software engineering.

The contributions of research in programming methodology are found in the work on structured programming, program verification, and information hiding. Consequently, we now have a better understanding of the distinction between specification and implementation and of the various forms of abstraction. Software Engineering is primarily concerned with the issues that arise in the construction and maintenance of large systems. The results of this research have clarified the need for modularity, various forms of abstractions, exception handling, concurrency and hardware representations.

The Ada language, which was first published in 1980, reflects not only the results of language design in the 1960's, but also includes support for the new insights of the 1970's. The traditional constructs of the 1960's are discussed in the next section, while the specific Ada features that support software engineering are discussed in the last section of this chapter.

1.2 The Traditional Language Constructs

The traditional programming language constructs can be partitioned into the following categories:
- type declarations
- data declarations
- expressions
- control statements
- subprograms and parameters
- scope rules.

We will briefly discuss each of these categories and compare the features provided by both languages.

Type Declarations

Pascal and Ada both provide standard types for integers, floating point numbers, characters and Booleans. In addition, both languages provide four kinds of user-defined types:
- enumeration types;
- array types;
- record types;
- pointer types (called access types in Ada).

The following examples show that the differences between the declarations of user-defined types in the two languages are only minor.

```
type   direction   =   (North, East, South, West);         {Pascal}
       score       =   array[1 . . 10] of integer;
       account     =   record actnr, credit : integer end;
       actptr      =   ↑ account;
```

```
type   direction   is (North, East, South, West);          -- Ada
type   score       is array(1 . . 10) of INTEGER;
type   account     is record actnr, credit : INTEGER; end record;
type   actptr      is access account;
```

Note that the keyword **type** is used only once in Pascal, but is used for every type declaration in Ada. The key symbol "=" in Pascal corresponds to the keyword **is** in Ada. Two other slight differences are the use of square brackets in the Pascal array type declarations versus the parentheses in Ada and the use of the closing delimiter **end record** in Ada versus the single keyword **end** in Pascal. The fields of a record in Ada are always terminated by a semicolon, while in Pascal the last field in a record declaration is not terminated by a semicolon. Finally, the keyword **access** in Ada has exactly the same meaning as the symbol " ↑ " in Pascal type declarations.

We did not list Pascal's subrange type among the user-defined types, because this concept does not correspond to a *type* in Ada, but to the notion of a *scalar subtype*. A declaration of a scalar subtype does not introduce a new type, but defines a contiguous set of values of the base type.

> **type**   weekday   = Monday . . Friday;   {Pascal}
> **subtype** weekday   **is** day **range** Monday . . Friday;   -- Ada

The keyword **type** for a subrange type in Pascal is in fact inappropriate, because, just as in Ada, Pascal's subrange type introduces no new type, but identifies a subset of values of an existing type. Note the difference in syntax: Ada's subtype definition requires the name of the base type and the keyword **range**.

Ada provides two other kinds of subtypes: array subtypes and record subtypes. One can initially declare an array type without fixing the index bounds, but one must then fix the bounds at a later time by a subtype declaration. Record types can be declared with value parameters as one normally finds in a function or procedure declaration. The value of a record parameter is specified in a subtype declaration in a way similar to that of fixing the array bounds. These issues are discussed in detail in Chapters 3 and 4.

Both languages provide some predefined functions that apply to arguments of various types. Pascal provides the predefined function *ord* for all enumeration types and the predefined functions *pred* and *succ* for all scalar types except real. In Ada, predefined functions associated with types are called ATTRIBUTES of the type. The attribute POS corresponds to the Pascal function *ord* and the attributes PRED and SUCC correspond to the Pascal functions *pred* and *succ*. Ada has many more attributes than those listed here. For example, scalar types have the attributes FIRST and LAST, enumeration types the attributes POS and VAL and array types the attributes FIRST, LAST, LENGTH and RANGE. Attributes are also defined for fixed and floating point types, for record types, for access types and for tasks and entries (ARM appendix A, A-1). These attributes will be discussed in subsequent chapters as the need arises.

Ada has a very important type that does not occur in Pascal, namely the type **task type**. While other types are templates for data objects, task types are templates for process objects. Task types are used extensively in the third part of the book which deals with multitasking.

Data Declarations

Both languages have data declarations of the following kinds:
- constant declarations
- scalar declarations
- array declarations
- record declarations
- pointer declarations.

A major distinction between the two languages is that Pascal's data declarations are static, while Ada's data declarations are dynamic. This means that in Pascal declarations are expressed in terms of constants that are known at compile time, while in Ada declarations may be expressed in terms of program variables. Consequently, the size of structured objects in Ada may not be known at compile time, but is computed when the declaration is processed.

Another important distinction between the two languages is that in Ada a data object may be initialized in the declaration. This feature assures that data objects start their life in a well-defined initial state when that is needed. Other minor differences between the two languages are illustrated by the following examples.

```
const    pi        = 3.141592;                          {Pascal}
         capa      = 'A';
var      dir       : direction;
         x, y      : weekday;
         myscore   : score;
         timecard  : array [weekday] of integer;
         myact     : account;
         time      : record hr : 1 . . 24; min, sec : 1 . . 60 end;
         myactptr  : actptr;
         scoreptr  :   ↑ score;
```

```
pi        :  constant FLOAT := 3.141592;                  -- Ada
capa      :  constant CHARACTER := 'A';
upperb    :  constant INTEGER := N + 1;
stdscore  :  constant score := (1 . . 4 => 10, others => 15);
stdact    :  constant account := (1, 199);
dir       :  direction;
x ,y      :  weekday := Monday;
myscore   :  score := stdscore;
timecard  :  array (weekday) of INTEGER;
dynarray  :  array (1 . . N) of FLOAT := (1 => 1.0, others => 0.0);
myact     :  account;
youract   :  account := (820809, 340);
myactptr  :  actptr;
```

Note that Pascal uses the keywords **const** and **var** once to introduce the constant and variable declaration sections, while Ada does not use an introductory keyword for data declarations at all. The Ada constant *upperb* (third in the list) is an example of a dynamic constant: its value depends on the value of variable N at the time this declaration is processed. Arrays and records are initialized in Ada by array and record literals which are called *aggregates*. Details of their format and use are discussed in subsequent chapters. The declaration of *dynarray* (fourth from the bottom) is an example of a dynamic array: its size depends on the value of N at the time the declaration is processed. There is one kind of declaration in Pascal that has no equivalent in Ada. The last declaration in the list of Pascal declarations is an example of this kind. In this declaration a pointer type is created by prefixing an existing type with the symbol " ↑ ". Finally, note that Ada uses the separator ':' for both constant and variable declarations, while Pascal uses ' = ' for constants and ':' for variables.

Expressions

Both languages allow expressions to be written in the normal infix notation, using parentheses to override the precedence of operators. Both languages provide arithmetic operators, relational operators and Boolean operators. One major difference between the languages is that Pascal attaches an unusual precedence to Boolean operators, while Ada follows the normal rules. In Pascal the operator **not** has the highest precedence, the operator **and** has the same precedence as multiplication and the operator **or** has the same precedence as addition. In Ada, the precedence of all Boolean operators is lower than that of relational operators.

      if (i > 0) **and** (i < 7) **then** . . . {Pascal}

      if i > 0 **and** i < 7 **then** . . .   -- Ada

The parentheses are necessary in the Pascal example, because the operator **and** has higher precedence than the relational operators. The Ada version would be erroneous in Pascal.

Ada has two conditional variations on the Boolean operators **and** and **or**, denoted by **and then** and **or else**.

      if i > 0 **and** i < 7 **then** . . .   -- Ada

      if i > 0 **and then** i < 7 **then** . . .   -- Ada

In the first statement the subexpressions $i > 0$ and $i < 7$ are both evaluated and the result of the Boolean expression is the conjunction of the results. In the second statement the lefthand subexpression $i > 0$ is evaluated, while the righthand subexpression is evaluated only if the lefthand subexpression yields TRUE. If $i > 0$ is FALSE, the evaluation of the subexpression $i > 7$ is suppressed and the end result is immediately set to FALSE. Likewise, "A **or else** B" means if A is FALSE, then the result depends on B, but if A is TRUE, B is not evaluated and the result is set to TRUE.

The relational operators are defined in both languages for scalar objects and for strings (arrays of characters). Ada goes further and provides equality (and inequality) relations for array and record objects. Other minor differences between expressions in the two languages will be discussed when they arise.

Control Statements

The control statements found in both languages are of the following kinds:
- assignment statements
- procedure statements
- conditional statements
- iteration statements
- control flow statements.

In addition to permitting assignment to structured variables (which is allowed in both languages), Ada allows assignments to parts of arrays (called *slices*). Moreover, since Ada has the notion of array and record literals (the aggregates), the righthand side of an assignment can truly be an expression while the righthand side in Pascal can only be the name of an array or record.

```
myact    := youract;    -- where both variables are of type account
myscore  := yourscore;  -- where both variables are of type score
myact    := (820626, 425);
myscore (1 . . 4) := (7, 7, 6, 8);
```

The first two assignments are allowed in both languages, the last two only in Ada.

Procedure statements are very similar in both languages. Some additional features of Ada are described in the next section. The conditional statements provided by both languages are two forms of an **if** statement and a **case** statement.

```
if i < 0 then i := -i;                                    {Pascal}
if (p > 0) and (p > q)
    then    begin p := p - q; q := p + q end
    else    begin p := p + q; q := p - q end;
case x of
        North :  x := East;
        East  :  x := South;
        South :  x := West;
        West  :  x := North
end;
```

```
if i < 0 then i := -i; end if;                                    -- Ada
if p > 0 and p > q
      then  p := p - q; q := p + q;
      else  p := p + q; q := p - q;
end if;
case x is
      when North  => x := East;
      when East   => x := South;
      when South  => x := West;
      when West   => x := North;
end case;
```

Since control statements in Ada are consistently terminated by a closing delimiter
(such as **end if** or **end case**), there is no need to place a sequence of statements in
a compound statement as is required in Pascal (see the *p, q* example). Another
difference we notice is that statements in Ada, including the last statement of a
statement list, are always terminated by a semicolon. The Pascal programmer
uses the semicolon as a separator for statements (instead of as a terminator) and,
consequently, omits the semicolon after the last statement of a list. In Ada one
often finds a semicolon immediately preceding keywords such as **end** or **else**,
while this is never the case in Pascal.

The iteration statements in Pascal are the while, the repeat and the for
statement. Ada has one single loop statement which can be used by itself or can
be prefixed with a for or a while clause.

```
for n := 1 to 100 do A[n] := n;                                 {Pascal}
while (i < 10) and (A[i] > 0) do
      begin
      A[i] := A[i] - 1; i := i + 1
      end;
k := 0; repeat k := k + 1; A[k] := k until k = 100;

for n in 1 .. 100 loop A(n) := n; end loop;                      -- Ada
while i < 10 and then A(i) > 0 loop
      A(i) := A(i) - 1; i := i + 1;
end loop;
k := 0; loop k := k + 1; A(k) := k; end loop;
```

The control variable of a for loop is a declared variable in Pascal, but is a local
variable of the for statement in Ada. Since this variable does not exist outside of
the for statement, the problem caused in Pascal programs by the fact that the value
of the iteration variable is undefined when the loop terminates does not arise in
Ada.

Ada has no repeat statement like Pascal's, while Pascal has no loop statement
like Ada's. Note that in the example the last Ada loop has no termination

condition and will therefore eventually cause the error of an array index out of bounds. This infinite loop can be broken by inserting a conditional statement, which checks for the termination condition, in conjunction with an exit, return or goto statement.

k := 0; **loop** k := k + 1; A(k) := k; **exit when** k = 100; **end loop**;

This example now has all the characteristics of a repeat until construct. The exit statement performs an orderly exit from the loop. A goto statement branching to a label immediately after the loop accomplishes the same purpose. Pascal and Ada both provide a goto statement that has the effect of an unconditional branch. The exit statement does not exist in Pascal and is used in Ada only to terminate, and exit from, loops. The return statement will be discussed in the next section.

Subprograms and Parameters

Procedures and functions (referred to as subprograms in Ada) are basically the same in both languages. The general structures are similar (function or procedure heading, declarations, and a sequence of statements) and their invocations of subprograms are similar as well. The minor syntactic differences are easily noticed.

```
procedure P(x : integer; var y : integer);                    {Pascal}
        {local declarations}
begin
        {sequence of statements}
end;

function F1(x : integer; var y : integer) : integer;
        {local declarations}
begin
        {sequence of statements}
        F1 := some value
end;

function F2 : integer;
begin
        {sequence of statements}
        F2 := some value;
        {more statements if you wish}
end;

P(5, somevariable);
variable1 := F1(10, variable2) + F2
```

```
procedure P(x : in INTEGER; y : out INTEGER) is          -- Ada
    -- local declarations;
begin
    -- sequence of statements;
end P;

function F1(x ,y : in INTEGER) return INTEGER is
    -- local declarations;
begin
    -- sequence of statements;
    return some value;
    -- more statements if you wish;
end F1;

function F2 return INTEGER is
    -- local declarations;
begin
    -- sequence of statements;
    return some value;
    -- more statements if you wish;
end F2;

P(5, variable1, variable2);
variable1 := F1(10, variable1) + F2;
```

Note the difference in how values are returned from functions. In Pascal, the returned values are assigned to the implicit variable that has the same name as the function. In Ada, the value is explicitly returned by means of the return statement, which both returns the value and terminates the function execution.

Other more significant differences between Pascal and Ada exist with respect to parameter modes, side effects and structured results. We defer the discussion of parameter modes to subsequent chapters where they will be treated extensively. In Pascal, no restrictions are made concerning side effects. In Ada, however, side effects are not allowed on parameters but are allowed on global data. This implies that functions in Ada can only have in parameters. For return values from functions, Pascal allows only scalar values, while Ada makes no restrictions whatever. If the object can be used in an assignment statement in the righthand side, it may be returned as a value of a function.

```
type matrix is array (1 . . 20) of INTEGER;
function INCRMAT (m : in matrix; x : in INTEGER := 1) return matrix;
```

There are three extensions that Ada provides for subprograms: default values for in parameters, parameter association by name, and overloading of subprogram names. The example of INCRMAT above illustrates the use of default values: the second parameter may be omitted if the value 1 is to be added to each element of the matrix.

Parameter association by name enables the programmer to disregard the order of the parameters and explicitly associate the particular value with the desired parameter.

    mat : = INCRMAT (x = > 5, m = > mat);

While this feature is particularly useful in production programs for its documentary value, we use the positional association throughout the remainder of the book.

Ada allows the introduction of identical names for functions and procedures where Pascal requires that all function and procedure names be unique. The overloaded subprograms are then distinguished on the basis of their parameters. We discuss this in detail in Chapter 3, Section 4.

Scope Rules

Pascal has Algol60 scope rules: visibility of names comes from the current and outer scopes; there is no visibility inward into nested scopes. This same scope mechanism is the basis for Ada's scope rules, even though Ada has a larger variety of scoping units than Pascal (e.g., blocks, packages, and tasks). The scope rules for blocks are identical to those for procedures and functions. The naming convention for task entries is the same as that for record fields: a particular entry is selected by prefixing its name with the task name. For instance, if *credit* is a field of record *myaccount* and SEND is an entry of task MAILBOX, one writes

    myaccount.credit   and   MAILBOX.SEND(some message).

Package interfaces are slightly different. The items defined in a package can be made visible in one of two ways. First, the package items can be referenced by name qualification analogously to task and record components. Second, the package interface may be opened completely by a **use** statement which allows one to reference the items directly without prefix. These extended scoping rules will be discussed further as they arise in the context of subsequent chapters.

1.3 Software Engineering Issues

Software Engineering is concerned with the design, organization, implementation and maintenance of large systems. The main concern of software engineering is the complexity that results from the largeness of these systems. Rules of behavior that work for two and three page programs do not automatically extend to even small systems described in two hundred to three hundred page programs. While small programs can be written and maintained by an individual who keeps all details in his head, large systems are produced and maintained by a team of programmers who must rely on software engineering techniques for keeping their task within manageable bounds.

Most programming languages do not provide facilities in the language itself that support software engineering techniques. When such languages are used for systems programming, the programmers team must rely on self invented conventions such as naming schemes and disciplined behavior regarding access to shared variables. We believe that such self-imposed rules are easily violated and difficult to enforce. It is therefore desirable to use a programming language that provides specific language constructs and language rules that facilitate the application of software engineering techniques. We show in this section that Ada is a programming language that indeed provides this desirable support.

The first lesson to be learned from software engineering investigations of the past decade is that constructing a system as a single monolithic program results in a totally unmanageable product. Such an approach makes it hard to find where and how a variable is used and causes even the smallest revision to have unpredictable effects. Therefore, the conclusion of this lesson is that a system should be partitioned into a number of components that can be managed separately.

In order for these individual components to fit together to form a coherent system, it is necessary to specify the interfaces precisely. Discussions during the past decade have resulted in the conviction that interfaces should minimize the connectivity between components. This is accomplished by restricting the specification to the logical aspects that must be known in order to use that component properly. Since, in most cases, the implementation is irrelevant to that proper use, little or nothing is included in the specification about the implementation. This minimization principle is generally known as *information hiding*.

In order to understand what features should be included in a programming language in support of software engineering, it is useful to review briefly the major concepts that have emerged during the past decades. These concepts include
- modularity
- various forms of abstraction
- concurrency
- exception handling
- hardware interface

We will discuss each of these concepts and introduce the specific features of Ada that support them (a more detailed discussion will be found in later chapters).

Modularity

We have already noted the need for modularity in order to partition the system into separately manageable pieces. Ada supports this need in two ways: by program unit constructs and by separate compilation. Besides the traditional modularization constructs of subprograms (i.e., procedures and functions), Ada provides the task and package constructs. The latter is particularly important because it enables the designer to group related program pieces into larger units and thus provides a more powerful modularization mechanism than subprograms. (We defer the discussion of tasks to the section on concurrency.)

A package consists of two distinct parts: the visible specification and the implementation body. The visible part is accessible to the user of the package and may contain declarations of types, constants, data objects, subprograms, tasks, and even packages. The implementation, however, is hidden from the user. For example, there is no way in which a user can access data local to the implementation body of a package.

```
package P is
        -- visible type, data objects, subprogram, etc., specifications
end P;


package body P is
        -- local data, subprogram, package, task declarations
        -- implementation of visible subprograms, packages, tasks
begin
        -- local initializations
end P;
```

It is not necessary that the implementation immediately follows its visible part. One can first write a collection of visible parts and later add the implementation bodies at the end of the program. In this way, a programmer can first concentrate on the specification of system components and worry about implementation details at a later time.

The ability to separate the specification is further strengthened by separate compilation. This feature of Ada makes it possible to compile the visible part of a package independently of its implementation body. However, each component is compiled in a certain context, namely, the collection of visible parts used in the component being compiled. Note that the implementation bodies of the used packages are not part of the context.

Separate compilations together with the separation of the visible part and the implementation provide the means of clearly specifying the interfaces of the different modules of a system. This approach is of paramount importance in developing large systems with large numbers of programmers because it enables the programmers to produce and test modules concurrently and in relative isolation from each other.

Abstraction

The term *abstraction* denotes the idea of emphasizing common and essential features in a collection of objects while disregarding the dissimilar and unimportant features. For example, the concept of mammal emphasizes the features in common between man and animal, and disregards such features as weight, fur, stance, habitat, etc. Likewise, the concept of manhood emphasizes the distinction between man and animals but disregards the distinction between men and women. Thus abstraction is a tool that enables us to focus our attention on different aspects of objects at different times. In this way, the various forms of abstraction allow the programmer to manage the complexity of a system by reducing the amount of information that must be dealt with at any given time.

One form of abstraction, *computational abstraction*, is found in every programming language. This form is supported by the procedure, function or subroutine construct. In Ada, computational abstraction is provided by two basic constructs: subprograms and tasks. We have dealt with subprograms earlier in this chapter and will discuss tasks in a subsequent section on concurrency.

Ada provides two further forms of abstraction seldom found in other programming languages: *data abstraction* and *type abstraction*. We distinguish a weak and a strong form of data abstraction: data encapsulation and structural abstraction. A common form of data encapsulation is where a data type is associated with a set of basic operations that applies to objects of that type. For example,

```
package RealStack is
       type stack is array (1 . . 533) of FLOAT;
       procedure PUSH (f : in FLOAT; s : in out stack);
       procedure POP   (f : out FLOAT; s : in out stack);
end RealStack;
```

The stronger form of data abstraction, structural abstraction, usually includes data encapsulation but also hides the structure of the encapsulated type. For example,

```
package RealStack is
       type stack is private;
       procedure PUSH (f : in FLOAT; s : in out stack);
       procedure POP   (f : out FLOAT; s : in out stack);
       . . .
end RealStack;
```

The distinction between these two examples is that in the first one can operate directly on any element of a stack whereas in the second, one has access to a stack only through the supplied operations PUSH and POP. (Note: The term *data abstraction* is often used in the literature in the narrower sense of *structural abstraction.*)

Data abstraction is often used as a principle for partitioning a system into coherent units. It is, therefore, often the case that the modular structure of a system is the result of the application of data abstraction. For this reason, Ada provides one mechanism, the package, to provide support for both data abstraction and modularity. We will discuss these issues in great detail in subsequent chapters.

Type abstraction is a crucial prerequisite for writing reusable software. In languages without type abstraction, the programmer must rewrite the entire specification and implementation of a package when only minor details are changed, such as the stack element type in the example above. In Ada, one can solve this problem by generic units. For example, one can create a program schema for stacks that is independent of the stack element type and which can be instantiated for any desired stack element.

```
generic type element is private;
package StackModule is

    type stack is private;

    procedure PUSH (e : in element; s : in out stack);
    procedure POP   (e : out element ; s : in out stack);
    . . .
end StackModule;
```

Basically, the generic unit is a template or program scheme for program units that can be created by instantiating the generic unit. The relationship between a generic unit and its instantiations is similar to that between a data type and its corresponding data objects. For example, we can now declare a variety of stack modules.

```
package RealStack  is new StackModule (FLOAT);
package IntStack   is new StackModule (INTEGER);
package ActStack   is new StackModule (Account);
package ScoreStack is new Stack Module (Score);
```

Generic program units are useful especially if one wants to define a structure, and operations on that structure, independent of the particular type of elements that can be stored in that structure. This form of type abstraction serves the purpose of writing reusable software. We will come back to this issue in several subsequent chapters.

Concurrency

There are problems that can only be solved by using concurrent processes, such as operating systems, airline reservation systems, banking systems and expert systems. There are also many problems that allow for a natural decomposition into systems of concurrent processes, such as some of the sorting algorithms and Dijkstra's garbage collection algorithm. One can even find concurrent solutions for problems that are usually treated sequentially. For example, consider the statement

```
x := F (y) + G (z);
```

where the function calls F and G are executed concurrently, rather than sequentially, before the results are added.

Systems that require concurrent processes are very difficult to write correctly in languages that do not support concurrency. Problems arise in areas such as access to shared data and sharing resources. For instance, it should not be possible for two processes to reserve the same resource or to overwrite one another's data. In these languages, the solutions often rely on ad hoc extensions of the language with features that are derived from the underlying operating system.

Ada is one of the few programming languages that provides support for concurrent processes in the language itself. The construct supporting concurrency in Ada is the task construct. Structurally a task is similar to a package: it consists of a visible part and an implementation body. Just as with packages, the specification of the user interface is completely separate from the task implementation. This separation makes the task construct extremely useful as a modularization construct. Tasks also behave identically to packages with respect to separate compilation.

Notwithstanding the similarities between tasks and packages, there are two basic differences: in contrast to a package body, a task body defines an independent activity and the task interface defines a number of entry points in the task. For example, consider the task that manages a flight list.

```
task FlightList is

    entry RESERVE (s : out seat);
    entry CANCEL  (s : in seat);

end FlightList;
```

Other tasks communicate with the FlightList task by calling these entry points in a manner similar to procedure calls.

```
FlightList.RESERVE(x);
FlightList.CANCEL(y);
```

A severe shortcoming in this example is that there is only one FlightList. One would like to be able to create as many flight lists as are needed. This can be achieved in Ada by declaring a task type instead of a single task.

```
task type FlightList is
        entry RESERVE (s : out seat);
        entry CANCEL  (s : in seat);
end FlightList;
```

Task types are similar to data types in that task objects can be declared as instantiations of a task type just as data objects can be declared as instantiations of a data type.

```
FlightTW510, FlightPE137 : FlightList;
```

We present numerous examples of tasking in the third part of this book.

Exception Handling

A significant part of a large system is concerned with handling errors. Every program consists of two classes of program parts: those parts which implement the normal algorithm, and those parts which handle errors (the abnormal algorithm so to speak). Programs in which these two classes are intertwined are inherently more complex than programs in which these classes are separated. Ada provides an exception handling mechanism that makes it possible to separate these two classes of program parts. In Ada, the error handling code is always the last part of a program block and conspicuously separated from the normal part. We make extensive use of exceptions where they are appropriate.

Physical Representation

For many systems, programmers must deal with special characteristics of the hardware. In most languages, no support is provided for the representation of the hardware interfaces. This support must then be found outside the language, typically by resorting to assembly language coding. It is useful to be able to address these issues at the same logical level as non hardware-type interfaces. To accomplish this, Ada provides the facilities to map logical structures onto physical representations. For example, records can be mapped onto bit positions, data can be mapped onto particular addresses and entries can be mapped onto particular interrupts. These issues are discussed in Chapters 14 and 15.

Conclusion

The overview shows that Ada is a rich language. It has a wealth of features that support the programmer in the design and maintenance of large systems. This does not imply, however, that compilation of Ada programs results in elaborate machine code. The emphasis of the language is on compile time checking and the elaboration of object formats in their declarations. Much of the expressiveness at the design level is compiled out and leaves no trace in the object code.

In conclusion, we see that Ada is similar to Pascal in its goal of run-time efficiency but strongly differs from Pascal in its elaborate support for software engineering.

1.4 Reminders

1. Features that are similar in Pascal and Ada
    - base types
    - enumeration, array, record, pointer and range (sub)types
    - static constants
    - predefined functions
    - scalar, array, record and pointer declarations
    - expressions
    - assignment statements
    - control statements
    - procedures and functions
    - parameter modes
    - subprogram scope rules
    - file I/O.

2. Features in Ada that are extensions to Pascal
    - dynamic array types
    - subtypes (dynamic array types and parameterized record types)
    - type attributes
    - task types
    - dynamic constants
    - initialization of declarations
    - array and record literals (aggregates)
    - short circuit Boolean operators
    - assignment of structured expressions
    - return statement
    - task control statements
    - default values for **in** parameters
    - package, task and block scopes.

3. Concepts in Ada not found in Pascal
    - packages and tasks
    - separation of specification and implementation
    - separate compilation
    - abstract data types
    - generic program units (program schemes)
    - multitasking
    - exception handling
    - physical representation
    - low-level I/O.

1.5 Problems

1. The eight compass directions can be represented in both languages by an enumeration type.

>   **type** winddir = (N, NE, E, SE, S, SW, W, NW);   {Pascal}
>   **type** winddir **is** (N, NE, E, SE, S, SW, W, NW);   -- Ada

A Boolean function that determines whether or not two given wind directions are opposite, returns the value TRUE if and only if the positions of the input values in the declared type differ by four. Function OPPOSITE is written in Pascal and in Ada as follows

>   **function** OPPOSITE(u, v : winddir) : boolean;   {Pascal}
>   **begin**
>   **if** ord(u) > ord(v) **then** OPPOSITE := (ord(u) - ord(v) = 4)
>   **else** OPPOSITE := (ord(v) - ord(u) = 4)
>   **end**;

>   **function** OPPOSITE(u, v : **in** winddir) **return** BOOLEAN **is**
>   **begin**   -- Ada
>   **if** winddir'POS(u) > winddir'POS(v)
>   **then return** winddir'POS(u) - winddir'POS(v) = 4;
>   **else return** winddir'POS(v) - winddir'POS(u) = 4;
>   **end if**;
>   **end** OPPOSITE;

In the first program we made use of the predefined function *ord* in Pascal that returns the ordinal position of a value of some enumeration type. The Ada language has a similar predefined function, called POS. In Ada, the use of POS is qualified by a prefix that indicates the particular enumeration type to which the predefined function is applied.

Write a Boolean function in Pascal and in Ada that determines whether or not two directions are perpendicular.

2. Both languages allow the declaration of local variables. The amount of computing in function OPPOSITE of the preceding problem can be reduced by introducing a local variable *dif* that holds the difference of the positions of the input directions. In Ada the value of *dif* can be fixed once and for all in the declaration. The use of the local variable leads to the following versions.

>   **function** OPPOSITE(u, v : winddir) : boolean;   {Pascal}
>   **var** dif : integer;
>   **begin**
>   dif := ord(u) - ord(v);
>   **if** dif > 0 **then** OPPOSITE := (dif = 4) **else** OPPOSITE := (dif = -4)
>   **end**;

```
function OPPOSITE(u, v : in winddir) return BOOLEAN is    -- Ada
    dif : constant INTEGER := winddir'POS(u) - winddir'POS(v);
begin
    if dif > 0 then return dif = 4; else return dif = -4; end if;
end OPPOSITE;
```

Write the new versions of function OPPOSITE in both languages that use a local variable, but that do not use an if statement. In this new version, the Pascal program contains a single assignment to the function name and the Ada program a single return statement. (Hint: Use the Boolean operator **or**.)

3. An array of integers is in ascending order if (and only if) the value of each element is less than that of its right neighbor (if any). The following four programs attempt to determine whether or not a given array is in ascending order. One of the four programs is incorrect.

```
const size = 13;    {Pascal}
type intar = array[1 . . size] of integer;
function ASCENDING(U : intar) : boolean;                     {Pascal}
    var i : integer;
begin
    i := 1; while i < size and U[i] < U[i + 1] do i := i + 1;
    ASCENDING := (i = size)
end;
```

```
function ASCENDING(U : intar) : boolean;                     {Pascal}
    var i : integer;
begin
    i := 1; while i < size do
        if U[i] < U[i + 1] then i := i + 1 else i := size + 1;
    ASCENDING := (i = size)
end;
```

```
size : constant INTEGER := 13;                              -- Ada
type intar is array(1 . . size) of INTEGER;
```

```
function ASCENDING(U : in intar) return BOOLEAN is          -- Ada
    i : INTEGER := 1;
begin
    while i < size and then U(i) < U(i + 1)
        loop i := i + 1; end loop;
    return i = size;
end ASCENDING;
```

```
function ASCENDING(U : in intar) return BOOLEAN is        -- Ada
    i : INTEGER := 1;
begin
    loop
        if i = size then return TRUE; end if;
        if U(i) < U(i + 1)
            then i := i + 1;
            else return FALSE;
        end if;
    end loop;
end ASCENDING;
```

The first Pascal program is incorrect, because for an ascending input array U the while loop is supposed to terminate when i = size. The test fails, however, because it tries to compare the element U[i = size] with a non-existing element U[i + 1 = size + 1]. This problem is avoided in the first Ada program by the use of the short circuited Boolean operator **and then**. Check whether the second Pascal program and the two Ada programs work correctly for various positive values of the constant *size*, in particular if *size* is defined to be equal to one.

4. An instant or an interval of time expressed in hours, minutes and seconds can be represented in both languages by a record consisting of three components, one for the hours, one for minutes and one for seconds. The three time units themselves can be defined as types in Pascal and as subtypes in Ada.

```
type hour   = 0 . . 23;                                   {Pascal}
type minute = 0 . . 59;
type second = 0 . . 59;
type time   = record hr : hour; min : minute; sec : second end;
```

```
subtype hour   is INTEGER range 0 . . 23;                  -- Ada
subtype minute is INTEGER range 0 . . 59;
subtype second is INTEGER range 0 . . 59;
type time is record hr : hour; min : minute; sec : second; end record;
```

It makes sense to add or subtract time intervals. The arithmetic of minutes and seconds is performed modulo 60 and that of hours modulo 24.

```
procedure ADDTIME(u, v : time; var w : time);             {Pascal}
    var a, b, c : integer;
begin
    c := u.sec + v.sec;           w.sec := c mod 60;
    b := u.min + v.min + c div 60;  w.min := b mod 60;
    a := u.hr + v.hr + b div 60;   w.hr := a mod 24
end;
```

In Ada we overload the " + " operator for time addition.

```
function " + "(u, v : in time) return time is          -- Ada
    a, b, c : INTEGER;
begin
    c := u.sec + v.sec;
    b := u.min + v.min + c / 60;
    a := u.hr + v.hr + b / 60;
return(a mod 24, b mod 60, c mod 60);
end " + ";
```

Write the corresponding Pascal procedure and Ada function for subtraction of time intervals.

5. A natural number is prime if it has no other divisors than the number one. A test for potential divisors of a number n can be restricted to the interval 2 . . ROUND(SQRT(N) - 0.5), where function ROUND rounds a real value to the nearest integer and function SQRT yields the square root of a natural number n.For instance, ROUND(3.1415) and ROUND(2.718) both return the integer number 3. The number of tests can be reduced to one third of the interval by omitting all multiples of 2 or 3 (except these numbers themselves). One can easily show that the natural numbers that are not multiples of 2 or 3 are multiples of six plus or minus one: (5, 7, 11, 13, 17, 19, . .). The distance between these numbers is alternatively two and four. Taking this analysis into account, a program for determining whether or not a given natural number is prime is

```
function ISPRIME(N : integer) : boolean;                    {Pascal}
    var limit, divisor, step : integer;
begin
    limit := SQRT(N) - 0.5;       {Pascal rounds automatically}
    divisor := 5; step := 2;
    if (N mod 2 = 0) or (N mod 3 = 0) then
        divisor := limit
    else while (divisor <= limit) and (N mod divisor > 0) do
        begin
        divisor := divisor + step; step := 6 - step
        end;
    ISPRIME := (divisor > limit)
end;
```

In Ada one cannot mix integer and real arithmetic. However, an integer number can be converted into a floating point number by the predefined function REAL, and a floating point number can be truncated to the nearest integer number by the predefined function INTEGER (ARM 4.6, 4-23).

```
function ISPRIME(N : in POSITIVE) return BOOLEAN is        -- Ada
    limit : constant POSITIVE := INTEGER(SQRT(N) - 0.5);
    divisor : POSITIVE := 5; step : POSITIVE := 2;
begin
    if N mod 2 = 0 or N mod 3 = 0 then return FALSE; end if;
    loop
        if divisor > limit then return TRUE; end if;
        if N mod divisor = 0 then return FALSE; end if;
        divisor := divisor + step; step := 6 - step;
    end loop;
end ISPRIME;
```

Subtype POSITIVE guarantees in the Ada program that the input value is a positive integer. The subtype indication POSITIVE is in fact superfluous for the local variables *divisor* and *step*, because the way these variables are initialized and are changed in the program guarantees that their values are always POSITIVE numbers. The Pascal program has no protection built in for the input value. Modify the Pascal program so that function ISPRIME rejects zero or a negative integer as input value. Can this be done by introducing a type POSITIVE in Pascal? (Hint: Range types in Pascal are defined by their upper and lower bound.)

Two

Data Encapsulation.

Topics: array variables, enumeration types, qualified expressions, if statements, in parameters, local declarations, packages, procedures, functions, range types, subtypes, constants, attributes.

Issues: initialization, implementation hiding, conditional expressions, derived types, anonymous types, and type equivalence.

2.1 Problem Statement

There are a number of different ways of referring to a particular day. One way is by the Julian date which designates the nth day of the year. Another is by the day of the week. These are the most common forms of reference to days within a rather local framework, such as within a period of one or two weeks. Beyond this local period of reference, the most common form of reference is a three-component date consisting of a month, a day, and a year.

Given these different forms of reference, it is often useful to be able to convert from one form to another. For this chapter, the problem is to provide a conversion routine that converts a three-component date into the day of the week. Important to this conversion process is the leap year rule: every fourth year is a leap year (and hence a year with one extra day) with the exception of centenary years that are not divisible by 400. Thus, the years 1000 and 1703 are not leap years, but 1200 and 1864 are. For reasons of simplicity (in avoiding the centenary leap year problems) we limit the conversions to the twentieth and twenty-first centuries.

2.2 Problem Discussion

The conversion process depends upon the relationships between weekdays and the different components of the three-component date. We will first discuss the relationship between weekdays and dates within a month, then the relationship between weekdays and months and finally the relationship between weekdays and years.

Let the weekdays Sunday, Monday, . . . , Saturday be numbered 0, 1, . . . , 6. In a particular month, M, if the dates 1, 8, 15, 22 and 29 fall on weekday k, then the dates 2, 9, 16, 23 and 30 fall on the next weekday, which is $(k+1) \bmod 7$. The weekday of an arbitrary date in that particular month M can be derived from the weekday of the first day of that month by the formula

weekday(month M, day n) =   (1)
[weekday(month M, day 1) + (n - 1)] **mod** 7.

In order to simplify problems encountered with leap years, we consider a year to be a contiguous period beginning on March 1 and running through the end of February. Within such a period there is a fixed relationship between the weekdays of the first day of every month. If March 1 is on weekday k, April 1 is on weekday $(k+31) \bmod 7$ (because March has 31 days), May 1 is on weekday $(k+61) \bmod 7$ (because March has 31 days and April has 30 days), etc. The weekday of the first of every month in relation to the preceding occurrence of March 1 is given by the following table.

March	0	June	1	September	2	December	2
April	3	July	3	October	4	January	5
May	5	August	6	November	0	February	1

For example, if the 1st of March is on Sunday, then the 1st of April is on Wednesday. Given this table we can compute the relationship between any date and the preceding March 1.

weekday(month, day) =   (2)
[weekday(March 1) + table[month] + (day-1)] **mod** 7.

The weekday advances one day each year, because $365 \bmod 7 = 1$. Over a period of many years, an extra day must be added for every interval of four years. Because 2000 is a centenary leap year, the period March 1, 1900 through February 28, 2100 contains no exceptions. The weekday of March 1 in a particular year Y in that period can be derived from the weekday of March 1, 1900 by the formula

weekday(March 1, Y) =   (3)
[weekday(March 1, 1900) + (Y-1900) + (Y-1900) **div** 4] **mod** 7.

For example, March 1, 1905 is six weekdays after March 1, 1900.

The weekday of an arbitrary date in the given time interval can now be calculated by combining 2 and 3. For a date between March 1 and December 31 the formula is

weekday(month, day, year) =
  [weekday(March 1, year) + table[month] + (day-1)] **mod** 7 =   (4)
  [weekday(March 1, 1900) + (Y-1900) + (Y-1900) **div** 4 +
    table[month] + (day-1)] **mod** 7.

Because we have arranged the year to simplify leap year accounting, a date in the month of January or February must use the March 1 in the preceding year as its reference. Thus, for these two months the year must be decreased by one.

weekday(month(is January or February), day, year) = . . . =   (5)
  [weekday(March 1, 1900) + (Y-1-1900) + (Y-1-1900) **div** 4 +
    table[month] + (day-1)] **mod** 7.

A small optimization of this formula is obtained by including the constants weekday(March 1, 1900) at the beginning of the formula and the constant -1 at the end of the formula in the values of the table. We use the name *offset* for the modified table. The relationship between *offset* and *table* is

offset[month] =   (6)
  (table[month] + weekday(March 1, 1900) - 1) **mod** 7

Since March 1, 1900 fell on a Thursday, equations 6 for *offset*, 4 for dates in March through December and 5 for dates in January and February can be rewritten as the following formulae.

offset[month] = (table[month] + 3) **mod** 7   (7)
weekday(month, day, year) =   (8)
  [offset[month] + (Y-1900) + (Y-1900) **div** 4 + day] **mod** 7
weekday(month, day, year) =   (9)
  [offset[month] + (Y-1901) + (Y-1901) **div** 4 + day] **mod** 7

The offset values are for each month are as follows.

March	3	June	4	September	5	December	5
April	6	July	6	October	0	January	1
May	1	August	2	November	3	February	4

Using the *offset* table, we find that newyears day in the year 2000 is on day [1 + 99 + 99 **div** 4 + 1] **mod** 7, which is a Saturday.

2.3 A Pascal Solution

Enumeration and Range Types

In the problem discussion, the days of the week were represented by numbers to facilitate the computation, and the months were implicitly represented by numbers to index into the offset table. This implicit mapping between integers and weekdays and months is not a particularly safe one. Much more suitable, explicit and self-documenting are Pascal's enumeration types. (We shall see below that we do encounter some computation problems by abandoning the implicit integer mapping.)

> **type**   weekday = (Sun, Mon, Tue, Wed, Thu, Fri, Sat);
>   month   = (Jan, Feb, Mar, Apr, May, Jun,
>   Jul, Aug, Sep, Oct, Nov, Dec);

Since days of a month are restricted to a specific range, an appropriate type definition for days of the month is the range of integers from 1 to 31.

> **type**   day = 1 . . 31;

Note that this range is uniform for all months even though a particular month may have fewer days. It is possible to refine the definitions to four different range types, distinguishing between months of 31, 30, 29 and 28 days.

> **type**   longmonthday   = 1 . . 31;
>   shortmonthday = 1 . . 30;
>   leapmonthday   = 1 . . 29;
>   februaryday   = 1 . . 28;

(Note that all type definitions in Pascal are terminated by a semicolon, including the last definition. For type definitions, the semicolon is used as a *terminator*, while for statements the semicolon is used as a *separator*. Subsequent statements in Pascal are separated by a semicolon, but the last statement of a statement list is not followed by a semicolon.) Refining the definitions in so much detail causes a problem in using objects of these types as actual parameters to functions or procedures. One solution is to write four copies of each function under different names, where each copy has one of the four types as its formal parameter. The obvious drawbacks here are the amount of duplication and the need to distinguish between the various functions at every function call. Another solution is to write a single function *f*(x : integer), using the base type of all four types for the parameter so that *f* can accept objects of any one of the four types as actual parameters. Unfortunately, type checking is lost and that is the main reason for introducing the distinct types in the first place. A third solution is some form of variant record type where the variants distinguish between the four ranges. This solution encounters unsolvable difficulties for the month of February. It is all right to use the month as a discriminant to distinguish between *longmonthday* and *shortmonthday*, but the month is inadequate for discriminating between *leapmonthday* and *februaryday*. Therefore, we conclude that it is not very useful to make such a fine distinction between the possible ranges for days of the month.

Since dates are to be allowed only in the twentieth and twenty-first century, years are restricted to the range from 1900 to 2099. Thus, a suitable type definition for years specifies this range.

> **type** year = 1900 . . 2099;

Array Variables

At the end of the discussion we listed the offsets for all twelve months. A straightforward representation in Pascal is an array of twelve elements, indexed by the enumeration type *month*. Since we have only one such object, we combine the declaration and the type definition and define the array *offset* to be an anonymous array type.

> **var** offset : **array**[Jan . . Dec] **of** weekday;

The correct values are filled into array *offset* by an initialization procedure.

```
procedure OFFSETINIT;
begin
        offset [Jan]    := Mon   ;     offset [Feb]    := Thu    ;
        offset [Mar]    := Wed   ;     offset [Apr]    := Sat    ;
        offset [May]    := Mon   ;     offset [Jun]    := Thu    ;
        offset [Jul]    := Sat   ;     offset [Aug]    := Tue    ;
        offset [Sep]    := Fri   ;     offset [Oct]    := Sun    ;
        offset [Nov]    := Wed   ;     offset [Dec]    := Fri
end;
```

Functions and Statements

The computation that converts a given date to its weekday is performed by the function WEEKDAYOF that takes a date as parameter and returns a *weekday*.

> **function** WEEKDAYOF(m : month; d : day; y : year) : weekday;

Formulae 8 and 9 define the conversion from the input date into the correct weekday. By factoring out the differences (namely Y - 1900 and Y - 1901) we can combine the two formulae into a single computation. One is inclined to simplify *y* by the statement:

> **if** (m = Jan) **or** (m = Feb) **then** y := y - 1901 **else** y := y - 1900

However, this statement results in a range error, because the values of the expressions y - 1901 or y - 1900 are not in the proper range assignable to *y*. In other words, the results are in the range 0 . . 199 instead of in the range 1900 . . 2099. This problem can be solved either by using a local variable *z* or by not introducing a type for the year component. We reject the latter solution because the type definition guarantees that the argument passed to the function is in the range for which the conversion is defined. In choosing the first alternative, there is no need to restrict the range of *z* (although we could) because the necessary type check has already been applied to the input parameter *y*. Formulae 8 and 9 become one statement by substituting *z* for (Y - 1900) and (Y - 1901) respectively. For convenience, we retain the result in a local variable *weekdaynum*.

> **function** WEEKDAYOF(m : month; d : day; y : year) : weekday;
>   **var** z : integer; weekdaynum : 0 . . 6;
> **begin**
>   **if**(m = Jan) **or** (m = Feb) **then** z := y - 1901 **else** z := y - 1900;
>   weekdaynum := (ord(offset[m]) + z + z **div** 4 + d) **mod** 7;
>   . . .
> **end**

The function *ord* is the standard Pascal function that returns the ordinal position of a value belonging to an enumeration type (PRM 107).

If an enumeration type in Pascal were interpreted as a constant array and the definition of that type as the initialization of that array, we could have written weekday[weekdaynum] to select the correct return value, and written

> WEEKDAYOF := weekday[weekdaynum]

to return that value as the result of function WEEKDAYOF. (Remember that a value is returned from a function by assigning to the function name in the function body (PRM 162).) However, this is not Pascal's interpretation of enumerated types. We must therefore return the proper weekday by a case statement where the components associate the resulting integer value with the appropriate weekday value.

> **case** weekdaynum **of**
>   0 : WEEKDAYOF := Sun;
>   1 : WEEKDAYOF := Mon;
>   2 : WEEKDAYOF := Tue;
>   3 : WEEKDAYOF := Wed;
>   4 : WEEKDAYOF := Thu;
>   5 : WEEKDAYOF := Fri;
>   6 : WEEKDAYOF := Sat
>   **end**

Note that it is in fact not necessary to introduce the variable *weekdaynum*. Instead, we could have used the expression assigned to *weekdaynum* directly in the case statement at the place of *weekdaynum*.

2.4 An Ada Solution

Enumeration Types

The enumeration types *weekday* and *month* can be defined in Ada just as in Pascal. There is a slight difference in notation in that Ada uses the keyword **is** instead of the Pascal symbol "=" and requires the keyword **type** before each declaration (ARM 3.3.1, 3-7).

> **type** weekday **is** (Sun, Mon, Tue, Wed, Thu, Fri, Sat);
> **type** month **is** (Jan, Feb, Mar, Apr, May, Jun,
> Jul, Aug, Sept, Oct, Nov, Dec);

The values of an enumeration type can be referred to by their name just as in Pascal. In addition, if there is any possibility of ambiguity, an enumeration value can be referred to by a qualified expression that is constructed by prefixing the value name with the type name (ARM 4.7,4-24). For example, weekday'(Wed) and month'(Jan) unambiguously denote Wednesday and January respectively. As a consequence of this convention in Ada, different enumeration types are allowed to have values with identical names. For example, *Jan* might be a value in the type *month* and also in an enumerated type for girls' nicknames.

Subtypes and Derived Types

Ada recognizes the fact that ranges are formed as restrictions to an existing type. The latter is called the *base type* and the restriction is called the *subtype* (ARM 3.3.2, 3-8). A subtype declaration is opened by the keyword **subtype** and describes a constrained version of the base type. This subtype is not a new type, but the specification of a limited subset of the set of possible values that belong to the base type. Consider, for example, the subtype definitions for *day* and *year*.

> **subtype** day **is** INTEGER **range** 0 . . 31;
> **subtype** year **is** INTEGER **range** 1900 . . 2099;

Objects declared of subtype *day* or *year* are of type INTEGER, but the values they may assume are restricted as indicated in the subtype definitions. As in Pascal, range restrictions can be applied to any scalar type to form subtypes. However, this is not the only way to construct subtypes. In subsequent chapters we will encounter other subtypes, in particular array subtypes and record subtypes.

An alternative approach for the definitions of *day* and *year* is to declare them as *derived types* (ARM 3.4, 3-10). Where a subtype restricts the legal values of the base type, a derived type is a completely new type based on its parent type. It inherits all the values and the basic operations from the parent type but these values and operations are distinct from those of the parent type or any other type derived from the parent type. Therefore, objects of the derived type cannot be mixed with objects of the parent type either in the derived types' operations or in the parent types' operations.

This latter property is the main reason why we do not wish to use derived types for *day* and *year*. Suppose we declare *day* and *year* as derived types.

> **type** day **is new** INTEGER **range** 1 . . 31;
> **type** year **is new** INTEGER **range** 1900 . . 2099;

It is correct to use an expression such as d + 1 or d1 + d2, where d, d1 and d2 are of type *day*, because the derived type *day* inherits the operation ' + ' and the constant 1 from the parent type INTEGER. Likewise, it is correct to write an expression such as y + 1, where y is a year. However, it is not correct to write an expression such as y + d, because evaluation of this expression would result in an error message stating that the types of the two operands of the plus operation don't match. Since we need mixed arithmetic of days and years (cf. equation 8), derived types are unsuitable for this program.

The problem of mixed type operations can be solved by type conversion where the types have the same parent type or involve the parent type (ARM 4.6, 4-21). For example, if *d* and *y* are of derived types *day* and *year*, the following expressions are proper in Ada.

> INTEGER(d) + INTEGER(y)
> year(INTEGER(d)) + y
> year(INTEGER(y) + INTEGER(d))

The first expression is of type INTEGER, while the second and third are of type *year*. It is incorrect to write *year*(d), because type *day* is not derived from type *year*, but from type INTEGER. While this enables one to mix derived types and produce results of a desired type, there is a distinct loss of computational clarity.

Since we are primarily interested in range checking and this is provided by both approaches, we choose the simpler one. Subtypes provide exactly what we need while derived types provide more than we need. The extra power that derived types have over subtypes is in the additional check for type uniformity in expressions and assignment.

Note that, for derived types, instead of

    type day **is new** INTEGER **range** 1 . . 31;

we may use the shorthand notation

    type day **is range** 1 . . 31;

This shorthand is allowed only for types derived from the parent type INTEGER (ARM 3.5.4, 3-15). We do not recommend the use of this shorthand, because a similar abbreviation is not allowed in subtype definitions involving the base type INTEGER.

Packages

We now come to one of the major advances of Ada over Pascal. Pascal is an improvement over ALGOL60, FORTRAN and other languages in that it allows users to define their own data types. Inherent to this concept of data type is the notion of a collection of procedures and functions that operate on objects of that type. However, in Pascal there is no language mechanism that establishes the connection between a data type definition and the declaration of functions and procedures that operate on objects of that type. That is, there is no data encapsulation mechanism.

The major advance of Ada is that there is such a data encapsulation mechanism which bundles data types together with their functions and procedures. This mechanism is provided by Ada packages which serve an additional purpose, that is, to allow programmers to make a clear distinction between what a user should know in order to use the defined data types, functions and procedures, and what the programmer knows about the implementation of these data types, functions and procedures. This separation of user interface and implementation is achieved by writing the definition of a package as two distinct pieces: the *visible* part, containing the user interface, and the *package body*, containing the necessary implementations of data structures, procedures and functions.·

In exceptional cases, primarily where a package consists of some open type and constant definitions but contains no procedure or function declarations, a package may consist of only the visible part (ARM 7.2, 7-2). However, it is more common that the interface specifies several procedures and functions whose bodies are included in the package body. The package body may be used not only for hiding the implementation of items defined in the visible part, but also for hiding the existence (i.e., the declaration and implementation) of shared data objects and local procedures or functions.

Solving our particular problem, we use a package CALENDAR that consists of a visible part and an implementation body of the following form.

```
package CALENDAR is
      <type and subtype definitions>
      <procedures and function specifications>
end CALENDAR;


package body CALENDAR is
      <local declarations, including initializations>
      <procedure and function implementations>
      <package initialization statements if needed>
end CALENDAR;
```

Note that we must use the same name for a package body as for its visible part; there is at most one body for every visible part (ARM 7.1, 7-1).

It is obvious that we must inform users of package CALENDAR about the enumeration types *weekday* and *month*, and about the subtypes *day* and *year*. Most importantly, a user needs the specification of the function WEEKDAYOF because it is the function to be called if one wishes to find the weekday of a given date. However, there is no need to let the user know about the array *offset*. In fact, the user does not need to know how the conversion is done at all. We conclude, therefore, that array *offset* should be hidden from the user and should be included solely in the package body. This reasoning leads to the following visible part.

```
package CALENDAR is
   type      weekday  is (Sun, Mon, Tue, Wed, Thu, Fri, Sat);
   type      month    is (Jan, Feb, Mar, Apr, May, Jun, Jul,
                                Aug, Sep, Oct, Nov, Dec);
   subtype   day      is INTEGER range 1 . . 31;
   subtype   year     is INTEGER range 1900 . . 2099;
   function WEEKDAYOF(m : in month; d : in day; y : in year) return weekday;
end CALENDAR;
```

Note that in Ada the type of the return value is preceded by the keyword **return** instead of by a colon as in Pascal. The mode specification **in** means that the function will use the arguments passed to it as input values. We will see below, however, that Ada's in parameters are not identical to Pascal's value parameters.

The visible part contains no more than the user needs to know to use the CALENDAR package and does not include irrelevant information such as the implementation of function WEEKDAYOF or the auxiliary array *offset*. These are included in the package body of CALENDAR which has the following form.

```
package body CALENDAR is
      <declaration and initialization of array offset>
      <declaration, program body of function WEEKDAYOF>
end CALENDAR;
```

Array Declarations, Constants and Initialization

Ada provides two very useful features for declarations that are lacking in Pascal. For example, one can initialize variables and constants at their declaration. Second, one can declare structured objects to be constant, in contrast to Pascal where constants can only be scalar objects. Finally, initialization of structured objects is accomplished by using aggregates (ARM 4.3 4-7) which specify all the values for the object.

It is obvious that array *offset* will never be changed in the weekday computations. In Ada one is able to express this fact by declaring the array to be constant where in Pascal it was necessary to write an initialization procedure that assigns the appropriate values to the elements of array *offset* and which must be called once and prior to any weekday computation. Moreover, in Pascal the user is made aware of the existence of the array (in order to initialize it properly) and could even change the values of the array, because the array is not constant. The ability to initialize structured objects in Ada makes it possible to declare the array to be constant and makes the initialization procedure superfluous. An additional advantage in Ada is that the existence of array *offset* remains hidden from the user because its declaration is included in the implementation body of package CALENDAR but not in its visible part.

```
offset: constant array (month) of weekday : =
        (Mon, Thu, Wed, Sat, Mon, Thu, Sat, Tue, Fri, Sun, Wed, Fri);
```

Anonymous Types and Type Equivalence

In the preceding example, we did not declare a separate type name for the array but defined the array type as part of the constant declaration. This form of object definition raises an important issue in typing: type equivalence. How do you decide when two objects have the same type?

Pascal and Ada both adhere to the rule of name equivalence. In other words, two objects are of the same type if they use the same type name in their declaration and are within the same scope for that name. (Because of scope rules, the same name may designate different types in different scopes.) Consider the following declarations.

```
type t is record a, b : INTEGER ; end record;
type s is record p, q : INTEGER ; end record;
x      : t;
u, v   : s;
y      : t;
```

Both Pascal and Ada consider *x* and *y* to be of the same type, *u* and *v* to be of the same type, but *x* and *u*, *x* and *v*, *y* and *u*, and *y* and *v* are of different types.

The problem is not so easily decided for anonymous types as in our declaration of *offset*. Suppose that we have three arrays.

      offset1 : **constant array** (month) **of** weekday;
      offset2, offset3 : **constant array** (month) **of** weekday;

Are they of the same type or not? Their structure is identical: they have the same component type and are indexed by the same type. In short, they are structurally equivalent. However, Ada uses name, not structural, equivalence to determine type equivalence. Here Ada has adopted the rule that every occurrence of an anonymous type is as if a type declaration took place. It essentially attaches an internal name to the anonymous type without letting the user know what this name is. As a consequence of the name equivalence rule and this interpretation of the use of anonymous types, Ada considers *offset2* and *offset3* to be of the same type because they are declared together, and hence of the same anonymous type; but, since *offset1* was declared separately, its anonymous type is distinct from that of the others and therefore has a different type.

Subtype Equivalence

These implications of name equivalence do not apply to subtypes. A subtype declaration can be considered an abbreviation of a fuller expression that explictly constrains the base type. In one sense, the equivalence of subtypes depends upon the equivalence of the base types. Subtypes cannot be equivalent if their base types are different. In a more complete sense, subtype equivalence depends upon the constraints placed upon the base type. If the constraints are identical, the subtypes are equivalent. Consider the following declarations.

      subtype s **is** INTEGER **range** 0 . . 6;
      x   : s;
      y   : INTEGER **range** 0 . . 6;
      u, v : INTEGER **range** 1 . . 31;

All four variables are of the same type: the base type INTEGER. Objects *x* and *y* have the same subtype, even though *y* was not declared with an explicit subtype name, because the constraints are the same. However, *x* and *y* have different subtypes from *u* and *v*.

Subtype equivalence is important in assignment (including the implicit assignment to **in** and **out** parameters). If the subtypes of both objects in an assignment statement are equivalent, no run-time check needs to be made -- the constraints are identical. However, if the subtypes are not equivalent, then a check must be made before the assignment to guarantee that the constraints will be satisfied by the assignment. If the constraints are not met, a constraint error is raised at runtime.

Functions

In order to show the similarity between the language constructs of Pascal and Ada, we first write a program for function WEEKDAYOF that follows exactly the implementation of the corresponding Pascal program. The function heading of *weekday* as it appears in the visible part of the package CALENDAR is repeated in the package body of CALENDAR, except for the terminating semicolon. The latter symbol is replaced by the keyword **is**, announcing that the implementation follows. The heading of a function or procedure declaration is followed by local declarations, and then by the body of the function. Thus, the function declaration and implementation is outlined as follows.

function WEEKDAYOF(m : **in** month ; d : **in** day ; y : **in** year) **return** weekday **is**
    z : INTEGER ;
    weekdaynum : INTEGER **range** 0 . . 6 ;
begin . . . **end**;

In Parameters

The concept of an *in parameter* in Ada differs from that of a *value parameter* in Pascal. A value parameter is a local variable of a procedure or function and distinguishes itself from other local variables in that its value is initialized from the argument when the procedure or function is called. However, the in parameter of an Ada function or procedure is not a variable, but a name for a value and represents the value of the argument passed to the function or procedure. As a consequence, an in parameter is considered a constant in the body of a function or procedure and, therefore, one cannot assign to an in parameter. In our particular example, any assignment such as $y := $ expr is illegal.

If Statement

The if statement used in the Pascal program for adjusting the year parameter for the months of January and February is equally needed in the Ada program. Note that both languages lack a conditional expression that would allow us to write an unambiguous assignment statement of the form

    z := **if** m = Jan **or** m = Feb **then** y - 1901 **else** y - 1900 **fi** -- illegal

Instead, the assignment to local variable z must be included in both alternatives of a conditional statement that takes the following form in Ada.

    if m = Jan **or** m = Feb **then** z := y - 1901; **else** z := y - 1900; **end if**;

Note that it is not necessary, as in Pascal, to put parentheses around the subexpressions m = Jan and m = Feb. Ada, in contrast to Pascal, recognizes the proper precedence rules of relational and Boolean operators (ARM 4.5, 4-12).

Enumeration Type Attributes

The expression that is at the heart of function WEEKDAYOF is denoted almost in the same way in Ada as in Pascal.

weekdaynum := (weekday'POS(offset(m)) + z + z / 4 + d) **mod** 7;

The composite name weekday'POS represents the position function applied to the enumeration type *weekday* and corresponds to the Pascal standard function *ord*. The function POS is called an ATTRIBUTE of enumeration types. Each of the type generators (e.g., enumeration, records, arrays, etc.) has an associated set of attributes that enable the programmer to query certain basic properties of the type and perform certain basic conversions. For enumerations, the attributes are POS, VAL, FIRST and LAST (ARM 3.5.5, 3-16). FIRST and LAST return the first and last values respectively of the enumeration type while POS and VAL are conversion functions. For example,

```
weekday'FIRST        = Sun
weekday'LAST         = Sat
weekday'POS(Wed)     = 3
weekday'VAL(3)       = Wed
```

The case statement was necessary in the Pascal program because Pascal does not have an inverse function for the standard function *ord*: one that would map a ordinal number n into the nth constant value of an enumeration type. This problem does not arise in Ada. If we make use of the attribute VAL, the case statement becomes entirely superfluous. In place of

```
case weekdaynum is
        when 0    => return Sun;
        when 1    => return Mon;
        when 2    => return Tue;
        when 3    => return Wed;
        when 4    => return Thu;
        when 5    => return Fri;
        when 6    => return Sat;
end case;
```

we can write

return weekday'VAL(weekdaynum);

At the end of the Pascal program discussion, we observed that there is really no need to introduce the variable *weekdaynum*, because the expression stored into it preceding the case statement may be used directly as the expression of the case clause. There is even more reason to omit the variable *weekdaynum* from the Ada program if the case statement is replaced by a single return statement. This simplification leads to ending function WEEKDAYOF with the following single statement.

return weekday'VAL((weekday'POS(offset(m)) + z + z / 4 + d) **mod** 7);

2.5 The Complete Programs

The Pascal Program

```
type  weekday  =  (Sun, Mon, Tue, Wed, Thu, Fri, Sat);
      month    =  (Jan, Feb, Mar, Apr, May, Jun,
                        Jul, Aug, Sep, Oct, Nov, Dec);
      day      =  1 . . 31;
      year     =  1900 . . 2099;

var   offset     :  array[month] of weekday;

procedure OFFSETINIT;
begin
        offset [Jan]   : =  Mon  ;      offset [Feb]   : =  Thu   ;
        offset [Mar]   : =  Wed  ;      offset [Apr]   : =  Sat   ;
        offset [May]   : =  Mon  ;      offset [Jun]   : =  Thu   ;
        offset [Jul]   : =  Sat  ;      offset [Aug]   : =  Tue   ;
        offset [Sep]   : =  Fri  ;      offset [Oct]   : =  Sun   ;
        offset [Nov]   : =  Wed  ;      offset [Dec]   : =  Fri
end;

function WEEKDAYOF(m : month; d : day; y : year) : weekday;
        var z : integer; weekdaynum : 0 . . 6;
begin
        if(m = Jan) or (m = Feb) then z : = y - 1901 else z : = y - 1900;
        weekdaynum : = (ord(offset[m]) + z + z div 4 + d) mod 7;
        case weekdaynum of
                0 :     WEEKDAYOF : = Sun;
                1 :     WEEKDAYOF : = Mon;
                2 :     WEEKDAYOF : = Tue;
                3 :     WEEKDAYOF : = Wed;
                4 :     WEEKDAYOF : = Thu;
                5 :     WEEKDAYOF : = Fri;
                6 :     WEEKDAYOF : = Sat
        end
end;
```

The Ada Program

package CALENDAR **is**

    type   weekday **is** (Sun, Mon, Tue, Wed, Thu, Fri, Sat);
    type   month   **is** (Jan, Feb, Mar, Apr, May, Jun,
                                   Jul, Aug, Sep, Oct, Nov, Dec);
    subtype day   **is** INTEGER **range** 1 . . 31;
    subtype year   **is** INTEGER **range** 1900 . . 2099;

    function WEEKDAYOF
            (m : **in** month; d : **in** day; y : **in** year) **return** weekday;

end CALENDAR;

package body CALENDAR **is**

    offset : **constant array** (month) **of** weekday : =
        (Mon, Thu, Wed, Sat, Mon, Thu, Sat, Tue, Fri, Sun, Wed, Fri);

    function WEEKDAYOF
      (m : **in** month; d : **in** day; y : **in** year) **return** weekday
    is
      z : INTEGER;
    begin
      if m = Jan **or** m = Feb **then** z := y - 1901; **else** z := y - 1900; **end if**;
      return weekday'VAL((weekday'POS(offset(m)) + z + z/4 + d) **mod** 7);
    end WEEKDAYOF;

end CALENDAR;

2.6 Reminders

1. The value list in an enumeration type definition is enclosed by parentheses in both languages.

2. Declarations are terminated by a semicolon in both languages.

3. In Ada the same convention is used for statements. In Pascal the last statement of a list must not be terminated by a semicolon.

4. A subtype in Ada does not introduce a new type but delineates a subset of the set of values belonging to the base type. The type of an object declared to be of a particular subtype is the base type (not the subtype). The values it may assume are restricted to the subset determined in the subtype definition.

5. Ada packages allow for a separation of the user interface and the corresponding implementation. The use of packages is strongly recommended for data type encapsulation and for information hiding.

6. In Pascal, Boolean operators have higher precedence than relational operators. Ada follows the more natural rule of giving relational operators higher precedence than Boolean operators.

7. The result of a Pascal function is returned through an assignment to the function identifier. Ada functions pass their result to the call site through a return statement.

8. Integer subtypes in Ada correspond to integer subrange types in Pascal.

9. Enumeration type attributes such as POS, VAL, FIRST and LAST are prefixed by the enumeration typename and a single quote (pronounced *tic*).

10. Subtypes are useful if one wishes to work with constants or variables whose values are guaranteed to be in a restricted subset of values that belong to a given base type. Derived types have the same potential and, in addition, ensure that objects of different derived types and of the parent type cannot be mixed.

11. In Ada one can initialize scalar and structured variables when they are declared. This makes it possible to declare any object to be a constant.

12. Ada and Pascal both apply the name equivalence rule for types. In Ada, all distinct anonymous types are different type declarations and differ from all named types.

13. The type equivalence rule is applied to subtypes by applying it to the base type of that subtype.

14. A value parameter in Pascal is an initialized local variable. An in parameter in Ada is the name for a constant value that cannot be assigned to.

2.7 Problems

1. Would it be possible in the Pascal program to use a local variable *weakday* of type weekday instead of the local variable *weekdaynum* of range type 0 . . 6 in the function WEEKDAYOF? Would it be possible to do it in the Ada program? If possible, write a revised version of the assignment statement and the subsequent **case** statement for each of the two programs.

2. Find the maximum time interval that includes the years 1900 and 1901 for which the programs work properly. Revise the programs so that they work for the time starting at year zero and going indefinitely into the future.

3. Let the type *date* be defined as a record of three fields, respectively of type *month*, *day* and *year*. Rewrite the Pascal and Ada programs including a suitable definition of type *date* and use this type in the specification of a single parameter for the function WEEKDAYOF. Would it be possible in the Ada program to do away with the explicit type definitions for month, day and year by using anonymous types for the fields of date records? Would it be possible to eliminate the type *weekday* and use an anonymous type for the result of WEEKDAYOF? Why is the latter not a good idea?

4. A *Julian date* is a pair of numbers representing a day number in the range 1 . . 366 and a year. A Julian date can be represented in both languages by a record type. We want to have a program that takes a Julian date in a (non-negative) year and maps it into a date of the record type described in the preceding problems. In Ada, this program can be a function that returns a record value of the type *date*. In Pascal, a function can return a value of scalar type or pointer type, but not of structured type. This is related to the fact that in Pascal assignment statements are restricted to scalar and pointer type variables, while Ada allows assignment to structured objects.

The problem is solved in Pascal by using a procedure instead of a function and by giving that procedure a Julian date as a value parameter and a date as a var parameter (PRM 153). It is then possible to assign to the fields of that var parameter, one by one, in the body of the mapping procedure.

Write the Ada and Pascal programs for the described mapping.

5. One frequently encounters questions of the sort: "On which date is Labor Day this year?" (Labor Day is on the first Monday in September.) This question is a specific instance of the general question: Given an ordinal

number n, a weekday s, a month m and a year y, find the date of the n occurrence of weekday s in month m of year y. Write programs in Pascal and Ada that define suitable types for n, s, m and y, and that include a function that takes n, s, m and y as parameters and returns the corresponding date. Some cases to try are the next occurrence of Thanksgiving (the fourth Thursday in November), or Memorial Day (the last Monday of May). Programming *last* is in fact an interesting variation!

Three

Array Types

Topics: composite array variables, for statement, var parameters, overloading of names, exceptions, use clause, with clause.

Issues: vectors of various sizes, structured objects as function result, array type constraints, aliasing.

3.1 Problem Statement

The problem of this chapter is the design and implementation of vector and matrix arithmetic. For vectors we want operations for addition, subtraction, multiplication, division, scalar multiplication and inner product (six in total). For matrix arithmetic we are interested in multiplication with scalars, vectors and matrices. In addition to demonstrating the principle of encapsulation, the chosen example shows the flexibility of the variable size Ada arrays in contrast to the rigid fixed size Pascal arrays.

An n-dimensional *vector* is an ordered set of n values, referred to as the n *components* of that vector. Each vector component can be accessed as a separate unit. Assuming that components are arithmetic values, one can define vector operations as extensions of arithmetic operations. For instance, if the vector components are integer numbers, one can define vector addition for two n-dimensional vectors as an extension of integer addition by the rule

$\text{VECPLUS}(u, v) \Rightarrow w$, such that $w_k = u_k + v_k$.

Thus, applied to the vectors (1, 2, 3, 4) and (5, 10, 14, 7), we have

$$\text{VECPLUS}((1, 2, 3, 4), (5, 10, 14, 7)) =$$
$$(1+5, 2+10, 3+14, 4+7) = (6, 12, 17, 11) .$$

45

The rule defines the vector operation VECPLUS as the component-wise addition of two vectors. Subtraction, multiplication and division of vectors can be defined in a similar manner. Each of these extended operations computes an n-dimensional vector from two given n-dimensional input vectors.

In addition to the extensions of the component operations, we define the inner product of two n-dimensional vectors u and v by the rule

INNERPROD(u, v) $\Rightarrow$ s, where s = SUM(w) and w = VECPROD(u, v).

The inner product is the sum of the products of corresponding elements of two vectors. In other words, to get the inner product of two vectors, take the product vector and add all its elements. For example,

INNERPROD$((u_1, u_2, u_3, u_4), (v_1, v_2, v_3, v_4))$ =
$(u_1 * v_1 + u_2 * v_2 + u_3 * v_3 + u_4 * v_4)$.

Note that, in contrast to the extended operations, the result of computing an inner product is not a vector, but a value of the same type as the vector components.

An m$\times$n *matrix* is a rectangular array of m rows and n columns, where each row has n elements and each column m elements. One can view a matrix as consisting of m n-dimensional row vectors, or of n m-dimensional column vectors. Elements of a matrix M are denoted by a double indexed identifier such as M_{ij} or x_{ij}, where i is a number in the range 1 . . m and j in the range 1 . . n.

The matrix operations of interest to us are matrix multiplication and multiplication of matrices and vectors. These operations play a crucial role in vector transformations and in linear algebra. The product of matrix M and vector v is defined if the rows of M have the same dimension as v. The product is defined by the rule

M$\times$v $\Rightarrow$ w, such that w_i = INNERPROD(row$_i$, v).

The product is obtained by combining every row of the matrix with the vector and computing all inner products. The resulting vector w has one element for every combination of a row with the vector. Thus, the dimension of w is equal to the number of rows, which is the column-dimension of matrix M.

Example.
A 3$\times$4 matrix times a 4-component vector yields a 3-component vector.

1 2 3 4			(1, 2, 3, 4) . (2, 3, 3, 2)	25
5 6 6 5	$\times$ (2 3 3 2) =	(5, 6, 6, 5) . (2, 3, 3, 2) =	56
4 3 3 2			(4, 3, 3, 2) . (2, 3, 3, 2)	31

Multiplication of two matrices is defined if the row-dimension of the first matrix is equal to the column-dimension of the second matrix. The result is obtained by taking the inner products of all possible combinations of rows from the first matrix with columns from the second matrix. Element M_{ij} of the result matrix is the inner product of the ith row of the first matrix with the jth column of the second matrix. Hence, the result matrix has as many rows as the first matrix and as many columns as the second matrix.

Example. A 3×4 matrix times a 4×2 matrix results in a 3×2 matrix.

$$
\begin{matrix} 1 & 2 & 3 & 4 \\ 5 & 6 & 6 & 5 \\ 4 & 3 & 2 & 1 \end{matrix}
\quad \times \quad
\begin{matrix} 1 & 4 \\ 2 & 3 \\ 3 & 2 \\ 4 & 1 \end{matrix}
\quad = \quad
\begin{matrix} r_1 \cdot c_1 & r_1 \cdot c_2 \\ r_2 \cdot c_1 & r_2 \cdot c_2 \\ r_3 \cdot c_1 & r_3 \cdot c_2 \end{matrix}
\quad = \quad
\begin{matrix} 30 & 20 \\ 55 & 55 \\ 20 & 30 \end{matrix}
$$

Finally, we define scalar multiplication for both vectors and matrices. Let s be a value of the same type as the vector components or matrix elements. Scalar multiplication of scalar s and vector v or of scalar s and matrix M is defined as the vector or matrix that results from multiplying every component or element with s.

3.2 Problem Discussion

Let $u = (u_1, \ldots, u_n)$ and $v = (v_1, \ldots, v_n)$ be two n-dimensional vectors ($n \geq 1$). The result of adding these two vectors is an n-dimensional vector $w = (w_1, \ldots, w_n)$ such that

$$w_i = u_i + v_i \text{ for } i \in \{1 .. n\} \tag{1}$$

It is common to use the symbol $+$ not only for addition of real and integer numbers, but also for vector addition. Thus, we simply write $u+v$ instead of VECPLUS(u, v). The symbol $+$ is called an infix operator, because it is placed in between its operands u and v.(By the same token, VECPLUS is called a prefix operator, because it precedes both its operands.)

Without explicitly naming the result of a vector addition, the rule for addition takes the form

$$u+v = (u_1+v_1, u_2+v_2, \ldots, u_n+v_n). \tag{2}$$

or

$$(u_1, \ldots, u_n) + (v_1, \ldots, v_n) = (u_1+v_1, \ldots, u_n+v_n).$$

For example,

$$(1, 2, 4) + (5, 6, 8) = (1+5, 2+6, 4+8) = (6, 8, 12).$$

Note that $+$ represents vector addition on the lefthand side of these equations and integer addition on the righthand side. This is an example of overloading (cf. Chapter 1). A familiar case of overloading is the use of $+$ for both integer and real arithmetic.

An algorithm for computing the sum of two vectors adds corresponding vector components as described in 1. The algorithm may do the additions in any order, because the addition of one pair of corresponding components is completely independent of the addition of every other pair. The operations subtraction, multiplication and division can be handled similarly. The vector versions of these three operations are defined by the rules

$$u - v \Rightarrow w, \text{ such that } w_i = u_i - v_i \text{ for } i \in \{1 \ . \ . \ n\} \qquad (3)$$
$$u*v \Rightarrow w, \text{ such that } w_i = u_i*v_i \text{ for } i \in \{1 \ . \ . \ n\} \qquad (4)$$
$$u/v \Rightarrow w, \text{ such that } w_i = u_i/v_i \text{ for } i \in \{1 \ . \ . \ n\}. \qquad (5)$$

Sequential algorithms for computing the difference, the product and the quotient of two vectors work similarly to the one for addition: the operation is successively applied to all pairs of corresponding components u_i and v_i.

The inner product of two n-dimensional vectors is often denoted by the infix operator ".". Instead of INNERPROD(u, v) we write "u.v". The inner product is defined as

$$u.v = u_1*v_1 + u_2*v_2 + \ . \ . \ . \ + u_n*v_n \qquad (6)$$

Since it is the sum of the components of the product vector, the inner product can be computed in two steps: first, compute the product vector and then add all its elements. An experienced programmer will not be satisfied with this algorithm, because it wastes space: It uses memory space to store the n components of the intermediate product vector, while the components of this vector are not needed in the final result.

An accumulative sequential algorithm that uses no space for the intermediate product vector is the following one. Instead of first computing all products and then performing n - 1 addition, the algorithm alternates between multiplications and additions. Let *sum* be the name for the end result and let it be initialized to zero. Each time a product of two corresponding components u_i and v_i is computed, the result is immediately added to *sum*. It is clear that *sum* indeed contains the desired result once all products have been computed and added to *sum*. It is also clear that this algorithm uses no intermediate storage proportional to the length of the input vector.

Scalar multiplication for n-dimensional vectors and m×n matrices is defined by the rules

$$s*u \Rightarrow v, \text{ such that } v_i = s*u_i \text{ for } i \in \{1 \ . \ . \ n\} \qquad (7)$$
$$s*M \Rightarrow Q, \text{ such that } Q_{ij} = s*M_{ij} \text{ for } i \in \{1 \ . \ . \ m\} \text{ and } j \in \{1 \ . \ . \ n\} \qquad (8)$$

Sequential algorithms for computing scalar products are very simple. Such an algorithm steps through all components of a vector, or all elements of a matrix, and multiplies that component or element by the scalar factor s.Each multiplication generates a component of the result vector, or an element of the result matrix.

Since multiplying matrices or a matrix and a vector is defined in terms of inner products, the corresponding algorithms can make use of the algorithm for inner products. Let $m \times n$ matrix M consist of m n-dimensional row vectors $r_1, \ldots, r_m$. The product $M \times v$ yields an m-dimensional vector $w = (w_1, \ldots, w_m)$ that has a component for each row of M defined by

$$M \times v \Rightarrow w, \text{ such that } w_i = r_i.v \text{ for } i \in \{1 \ .. \ m\}. \tag{9}$$

A straightforward algorithm computes the m inner products of all rows r_i with vector v, traversing matrix M from left to right and from top to bottom. The same result is obtained by traversing matrix M from top to bottom and then from left to right, following the column structure of matrix M instead of the rows. To see how this algorithm works, we observe that the result w can be written as

$$M \times v = \begin{matrix} w_1 \\ . \\ . \\ . \\ w_m \end{matrix} = v_1 * \begin{matrix} c_{11} \\ . \\ . \\ . \\ c_{1m} \end{matrix} + \ldots + v_n * \begin{matrix} c_{n1} \\ . \\ . \\ . \\ c_{nm} \end{matrix} \tag{10}$$

where c_j is the jth column of matrix M and each product $v_j * c_j$ is a scalar multiplication of scalar v_j with vector c_j. The result vector is now written as the sum of n vectors. If the components of the result vector w are initialized to zero, each component w_i can be treated as variable *sum* in the inner product computation. Each product $c_{ij} * v_j$, is immediately added to component w_i. It is obvious that this quasi-parallel algorithm needs the same number of multiplications and additions as the straightforward algorithm mentioned earlier.

The product of an $m \times n$ matrix M and an $n \times p$ matrix P is the $m \times p$ matrix Q which is generated by computing all inner products $r_i.c_j$, where r_i is a row of matrix M and c_j a column of matrix P. The order in which these inner products are computed is immaterial. Another approach, similar to that of the quasi-parallel algorithm described above, is to design an algorithm that builds all elements of the result matrix simultaneously. This algorithm is based on the observation that each element x_{ij} of matrix M will be multiplied with each element y_{jk} of matrix P and that the resulting product contributes to element z_{ik} of the result matrix Q. Thus, if all elements z_{ik} of the result matrix are initialized to zero, the algorithm may compute the products $x_{ij} * y_{jk}$ in any order and add them to the appropriate element of the result matrix.

3.3 A Pascal Solution

Array Types and Variables

A natural representation for n-dimensional vectors in Pascal is as an array of n elements. Thus, we are inclined to write

> **type** vector = **array** [1 . . n] **of** real;

But, unfortunately, there is something wrong with this definition.   The upperbound of the array must be a constant value that is known at compile time (PRM 142, 143).   It is not just that the value of upperbound n must be known when the declaration is elaborated at runtime, it is entirely forbidden to use a variable in the bound specification.   This restriction forces us right from the beginning to work with vectors of a specific dimension.   In fact, if one wishes to work with vectors of various dimensions, one has to duplicate all the code as many times as there are different dimensions!

In order not to freeze the specific dimension in the code, we make use of the constant declaration feature to give the dimension a name.   This leads to the pair of declarations

> **const** vecdim =   16;
> **type**   vector   =   **array**[1 . . vecdim] **of** real;

For the addition of two vectors, one may want to write:

> **function** VECPLUS(u, v : vector) : vector ; {illegal result spec}
>   . . .
> **begin** . . . **end**;

Unfortunately, the result of a function cannot be a structured object such as an array or a record. It must be a scalar or a pointer (PRM 162). The standard way out of this problem is to use a var parameter for the output. A var parameter is often called a reference parameter. Such a parameter does not act as an initialized local (as a value parameter does), but as an internal name for the actual parameter that is passed when the procedure is called. Every time the procedure operates on a var parameter, it operates directly on the corresponding actual parameter and not on one of its own local variables (PRM 152, 153). The alternative is

> **procedure** VECPLUS(u, v : vector ; **var** w : vector);
>   . . .
> **begin**
>   . . .
> **end**;

For Statement

To compute the components of w, the addition of u[i] and v[i] must be repeated for all values of i in the range [1 . . vecdim]. The Pascal for statement is the convenient construct for this purpose (PRM 157).

>   **for** i := 1 **to** vecdim **do** w[i] := u[i] + v[i]

In Pascal, the control variable *i* must be a declared variable. Since the for statement will be placed in the body of procedure VECPLUS, the control variable can be declared as a local variable of this procedure. The complete declaration is

```
procedure VECPLUS(u, v : vector ; var w :  vector);
        var  i : integer;
begin
        for i := 1 to vecdim do w[i] := u[i] + v[i]
end;
```

The declarations for VECSUB, VECPROD, VECDIV are exactly the same except for the expression u[i] + v[i] which is respectively replaced by u[i] - v[i], u[i] * v[i] and u[i] / v[i].

Scalar multiplication is very similar to procedure VECPROD. The main difference is that the scalar takes the place of input vector u.

```
procedure SCALMUL(x : real ; v : vector ; var w :  vector);
        var  i : integer;
begin
        for i := 1 to vecdim do w[i] := x * v[i]
end;
```

It is immaterial in which order the components of w are computed. We have chosen to go from 1 to vecdim, but we could have reversed the order. Going backwards is indicated in the for statement by the keyword **downto**:

>   **for** i := vecdim **downto** 1 do w[i] := x * v[i]

Functions

The accumulative algorithm for computing the inner product uses a temporary variable *sum*, which can be declared as a local variable of the inner product function. This time we can write the desired program as a function, because the result is not a vector, but a scalar value of the same type as the vector components. As stated in the discussion, each time the product of two corresponding elements is computed, the result is added to variable *sum*.

```
function INPROD(u, v : vector) : real;
      var i : integer ; sum : real;
begin
      sum := 0;
      for i := 1 to vecdim do sum := sum + u[i] * v[i];
      INPROD := sum
end;
```

Note that it is not possible to use the function name as a temporary variable instead of variable *sum*. The function name represents the result when used on the lefthand side of an assignment (PRM 162). When used in a expression, a function name always represents a function call. Thus,

INPROD := INPROD + u[i] * v[i] ; {incorrect}

uses the name INPROD first as a variable to represent the result and then as a function designator. The latter is used incorrectly, because it must be used with an actual parameter list consisting of two input vectors.

Multidimensional Arrays

A matrix structure can be defined in one of two ways: either as 'a two dimensional vector or as a composition of an array of arrays. We present declarations for both and then continue writing the remaining programs using the composite array structure.

First alternative: two dimensional arrays.

```
const     lastrow  =  12;
          lastcol  =  16;
type      matrix   =  array[1 . . lastrow, 1 . . lastcol] of real;
```

Second alternative: composite arrays.

```
const     lastrow  =  12;
          rowdim   =  16;
type      matrix   =  array[1 . . lastrow] of array[1 . . rowdim] of real;
```

The latter type definition suggests that a matrix is an ordered set of row vectors. This view seems to be biased against treating a matrix as a collection of column vectors. The following programs show that this is indeed a problem for matrix multiplication when column vectors are needed. However, the two dimensional array representation does not work any better for column vectors than the composite array structure does. The two dimensional array structure is worse than either a row vector or a column vector representation, because it recognizes no vector structure at all.

Nested For Statements

Stepping through an array in two directions, from left to right and from top to bottom, is represented in a program by a nested for statement of the form:

> **for** i := 1 **to** lastrow **do**
>   **for** j := 1 **to** rowdim **do** . . .

Variable i, the control variable of the outerloop, indicates successive rows, while variable j, the control variable of the innerloop, steps through the components of the ith row vector.

Scalar multiplication is accomplished by accessing each matrix element once and multiplying it by the scalar value. Since the result is a structured object, we must transfer the output through a **var** parameter.

> **procedure** MATSCALMUL(x : real ; M : matrix ; **var** P : matrix);
>   **var** i, j : integer;
> **begin**
>   **for** i := 1 **to** lastrow **do**
>   **for** j := 1 **to** rowdim **do** P[i][j] := x * M[i][j]
> **end**;

Arrays Revisited

An alternative approach would be to make use of the procedure already defined for multiplying a vector with a scalar. That version is derived from the one above by replacing the innerloop by a call to procedure SCALMUL.

> **procedure** MATSCALMUL(x : real ; M : matrix ; **var** P : matrix);
>   **var** i : integer;
> **begin**
>   **for** i := 1 **to** lastrow **do** SCALMUL(x, M[i], P[i])
> **end**;

This version shows the advantage of the composite array representation over the two dimensional array representation, because the latter would not have allowed us to pass the vectors M[i] and P[i] as arguments to procedure SCALMUL.

With the multiplication of a matrix and a vector we run into Pascal's well-known problem caused by fixed size arrays. The problem is that the input vector, v, in the multiplication M×v $\Rightarrow$ w has the dimension *rowdim* (the same as that of the matrix rows), but the result vector, w, has the dimension *lastrow*, which is the column-dimension of M.Thus,

> **procedure** MATVECMUL(M : matrix ; v : vector ; **var** w : vector);
> **begin** . . . **end**;

is correct only for square matrices, for which the constants *lastrow* and *rowdim* happen to be the same. To handle the general case, it is necessary to introduce two different vector types that correspond to rows and columns respectively. In order to avoid rewriting all vector procedures and functions for both types of vectors, we will use *vector* to mean *rowvector* and introduce a new type *colvector*. Now we need the following declarations:

```
const   vecdim  =  16;
        coldim  =  12;


type    vector    =  array[1 . . vecdim] of real;
     colvector    =  array[1 . . coldim] of real;
        matrix    =  array[1 . . coldim] of vector;
```

Note that the procedures and functions we wrote for vectors, VECPLUS, VECSUB, . . . , INPROD, are defined for type vector, but not for type colvector! In Pascal, one would have to rewrite them all for type colvector under different names such as COLVECPLUS, . . . , COLINPROD.

A procedure for matrix and vector multiplication can now be written using the proper type specifications.

```
procedure MATVECMUL(M : matrix ; v : vector ; var w :  colvector);
        var  i : integer;
begin
        for i := 1 to coldim do w[i] := INPROD(M[i], v)
end;
```

The quasi-parallel algorithm explained in the discussion section steps through successive columns, multiplies the jth column with the jth component of input vector v and adds each product to the corresponding output component. The output vector must be initialized to all zeros before the intermediate products can be accumulated.

```
procedure MATVECMUL(M : matrix ; v : vector ; var w :  colvector);
        var  i, j : integer;
begin
        for i := 1 to coldim do w[i] := 0;
        for j := 1 to vecdim do
                for i := 1 to coldim do w[i] := w[i] + M[i][j] * v[j]
end;
```

A slightly better version is obtained by interchanging the two for clauses of the nested for statement. If *j* is the controlled variable of the innerloop (we step through the rows again instead of through the columns), then w[i] does not vary while *j* varies. We can then first compute the value of w[i] in a local variable and assign it at the end of the outer loop. The advantage is that indexing into array w is no longer done in the body of the nested for statement. The revised program is

```
procedure MATVECMUL(M : matrix ; v : vector ; var w :  colvector);
      var  i, j : integer; inprod : real;
begin
      for i := 1 to coldim do
      begin
            inprod := 0;
            for j := 1 to vecdim do inprod := inprod + M[i][j] * v[j];
            w[i] := inprod
      end
end;
```

The fact that rows of the first matrix are combined with columns of the second matrix makes it hard to take advantage of a vector representation if we are forced to choose between a rowvector representation or a columnvector representation. Therefore, we use the algorithm that accumulates all products $x_{ij} * u_{jk}$ in element z_{ik} of the result matrix.

One would like to compute the value of element z_{ik} in a way similar to that of component w[i] in the preceding algorithm. For given values of i and k, the statement would be:

```
begin
      inprod := 0;
      for j := 1 to vecdim do inprod := inprod + x[i][j] * y[j][k];
      z[i][k] := inprod
end
```

The upperbound of controlled variable *j* should be *vecdim*, because the algorithm should step through the rowvectors of the first matrix. However, the problem caused by the fixed size arrays arises again. The two matrices cannot be of the same Pascal type (unless both matrices are square and have the same number of elements), because that would violate the requirement that the row-dimension of the first be equal to the column-dimension of the second. To make things even worse, the result matrix must be of a third type, because its dimensions are different from both input matrices! These considerations lead to the following revised declarations.

```
const   vecdim  =  16;
        coldim  =  12;
        secdim  =  20;

type    vector    =  array[1 . . vecdim] of real;
        colvector =  array[1 . . coldim] of real;
        matrix    =  array[1 . . coldim] of vector;
        secmatrix =  array[1 . . vecdim] of array[1 . . secdim] of real;
        resmatrix =  array[1 . . coldim] of array[1 . . secdim] of real;
```

The compound statement that computes the value of an element z_{ik} of the result matrix must be executed for all i and k, where i ranges over the rows of the first matrix and k over the columns of the second matrix. Thus, the compound statement must be embedded into the nested for statement whose clauses are

> **for** i := 1 **to** coldim **do for** k := 1 **to** secdim **do** . . .

The complete program for procedure MATMUL is

```
procedure MATMUL(x : matrix ; y : secmatrix ; var z :  resmatrix);
    var i, j, k : integer; inprod : real;
begin
    for i := 1 to coldim do
        for k := 1 to secdim do
        begin
            inprod := 0;
            for j := 1 to vecdim do inprod := inprod + x[i][j] * y[j][k];
            z[i][k] := inprod
        end
end ;
```

There is no need for different matrix and vector types if we restrict ourselves to square matrices (although one still has to rewrite all procedures and functions for every different matrix size and vector dimension). In the case of square matrices and matching vectors, one uniform dimension suffices. The declarations can then be reduced to two type definitions, one for vectors and one for matrices.

```
const   vecdim  =  16;

type    vector  =  array[1 . . vecdim] of real;
        matrix  =  array[1 . . vecdim] of vector;
```

The multiplication procedures no longer cause the type specification problems. Their headings are:

```
procedure MATVECMUL  (M : matrix ; v : vector ; var w :  vector);
procedure MATMUL      (x, y : matrix ; var z :  matrix);
```

Aliasing

Passing a matrix as an input parameter is somewhat costly, because every time a procedure with an input parameter is called, the actual parameter is copied into the corresponding parameter that acts as an initialized local. One might consider passing sizeable objects, such as matrices, as var parameters in order to save the copying at the call. Applied to the last two procedures, the specification would be:

```
procedure MATVECMUL  (var M : matrix ; var v, w :  vector);
procedure MATMUL      (var x, y, z :  matrix);
```

However, the phenomenon of *aliasing* causes a problem that arises if one of the input parameters is the same as the output parameter. For example, let A and B be square matrices with $vecdim^2$ elements each in the program call

```
MATMUL(A, B, B); {an example of aliasing}
```

The various programs for matrix multiplication do not take into account the possibility that the elements y_{jk} and z_{ik} are located in the same matrix B. The problem is that the values of some elements of output matrix B are changed when addressed as z, while in the next multiplication the same elements are taken from input matrix B when addressed as y. At that point the old value should have been used and not the newly computed one. To give a specific example, element z_{11} is the first one to be computed; later, when element z_{21} is computed, the element y_{11} is used which is the same as the newly computed element z_{11}. Aliasing is avoided by first computing the result in a local variable and then copying the value of that local object into the actual output parameter. But this amounts to writing out what otherwise is done implicitly by copying the input parameter into the local value parameter. Thus, in order to avoid the problem caused by aliasing, we recommend that value parameters be used for input to Pascal procedures or functions and that var parameters be used for output only.

3.4 An Ada Solution

In Ada we write two packages: one for vector manipulations and one for matrix manipulations. Writing the necessary programs in Ada is much simpler than in Pascal, because there is no fixed-size problem and functions may return structured objects. Also in contrast to Pascal, the programs are valid for any dimension. There is no need to rewrite all procedures and functions for every vector dimension and matrix size.

Overloading

We mentioned in Chapter 1 Ada's feature of *overloading* procedure and function names. Two procedures or two functions may have identical names in the same scope provided that their *profiles* are different. The profile of a subprogram is the ordered list of the base types of the parameters and, for functions, the base type of the result as well (ARM 6.6, 6-10). Overloading makes it possible, for instance, to define two functions

```
function MAX(v : in vector)   return FLOAT;
function MAX(M : in matrix)   return FLOAT;
```

that have the same function name, but apply to different parameter base types. The profile of the first function is (vector, FLOAT) and that of the second function (matrix, FLOAT). Ada's type FLOAT corresponds to Pascal's type real.

The feature of overloading applies not only to user defined subprogram names, but also to the standard operator symbols such as + , - , etc. With the use of these features, the package specifications for vectors and matrices are:

```
package VECMANAGEMENT is
    type vector    is array(index range <>) of FLOAT;
    function "+"   (u, v : in vector) return vector;
    function "- "  (u, v : in vector) return vector;
    function "*"   (u, v : in vector) return vector;
    function "/"   (u, v : in vector) return vector;
    function "*"   (x : in FLOAT; v : in vector) return vector ;
    function INPROD(u, v : in vector) return FLOAT;
end VECMANAGEMENT;

package MATMANAGEMENT is
    use VECMANAGEMENT;
    type matrix    is array(index range <>) of vector;   -- incorrect
    function "*"   (M : in matrix ; v : in vector) return vector;
    function "*"   (x : in FLOAT ; M : in matrix) return matrix;
    function "*"   (x, y : in matrix) return matrix;
end MATMANAGEMENT;
```

The Use Statement

Three issues require further explanation: the *use* declaration; the array definitions in the type declarations of vector and matrix; and the representation of a matrix as a composite array or as a two dimensional array. A use declaration in scope s has the effect of making the content of a package known in scope s (ARM 8.4, 8-6). In this particular case, scope s is package MATMANAGEMENT (the scope in which the use declaration occurs), and the package that is imported is VECMANAGEMENT. The effect is that the content of package VECMANAGEMENT (subtype *index*, type *vector* and all vector operations) is now available in package MATMANAGEMENT. Without the use declaration, it would have been illegal to use the subtypename *index* and the typename *vector* in the declarations of type *matrix* and the matrix operations. It would have been all right to refer to the content of VECMANAGEMENT by prefixing each item with the package name.

VECMANAGEMENT.vector, VECMANAGEMENT.index, etc.

Ada Programs

An Ada program is stored in a *program library* which one can think of as an incomplete package, called STANDARD (ARM 8.6, 8-10). A program library contains three kinds of objects:

- standard types and subprograms for Booleans, integers, floating point numbers, characters and strings;
- predefined packages for I/O, Operating System and Hardware dependencies;
- user defined program units, primarily packages and tasks, but also subprograms and generic units.

A program library resembles an ordinary package in that all predefined and user defined units have access to the types and subprograms defined in STANDARD. No name qualification is needed for Boolean operations, integer operations, etc. However, a program library differs from an ordinary package with respect to the order of the units it contains. In ordinary packages, the order of declarations is significant and supports the rule *declaration before use*. In a program library, on the other hand, the order of predefined and user defined units has no significance. The order can be changed arbitrarily and a new user defined package can be placed anywhere in the program library.

In other program languages the order in which program units are written usually coincides with the order in which these units are compiled. Since Ada wants to provide great flexibility in separate compilation, a similar rule does not apply in Ada. Instead of relying on the order in which units are written, each library unit in Ada explicitly names the units it depends on. If a user defined package P depends on a predefined package D and on other user defined packages A and B, the library unit for package P has the format:

    with A, B, D;
    package P **is** . . . **end** P;

The with clause informs the compiler that the specification parts of units A, B and D are needed for a (separate) compilation of unit P (ARM 10.1.2, 10-3).

One should not confuse the with clause with the use statement. The former expresses compilation dependencies while the latter opens a scope so that objects in that scope can be named without name qualification. If it uses objects x and y from unit A and objects p and q from unit B, package P must refer to these objects by the full names A.x, A.y, B.p and B.q no matter whether P is prefixed with a with clause or not. However, if we add a use statement for A and B, then the unqualified names x, y, p and q can be used in package P (assuming there are no local name conflicts). The additional use statement can be written either inside package P or as an extension of the with clause.

with A, B, D; **use** A, B;
package P **is** . . . **end** P;

with A, B, D;
package P **is**
    use A, B;
    . . .
end P;

Other forms in which one is placed inside and the other as an extension of the
with clause are allowed too. In our example, components of units A and B can be
addressed inside package P by unqualified names, because A and B are included
in a use clause. The components of D must be addressed with their full names,
because unit D is not included in a use statement of P.(One can, of course, also
add D to one of the use statements.)

Suppose unit B depends on some other unit X.Should unit X also be included
in the with clause of package P? The answer is NO: the with clause must not
contain indirect dependencies. Only those units whose components are explicitly
used in P must be included in P's with clause and no others.

Since we want to write realistic Ada programs that one can compile, from now
on we will include the with clause in program units that need them. In our
example of preceding sections, there is a dependency of matrices on vectors.
Both also use integer, Boolean and floating point arithmetic, but these operations
form the standard part of every program library for which no with clause is
required. Thus, for our particular example, no with clause is needed for package
VECMANAGEMENT, while package MATMANAGEMENT must be augmented
by a with clause expressing the dependency on VECMANAGEMENT.

with VECMANAGEMENT; **use** VECMANAGEMENT;
package MATMANAGEMENT **is** . . . **end** MATMANAGEMENT;

Arrays

An array used in an Ada type declaration can be *constrained* or *unconstrained*.
In the former case the bounds are fixed, in the latter only the range within which
the bounds must be chosen is given (ARM 3.6, 3-28).

type table **is array**(1 . . 10) **of** something;   -- constrained
type vector **is array**(index **range** <>) **of** something; -- unconstrained

The symbol "<>" (pronounced box) indicates that the size of the array type is
not fixed and will be specified when objects of that type are declared. Objects
declared of type *table* all have the same size and index range; objects declared of
type *vector* may use different subtypes that define different sizes and different

index ranges. For example,

```
u, v    : vector(1 . . 16);
unit    : constant vector := (1 . . 5 => 1);
w       : vector(0 . . 4) := (1, 3, 5, 7, 9);
pent    : vector(1 . . 5);
```

The type of all objects declared here is *vector*. The objects are all of the same type, but not of the same subtype. Objects of the same subtype are u and v, and also unit and pent. Thus, assignments such as

```
u := v; pent := unit;
```

are allowed, but not

```
u := unit; pent := v;
```

Since the length of vector w is the same as that of unit and pent, Ada also allows assignments for these arrays although their subtypes are not identical. The subtype of vector *unit* is defined by the initialization. Since vector *unit* is declared as constant, the values of its five components cannot be changed.

The matrix type declaration in package MATMANAGEMENT is incorrect because the components of a composite array must be of a defined subtype (ARM 3.6, 3-27). In other words, the components of a composite array must be constrained and cannot be left unconstrained until objects of that composite array type are declared. It would have been all right to declare

type matrix **is array**(index **range** <>) **of** vector(1 . . vecdim);

where *vecdim* is some constant or variable that has a value by the time that this declaration is elaborated. But this precludes matrices of arbitrary size.

Fortunately, a similar restriction is not imposed on multi-dimensional arrays: if a matrix is declared as a two dimensional array, then both bound pairs may remain unconstrained until matrix objects are declared (ARM 3.6.1, 3-30). Thus, to retain flexibility, we recommend the use of the multi-dimensional array representation for matrices.

type matrix **is array** (index **range** <>, index **range** <>) **of** FLOAT;

For Statement

We noted in Chapter 1 that in Ada the control variable is a local constant of the for statement (ARM 5.5, 5-7). No explicit declaration in the scope of the for statement is needed. Each time the body of the for statement is executed, the control variable is set to the next value in the specified range. The control variable is treated as a constant (i.e., no assignment or use as an out parameter).

```
function " + "(u, v : in vector) return vector is
    dim : constant INTEGER : = u'LENGTH;
    w : vector(1 . . dim);
begin
    for i in 1 . . dim loop w(i) : = u(i) + v(i) ; end loop;
    return w;
end VECPLUS;
```

Remember that LENGTH is an attribute defined for arrays. We were able to define VECPLUS as a function in Ada, but that function needs a local variable *w* for constructing the result. This local variable was not needed in the Pascal procedure, because the reference parameter was directly used for assembling the result.

Exceptions

A glaring omission in this version of VECPLUS is a check for equal dimensions of the input vectors *u* and *v*. This problem did not occur in Pascal, because all vectors were of fixed and equal length. In Ada, vectors can be of different length, but vector addition is defined only if applied to vectors of equal length. It is clear what should be done if the lengths are equal, but we must also consider what should be done if their lengths are not equal. The suitable mechanism in Ada for dealing with unexpected situations is that of *exceptions*.

An exception is declared just as constants and variables. The declaration consists of a name and the keyword **exception** (ARM 11.1, 11-1). Its position determines its scope, just as for constants and variables.

IncompatDims : **exception**;

At a point in the program where the exception may occur one writes a raise statement (ARM 11.3, 11-4).

raise IncompatDims;

A raise statement for a particular exception may be written in many different places within the scope of that exception. At the end of the scope of the exception declaration, or at the end of every inner block of that scope, one can write an exception handler (ARM 11.2, 11-3). These handlers are the last statements before the end of a scope and their general format is

```
exception
    when x = >  <statement>      -- where x is some declared exception
        <other handlers>
end;
```

The program section containing exception handlers is opened by the keyword **exception** and always occurs at the end of a block. A particular handler is identified by a when clause. When an exception is raised in a raise statement, program execution is transferred to the exception handler with a matching name that is the highest in the runtime subprogram callstack (ARM 11.4, 11-5). For example, let procedures F and G contain handlers for an exception x that is raised in a procedure H.

```
x : exception;                    procedure H( . . . ) is
procedure F( . . . ) is           begin . . . raise x . . . end H;

   . . .
begin                             procedure G( . . . ) is
   -- G -- exception handled by G    . . .
   . . .                          begin
   -- H -- exception handled by F    -- H -- exception handled by G
   . . .                             . . .
exception                         exception
   when x => . . .                   when x => . . .
end F;                            end G;
```

If F calls G and G calls a procedure H which raises exception x, then the handler in G will be executed. If F calls H directly and H raises exception x, then the handler in F will be executed.

A typical example of declaring different handlers in different scopes for the same exception is that of division by zero. In scalar arithmetic division by zero is a plain error, but in matrix arithmetic it means that we are dealing with a singular matrix. By placing an exception handler in a procedure such as matrix inversion, one can produce the message "singular matrix" rather than "divide error" when the matrix inversion procedure is on top of the call stack. The proper scope for the exception IncompatDims is package VECMANAGEMENT. That allows us to raise the exception in both vector and matrix operations, because the vector package was imported into package MATMANAGEMENT by the use declaration. The exception declaration is included in the visible part of package VECMANAGEMENT at the end of this chapter.

The check for equal dimensions must be included in all vector functions that take two vectors as input. For example, the revised version of vector addition is:

```
function " + "(u, v : in vector) return vector is
        dim : constant INTEGER := u'LENGTH;
        w : vector(1 . . dim);
begin
        if v'LENGTH /= dim then raise IncompatDims; end if;
        for i in 1 . . dim loop w(i) := u(i) + v(i) ; end loop;
        return w;
end VECPLUS;
```

The addition could have been performed in reverse order by

for i **in reverse** 1 . . dim **loop** . . . **end loop**;

The proper place for exception handlers for exception IncompatDims is the scope that contains calls to vector and matrix operations. It is the user of these operations, who should worry about what to do if he passes incompatible vectors to a vector operation. But since the calling environment is hardly ever included in our examples, exception handlers will usually not appear in our programs.

As in Pascal, the Ada programs VECSUB, VECMUL and VECDIV can be derived from the program VECPLUS by respectively substituting u(i) - v(i), u(i)*v(i), and u(i)/v(i) for the addition u(i) + v(i). The scalar-vector multiplication program is also easily derived from VECPLUS by replacing expression u(i) + v(i) by the product x*v(i), where x is the input scalar. The resulting program is:

```
function "*"(x : in FLOAT ; v : in vector) return vector is    -- scalmul
    dim : constant INTEGER := v'LENGTH;
    w : vector(1 . . dim);
begin
    for i in 1 . . dim loop w(i) := x*v(i) ; end loop;
    return w;
end "*";
```

There is no need to raise an exception in this function, because the question of incompatible vector dimensions does not arise for a single input vector.

The check for incompatible vector dimensions is needed again in the function that computes the inner product. The Ada program for inner product is basically the same as the corresponding Pascal program with the important distinction that the Ada program is valid for vectors of arbitrary dimension, whereas the Pascal program is valid for vectors of exactly one particular dimension only.

```
function INPROD(u, v : in vector) return FLOAT is
    dim : constant INTEGER := u'LENGTH;
    sum : FLOAT := 0;
begin
    if v'LENGTH /= dim then raise IncompatDims; end if;
    for i in 1 . . dim loop sum := sum + u(i) * v(i) ; end loop;
    return sum ;
end INPROD;
```

The three programs for multiplying a matrix with a scalar, a vector or another matrix are, again, very similar to the corresponding Pascal programs, with the important distinction that the programs work for any pair of compatible objects and not just for a fixed dimension. Another difference is that the various matrix dimensions are not introduced as global constants, but as local constants that are initialized each time the procedures are called. For instance, the matrix multiplication function in Ada is:

```
function "*"(x, y : in matrix) return matrix is
    coldim : constant INTEGER := x'LENGTH(1);
    rowdim : constant INTEGER := x'LENGTH(2);
    secdim : constant INTEGER := y'LENGTH(2);
    z : matrix(1 . . coldim, 1 . . secdim);
    -- size(z) = coldim(x) × rowdim(y)
    INPROD : FLOAT;
begin
    if rowdim /= y'LENGTH(1) then raise IncompatDims ; end if;
    for i in 1 . . coldim loop
        for k in 1 . . secdim loop
            INPROD := 0.0;
            for j in 1 . . rowdim
                loop INPROD := INPROD + x(i, j) * y(j, k) ; end loop;
            z(i, k) := INPROD;
        end loop;
    end loop;
    return z;
end "*";
```

Aliasing in Ada

The problem caused by aliasing does not arise in Ada because we use functions instead of procedures with var parameters. However, another form of aliasing may arise when a subprogram uses a non-local variable that happens to coincide with one of the parameters. An example is

```
global : INTEGER := 1;
function ADDGLOBAL(x : in INTEGER) return INTEGER is
begin
        global := global + x; return global + x;
end ADDGLOBAL;
```

Fortunately, aliasing causes no problem in Ada, because the input variable is treated as an initialized constant. Thus, the result of the call ADDGLOBAL(global) is 3 and not 4.

3.5 The Complete Programs

The Pascal Program for Vector Arithmetic

```
const  vecdim   =  16;
type   vector   =  array[1 . . vecdim] of real;

procedure VECPLUS(u, v : vector ; var w :  vector);
      var  i : integer;
begin
      for i : =  1 to vecdim do w[i] : = u[i]  +  v[i]
end;
```

<<Likewise for procedures VECSUB, VECPROD and VECDIV>>

```
procedure SCALMUL(x : real ; v : vector ;  var w :  vector);
      var  i : integer;
begin
      for i : =  1 to vecdim do w[i] : = x ∗ v[i]
end;

function INPROD(u, v : vector) : real;
      var    i : integer;
             sum : real;
begin
      for i : =  1 to secdim do sum : = sum + u[i] ∗ v[i];
      INPROD : = sum
end;
```

The Ada Program for Vector Arithmetic

```ada
package VECMANAGEMENT is

        subtype index   is INTEGER range 0 . . INTEGER'LAST;
        type vector     is array(index range <>) of FLOAT;
        IncompatDims    : exception;

        function " + "  (u, v : in vector) return vector;
        function " - "  (u, v : in vector) return vector;
        function "*"    (u, v : in vector) return vector;
        function "/"    (u, v : in vector) return vector;
        function "*"    (x : in FLOAT ; v : in vector) return vector;
        function INPROD(u, v : in vector) return FLOAT;

end VECMANAGEMENT;

package body VECMANAGEMENT is
        function " + " (u, v : in vector) return vector is
                dim : constant INTEGER := u'LENGTH;
                w : vector(1 . . dim);
        begin
                if v'LENGTH /= dim then raise IncompatDims ; end if;
                for i in 1 . . dim loop w(i) := u(i) + v(i) ; end loop;
                return w;
        end " + ";  -- Likewise for vector version of " - ", "*" and "/"

        function "*" (x : in FLOAT ; v : in vector) return vector is
                dim : constant INTEGER := v'LENGTH;
                w : vector(1 . . dim);
        begin
                for i in 1 . . dim loop w(i) := x * v(i) ; end loop;
                return w;
        end "*";

        function INPROD(u, v : in vector) return FLOAT is
                dim : constant INTEGER := u'LENGTH;
                sum : FLOAT := 0.0;
        begin
                if v'LENGTH /= dim then raise IncompatDims ; end if;
                for i in 1 . . dim loop sum := sum + u(i) * v(i) ; end loop;
                return sum;
        end INPROD;

end  VECMANAGEMENT;
```

The Pascal Program for Matrix Arithmetic

```
const  coldim    =  12;
       secdim    =  20;
type   colvector  =  array[1 . . coldim] of real;
       matrix     =  array[1 . . coldim] of vector;
       secmatrix  =  array[1 . . vecdim] of array[1 . . secdim] of real;
       resmatrix  =  array[1 . . coldim] of array[1 . . secdim] of real;

procedure MATSCALMUL(x : real ; M : matrix ; var P :  matrix);
       var  i, j : integer;
begin
       for i := 1 to vecdim do for j := 1 to coldim do P[i][j] := x * M[i][j]
end;

procedure MATVECMUL(M : matrix ; v : vector ; var w :  colvector);
       var  i, j : integer ; inprod : real;
begin
       for i := 1 to coldim do
               begin
               inprod := 0.0;
               for j := 1 to vecdim do inprod := inprod + M[i][j] * v[j];
               w[i] := inprod
               end
end;

procedure MATMUL(x : matrix ; y : secmatrix ; var z :  resmatrix);
       var  i, j, k : integer ; inprod : real;
begin
       for i := 1 to coldim do for k := 1 to secdim do
               begin
               inprod := 0.0;
               for j := 1 to vecdim do inprod := inprod + x[i][j] * y[j][k];
               z[i][k] := inprod
               end
end;
```

The Ada Program for Matrix Arithmetic

```ada
with VECMANAGEMENT;  use VECMANAGEMENT;
package MATMANAGEMENT is

        type matrix  is  array(index range <>, index range <>) of FLOAT;

        function "*" (x : in FLOAT ; M : in matrix) return matrix;
        function "*" (M : in matrix ; v : in vector) return vector;
        function "*" (x, y : in matrix) return matrix;

end MATMANAGEMENT;

package body MATMANAGEMENT is

        function "*" (x : in FLOAT; m : in matrix) return matrix is
                coldim : constant INTEGER := M'LENGTH(1);
                rowdim : constant INTEGER := M'LENGTH(2);
                z : matrix(1 . . coldim, 1 . . rowdim);
        begin
                for i in 1 . . coldim loop
                        for j in 1 . . rowdim loop z(i, j) := x * M(i, j); end loop;
                end loop;
                return z;
        end "*";

        function "*" (M : in matrix ; v : in vector) return vector is
                coldim : constant INTEGER := M'LENGTH(1);
                rowdim : constant INTEGER := M'LENGTH(2);
                w : vector(1 . . coldim) ; inprod : FLOAT;
        begin
                if rowdim /= v'LENGTH then raise IncompatDims ; end if;
                for i in 1 . . coldim loop
                        inprod := 0.0;
                        for j in 1 . . rowdim loop
                                inprod := inprod + M(i, j)*v(j);
                        end loop;
                        w(i) := inprod;
                end loop;
                return w;
        end "*";
```

```
function "*" (x, y : in matrix) return matrix is
        coldim : constant INTEGER := x'LENGTH(1);
        rowdim : constant INTEGER := x'LENGTH(2);
        secdim : constant INTEGER := y'LENGTH(2);
        z : matrix(1 . . coldim, 1 . . secdim); inprod : FLOAT;
begin
        if coldim /= y'LENGTH(1) then raise IncompatDims ; end if;
        for i in 1 . . coldim loop for k in 1 . . secdim loop
                inprod := 0.0;
                for j in 1 . . rowdim loop
                        inprod := inprod + x(i, j)*y(j, k);
                end loop;
                z(i, k) := inprod;
        end loop ; end loop;
        return z;
    end "*";
end  MATMANAGEMENT;
```

3.6 Reminders

1. The size of Pascal arrays is fixed at compile time. Array bounds may not depend on variables of the program.

2. Ada arrays may be constrained or unconstrained. Even if an array is constrained, the constraints may depend on program variables and do not have to be known at compile time. The bounds of an unconstrained array must be fixed either in a subtype declaration or when an object of that array type is declared.

3. In Pascal function and procedures can operate on arrays of specific size only. One must rewrite these functions and procedures for each distinct array size.

4. In Pascal, names of functions and procedures cannot be overloaded. In Ada,they can. One subprogram is distinct from another subprogram if the list of parameter (and result) base types of the one is different from that of the other.

5. Ada functions can be represented by infix operator symbols such as ″+″, ″*″, etc.

6. The control variable of a Pascal for statement must be declared in the surrounding environment. The control variable of an Ada for statement is a local constant of that for statement. That constant is initialized to the next value in the range each time the controlled statement is repeated.

7. A Pascal function assigns its result to the function name. An Ada function contains one or more return statements.

8. Both languages allow the composition of arrays with arrays.

9. For multiplying rectangular matrices in Pascal, three different types of matrices are required because of the different array sizes. One also must distinguish between two types of vectors: rowvectors and columnvectors. It is not possible to write an inner product function in Pascal that applies to both types of vectors.

10. For composite arrays, Ada requires that the components are specified by a subtype and not just by a type. This rules out the possibility of postponing the computation of the component size until objects are declared.

11. The content of a package can be provided to (imported into) another package by the declaration of a use statement. This feature is not unlike the Pascal with statement.

12. Ada provides standard attributes for arrays such as LENGTH.

13. Unexpected or abnormal situations are handled by Ada's exception mechanism. Exceptions are raised where the exceptional condition is detected and exceptions are usually handled in the scope of the calling environment in which the user operates.

3.7 Problems

1. The matrix-vector multiplication programs in Pascal and Ada were written so that successive components of the result vector are computed. The advantage of this arrangement is that the output components w_i are not repeatedly accessed in the innerloop. One might make the same argument for the components v_j of the input vector. As it stands, these components are accessed repeatedly in the innerloop. Instead, we propose that the value of a component v_j be stored in a local variable, that all elements m_{ij} for $i \in \{i \, . \, . \, \text{coldim}\}$ be multiplied by that local variable and that the results be added to the output components w_i. This algorithm amounts to the quasi-parallel algorithm described in the discussion. Write the Pascal and Ada programs that implement the described algorithm and include the proposed optimization. Make sure the **for** clauses are in the right order and the ranges are correct. Since the optimization of avoiding access to the output components in the innerloop will be lost in your version, compare the various versions and determine which one is more efficient in space and/or time.

2. The inner product function is defined both in Pascal and Ada as a function that requires two vectors as input. In Pascal, matrix-vector multiplication had to be written as a procedure that uses a var parameter as output. In Ada, matrix-vector multiplication is written as a function. We try to translate the Ada expression

    if INPROD(u, v) = INPROD(M*u, M*v) **then** . . . ; **end if**;

into Pascal, where M is a non-square m×n matrix and *u, v* are n-dimensional vectors. In Pascal we need two intermediate vector variables, *x* and *y*, to store the result of the matrix-vector multiplication. Thus, one might expect the following piece of program to work correctly:

    MATVECMUL(M, u, x) ; MATVECMUL(M, v, y) ;
    if INPROD(u, v) = INPROD(x, y) **then** . . . ;

    Given the values of *m* and *n* (which may be treated as Pascal constants), define the proper type definitions and declarations of all variables involved. You may be surprised to find that the Pascal program does not work even if you have all the types designed correctly!!

3. For Ada we have chosen the multi-dimensional array representation, because the composite array representation requires that the subtype of the rows, including their size, be fixed when the matrix type is declared. By doing so, we lose the advantage of viewing a matrix as an ordered set of row vectors. We used the composite array representation in the Pascal programs and were thus able to make use of the earlier defined inner product functions for vectors. If we want to do a similar thing in Ada, we need a function ROW that takes a matrix and an index as input parameters and returns the ith row of that matrix. If we also design a function COL that takes the same kind of input parameters and returns the ith column, then even matrix multiplication can be written making use of the inner product function. Write Ada programs for the functions ROW and COL and rewrite the multiplication functions for a matrix with a vector and for two matrices using the functions ROW, COL and INPROD.

4. The problem caused by aliasing arises in Pascal if one uses var parameters for input and output. The problem does not arise in Ada, because Ada functions may return structured values. We found, however, that the Ada programs needed local variables for constructing the result. Review the Pascal programs for vector and matrix operations with var parameters and determine which ones are affected by the aliasing problem. For the ones that are, write a revised procedure body that avoids the problem.

5. A matrix is called *orthogonal* if every pair of different rowvectors of the matrix is perpendicular. Two vectors are perpendicular if their inner product is equal to zero. Write programs in Pascal and in Ada that determine whether or not an arbitrary matrix is orthogonal. Assuming the test function occurs in a package distinct from the matrix package, be careful about the correct naming of the vector and matrix operations defined in the vector and matrix packages.

Four

Parameterized Types

Topics: array types, while loops, return statements, structured functional
              values, array slices, string concatenation, array assignment,
              parameterized record types.

Issues: variable strings, differences in array types, open type with
              operations, overloading of functions.

4.1 Problem Statement

String manipulation is useful in many contexts. Pattern matching and deletion
form an important subset of these operations. The problem for this chapter
combines both matching and deletion in the implementation of the string
subtraction operation: given a string of characters, remove the leftmost occurrence
of a specified substring. A reasonable maximum string length may be specified.

4.2 Problem Discussion

The problem is essentially that of matching character strings. The most
straightforward and naive solution is the one that tries to match the first character
of the substring with each successive character in the string. When a match is
found, each succeeding character in the substring is matched against the string
until the match is complete or it fails. If failure occurs, the matching process
begins again at the character in the string immediately after the beginning of the
preceding match. For example, suppose the match begins at character position k
in the string and the match eventually fails. The matching process then begins
again at character position $k + 1$.

Several observations suggest that this algorithm can easily be improved. The first is that there is no need to look for a match if the number of characters remaining in the string is less than the length of the substring to be matched. The second is illustrated with the following example. Let the substring be *aaab* and let the string be *aaaaaaab*. In the first four attempts to match the substring, the first three characters match and failure occurs on the fourth character of the substring. The successful match begins on the fifth character of the string. The match process looks like

```
aaaaaaab
aaab
 aaab
  aaab
   aaab
    aaab
```

with four attempts that fail on the last character, before finally succeeding on the fifth attempt. The total number of comparisons is 5*4 = 20. In this case the strategy of beginning each new attempt with the first character of the substring yields the worst case possible with respect to the number of comparisons.

A different strategy is suggested by this example: continue the search with the character in the substring that failed in the match and compare it with the next character in the string after the character on which it failed. When a match does occur, continue the matching until the end of the substring and then wrap around to the beginning of the substring until it has been completely matched. This results in considerably less backtracking and redundant matching.

```
aaaaaaab
aaab
    b
     b
      b
   aaab
```

Only 11 comparisons are required to find the substring in the string.

A useful image in considering the match process is that of a window that slides along the string. The window delineates the particular slice of the main string that we are momentarily comparing with the substring. Assuming we will slide the window from left to right, the position of the window can be characterized by the number of character positions in the main string to the left of the window. If *windowpos* represents the number of character positions to the left of the window, the leftmost character in the window is found in position *windowpos* + 1. Two additional items of information are needed: an index into the string in which we are looking for the occurrence of the substring and second, an index into the substring we are trying to match and the number of characters matched thus far in an attempt to match the substring in the current window. With this in mind, we have the following invariant relationship between the *string index*, the *substring index* and the beginning position of the match window:

string index = window position + substring index.

For example,

      ↓
   adamant
   ant
   ↑

string index = 3, substring index = 1
windowpos = 2, leftmost windowchar = 3

Because of this invariant, we may omit the string index and remember the window position instead. This simplifies the comparison mechanism between the string and the substring and simplifies the bookkeeping when the substring index wraps around from the end of the substring to the beginning.

At the beginning of the search, the window is all the way to the left and the substring index starts with the first character. Thus, substring index should be initialized to one and *windowpos* to zero, because in the initial position there are no character positions in the main string to the left of the window. Variable *matchcount* should also be initialized to zero, because in the initial state we have not yet found any matching characters.

Two cases occur in the character by character match process. In the case where the indexed character in the substring matches the corresponding character in the string the match count must be incremented and the *substring index* incremented modulo the length of the substring. In the other case where the characters do not match, the match count must be reset to 0 (no characters matched) and the match window must be moved one position to the right in the string.

Success in the matching attempt occurs when the match count is equal to the length of the substring. We have then matched all the characters in the substring regardless of where the match started in the substring. The possibility of a match occurring is determined by whether or not there remains a sufficient number of characters in the string to fill the window. This possibility exists when

window position + substring length ≤ string length.

Clearly, we are finished when either there is a match or there is no longer the possibility of a match. If a match does occur, then the substring must be removed from the string.

4.3 A Pascal Solution

Pascal Strings

Pascal string literals are sequences of characters enclosed in single quotes and are representable in Pascal by a packed array of characters.

packed array[1 . . n] **of** char;   {n must be a constant}

Treating strings as arrays implies that all the problems associated with Pascal's arrays also apply to strings, in other words, arrays with the same components but different bounds are distinct types. A convenient solution -- though not without its drawbacks -- is to disregard the differences in length of the string arrays and define one standard length and use only that portion which is actually needed for a given object. The drawbacks, of course, are with regard to space efficiency and the variance of lengths that might occur. Careful analysis is required to accomplish a desirable balance between the two issues.

For the purposes of this problem, we select an arbitrary maximum size for strings and define the constant *strsize* to be the maximum size. Using this constant, we then define the index type for strings, *strindex*. *Strlen*, on the other hand, defines the permissible lengths for the strings and allows empty strings, that is, strings with a length of 0. The type *string* is defined as a packed array of characters indexed by the index type *strindex*.

const strsize   = 32;

type strindex   = 1 . . strsize;
      strlen   = 0 . . strsize;
      string   = **packed array** [strindex] **of** char;

There are several alternatives that might be chosen to indicate the actual size of the variable strings in the fixed size string array. One is to fill the unused portion of the character array with pad characters. This approach is desirable because, upon string assignment, parts of old strings are not left behind, but are overwritten with padding characters. However, this approach is possible only if one can afford to reserve a special padding character that will not be used in strings. Its major drawback is that the pad character must always be inserted -- possibly a time consuming process. Another approach, which eliminates the insertion of pad characters, is that which uses a terminating character to indicate the end of the actual string. The basic problem is choosing a suitable terminating character that will not occur in any string. Another drawback is the fact that the length must be computed when it is needed by scanning the string. Since the length of a string is of paramount importance to our algorithm, and to most string operations in general, a better approach than the previous two is to choose a record representation that defines a variable string type. The record consists of the length of the string and the fixed string array. In this way, the length need not be computed but is immediately available.

> **type** vstring = **record** len : strlen ; str : string **end**;

Pascal Procedures

Because Pascal functions can only return scalar values, we are forced to make the substring removal operation a procedure and use a var parameter for its result. Instead of writing a function, we must write a procedure

> **function** STRINGSUB (whole, part : vstring) : vstring; -- illegal

> **procedure** STRINGSUB (whole, part : vstring; **var** result : vstring);

for the operation of locating and removing a given substring. The value parameter *whole* is the string from which to remove the string specified in the value parameter *part*. The result of the operation is returned in the reference parameter *result*.

Procedure STRINGSUB uses an internal procedure, EXTRACT, which actually removes the substring once it has been found. The removal is accomplished by copying the remaining parts from the input parameter *whole*. The part of *whole* to be copied first into the reference parameter *result* is specified by the value parameter *windowpos*. It specifies the number of characters in *whole* that occurs before the substring to be removed. The value parameter *len* indicates the number of characters to be skipped before copying the remainder of *whole* into *result*.

> **procedure** EXTRACT (whole : vstring;
> windowpos, len : strlen;
> **var** result : vstring);

For Loops

The body of EXTRACT consists primarily of two loops to copy the parts of the input string preceding and following the leftmost occurrence of the substring. First the string up to and including the character indexed by *windowpos* is copied into *result*, a character at a time. The substring is then skipped and any remaining characters are copied. Both of these actions are accomplished by for loops. (We shall see below where array assignment as a whole in a single statement can be accomplished. Here copying must be done one character at a time, because the input and output arrays are not of the same type due to their different lengths.) The length of the resulting string is the difference of the lengths of the input string and the substring.

```
        begin
                for i := 1 to windowpos do result.str[i] := whole.str[i];
                for i := windowpos + len + 1 to whole.len
                do result.str[i - len] := whole.str[i];
                result.len := whole.len - len
        end;
```

Local Variables

As mentioned in the algorithm discussion, there are two pointers and one counter that are needed to implement the search algorithm: the window position (here defined as *windowpos*), the substring index (*subindex*) and the match count (*matchcount*).

        var matchcount, windowpos : strlen;   subindex : strindex;

The necessary initialization is accomplished by the following statements.

        matchcount := 0 ; windowpos := 0 ; subindex := 1;

Loop Exit

The heart of the search algorithm is performed in a loop that matches characters, or moves the window until either there is a match or there is no longer the possibility of a match. Since there is no means of exiting from the middle of a loop other than by using a goto statement, the order of the loop test and the sequence of statements within the loop are very important. First, because a successful match occurs when the match count is equal to the length of the substring, we know that we can continue looping while the match count is less than the substring length. Second, as long as there is a possibility of a match (i.e., as long as the window does not go beyond the end of the input string), the loop should be continued.

        while (matchcount < part.len) **and**
                (windowpos + part.len <= whole.len)
        do . . . ;

The loop body is an if statement that determines whether or not the indexed characters in *whole* and *part* match. If they do, the match count is incremented and the substring index is incremented and wrapped around to the beginning of the substring if necessary. If the characters do not match, the match count is reset to zero and the window moved one character to the right. In either case, the terminating conditions may have been created. If there is a match, then it might have been the last match required to complete the match. Otherwise, the window might have moved past the end of the input string.

```
if whole.str[windowpos + subindex] = part.str[subindex]
    then  begin
              matchcount : = matchcount + 1;
              subindex : = subindex mod part.len + 1
          end
    else  begin
              matchcount : = 0;
              windowpos : = windowpos + 1
          end;
```

Array and Record Assignment

In discussing procedure EXTRACT it was stated that the characters in the array had to be copied into the resulting array one at a time. There is one case, however, where an array may be assigned as a unit: when array types of the two variables are identical. In the operation STRINGSUB, if no match is found, then the entire string is returned as the result. In that case one can write

```
result.str : = whole.str;

result.len : = whole.len;
```

The array assignment of the first statement is allowed because the lefthand side and the righthand side are of the same type. In this particular case we can go further and combine the two statements into a single record assignment statement

```
result : = whole;
```

The assignment is allowed because the types of the two records are the same (PRM 149).

The last statement in STRINGSUB, then, determines whether a substring has been found. If it has been found, then remove the substring; otherwise, return the input string.

```
if matchcount = part.len
    then  EXTRACT(whole, windowpos, part.len, result)
    else  result : = whole
```

4.4 An Ada Solution

Ada Strings

Ada provides both string literals and a predefined string type. String literals in Ada are enclosed in double quotes rather than in single quotes as in Pascal. Characters, on the other hand, are enclosed in single quotes in Ada.

The string type in Ada is predefined as an unconstrained, one dimensional array of characters whose unconstrained index is of subtype POSITIVE.

type STRING **is array** (POSITIVE **range** <>) **of** CHARACTER;

The unconstrained index specification requires that a range be specified for each object declared to be of type STRING. For example

```
name          : STRING(1 . . 20);
errormessage  : constant STRING : = "error in program";
sentence      : STRING(1 . . 200);
text          : STRING(1 . . 65000);
```

Thus, each string object has a particular size and this size determines the specific subtype of the type STRING. We will see below that this causes certain programming problems even though Ada does solve the problems that Pascal has with fixed size string arrays.

Parameterized Record Types

For purposes of comparison, we will first write the Ada programs analogous to the Pascal programs in order to illustrate some of the basic differences. We will then revise the Ada programs to exploit Ada's expressiveness.

One useful way to attain variable length arrays, and hence variable strings, is to include the declaration of the array object in a record and specify the upperbound of the array as a record parameter.

type vstring(len : NATURAL) **is record**
    str : STRING(1 . . len);
end record;

This type definition has the parameter *len* which must be specified when an object is declared (this is the same as the requirement for objects of type STRING above). The primary advantage of this definition over the one in Pascal is that there is no wasted space: the array is precisely of the length specified. Thus, we have a type definition in Ada that captures the flavor of variable length strings.

However, there is one major drawback with this definition. Consider the variable following declarations.

S1, S2 : vstring(10);
S3, S4 : vstring(20);

These declarations fix the subtypes of the objects S1, S2, S3 and S4 and the objects themselves are constrained to those particular subtypes. (ARM 3.7.2, 3-36). The constraints expressed by the parameter values cannot be changed for these objects once they have been declared. Thus, while the assignment statements

S1 := S2 ; S2 := S1 ; S3 := S4 ; S4 := S3;

are legal in Ada,

S1 := S4 ; S2 := S3 ; S3 := S1 ; S4 := S2;

are not legal, because the objects S1 and S2 are constrained to sizes different from S3 and S4.

The restrictions on assignment to objects of a specific subtype can be avoided if the base type can be defined so that variables can be declared without specifying the size constraints (i.e., without constraining the subtype of the objects). Ada indeed allows variable declarations that do not specify the subtype constraint provided that the constraint parameter in the type definition has a default value! Thus, by this rule, if the *len* parameter is given a default value as in

type vstring (len : NATURAL := 32) **is record**
    str : STRING(1 . . len);
end record;

then it is not necessary to constrain objects (variables) to a particular subtype when they are declared. Examples of legal declarations that use this version of *vstring* are:

S1, S2 : vstring;
S3, S4 : vstring(20);

Though initially of length 32, the objects S1 and S2 are unconstrained and can, as an important side effect of this form of definition, be assigned a value of any subtype of the base type *vstring*. S3 and S4, on the other hand, have been constrained at their declaration and can hold only strings of 20 characters. The assignment statements

S1 := S2 ; S2 := S1 ; S1 := S3 ; S2 := S4 ; S3 := S4 ; S4 := S3;

are all legal -- the first four because S1 and S2 can be assigned any values and the last two because S3 and S4 are constrained to the same subtype. However, the legality of the assignments

        S3 := S1 ; S4 := S2;

depends on the current values of S1 and S2. If these are of the same subtype
(i.e., strings of 20 characters) then the assignments will be performed; otherwise,
the assignments will produce a runtime error because the subtype constraints of S3
and S4 have not been met.

   There are certain restrictions on assignment to fields of variant records. The
restriction applies if the record field depends on the discriminant which is one of
the record type parameters. A field depends on a discriminant if the definition of
the field contains the discriminant parameter or if the record field is part of a
variant that is determined by the discriminant (cf. Chapter 10). In the case where
a dependency exists, assignment is allowed only if the current value of the
discriminant is the one the record field depends on. This rule excludes direct
assignment to the discriminant itself because one could assign no other value than
the one the discriminant already has. There is, however, a way around this
restriction.   Ada does allow the assignment of a complete aggregate to a record
variable independent of the current value of the discriminant. This mechanism
allows for a simultaneous change of all record fields, including the discriminants
and the components that depend on those discriminants. Given that

        S1 := vstring(5, "hello");

then

        S1.str := "jello";

is legal but

        S1.str := "hi";

is not because *str* depends on *len* whose current value is 5. Alternatively,

        S1.len := 6;

is not allowed in Ada because *len* is the discriminant and cannot be changed
arbitrarily. Note that assignment to a discriminant is possible in Pascal which in
turn makes it possible to reinterpret the component values. This form of type
subversion is not allowed in Ada because the discriminant can be changed only as
part of a complete record assignment such as occurs in the following Ada
statements.

        S1 := S2;
        S1 := (2, "Hi");

   The second assignment statement is an example of a record aggregate
assignment using positional notation to specify the component values (ARM 4.3,
4-7).   Record parameters occur implicitly at the beginning of the record in the
order in which they are declared in the parameter list.   Aggregate positional
notation provides values for the components according to their order of declaration

in the record. Alternatively, component name notation could have been used and the order of the components may be ignored.

S1 := (str => "hi", len => 2)

We rarely use the named component notation.

Overloading

In Pascal it is not possible to overload language provided operators, nor is it possible to overload user defined operations. With the exceptions of the membership operation **in** and the short circuit control operations **and then** and **or else**, it is possible in Ada to overload both language supplied operations and user defined operations (ARM 6.6, 6-10 and 6.7, 6-11). Thus, for string subtraction we are allowed to use the infix subtraction operation "-" and overload it to operate on *vstrings*.

function "-" (whole, part : **in** vstring) **return** vstring;

The compiler determines the correct function on the basis of context. Where the correct operation cannot be determined because of ambiguities, the programmer must fully qualify either the name of the component, or the values of the arguments or the results.

Package Specification

So far we have been concerned only with the aspects that define what the user needs to know about variable strings and the single operation defined for them. This information is consolidated into the following interface specification

package StringExtension **is**

    type vstring(len : NATURAL := 32) **is record**
        str : string(1 . . len);
    end record;

    function "-" (whole, part : **in** vstring) **return** vstring;
    . . .
end StringExtension;

where the ellipses indicate the other operations that one normally expects to find with strings.

This example illustrates the use of a package as the basic mechanism for data encapsulation -- supplying a type definition and the basic operations on that type.

The only hiding that occurs is that for the implementation of the operations. No hiding at all has been applied to the type definition: the structure of vstrings is completely visible and accessible to the user.

Local Declarations

Local to the subtraction function are the declarations for the variables *macthcount*, *windowpos* and *subindex*.

```
matchcount  : NATURAL   := 0;
windowpos   : NATURAL   := 0;
subindex    : POSITIVE   := 1;
```

Note that the variables have been defined to be of type INTEGER but of two different subtypes and that they have been assigned initial values. The initial values are set each time the function is invoked. The proper place for these variables is local to the function and not local to the package body (which would mean global to the function). Global variables would have to be re-initialized for each use and the initial values would be superfluous.

While and Return Statements

The loop to search for matching substrings in Pascal continues until the match was found or a match was no longer possible. Because of the nature of Ada's return statement and its exiting properties, the while expression can be shortened to consider only the possibility of a match. The return statement will cause an exit both from the loop and from the function with the value specified in the statement. The overall structure of the function body is

```
begin
      while windowpos + part.len <= whole.len loop
            . . .
            return   . . . ;
            . . .
      end loop;
      return whole;
end "-";
```

At the first return statement in the program skeleton, it has been determined that a match has occurred and the relevant parts of input string *whole* are returned as the result of the function. At the second return statement, no match has occurred (because the loop has been completed when a match is no longer possible) and, hence, the entire input string *whole* is returned as the function value.

Array Slices and String Concatenation

Array slicing provides the ability to select a segment of an array (which is a sequence of contiguous components) and address them as a unit. For example,

A(1 . . 5),   B(20 . . 20+k),   and C(D . . E)

are all examples of array slicing where the bounds can be either statically or dynamically determined (ARM 4.1.2, 4-2). Since strings are defined in terms of arrays, array slicing can be used to construct or delineate substrings.

S1.str(1 . . 5),   S2.str(20 . . S2.len)

are examples of string slicing that might be used for objects of the type *vstring*.

In order to delete a substring from a string, two substrings are of interest. First, the substring from the beginning of the string to the character before the substring to be removed and second, the substring that begins after the substring to be removed and continues to the end of the string. These parts are represented by the array slices

whole.str(1 . . windowpos)

and

whole.str(windowpos + part.len + 1 . . whole.len).

There are two boundary cases to be considered: when the string to be removed is at the beginning and when it is at the end. If the former case applies, then *windowpos* will be 0 and the string will be, effectively, *whole*.str(1 . . 0). The Ada convention is to treat this slice as an empty object. The same applies to the removal of the string at the end. A slice where the second bound is one less than the first denotes the null range (ARM 3.5, 3-13) and, hence, a slice that contains no components. Thus, the representation of the relevant parts is also correct for the boundary conditions.

The concatenation operator & is then used to glue the two string slices back into one string.

passed := windowpos + part.len + 1;
whole.str(1 . . windowpos) & whole.str(passed . . whole.len);

The result of concatenation is a string.

The context in which the strings are concatenated together is the if statement that determines whether or not characters match. If they do and the match is complete, the constructed string is returned as part of the *vstring* aggregate. Otherwise, the match continues or restarts.

```
if whole.str(windowpos + subindex) = part.str(subindex)
then   matchcount := matchcount + 1;
       if matchcount = part.len then
            passed := windowpos + part.len + 1;
            return ((whole.len - part.len),
                    whole.str(1 .. windowpos) &
                    whole.str(passed .. whole.len));
       end if;
       subindex := subindex mod part.len + 1;
else   matchcount := 0;
       windowpos := windowpos + 1;
end if;
```

Strings Revisited

In the Pascal version, the type *vstring* was introduced to circumvent Pascal's problems with array types by removing the variations in the size of the array. In the Ada version, the type *vstring* was retained for reasons of analogy as well as to circumvent some problems in Ada concerning variable length strings. However, since Ada does have a specific string type and does allow parameters to be declared as the unconstrained array base types, we could instead write a string subtraction operation for Ada's predefined type STRING. This is made possible by the attributes that are available for arrays. The important attribute here is LENGTH which returns the number of index values in the index range for the array. In our subsequent discussion, we make one simplifying assumption: that all index ranges of strings are declared to have the lower bound of 1.

```
function "-" (whole, part : in STRING) return STRING is
    matchcount, windowpos : NATURAL := 0;
    subindex : POSITIVE := 1;
begin
    while windowpos + part'LENGTH <= whole'LENGTH loop
        if whole(windowpos + subindex) = part(subindex)
        then matchcount := matchcount + 1;
            if matchcount = part'LENGTH then
            return whole(1 .. windowpos) &
                whole(windowpos + part'LENGTH + 1 .. whole'LENGTH);
            end if;
            subindex := subindex mod part'LENGTH + 1;
        else matchcount := 0;
            windowpos := windowpos + 1;
        end if;
    end loop;
    return whole;
end "-";
```

As shown by the function implementation, there is no problem writing a subtraction function for Ada's predefined type STRING. The problem lies in using it. Whereas parameterized record types allow the programmer the option of declaring constrained or unconstrained objects by means of the default parameter value mechanism, there is no such option for unconstrained array types. The type STRING is such an unconstrained array type. Each object of type STRING must be constrained to a specific range at declaration time. Their bounds specification cannot be delayed until assignment. Thus, if S1, S2 and S3 are variables of type STRING, the following assignment statement is, in general, not likely to work.

S1 := S2 - S3;

If the string resulting from S2 - S3 happens to be exactly the size that S1 is constrained to, then all is well. But in a dynamic string handling program, that is not very likely. The one case where it can be used to advantage is to provide the initial value in a declaration and to provide the size constraint based upon the initial value.

S3 : **constant** STRING := S1 - S2;

It is precisely for these reasons of inflexibility that the record type *vstring* should be used over the Ada supplied STRING type.

4.5 The Complete Programs

The Pascal Program

```
const  strsize    = 32;

type   strindex   = 1 . . strsize;
       strlen     = 0 . . strsize;
       string     = packed array [strindex] of char;
       vstring    = record len : strlen ; str : string end;

var    matchcount, windowpos : strlen;
       subindex  : strindex;

procedure STRINGSUB(whole, part : vstring; var result : vstring);

       procedure EXTRACT
              (whole : vstring; windowpos, len : strlen; var result : vstring);
              var i : integer;
       begin
              for i := 1 to windowpos do result.str[i] := whole.str[i];
              for i := windowpos + len + 1  to whole.len
              do result.str[i-len] := whole.str[i];
              result.len := whole.len - len
       end;

begin
       matchcount := 0 ; windowpos := 0 ; subindex := 1;
       while (matchcount < part.len)
       and (windowpos + part.len <= whole.len)
              do if whole.str[windowpos + subindex] = part.str[subindex]
                     then  begin
                            matchcount := matchcount + 1;
                            subindex := subindex mod part.len + 1
                            end
                     else  begin
                            matchcount := 0;
                            windowpos := windowpos + 1
                            end;
       if matchcount = part.len
              then   extract(whole, windowpos, part.len, result)
              else   result := whole
end;
```

The Ada Program

package StringExtension **is**

      type vstring(len : NATURAL : = 32) **is record**
          str : string(1 . . len);
      end record;

      function "-" (whole, part : **in** vstring) **return** vstring;

end StringExtension;

package body StringExtension **is**

      function "-" (whole, part : **in** vstring) **return** vstring **is**

          matchcount : NATURAL   : = 0;
          windowpos : NATURAL   : = 0;
          subindex   : POSITIVE   : = 1;

    begin
      while windowpos + part.len < = whole.len **loop**
        if whole.str(windowpos + subindex) = part.str(subindex)
      then   matchcount : = matchcount + 1;
          if matchcount = part.len **then**
            return (whole.len - part.len,
               whole.str(1 . . windowpos) &
               whole.str(windowpos + part.len + 1 . . whole.len));
          end if;
          subindex : = subindex **mod** part.len + 1;
      else
          matchcount : = 0;
          windowpos : = windowpos + 1;
      end if;
      end loop;
      return whole;

    end "-";

end StringExtension;

4.6 Reminders

1. Pascal's array typing problems can be avoided in Ada by the use of unconstrained array type definitions.

2. Record and array assignments are available in both languages, but Pascal has no aggregates or slices that can serve as genuine record or array expressions respectively.

3. Array slicing is available in Ada to deal with segments of arrays as single units. The slice where the upperbound is less than the lowerbound is the null slice.

4. Ada provides finer control over loop exits. In particular, the return statement can be used to exit from the interior of a loop statement and, thus, to reduce the amount of control required in the while clause.

5. Strings are a predefined type in Ada. The underlying base type is that of an unconstrained array of characters whose index type is POSITIVE.

6. String literals are enclosed in double quotes in Ada but in single quotes in Pascal. In Ada, single characters are enclosed in single quotes.

7. String objects must be declared to be of a certain size, in other words, the constraints for the index must be specified when the object is declared.

8. The concatenation operator & is defined in Ada for strings and one dimensional arrays to form new strings or one dimensional arrays, respectively.

9. Ada provides parameterized record type definitions. The parameters define discriminants that determine the possible subtypes of the record type. Objects may be declared as constrained or unconstrained with respect to the parameters depending upon the absence or presence of default values for the parameters.

10. Dynamically variable array sizes can be constructed in Ada by enclosing them within a parameterized record type where the upper bound of the array is one of the parameters.

11. Constrained objects can only have values of the subtype indicated by the particular constraint. Unconstrained objects can have any value appropriate to the type definition.

12. Component assignment in unconstrained records is subject to certain restrictions: the discriminant can only be changed by complete record assignment; variant components can be changed only if the variant is current; and components depending on the constraints are limited to value of subtype determined by that current constraint.

13. Record aggregates can be constructed in Ada by either positional or named notation.

14. Ada allows the overloading of all operators, functions and procedures except for the operators **in**, **and then**, and **or else**. Ambiguities that arise must be resolved by name qualification.

15. It is strongly recommended to include only declarations relevant to the user in a package specification.

16. Functions in Ada may return structured values. The returned value is specified in the return statement (where in Pascal the value is returned by assigning the value to the function name).

17. Ada's return statement exits all inner scopes, terminates the execution of the function and returns the computed value.

18. Attributes of arrays can be used to determine dynamically the particular constraints for parameters declared as unconstrained. FIRST, LAST, LENGTH and RANGE are defined for each index of an array.

4.7 problems

1. A simplifying assumption was made in the implementation of the subtract function for the type STRING. Modify the implementation so that the function will work for any index constraints in the string and substring, regardless of whether or not the lowerbound is equal to 1.

2. Slicing and concatenation are provided for strings but not for *vstrings*. Write slicing and concatenation functions for *vstrings* and modify the function "-" to use *vstring* slicing and concatenation. How does your *vstring* slicing compare with the language supplied string slicing? Are the two concatenation operations identical, similar or different? Should these operations be local or exported?

3. Write a *vstring* removal operation that removes all occurrences of a specified substring. Can the subtraction operator "-" be overloaded for this operation? Is there some other language supplied operation that can be overloaded?

4. The example search in the problem discussion would have terminated immediately if the search had started at the end of the string rather than at the beginning. Rewrite the Ada function to start at the end rather than at the beginning. (The objective is still to remove the leftmost occurrence.)

5. The Boolean operator "<" is defined for strings in both Pascal and Ada but as yet has not been defined for *vstrings*. Write the Boolean function "<"

for *vstrings* in both Ada and Pascal and compare the programs. Discuss the similarities and the differences of your programs in both languages with regard to syntax notation, semantics of the used control statements, generality of the programs for strings of various lengths and efficient use of memory space.

Five

Data Abstraction

Topics: private types, data encapsulation, generics, procedures and functions
            as parameters.

Issues: hiding of data implementation, similarity between types, type
            extensions.

5.1 Problem Statement

Complex numbers, fractions and two dimensional vectors in the Cartesian plane
can all be viewed as special cases of number pairs.   Complex numbers are
composed of a real and an imaginary part, fractions of a numerator and a
denominator, and two dimensional vectors of an abscis (the x-coordinate) and an
ordinate (the y-coordinate).   The characteristics that distinguish complex numbers,
fractions and two dimensional vectors from one another are mainly determined by
the operations we associate with them.   Addition and subtraction are defined for
all three types, but the way fractions are added or subtracted differs from that of
complex numbers and two dimensional vectors.   ·Multiplication is defined for
fractions and complex numbers, but the way this operation works for each of these
types is again quite different.

The examples of n-dimensional vectors and matrices in Chapter 3 introduced the
idea of defining data types together with the operations that can be applied to
objects of these types.   In this chapter we extend this concept with two major
additions: first, we wish to build new types as extensions of existing types;
second, we wish to hide the particular data structure that we choose as the
representation of objects of these types.   The motivation for building new types as
extensions of existing types is the general principle of *reusable software*: assemble
new objects out of already existing parts.   The motivation for hiding
implementation details is to make it easier to revise and modify programs.

95

In the preceding chapters we showed how package bodies can hide the implementation of procedures and local variables they share. But in all preceding examples the data structures used for implementing types were included in the visible part of the packages, with the result that users have access to these data structures. If the data structure of a typed object is displayed to the user, it is certain that user programs will directly refer to parts of such a structure. The result is that a system contains strong dependencies between the program part that defines the implementation and the program parts that use the defined objects. If one ever modifies the implementation, one must check all programs to see whether the change has an effect on the way the object is used. Experienced programmers know that it is very hard to check all places of usage and that it is almost impossible to keep track of where all these places are located in the mass of programs that are written for a system.

In our particular example, there are several ways in which the three types can be represented. In case of fractions one has the choice between reducing fractions to their canonical form and leaving common factors in the representation (i.e., 2/3 instead of 4/6 or 14/21). In the case of complex numbers and two dimensional vectors, one has the choice between cartesian coordinates and polar coordinates. If the choice remains hidden from the user, one can be sure that changing that representation will not affect any part of the user's programs. All changes are then limited to the program containing the hidden implementation.

In the case of vectors, strings or matrices, one purposely gives the user access to the structure of the objects. A user should be able to operate on components of vectors, on elements of matrices and she should be able to access individual characters or slices of strings. In these cases it is justified to display the internal structure to the users. (One hopes that the implementor will not often find good reasons for changing the representation of such types.) However, in the case of complex numbers and fractions it is doubtful whether a user should have access to the internal structure. Of course, hiding the internal structure does not prevent us from providing functions that produce the value of attributes such as the real part of a complex number or the denominator of a fraction.

The specific task for this chapter is the following. First we design and implement number pairs with operations for assembling a number pair from two real numbers and for addition, subtraction, multiplication and scalar multiplication. Next we design and implement the three data types *complex*, *planevector* and *fraction* whose internal structure will not be accessible to the users. The operations defined for these types are assembly, addition, subtraction, scalar multiplication and multiplication. The latter has a distinct implementation for each type which in case of planevectors is the INNERPROD. The intent is to build the three data types as much as possible on numberpair arithmetic.

5.2 Problem Discussion

All operations apply to objects that consist of two parts. Each part is of a scalar type to which the standard operations of addition, multiplication, etc. apply.

Operations on Numberpairs

We name the two components of numberpairs *first* and *second*. Assembling a numberpair out of two input numbers p and q is accomplished by setting *first* to p and *second* to q. Adding to numberpairs is basically the same as adding vectors (cf. Chapter 3). The sum is the numberpair whose components are obtained by adding the corresponding components of the input numberpairs. Subtraction and multiplication are defined likewise.

Scalar multiplication is also very similar to the corresponding operation for n-dimensional vectors (cf. Chapter 3). The scalar multiplication rule is

$$\text{SCALMUL}(s, y) = (s * \text{first}(y), s * \text{second}(y)) \tag{1}$$

This rule says that the scalar product of a scalar s and a numberpair y is again a numberpair whose components are obtained by multiplying each of y's components by scalar s.

Operations on Complex Numbers, Planevectors and Fractions

We observe that some numberpair operations are usable for complex numbers and plane vectors, but not for fractions. With multiplication the situation is just the opposite: the numberpair multiplication can be used for multiplying fractions, but not for plane vectors or complex numbers. We realize at this point that one should not be misled by apparent similarity. Although we speak of addition of complex numbers and fractions, and although we often use the same symbol " + " to denote these operations, their semantics are quite different! This is true not only for addition (or subtraction) of fractions and of complex numbers, but for scalar multiplication as well. For instance, the result of 3 ∗ (2/5) is not (6/15), but (6/5).

The operations that differ from those of numberpairs are

$$\text{FRACADD}(a/b, p/q) \qquad\qquad = \ (a*q + b*p) \ / \ (b*q) \tag{2}$$
similarly for subtraction
$$\text{FRACSCALMUL}(s, p/q) \qquad\quad = \ (s*p) \ / \ q \tag{3}$$
$$\text{INNERPROD}((u_1, u_1), (v_1, v_2)) \ = \ u_1*v_1 + u_2*v_2 \tag{4}$$
$$\text{COMPLMUL}((x_r, x_i), (y_r, y_i)) \ = \ (x_r*y_r - x_i*y_i, \ x_r*y_i + x_i*y_r) \tag{5}$$

Implementation of Fraction Operations

If fractions are kept in canonical form, the result of a fraction operation may need to be reduced by dividing out the common factor of the resulting numerator and denominator. However, if we first compute products of numerators and denominators (such as a∗q, b∗p, etc.) and wait until the end before we eliminate common factors, the intermediate results may become too large and cause numeric overflow. Therefore, it is better to eliminate common factors by division before components are multiplied. This improvement leads to the following fraction operations (replacing 2 and 3):

$$\text{FRACADD}(a/b, \ p/q) \qquad = \quad (a*q' + b'*p) \ / \ (b'*q'*g) \tag{6}$$
where b' = b/g, q' = q/g and g = GCD(b, q)

$$\text{FRACSCALMUL}(s, \ p/q) \qquad = \quad (s'*p) \ / \ q' \tag{7}$$
where s' = s/g, q' = q/g and g = GCD(s, q)

$$\text{FRACMUL}(a/b, \ p/q) \qquad = \quad (a'*p') \ / \ (b'*q') \tag{8}$$
where a' = a/g, b' = b/h, p' = p/h, q' = q/g,
and g = GCD(a, q), h = GCD(b, p)

5.3 A Pascal Solution

A natural choice for the type of the parts of numberpairs, complex numbers and planevectors is type *real* and for the parts of fractions, type *integer*. Choosing a type for numberpairs, we have a choice between an array type or a record type.

    type   NUMBERPAIR   = **array**[1 . . 2] **of** real;
            numberpair   = **record** first, second : real **end**;

The first type looks almost the same as the second type if we introduce an enumeration type whose values are *first* and *second*, and use this enumeration type for the index range of type NUMBERPAIR.

    type   pair   = (first, second);
            NUMBERPAIR   = **array** [pair] **of** real;

Components of NUMBERPAIR and numberpair objects *u* and *x* are accessed as *u*[first], *u*[second], *x*.first and *x*.second. There is in fact very little difference between the two type definitions for numberpairs. We need only one of the two and we choose to use the record type because of the slightly simpler type declaration.

Numberpair Operations

Since Pascal functions cannot return structured objects, the numberpair operations must be implemented as procedures that return their result in var parameters. Two examples are procedure ASSEM which takes two real numbers and assembles these into a numberpair and procedure ADDPAIR which returns the sum of two numberpairs.

```
procedure ASSEM(p, q : real ; var u :  numberpair);
begin
        u.first := p ;  u.second := q
end;

procedure ADDPAIR(x, y : numberpair ; var z :  numberpair);
begin
        z.first    := x.first + y.first;
        z.second := x.second + y.second
end;
```

SUBPAIR and MULPAIR are derived from ADDPAIR in the obvious way. Scalar multiplication is implemented by

```
procedure SCALMUL(s : real ; y : numberpair ; var z :  numberpair);
begin
        z.first := s * y.first; z.second := s * y.second
end;
```

Complex Numbers and Planevectors

It seems that numberpairs can be used effectively for the implementation of. complex numbers and planevectors if we choose cartesian coordinates and a record structure for their representation.

```
type   complex     = record realpart, imagpart : real end;
       planevector = record abscis, ordinate : real end;
```

Unfortunately, there is no way to associate the types complex and planevector with type numberpair, even though their representations are identical. There are three ways of solving this dilemma. First, we can write four conversion procedures that map complex numbers and planevectors into numberpairs and vice versa. Second, we can simply rewrite the procedures for addition, subtraction and scalar multiplication for the types complex and planevector. Third, we can make complex numbers and planevectors of the same type as numberpairs by using the existing type numberpair instead of introducing two new record types. We will investigate each of these three alternatives.

If we use conversion routines, we need procedures such as

```
procedure COMPLEXTOPAIR(x : complex ; var u :  numberpair);
begin u.first : = x.realpart; u.second : = x.imagpart end;
```

The other conversion routines are similar to this one.   Using the conversion
routines for defining complex and planevector operations, complex addition would
be written as

```
procedure COMPLADD(x, y : complex; var z :  complex);
        var u, v : numberpair;
begin
        COMPLEXTOPAIR(x, u) ; COMPLEXTOPAIR(y, v);
        ADDPAIR(u, v, u) ; PAIRTOCOMPLEX(u, z)
end;
```

Following the second idea of simply copying the code, one simply writes

```
procedure ADDCOMPL(x, y : complex ; var z :  complex);
begin
        z.realpart: = x.realpart + y.realpart;
        z.imagpart: = x.imagpart + y.imagpart
end;
```

Writing this procedure is far less work than writing the conversion routines and
the complex operations that use them.   It is also obvious that procedure
ADDCOMPL is less expensive in execution time than procedure COMPLADD. Thus,
copying the code compares favorably with introducing conversion routines.

The third alternative of not introducing new types for complex numbers and
planevectors is the easiest and least costly. In that case there is no need to write
any additional code, because the numberpair operations apply to complex numbers
and planevectors. However, a great disadvantage is that one now has to declare

```
var    x : numberpair;
       v : numberpair;
```

where in reality a complex object *x* and a planevector *v* are intended. Moreover,
one can now mix complex numbers and planevectors in statements such as

```
x := v ; COMPLMUL(x, v) ; INNERPROD(x, v)
```

This lack of type safety is such a serious drawback that we strongly prefer the
alternative of copying the code. The duplicated code is included in the complete
programs at the end of this chapter.

Both types complex and planevector have a multiplication operation that differs
from the multiplication operation for numberpairs. The multiplication programs
we need implement lines 4 and 5.

```
function INNERPROD(u, v : planevector) : real;
begin
    INNERPROD := u.abscis * v.abscis + u.ordinate * v.ordinate
end;
```

```
procedure COMPLMUL(x, y : complex ; var z : complex);
begin
    z.realpart := x.realpart * y.realpart - x.imagpart * y.imagpart;
    z.imagpart := x.realpart * y.imagpart + x.imagpart * y.realpart
end;
```

The INNERPROD can be written as a function, because the result is of scalar type.

Fraction Arithmetic

The similarity between fractions and numberpairs is only superficial. Assembly and multiplication are the only procedures that are somewhat similar, although little similarity remains if we keep intermediate results as small as possible in order to avoid numeric overflow. In addition, we wish to reduce fractions to their canonical form in which numerator and denominator have no factor in common.

A suitable type definition for fractions is

```
type frac = record num, denom : integer end;
```

The operation that assembles a fraction out of two integers divides these numbers by their GCD (greatest common divisor). The result is a pair of numbers that have no factor in common.

```
procedure ASSEM(a, b : integer ; var x : frac);
        var g : integer;
begin
        g := GCD(a, b);
        x.num := a div g ;
        x.denom := b div g
end;
```

When two fractions are multiplied, we want to remove the common factor of the first numerator and the second denominator as well as that of the second numerator and the first denominator before multiplying (see line 8). If x, y are the fractions to be multiplied and u, v are auxiliary fraction variables, the statements

```
ASSEM(x.num, y.denom, u) ; ASSEM(y.num, x.denom, v)
```

remove all possible common factors. Multiplication of x and y can now be replaced by multiplication of u and v.

```
procedure FRACMUL(x, y : frac ; var z :  frac);
     var u, v : frac;
begin
     ASSEM(x.num, y.denom, u) ; ASSEM(y.num, x.denom, v);
     z.num := u.num * v.num ; z.denom := u.denom * v.denom
end;
```

In fraction addition, the intermediate product can be kept as small as possible by dividing out the GCD of the denominators (see line 6). It is possible that the result can be reduced once again because of the addition in the numerator (see 6). Thus, the addition program begins with dividing the denominators by their GCD and ends with a call of ASSEM so that the result is delivered in canonical form.

```
procedure FRACADD(x, y : frac ; var z :  frac);
     var g : integer;
begin
     g := GCD(x.denom, y.denom);
     x.denom := x.denom div g ; y.denom := y.denom div g;
     z.num := x.num * y.denom + y.num * x.denom;
     z.denom := x.denom * y.denom * g;
     assem(a.num, z.denom, z)
end;
```

The procedure for subtraction is of course very similar to this procedure. The one for scalar multiplication is a variation of procedure FRACMUL. The complete set of Pascal programs is found at the end of this chapter.

5.4 An Ada Solution

Numberpair Arithmetic

A record type definition for numberpairs in Ada is

type numberpair **is record** first, second : FLOAT ; **end record**;

The natural thing to do in Ada is to encapsulate this type with the operations on numberpairs in a package PAIRARITHMETIC. The package exports the open type *numberpair*, the basic assembly operation ASSEM that constructs a numberpair, and the basic numberpair operations of addition, subtraction and the two forms of multiplication. Note that the numberpair functions are overloaded with the operations for integer and real arithmetic (cf. Chapters 1 and 3). The operations defined here are differentiated from the integer and real operations by their parameter and result profiles.

```
package PAIRARITHMETIC is

    type numberpair is record first, second : FLOAT ; end record;

    function ASSEM (x, y : in FLOAT) return numberpair;
    function "+"  (u, v : in numberpair) return numberpair;
    function "-"  (u, v : in numberpair) return numberpair;
    function "*"  (u, v : in numberpair) return numberpair;
    function "*"  (x: in FLOAT; v: in numberpair) return numberpair;

end PAIRARITHMETIC;
```

The implementation of these functions is described in the package body of PAIRARITHMETIC whose complete program is found at the end of this chapter. As an example of the implementation, we consider the addition of numberpairs. The program of this function is quite different from the corresponding Pascal program, not only because Ada functions may return structured objects, but also because Ada allows assignment of record expressions (aggregates) to record objects (cf. Chapter 1). We saw examples of record assignments for vstrings in Chapter 4. The Ada version of pair addition is in fact no more than a return statement in which the sum aggregate is assembled.

```
    function "+"(u, v : in numberpair) return numberpair is
    begin
            return (u.first + v.first, u.second + v.second) ;
    end "+";
```

Note that the parentheses following the keyword **return** do not enclose a parameter list, but delineate a record aggregate for which we used positional notation.

Generic Subprograms

Instead of rewriting the procedures for each of the operators as we had to do in Pascal, we would like to write a program schema that accepts the particular operator, "+", "-" or "*", as an actual parameter. While Pascal does allow functions and procedures to be passed as parameters, it does not allow language defined operators to be used as actual parameters. In Ada, a program schema can be written as a *generic* program unit consisting of a generic clause that precedes a subprogram, a package or a task. The generic clause specifies the generic parameters which can be data parameters (expressions, variables or constants), type parameters, procedure parameters or function parameters. Ordinary parameters to a function or a procedure must be data parameters and cannot be a type, a procedure or a function parameter.

```
procedure P(x : in FLOAT ; function f) :          -- illegal in Ada
function   F(u : in vector ; type T) ;            -- illegal in Ada
function   F(i, k : in INTEGER ; procedure P) ;   -- illegal in Ada
```

The first and last specifications, but not the second, are legal in Pascal: parameters in Pascal may be procedures or functions, but not types. In Ada, all three can be passed as generic parameters. The specification of a procedure or function parameter requires a complete list of parameters, including their types and, for functions, the result type. A subprogram parameter specification is identical to the procedure or function heading in a declaration.

```
generic with procedure P(u, v : in complex);
        with function F(x, y : in FLOAT ; v : in vector) return vector;
        . . .
        package name is
        . . .
        end name;
```

A generic function or procedure parameter is preceded by the keyword **with** in contrast to other generic parameters (such as data or type parameters) which are not preceded by this keyword (ARM 12.1, 12-2).

We saw in Chapter 1 that a generic program unit is comparable to a data type: it is a template for objects which can be created using the template as a model. The use of a generic unit for the creation of an object is called an *instantiation* of that unit. The syntactic form of an instantiation closely resembles a procedure call and has the general format

```
new genericunitname (actuals for the generic parameters)
```

For example, the instantiation

```
package Q is new name(LINE, EXCHANGE);
```

instantiates generic package name and attaches the name Q to the newly created object. The language system checks that the actual parameters LINE and EXCHANGE match the specifications of the generic paramters F and P.

Generic Pair Operations

We can express the commonality of the three operations addition, subtraction and multiplication as a generic unit and instantiate that unit once for each operation. The generic unit takes a function as formal parameter.

```
generic with function "&"(x, y : in FLOAT) return FLOAT;
        function PAIROP(u, v : in numberpair) return numberpair;
```

Note that "&" is a formal function name and not a specific operator.

The generic unit PAIROP is used to instantiate the functions "+", "-" and "*" for numberpairs. The implementation of these functions is placed in the body of package PAIRARITHMETIC, not in its visible part. Since the generic unit PAIROP is used only by the implementations of these functions, there is no need to make it visible. By including the generic unit in the implementation body, the visible part of package PAIRARITHMETIC displays only the necessary user interface. The package body contains the generic function declaration, the instantiations and the body of the generic function.

package body PAIRARITHMETIC **is**

```
generic with "&"(x, y : in FLOAT) return FLOAT;
function PAIROP(u, v : in numberpair) return numberpair;

function ASSEM (p, q : in FLOAT) return numberpair is
begin return (p, q) ; end ASSEM;

function " + " (u, v : in numberpair) return numberpair is
new PAIROP(" + ");

function "-" (u, v : in numberpair) return numberpair is
new PAIROP("-");

function "*" (u, v : in numberpair) return numberpair
is new PAIROP("*");

function "*"
         (x : in FLOAT; v : in numberpair) return numberpair is
begin return (x*v.left, x*v.right) ; end "*";

function PAIROP(u, v : in numberpair) return numberpair is
begin
         return (u.first & v.first, u.second & v.second) ;
end PAIROP;
```

end PAIRARITHMETIC;

The scalar multiplication cannot be defined as an instantiation of generic unit PAIROP, because their parameter lists do not match. The first parameter of PAIROP is u, a numberpair, while the first parameter of the scalar multiplication is scalar x, a FLOAT value. Note that a generic subprogram always consists of two parts: the generic declaration and a separate body. Putting the two together into a single local declaration is not permitted (ARM 12.1, 12.2).

Private Types

In the Problem Statement section we expressed a desire to hide the implementation not only of subprogram bodies, but also of the data structures used in type definitions. Ada allows us to indicate that the structure of a type remains hidden from the user by substituting the keyword **private** for the structure. For example,

> **type** complex   **is private**;
> **type** planevector **is private**;

One would expect to find the hidden definition of private types in the corresponding package body just as the function and procedure bodies. For users it is sufficient to find the typename of a private type in the visible part so that objects can be declared of that type and can be passed as parameters to operations defined for that type. Thus, in the case of complex numbers, one would expect the visible part of the package to contain the type specification and all the operations on that type in the following form.

> **package** COMPLARITH **is**   -- this visible part is not complete
>
>   **type** complex **is private**;
>
>   **function** ASSEM (x, y : **in** FLOAT) **return** complex;
>   **function** " + "   (u, v : **in** complex) **return** complex;
>   **function** "-"   (u, v : **in** complex) **return** complex;
>   **function** "*"   (u, v : **in** complex) **return** complex;
>   **function** "*"   (s : **in** FLOAT; v : **in** complex) **return** complex;
>   **function** RE   (u : **in** complex) **return** FLOAT;
>   **function** IM   (u : **in** complex) **return** FLOAT;
>
>   <and other relevant functions>
>
> **end** COMPLARITH;

As far as the user is concerned, the visible part indeed specifies all she has to know in order to declare complex variables and operate on them. Nevertheless, the visible part above is not correct Ada. The language requires that the structure of a private type be defined in the visible part in a separate section for which the keyword **private** serves as an opening bracket. The private section must be the last part of the visible part (ARM 7.4.2, 7-8). It sould be noted that subordinate type definitions needed to define the private types, but which are not exported in the visible interface, are also declared in the private part.

```
package name is
     type t is private;
     <other specifications>
private
     type t is <definition of type t>
     <other private elaborations>
end name;
```

Having a private section in the visible part of a package is motivated by compilation considerations. We mentioned in Chapter 1 that Ada's separate compilation facility is based on the idea that a visible part and an implementation body must be separately compilable. Of the packages used in a program unit only the visible parts should be included, but not their implementation bodies. Including visible parts without package bodies works fine for functions and procedures, but not for private types. The problem caused by private types is that, without having access to the implementation of private types, the compiler can not determine the size of declared objects. The problem is solved by including in the visible part a private section in which private types are elaborated. The presence of this section in the visible part of a package makes it possible for the compiler to process object declarations involving private types without including package bodies. We want to stress the fact that the private section at the end of a visible part is there to pass information to the compiler and should be treated by the user of a package as if it occurred in the package body. The content of a private section is of no concern to a user.

With the addition of a private section, the visible part of the complex arithmetic package is:

```
package COMPLARITH is

     type complex is private;

     function ASSEM (p, q : in FLOAT) return complex;
     function "+"    (u, v : in complex) return complex;
     function "-"    (u, v : in complex) return complex;
     function "*"    (u, v : in complex) return complex;
     function "*"    (x : in FLOAT; v : in complex) return complex;
     function RE      (u : in complex) return FLOAT;
     function IM      (u : in complex) return FLOAT;

private

     type complex is record realpart, imagpart : FLOAT ; end record;

end COMPLARITH;
```

Generic Packages

The packages for complex and planevector arithmetic are of course very similar to the numberpair package. Because of this similarity, Ada's generic facilities should again be very helpful in defining packages for all three types. We can define a generic package that models the common parts of the three types and then create the individual packages as instantiations of that generic unit. (We will see shortly that type *fraction* does not fit in this scheme because its similarity with the others is confined to its visible part and does not extend to its package body.)

A peculiar thing about the generic package for the three types is that it has no generic parameters.

> **generic**
> **package** PAIRS **is**
>
>   **type** pair **is private**;
>
>   **function** ASSEM   (x, y : **in** FLOAT) **return** pair;
>   **function** " + "   (u, v : **in** pair) **return** pair;
>   **function** "-"   (u, v : **in** pair) **return** pair;
>   **function** "*"   (u, v : **in** pair) **return** pair;
>   **function** "*"   (x : **in** FLOAT ; v : **in** pair) **return** pair;
>   **function** FIRST   (u : **in** pair) **return** FLOAT;
>   **function** SECOND (u : **in** pair) **return** FLOAT;
>
> **private**
>
>   **type** pair **is record** left, right : FLOAT ; **end record**;
>
> **end** PAIRS;

The body of this package is the same as that of PAIRARITHMETIC in Section 5.4.3.

The types *numberpair*, *complex* and *planevector* and their standard operations can be created by instantiations of generic package PAIRS. For instance, the declaration

> **package** COMPLBASICS **is new** PAIRS;

creates a new package that provides a record type of two FLOAT elements and the basic operations: assembly, addition, subtraction, multiplication, scalar multiplication and component extraction. To be precise, one must identify the items that came into being by this instantiation with the name as given in generic package PAIRS, but prefixed with the instantiation name to make clear to which package the items belong (ARM 12.3, 12-9). Thus, as a result of the instantiation, the items in existence are

type COMPLBASICS.pair and
function COMPLBASICS.ASSEM, COMPLBASICS."+", etc.

Renaming

The introduction of generic package PAIRS makes it possible to create the basic operations for the types *numberpair*, *complex* and *planevector* as instantiations of a single model. Although we gained in not having to copy the code for each of these three types, the resulting naming of the operation is not very satisfactory. At the end of the preceding subsection we encountered names such as COMPLBASICS.ASSEM, etc. One may expect similar verbosity for the other types, which have names such as NUMBERPAIR."-" and PLANEVECBASICS."*" instead of the more pleasing denotations "-" and "*".

To remove this difficulty, Ada provides a *renaming* facility that helps the user to identify program objects by short names or to remember part of a name evaluation (ARM 8.5, 8-8). The latter is not unlike the Pascal with statement as the following example shows.

type date **is record** mo : month ; d : day ; yr : year; **end record**;
type message **is record**
        datemark : date;
        sender : STRING(1 . . 24);
        text : STRING(1 . . 2000);
end record;
msg : message;

To fill in a particular date, one can write in Pascal

with msg.datemark **do**
        begin
                mo := Jul;
                d := 9;
                yr := 64
        end

A comparable statement in Ada is

declare
        dt : date **renames** msg.datemark;
begin
        dt := (Jul, 9, 64);
end;

The rename feature of Ada can be used to avoid the verbose names for operations on numberpairs, complex numbers and planevectors resulting from instantiations of the generic package PAIRS.

function ASSEM(x, y : **in** FLOAT) **return** complex
renames COMPLBASICS.ASSEM;

function "*"(u, v : **in** complex) **return** complex
renames COMPLBASICS."*";

etc.

The renaming feature will be used to define the bodies of the standard operations of the three types *numberpair*, *complex* and *planevector*. These function bodies are defined in the package bodies for each of these three types. The renaming scheme has the agreeable characteristic that no extra function call is introduced that would increase the execution of the programs. The renaming is interpreted by the lexical analyzer of an Ada compiler, but no trace of it is left in the object code.

Application of Generic Packages

We now have a generic package PAIRS that can produce the basic operations for types *numberpair*, *complex* and *planevector*. We have seen the notation for instantiating a package and we discussed the naming convention for instantiated objects such as COMPLBASIC.ASSEM. We also discussed the renaming feature that can be used for replacing verbose names by shorter ones without paying in runtime overhead. The purpose of this section is to discover where the instantiations should occur in the packages for numberpairs, complex numbers and planevectors and how these packages should make use of the instatiations.

Let us take package COMPLARITH as an example of instantiating generic package PAIRS. We want to explore
- how to introduce type *complex*
- where to put the instantiation of generic package PAIRS: in the visible part of package COMPLARITH or in its package body.

Instantiating the generic package PAIRS generates not only a set of standard functions, but also an instance of type pair. The instantiation

package COMPLBASICS **is new** PAIRS;

generates the type

type COMPLBASICS.pairs;

This type is the one that applies to the parameters of the generated standard functions COMPLBASICS."+", etc. and is the result type of all but COMPLBASICS.FIRST and COMPLBASICS.SECOND. Thus, if these functions are used for complex arithmetic, type complex must be the same as type COMPLBASICS.pairs.

One would expect that the renaming scheme for types to be the same as that for functions and procedures. Thus, one is inclined to write

type complex **renames** COMPLBASICS.pairs;

Unfortunately, Ada allows renaming of data objects, exceptions, subprograms, packages and tasks, but not of types! (ARM 8.5, 8-8). Types can be renamed in a unusual way by declaring a subtype *complex* and by letting the subtype be the entire parent type (i.e., the subtype is declared without any constraints) :

subtype complex **is** COMPLBASICS.pairs;

In the problem statement section we expressed the desire to keep the implementation of type complex hidden from the user. One might expect that this could be achieved by declaring a private subtype *complex* and by then elaborating its definition in a private section.

with PAIRS;
package COMPLARITH **is**

> **subtype** complex **is private** ;   -- this is illegal in Ada
> <all standardfunction specifications>

private
> **package** COMPLBASICS is **new** PAIRS;
> **subtype** complex **is** COMPLBASICS.pairs ;

end COMPLARITH;

Unfortunately, Ada does not allow a subtype to be declared as private. This feature exists only for types and not for subtypes. Since the renaming scheme forces us to declare *complex* as a subtype and since a subtype cannot be declared private, the subtype definition at the beginning of package COMPLARITH must be the actual definition in terms of COMPLBASICS.

It seems that the ability to hide the implementation of type *complex* is lost because we are forced to make complex a subtype and subtypes cannot be declared private. It is indeed true that the subtype definition cannot help us to hide the implementation, but, on the other hand, the parent type can! The subtype is implicitly private if the parent type is. Thus, subtype *complex* is implicitly private if its parent type COMPLBASICS.pair is private. The latter is private if and only if the generic package PAIRS defines its type *pair* to be private. Since this is indeed the case, it is certain that the structure of type *complex* remains hidden. The fact that hiding an instantiated type depends entirely on the generic definition, and not at all on the instantiation, has a slight drawback in that either all its instantiated types are private or none are. It is not possible, for example, to make the types *complex*, *planevector* private, but to make the type *numberpair* non-private.

The generic package PAIRS can be placed either in the visible part of package COMPLARITH or in its package body. Since it is not used in the specifications of the standard functions, the instantiation seems to belong in the package body. There is, however, a compelling reason for includung it in the visible part because the instantiation is used in the subtype definition of *complex*. This definition occurs in the visible part because several parameters and results of the functions listed in the visible part use that subtype. Since Ada has the rigorous rule "declaration before usage" (ARM 3.2.1, 3-4), the instantiation must precede the subtype definition of *complex*. This leads to the following visible part for complex arithmetic.

> **with** PAIRS;
> **package** COMPLARITH **is**
>   **package** COMPLBASICS **is new** PAIRS;
>   **subtype** complex **is** COMPLBASICS.pair;
>
>   **function** ASSEM(x, y : **in** FLOAT) **return** complex;
>   **function** " + " (u, v : **in** complex) **return** complex;
>   <and all other standard functions>
> **end** COMPLARITH;

The corresponding body declares the function bodies as renamed versions of the standard functions generated by the instantiation COMPLBASICS. The complete programs for both the visible part and the body are found at the end of this chapter.

Fraction Arithmetic

The visible part of fraction arithmetic looks very similar to all the others. The major difference is that the operation ASSEM and the scalar multiplication take an INTEGER parameter instead of a FLOAT parameter.

> **package** FRACARITH **is**
>   **type** frac **is private**;
>   **function** ASSEM   (x, y : **in** INTEGER) **return** frac;
>   **function** " + "   (u, v : **in** frac) **return** frac;
>   **function** "-"   (u, v : **in** frac) **return** frac;
>   **function** "*"   (u, v : **in** frac) **return** frac;
>   **function** "*"   (x : **in** INTEGER; v : **in** frac) **return** frac;
>   **function** NUMER   (v : **in** frac) **return** INTEGER;
>   **function** DENOM   (v : **in** frac) **return** INTEGER;
>   **function** RECIP   (v : **in** frac) **return** FRAC;
>   <other useful functions on fractions>
> **private**
>   **type** frac **is record** num, den : INTEGER ; **end record**;
> **end** FRACARITH;

Although the visible part of the package FRACARITH is very similar to the other packages, there is little purpose in creating this package as an instantiation of generic package PAIRS. The implementations are so different that the body of package FRACARITH cannot define the fraction operations by renaming the functions generated by generic package PAIRS. One should realize that generic instantiation involves not only the visible part of packages, but also their implementation. Creation of different type packages from a common generic model makes sense only if the operations included in these packages have the same specification and the same implementation.

In Ada, fractions are assembled out of INTEGERS by a function whose body consists of a single return statement.

> **function** ASSEM(x, y : **in** INTEGER) **return** frac **is**
>   g : **constant** INTEGER : = GCD(x, y);
> **begin**   **return** (x/g, y/g) ;   **end** ASSEM;

Note that in Pascal integer division is denoted by the keyword **div**. In Ada, the symbol "/" is overloaded and applies to either a pair of INTEGER operands or a pair of FLOAT operands.

Multiplication of fractions in Ada uses two auxiliary fractions, as in Pascal, to retain the intermediate results of common factor elimination (cf. 8).

> **function** "*" (u, v : **in** frac) **return** frac **is**
>   x : frac : = ASSEM(u.num, v.den);
>   y : frac : = ASSEM(v.num, u.den);
> **begin**   **return** (x.num*y.num, x.den*y.den) ;   **end** "*";

At a first glance, one might think that the field extractions: u.num, etc., are illegal, because all parameters and variables are of type *frac* and *frac* is a private type. It is indeed true that a private type hides its structure from all programs in other packages (or tasks) that use fractions. But the·multiplication function is located in the body of package FRACARITH which is part of the scope of the type definition. Since the structure of a private type is accessible in the scope of its definition (ARM 7.4.2, 7-7), the fields *num* and *den* are available in package body FRACARITH and nowhere else.

The addition of fractions in Ada is implemented as a function containing a return statement in which the result record is assembled in accordance with 6.

> **function** "+" (u, v : **in** frac) **return** frac **is**
>   g : **constant** INTEGER : = GCD(u.den, v.den);
>   b : **constant** INTEGER : = u.den/g;
>   d : **constant** INTEGER : = v.den/g;
> **begin**   **return** ASSEM(u.num*d + v.num*b, b*d*g);   **end** "+";

The indication that all three auxiliary items are constant is not strictly necessary because the body of function " + " does not contain any assignment statements. This time the expression of the return statement is a function call.

The function for subtraction is easily derived from the addition function. If we had defined a generic function, we could have created the addition and subtraction functions as instantiations of that generic function. This is done in the programs that follow.

5.5 The Complete Programs

Numberpairs in Pascal

type numberpair = **record** first, second : real **end**;

procedure ASSEM(p, q : real ; **var** u : numberpair);
begin u.first := p ; u.second := q **end**;

procedure ADDPAIR(x, y : numberpair ; **var** z : numberpair);
begin
      z.first := x.first + y.first;
      z.second := x.second + y.second
end;

procedure SUBPAIR(x, y : numberpair ; **var** z : numberpair);
begin
      z.first := x.first - y.first;
      z.second := x.second - y.second
end;

procedure MULPAIR(x, y : numberpair; **var** z : numberpair);
begin
      z.first := x.first * y.first;
      z.second := x.second * y.second
end;

procedure SCALMUL(s : real ; y : numberpair ; **var** z : numberpair);
begin
      z.first := s * y.first;
      z.second := s * y.second
end;

Generic Pairs in Ada

generic
package PAIRS **is**

      type pair **is private**;

          function ASSEM   (x, y : **in** FLOAT) **return** pair;
          function " + "   (u, v : **in** pair) **return** pair;
          function "-"   (u, v : **in** pair) **return** pair;
          function "*"   (u, v : **in** pair) **return** pair;
          function "*"   (s : **in** FLOAT ; v : **in** pair) **return** pair;
          function FIRST   (u : **in** pair) **return** FLOAT;
          function SECOND (u : **in** pair) **return** FLOAT;

private
      type pair **is record** left, right : FLOAT ; **end record**;
end PAIRS;

package body PAIRS **is**   -- not visible to users

      generic with function "&"(x, y : **in** FLOAT) **return** FLOAT;
      function PAIROP(u, v : **in** pair) **return** pair; -- declaration of PAIROP

      function ASSEM (x, y : **in** FLOAT) **return** pair **is**
      begin return (x, y) ; **end** ASSEM;

      function " + " (u, v : **in** pair) **return** pair **is**
      new PAIROP (" + ");

      function "-" (u, v : **in** pair) **return** pair **is**
      new PAIROP ("-");

      function "*" (u, v : **in** pair) **return** pair **is**
      new PAIROP ("*");

      function "*" (s : **in** FLOAT ; v : **in** pair) **return** pair **is**
      begin return (s*v.left, s*v.right) ; **end** "*";

      function FIRST(u : **in** pair) **return** FLOAT **is**
      begin return u.left ; **end** FIRST;

      function SECOND(u : **in** pair) **return** FLOAT **is**
      begin return u.right ; **end** SECOND;

      -- implementation of PAIROP
      function PAIROP(u, v : **in** pair) **return** pair **is**
      begin return (u.left & v.left, u.right & v.right) ; **end** PAIROP;

end PAIRS;

Complex Numbers in Pascal

```pascal
type complex = record realpart, imagpart : real end;

procedure ASSEMCOMPL(p, q : real ; var u :  complex);
begin u.realpart : = p ; u.imagpart : = q end;

procedure ADDCOMPL(x, y : complex ; var z :  complex);
begin
      z.realpart: =  x.realpart + y.realpart;
      z.imagpart: =  x.imagpart + y.imagpart
end;

procedure SUBCOMPL(x, y : complex ; var z :  complex);
begin
      z.realpart: =  x.realpart - y.realpart;
      z.imagpart: =  x.imagpart - y.imagpart
end;

procedure MULCOMPL(x, y : complex ; var z : complex);
begin
      z.realpart : = x.realpart * y.realpart - x.imagpart * y.imagpart;
      z.imagpart : = x.realpart * y.imagpart + x.imagpart * y.realpart
end;

procedure SCALCOMPL(s : real ; y : complex ; var z :  complex);
begin
      z.realpart : = s*y.realpart;
      z.imagpart : = s*y.imagpart
end;
```

Complex Numbers in Ada

```
with PAIRS;
package COMPLARITH is

        package COMPLBASICS is new PAIRS;
        subtype complex is COMPLBASICS.pair;

        function ASSEM   (x, y : in FLOAT) return complex;
        function "+"     (u, v : in complex) return complex;
        function "-"     (u, v : in complex) return complex;
        function "*"     (u, v : in complex) return complex;
        function "*"     (s : in FLOAT ; v : in complex) return complex;
        function REPART  (v : in complex) return FLOAT;
        function IMPART  (v : in complex) return FLOAT;

end COMPLARITH;


package body COMPLARITH is  --  not visible to users

        function ASSEM (x, y : in FLOAT) return complex
        renames COMPLBASICS.ASSEM;

        function "+" (u, v : in complex) return complex
        renames COMPLBASICS."+";

        function "-" (u, v : in complex) return complex
        renames COMPLBASICS."-";

        function "*" (s : in FLOAT ; v : in complex) return complex
        renames COMPLBASICS."*";

        function REPART (v : in complex) return FLOAT
        renames COMPLBASICS.FIRST;

        function IMPART (v : in complex) return FLOAT
        renames COMPLBASICS.SECOND;

        function "*" (u, v : in complex) return complex is
        begin
                return (REPART(u) * REPART(v) - IMPART(u) * IMPART(v),
                        REPART(u) * IMPART(v) + IMPART(u) * REPART(v));
        end "*";

end COMPLARITH;
```

Planevectors in Pascal

type planevec = **record** abscis, ordinate : real **end**;

procedure ASSEMPLANEVEC(p, q : real ; **var** u : planevec);
begin u.abscis : = p ; u.ordinate : = q **end**;

procedure ADDVEC(x, y : planevec ; **var** z : planevec);
begin
    z.abscis: = x.abscis + y.absics;
    z.ordinate: = x.ordinate + y.ordinate
end;

procedure SUBVEC(x, y : planevec ; **var** z : planevec);
begin
    z.abscis: = x.abscis - y.abscis;
    z.ordinate: = x.ordinate - y.ordinate
end;

function INNERPROD(x, y : planevec) : real;
begin
    INNERPROD : = x.abscis * y.abscis + x.ordinate * y.ordinate
end;

procedure SCALVEC(s : real ; u : planevec ; **var** v : planevec);
begin
    v.abscis : = s*u.abscis;
    v.ordinate : = s*u.ordinate
end;

Planevectors and Numberpairs in Ada

```
with PAIRS;
package PLANEVECARITH is

        package PLANEVECBASICS is new PAIRS;
        subtype planevec is PLANEVECBASICS.pair;

        function ASSEM (x, y : in FLOAT) return planevec
        renames PLANEVECBASICS.ASSEM;

        function " + "  (u, v : in planevec) return planevec
        renames PLANEVECBASICS." + ";

        function "-"  (u, v : in planevec) return planevec
        renames PLANEVECBASICS."-";

        function "*"  (u, v : in planevec) return FLOAT;

        function "*"  (s : in FLOAT ; v : in planevec) return planevec
        renames PLANEVECBASICS."*";

        function abscis  (v : in planevec) return FLOAT
        renames PLANEVECBASICS.FIRST;

        function ordinate  (v : in planevec) return FLOAT
        renames PLANEVECBASICS.SECOND;

end PLANEVECARITH;
```

with PAIRS;
package NumberPairs **is**

       package NPBASICS **is new** PAIRS;
       subtype numberpair **is** NPBASICS.pair;

       function ASSEM (x, y : **in** FLOAT) **return** numberpair
       renames NPBASICS.ASSEM;

       function "+" (u, v : **in** numberpair) **return** numberpair
       renames NPBASICS."+";

       function "-" (u, v : **in** numberpair) **return** numberpair
       renames NPBASICS."-";

       function "*" (u, v : **in** numberpair) **return** numberpair
       renames NPBASICS."*";

       function "*" (s : **in** FLOAT ; v : **in** numberpair) **return** numberpair
       renames NPBASICS."*";

       function LEFT (v : **in** numberpair) **return** FLOAT
       renames NPBASICS.FIRST;

       function RIGHT (v : **in** numberpair) **return** FLOAT
       renames NPBASICS.SECOND;

end NumberPairs;

package body PLANEVECARITH **is**
       function "*" (u, v : planevec) **return** FLOAT **is**
       begin
           return abscis(u) * abscis(v) + ordinate(u) * ordinate(v) ;
       end "*";
end PLANEVECARITH;

No extra information is passed to the user by including the rename definitions directly in the visible part. As a result, the body of PLANEVECARITH contains no more than the definition of the INNERPROD, while the body of NumberPairs is entirely empty! The latter can then be omitted entirely.Note that the body of PLANEVECARITH does not immediately follow its visible part. It is perfectly legitimate to write a number of visible parts first and include their bodies later in any order.

Fractions in Pascal

```
type frac = record num, den : integer end;

procedure ASSEMFRAC(p, q : integer ; var u :  frac);
     var g : integer;
begin
     g := GCD(p, q);
     u.num := p div g ; u.den := q div g
end;

procedure ADDFRAC(x, y : frac ; var z :  frac);
     var g : integer;
begin
     g := GCD(x.den, y.den);
     x.den := x.den div g ;  y.den := y.den div g;
     z.num := x.num*y.den + y.num*x.den;  z.den := x.den*y.den*g;
     assemfrac(z.num, z.den, z)
end;

procedure SUBFRAC(x, y : frac ; var z :  frac);
     var g : integer;
begin
     g := GCD(x.den, y.den);
     x.den := x.den div g ;  y.den := y.den div g;
     z.num := x.num*y.den - y.num*x.den;  z.den := x.den * y.den * g;
     assemfrac(z.num, z.den, z)
end;

procedure FRACMUL(z, y : frac ; var z :  frac);
     var u, v : frac;
begin
     assemfrac(x.num, y.den, u) ; assemfrac(y.num, x.den, v);
     z.num := u.num * v.num ; z.den := u.den * v.den
end;

procedure SCALFRAC(s : integer ; u : frac ; var v : frac);
begin v.num := s * u.num ; v.den := u.den end;
```

Fractions in Ada

```
package FRACARITH is
      type frac is private;
      function ASSEM    (a, b : in INTEGER) return frac;
      function " + "    (u, v : in frac) return frac;
      function "-"      (u, v : in frac) return frac;
      function "*"      (u, v : in frac) return frac;
      function "*"      (s : in INTEGER ; v : in frac) return frac;
      function NUMER    (v : in frac) return INTEGER;
      function DENOM    (v : in frac) return INTEGER;
      function RECIP    (v : in frac) return frac;
private
      type frac is record num, den : INTEGER ; end record;
end FRACARITH;

package body FRACARITH is
      function ASSEM(a, b : in INTEGER) return frac is
      g : constant INTEGER : = GCD(a, b);
      begin   return  (a/g, b/g) ;  end ASSEM;

      generic with function "&" (x, y : in INTEGER) return INTEGER;
      function FRACOP      (u, v : in frac) return frac;

      function "-" (u, v : in frac) return frac is new FRACOP("-");

      function "*" (u, v : in frac) return frac is
      x : frac : = assem(u.num, v.den); y : frac : = assem(v.num, u.den);
      begin   return  (x.num * y.num, x.den * y.den) ;   end "*";

      function "*" (s : INTEGER ; v : in frac) return frac is
      begin   return  (s * v.num, v.den) ;   end "*";

      function NUMER(v : in frac) return INTEGER is
      begin return v.num ; end NUMER;

      function DENOM(v : in frac) return INTEGER is
      begin return v.den ; end DENOM;

      function RECIP(v : in frac) return frac is
      begin return (v.den, v.num) ; end RECIP;

      function FRACOP(u, v : in frac) return frac is
            g : constant INTEGER : = GCD(u.den, v.den);
            b : constant INTEGER : = u.den/g;
            d : constant INTEGER : = v.den/g;
      begin   return assem(u.num*d & v.num*b, b*d*g); end FRACOP;
end FRACARITH;
```

5.6 Reminders

1. Pascal data types are *open types*. The user has access to the data structure described in the type definition. There is no way to hide the data representation.

2. Data types in Ada may be open types as in Pascal or private types. The data structure chosen to represent a private type remains hidden from the user. In other words, a user has no access to the record fields or array elements of objects declared to be of a private type.

3. Although record and array access are not possible, several language defined operations are available for objects declared to be of a private type: assignment, equality tests and parameter passing.

4. The implementor can change the representation of a private type (described in the type definition in the private section), without affecting any of the code that uses the private type.

5. In Pascal, new expressions must be assigned separately to successive record fields. In Ada one can compose and assign an *aggregate* that serves as a record expression.

6. In Pascal, there is no way to express the commonality of types. This is achieved in Ada by generic packages that serve a role for creating packages similar to what type definitions do for data object declarations.

7. Pascal allows function and procedure parameters. Such parameters are specified by their name; a specification of their parameters or the types of their parameters is not included.

8. Ada does not allow functions or procedures as subprogram parameters.

9. Generic program units can be functions, procedures, packages or tasks. Generic parameters can be data parameters (constants, variables and expressions) and also types, functions and procedures, but not packages or tasks.

10. Generic parameters are fully specified: A function or procedure parameter specifies all its parameters, including their modes and types, as well as the type of its result (if any).

11. Generic parameters are described in a generic clause preceding the generic program unit. A generic function or procedure parameter is preceded by the keyword **with**; all others require no special keyword.

12. Pascal's with statement helps to avoid repeated reference to a record name.

13. Ada allows a user to declare new names that rename existing objects. This feature is available for data objects, exceptions, procedures, functions, packages and tasks, but not for types. Renaming a type is achieved by declaring a subtype that is the same as the parent type. Since subtypes must be constrained, it is not possible to rename unconstrained types.

14. Ada has private types, but no private subtypes.

15. A private section of a package should be thought of as belonging to the package body. This implies that the data structures described in a private section are accessible in the corresponding package body and nowhere else.

16. Items created as part of a package instantiation are denoted by their name prefixed by the instantiation name.

17. If a type in a generic package is private, all its instantiations are private. As a result, the environment in which the instantiation occurs has no access to the structure of the instantiated type. (The body of the generic package in which the private type is defined is the only scope that has access to the structure of that type.)

18. Pascal uses **div** for integer division. In Ada the symbol "/" is overloaded and applies to two FLOAT operands with a FLOAT result, or to two integer operands with an INTEGER result.

19. Ada functions and procedures may need local constants or variables where Pascal does not, because Ada has no value parameters that act as initialized local variables as Pascal has.

5.7 Problems

1. The operator for integer division in Pascal is div and the remainder of integer division is denoted by mod. Integer division is denoted by the overloaded symbol "/" in Ada and the language has two remainder functions that work differently for negative operands. Write a program for the GCD (Greatest Common Divisor) for two integer numbers that may be positive, negative or zero. The algorithm can make use of the fact that
    - GCD(a, b) = GCD(b, a)
    - GCD(a, a) = a
    - GCD(a, b) = GCD(b, r), where r is defined by the remainder theorem $a = b * m + r$.

2. It seems that if generic package PAIRS did not export the functions FIRST and SECOND, function REPART could be defined as COMPLBASICS.pair.left, because COMPLBASICS.pair is identical to subtype complex. Why is this observation incorrect?

3. Instead of using a generic package PAIRS to create packages for Complex Numbers, Planevectors and NumberPairs, one can make use of derived types. First we write a package for NumberPairs (not generic, although a generic function in the body for creating the basic operations is all right). Then we introduce the standard operation of other types by declarations such as

> **type** complex **is new** numberpair;

A derived type inherits all constants and functions of its parent type. Thus, if there exists a function

> **function** " + " (u, v : **in** numberpair) **return** numberpair;

then the declaration of the derived type implicitly creates the function

> **function** " + " (u, v : **in** complex) **return** complex;

There is no need to declare this function explicitly. Write programs for complex numbers and planevectors that make use of types derived from type numberpair.

4. In Pascal one can write a procedure for multiplying two fractions that eliminates all common factors and needs only one auxiliary variable in order to avoid recomputations of GCD.

```
procedure FRACMUL(x, y : frac ; var z :  frac);
    var g : integer;
begin
    g := GCD(x.num, y.DENOM);
    z.num := x.num div g;
    z.denom := y.denom div g;
    g := GCD(y.num, x.denom);
    z.num := z.num * (y.num div g);
    z.denom := z.denom * (x.denom div g);
end;
```

Investigate whether this operation can be written as an Ada function also using just one auxiliary variable g.Do the same both in Pascal and in Ada for fraction addition.

5. Write a package for complex arithmetic that defines type complex as a private type and describes the structure of complex numbers (in the private section) in polar coordinates. The package should export functions for extracting the real and imaginary parts of a complex number. Discuss whether it would be useful to create this version of complex numbers as an instantiation of generic package PAIRS. When the package for complex numbers is done, write a package for planevectors that uses polar coordinates and builds on the already existing package for complex numbers.

6. Let passwords be defined as strings of 10 letters. It is essential that passwords cannot be read and cannot be assigned to. The necessary protection is obtained by declaring *pswd* as a limited private type. Declaring a type *private* (but not *limited* private) hides the structure, but allows assignment and comparison. For objects of a *limited* private type the structure is hidden and the default operations of assignment and comparison are not permitted. The visible part of a package that controls the use of passwords is:

```
package PSWDS is
    type pswd is limited private;
    subtype word is STRING(1 . . 10);
    function checkpswd(x : word; p : pswd) return BOOLEAN;
    procedure setpswd(x : word; p : out pswd);
private
    type pswd is
    record val : word; init : BOOLEAN : = FALSE; end record;
end PSWDS;
```

Write the package body for PSWDS containing code for subprograms CHECKPSWD and SETPSWD. The former returns TRUE if and only if a scrambled version of input string *x* is equal to the value of password *p*. Procedure SETPSWD initializes password *p* to a scrambled version of input string *x*. The scramble function can be defined local to the body of PSWDS.

Six

Function Parameters

Topics: function parameters, floating point numbers, repeat statement, loop statement, exit statement.

Issues: real-integer type conversion, numeric precision.

6.1 Problem Statement

The ability to pass a function as a parameter to another function is of great importance to the solutions for a class of standard numerical problems. In this chapter we discuss two examples of this class: computing a zeropoint of a function, and numeric integration. For both problems we assume that we are dealing with monotonic smooth functions, computable by an algebraic expression that is representable in Pascal and Ada. In the first problem we assume that a particular smooth monotonic function $f(x)$ has exactly one zeropoint in a given interval $a \leq x \leq b$ and determine the value $x = z$ for which $f(z) = 0$. Since an algorithm that works in finite time can do no more than approximate the actual zeropoint by a rational number, we must state which degree of accuracy is acceptable for a solution. For the second problem, given a smooth function $f(x)$, continuous on a given interval $a \leq x \leq b$, we compute the integral of f on that interval. Again, included as part of the input must be the required accuracy of the result.

6.2 Problem Discussion

We discuss two well known algorithms for computing the zeropoint of a smooth monotonic function $f(x)$ on a given interval $[a, b]$: the *binary search* algorithm, and a *linear regression* algorithm due to Newton. The first algorithm applies if function f(x) is continuous on the given interval, while the other algorithm applies if function f(x) is differentiable and has a continuous derivative that satisfies certain constraints.

Without loss of generality we may assume that function f(x) is monotonically increasing, and that f(a) < 0 and f(b) > 0. If it is the case that the given function is monotonically decreasing, we consider the function g(x) = -f(x) instead. Function g(x) is monotonically increasing and has the same zeropoint as f(x). If the zeropoint is x = z (i.e., f(z) = 0 and a < z < b), g(a) must be negative because g(a) < g(z) and g(b) positive because g(z) < g(b). Thus, we may restrict our discussion to a monotonically increasing function with a negative value in point *a* and a positive value in point *b*.

The Binary Search Algorithm

The binary search algorithm moves the lefthand interval boundary *a* or the righthand interval boundary *b* to the midpoint *m* of interval [a, b] depending on whether the value of function *f* in point *m* is negative or positive. If f(m) is negative, point *a* is moved to point *m*, if positive then point *b* is moved to point *m*. The result is a new interval [a, b] with the following properties:

> length(new[a, b]) = 1/2 length(old[a, b])
> f(a) < 0 **and** f(b) > 0
> zeropoint z ∈ new[a, b] since f(x) is monotonically increasing.

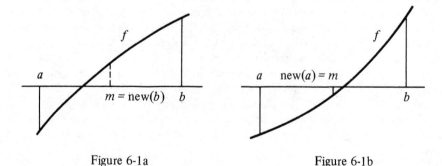

Figure 6-1a   Figure 6-1b

The property f(a) < 0 is retained because point *a* is moved to point *m* if f(m) < 0, but not if f(m) > 0. The property f(b) > 0 is likewise retained. In the unlikely event that f(m) = 0, the algorithm can terminate immediately and return the value *m* as its result. If f(m) is not zero, the algorithm moves the boundaries repeatedly, generating a sequence of intervals that are 1/2, 1/4, 1/8, . . . the length of the original interval.

If ε is the required accuracy, the algorithm may terminate when

length([a, b]) < ε.

The distance from either a or b to the zeropoint z is less than ε because $z \in [a, b]$. In addition, the midpoint m of the last computed interval is also closer than ε to the zeropoint because

a ≤ z ≤ b **and** a < m < b.

Thus, when the interval of proper length smaller than ε is found, the algorithm may terminate and return any one of the three values a, b or m as the result.

Executing a numeric algorithm on a computer causes problems because of the discrete representation of floating point numbers. The continuum of the real numbers (real in the mathematical sense, not in the Pascal sense) is represented in a computer by a finite set of rational numbers. Moreover, the distance between the representable rational numbers is fixed: it is not possible to represent any of the infinitely many rational numbers in between two representable rational numbers that are at the minimal distance apart. This limitation results in a computation of the midpoint of [x, y] that yields either x or y, but not the desired value in between.

Another result of this severe limitation on the representability of real numbers is the poor performance of the binary search algorithm if function f(x) is very flat in the neighborhood of x = z. Note that such functions are not rare and that simple functions such as $f(x) = x^2$ and $f(x) = x^3$ have this property.

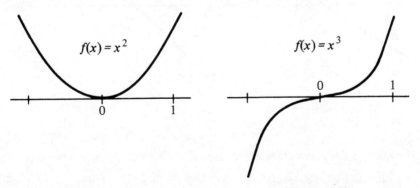

Figure 6-2a   Figure 6-2b

The problem that arises for a function f(x) that is very flat in the neighborhood of its zeropoint is that of *numeric underflow*. The computed value of f(m) may be smaller than the smallest representable floating point number without being exactly zero.

It is beyond the scope of this book to discuss these number representation problems and their effects in more detail. Extensive discussions on this problem and various ways to handle it are found in textbooks on Numerical Analysis.

Linear Regression

Another method for determining a zeropoint, particularly suitable for certain differentiable functions, is by a *linear regression* algorithm due to Newton. Let $f(x)$ be a differentiable function on interval [a, b] that contains exactly one zeropoint z of function $f(x)$. Let the derivative of $f(x)$ on interval [a, b] be $f'(x)$ and assume that $f'(x)$ is continuous and monotonic and that $f'(x) > 1/2$ on the entire interval.

Define the auxiliary function

$$p(x) = x - f(x)/f'(x), \tag{1}$$
for which $p(z) = z$, because $f(z) = 0$ and not $f'(z) = 0$.

Instead of solving $f(x) = 0$, we try to find a solution for the equation $p(x) = x$.

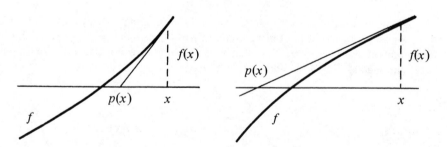

Figure 6-3a   Figure 6-3b

Point $p(x)$ is the intersection of the tangent in $f(x)$ with the x-axis because

$$f'(x) = f(x) / (x - p(x)).$$

In terms of the picture, Newton's algorithm proceeds as follows. After finding the intersection $p(x)$ of the tangent and the x-axis, it erects the function value in this new point $x_1 = p(x)$ and draws the tangent of function f in this new point. This new tangent intersects the x-axis in a point $x_2 = p(x_1)$. The procedure is executed repeatedly and generates a sequence of points

$$x_1 = p(x), \ x_2 = p(x_1), \ x_3 = p(x_2), \ \ldots$$

that approximate the zeropoint z.

The algorithm should terminate when it has found a point x_n within the required accuracy ε from zeropoint z. If $f'(x) > 1/2$ on the entire interval $[a, b]$, one can prove that the required accuracy has been reached when $|f(x_n)| < 1/2\ \varepsilon$. The reader who is not interested in the proof may wish to skip the remainder of this subsection and proceed to the discussion of numeric integration.

Let us assume that function f is concave and that the algorithm starts in $x = b$.

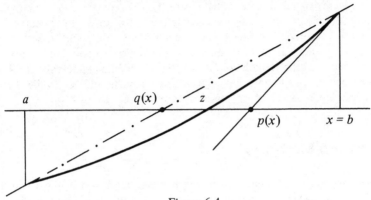

Figure 6-4

By Rolle's theorem there is a point $c \in [a, b]$ such that

$$f'(c) = (f(b) - f(a)) / (b - a).$$

The segment that connects $f(a)$ and $f(x = b)$ intersects the x-axis in a point $q(x)$ such that

$$q(x) = x - f(x)/f'(c),\ \text{because } x = b\ \text{and}$$
$$f'(c) = (f(b) - f(a)) / (b - a) = f(x) / (x - q(x)).$$

Since function f is concave, its zeropoint z lies in the interval $[q(x), p(x)]$. The distance between $p(x)$ and $q(x)$ is limited by

$$|p(x) - q(x)| = |f(x)| \times |1/f'(x) - 1/f'(c)|$$
$$\leq |f(x)| \times |1/m - 1/M| \leq 1/m \times |f(x)|$$

where m is the minimum and M the maximum of $f'(x)$ on interval $[a, b]$. Using the condition that $f'(x) > 1/2$ on the entire interval $[a, b]$, we find that $m = 1/2$ and that

$$|f(x)| < 1/2\ \varepsilon \Rightarrow |p(x) - q(x)| \leq \varepsilon$$

Since zeropoint z lies in the interval $[q(x), p(x)]$ which has a length smaller than ε, either $p(x)$ or $q(x)$ or any point in that interval is an acceptable approximation of z. It is obvious that one can give a similar proof for the case of a convex function f starting Newton's algorithm from the point $x = a$. Various detailed proofs are found in standard textbooks on Numerical Analysis.

An important difference between the binary search algorithm and Newton's algorithm is that the convergence of the former is independent of the particular function f(x) whereas the latter is not. (That is not to say that the accuracy of the result is independent of f(x)). We discussed briefly the impact of rounding real numbers to rational numbers and of the problems caused by discrete numbers representable in a machine on the accuracy of the result of a computation. In contrast to the binary search algorithm, the convergence of the linear regression algorithm does depend on the behavior of f(x) on the interval containing the zeropoint. This fact is precisely the characteristic that makes the linear regression method more attractive than the binary search algorithm. For smooth functions the linear regression algorithm converges much faster than the binary search algorithm because the length of the newly computed interval in Newton's algorithm goes rapidly to zero with the decreasing value of f(x), while that in the binary search algorithm decreases by a constant factor.

Integration Methods

The second problem for this chapter is numeric integration. Two well-known methods for computing the (definite) integral of a continuous function on a closed interval [a, b] are the *trapezoid* method and *Simpson's rule*. The former approximates an arc of f(x) between two points $f(x_i)$ and $f(x_{i-1})$ by a straight line segment. The latter approximates an arc going through three points $f(x_{i-1})$, $f(x_i)$ and $f(x_{i+1})$ by a parabola.

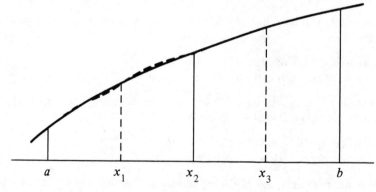

Figure 6-5

The parabola method is surprisingly accurate. (So much so, that it gives the exact integral for all polynomials of degree three or less.) We develop here the algorithm based on the parabola method and leave the trapezoid approximation as an exercise to the reader (see the problems at the end of this chapter).

Let the interval [a, b] be divided into an even number of intervals $[x_i, x_{i+1}]$ all of the same length, h. Consider two adjacent intervals $[x_{i-1}, x_i]$ and $[x_i, x_{i+1}]$. The general equation of a parabola whose axis is perpendicular to the x-axis is

$$y = Ax^2 + Bx + C$$

We wish to determine the coefficients A, B and C so that the parabola passes through the three function points $f(x_{i-1})$, $f(x_i)$ and $f(x_{i+1})$. Thus,

$$y_{-1} = f(x_{i-1}) = Ax_{i-1}^2 + Bx_{i-1} + C$$

$$y_0 = f(x_i) = Ax_i^2 + Bx_i + C$$

$$y_1 = f(x_{i+1}) = Ax_{i+1}^2 + Bx_{i+1} + C$$

For a continuous monotonic function $f(x)$ these three equations can be solved and the coefficients A, B and C can be computed. However, the coefficients are not really the goal of our computation, but the area enclosed by the interval $[x_{i-1}, x_{i+1}]$, the function f and the function values $f(x_{i-1})$ and $f(x_{i+1})$. We approximate this area by the area under the parabola. This area is

$$\int_{x_{i-1}}^{x_{i+1}} (Ax^2 + Bx + C)dx = \int_{-h}^{h} A(x_i+u)^2 + B(x_i+u) + C)du$$

Evaluation of this integral yields the result

$$1/3 * A[(x_i+h)^3 - (x_i-h)^3] + 1/2 * B[(x_i+h)^2 - (x_i-h)^2] + 2Ch$$
$$= 2/3hA[3x_i^2 + h^2] + 2hBx_i + 2Ch .$$

Making use of the values y_{-1}, y_0 and y_1, we find

$$y_{-1} + 4y_0 + y_1$$
$$= 4Ax_i^2 + A[(x_i-h)^2 + (x_i+h)^2] + 6Bx_i + 6C$$
$$= 6Ax_i^2 + 2Ah^2 + 6Bx_i + 6C .$$

From the last two lines we conclude

$$\text{Area(parabola)} = 1/3h * (y_{-1} + 4y_0 + y_1) \qquad (2)$$
$$= 1/3h * (f(x_{i-1}) + 4f(x_i) + f(x_{i+1})).$$

This line is known as *Simpson's Rule*. It expresses the area under the parabola passing through three points of $f(x)$ in terms of the interval length and the three function values.

The integral of $f(x)$ on the entire interval [a, b] is approximated by the sum of the parabola areas on each pair of two adjacent intervals. This sum is the result of adding

$$\text{Area}_1 = 1/3h * (f(x_0) + 4f(x_1) + f(x_2))$$

$$\text{Area}_3 = 1/3h * (f(x_2) + 4f(x_3) + f(x_4))$$

.

.

.

$$\text{Area}_{2n-1} = 1/3h * (f(x_{2n-2}) + 4f(x_{2n-1}) + f(x_{2n})) \ .$$

where $f(x_0) = f(a)$, $f(x_{2n}) = f(b)$ and $x_{j+1} - x_j = h$ for all $j \in [0 \ . \ . \ 2n - 1]$. Since every even term occurs in two successive areas (for example, $f(x_2)$ occurs in Area_1 and Area_3), except the very first and the very last, the approximation for the total area is as follows.

$$\text{TotalArea}(2n) = \qquad\qquad\qquad\qquad\qquad\qquad\qquad (3)$$
$$1/3h*[f(a) + 4f(x_1) + 2f(x_2) + 4f(x_3) + \ . \ . \ . \ + f(b)]$$

Another notation for the TotalArea(2n) is

$$\text{TotalArea}(2n) = 1/3h * [S_0 + 4 * \text{ODD} + 2 * \text{EVEN}]$$
$$\text{where } S_0 = f(a) + f(b), \text{ODD} = (f(x_1) + f(x_3) + \ . \ . \ .)$$
$$\text{and EVEN} = (f(x_2) + f(x_4) + \ . \ . \ . \ ).$$

Computing the Integral

The algorithm starts out with partitioning the interval into two equal parts.

$$\text{TotalArea}(2) = 1/3 * (b - a)/2 * [f(a) + 4f(m) + f(b)]$$
$$\text{with ODD} = f(m) \text{ and EVEN} = 0.$$

If the next approximation is obtained by incrementing n by one, most of the dividing points x_i for $n+1$ are different from the dividing points for n. This means that not much of the previous computation can be used again. A much better algorithm is obtained if we double n instead of increment n by one. If n is doubled, every existing interval is divided into two equal parts and all existing dividing points are retained. The advantage of this aproach is that the function values in half of the new dividing points are already available from the previous computation. Only the function values in the new odd dividing points must be computed. It is clear that the entire set of dividing points of Area(n) forms precisely the set of EVEN dividing points of Area(2n), because the latter is obtained from the former by placing a new dividing point in between each pair of successive points of the former. Thus,

$$\text{Area}(2n) = 1/3 * (b - a)/2n * (S_0 + 4 \ \text{ODD}(2n) + 2 \ \text{EVEN}(2n))$$
$$= 1/3 * (b - a)/2n * [S_0 + 4 \ \text{ODD}(2n) + 2(\text{ODD}(n) + \text{EVEN}(n))]$$
$$= 1/3 * (b - a)/2n * [4 \ \text{ODD}(2n) - 2 \ \text{ODD}(n)] + 1/2 \ \text{Area}(n)$$
$$= 1/3 * (b - a)/n \ * \ [2 \ \text{ODD}(2n) - \text{ODD}(n)] + 1/2 \ \text{Area}(n). \qquad (4)$$

Instead of starting with Area(2), we can introduce Area(1) and define

$$n = 1, h = (b - a), Area(1) = h * (f(a) + f(b))/3 \text{ and } ODD(1) = 0, \quad (5)$$
so that
$$Area(2) = 1/3 * (h/1) * [2f(m) - 0] + 0.5 * h * (f(a) + f(b))/3$$
$$= 1/3 * (b - a)/2 * [f(a) + 4f(m) + f(b)] .$$

The algorithm for approximating the integral starts with the initial values listed above, and repeats the following steps until the difference between two successive approximations is smaller than $0.5 \, \varepsilon$:

Compute NewODD, using the new ODD dividing points
Compute the new approximation by the formula: $\qquad$ (6)
NewArea $= (2*NewODD - OldODD)/(3*n)*h + 1/2*OldArea$
multiply n by 2 and repeat.

6.3 The Pascal Programs

Binary Search in Pascal

We assume that the function whose zeropoint we are going to compute is given by a Pascal function. In the predecessor of Pascal, Algol60, it was possible to pass an *expression* instead of a function as a parameter. In Algol60 one could write the following procedure.

```
procedure TABULATE(x, expr) ; real x, expr;
begin
        for x := 0.0 step 0.1 until 1.0 do
        begin
                NEWLINE ; PRINT(x) ; PRINT(expr)
        end
end;
```

The effect of the calls TABULATE(a, a*a + 1) and TABULATE(i, sin(i*(pi/2))) is that successive values of the expression $a^2 + 1$ are computed for $a = 0, 0.1, 0.2, \ldots$, 0.9, 1.0 and successive values of the sine function are computed in the first quadrant for 0, 0.05pi, 0.1pi, . . . , 0.45pi, 0.5pi. This desirable effect was achieved by a parameter mechanism known as *call by name* parameter evaluation. (It is essentially the same as the lazy evaluation idea in LISP: don't evaluate a parameter at the call, but wait until you need it.) Call by name parameters are not evaluated once when the procedure is called, but every time that the parameter is encountered. In the example above, the expression parameter is executed eleven times in each call to PRINT(expr) and produces a different value each time, because the argument *a* (or *i*) has changed in value.

Call by name parameters exist neither in Pascal nor in Ada. If the expression parameter is a value parameter in Pascal, or an in parameter in Ada, its value is computed once before procedure execution starts when procedure TABULATE is called. The desired effect of tabulating a series of function values then gets entirely lost because the *expr* parameter has the same value during the entire execution of TABULATE. There is no other possibility in either Pascal or Ada, because var parameters in Pascal and out parameters in Ada must be variables and cannot be expressions. Both Pascal and Ada allow assignment to var and out parameters and this excludes expressions as valid arguments.

Since an expression parameter cannot be evaluated repeatedly in the body of a procedure or function, the only acceptable alternative is to pass a function or procedure as an argument (PRM 10, 157). Applied to our binary search algorithm, an appropriate specification is

function BISEARCH(**function** f : real; a, b, eps : real) : real ;

where *f* is the function whose zeropoint we are looking for, *a* and *b* the boundaries of the interval and *eps* the required accuracy.

We argued in the discussion that we may assume that $f(a) \leq 0$ and $f(b) \geq 0$ without loss of generality. If the input violates this condition, it can be obtained by swapping the boundaries *a* and *b*. Upon initialization the algorithm must deal with the case that $f(a) = 0$ or $f(b) = 0$. This exceptional case is adequately handled by reducing the interval to zero.

if f(a) = 0 **then** b := a
else if f(b) = 0 **then** a := b
else if f(a) > 0 **then** swap(a,b)

After computing the value f(m), where *m* is the midpoint of interval [a, b], and storing it in a real variable *fm*, the algorithm compares this value with zero, and moves the boundaries so that $f(a) \leq 0$ and $f(b) \geq 0$ remains true. Moving boundary *a* or *b* according to the sign of *fm* was described in the discussion.

if fm = 0 **then begin** a := m ; b := m **end**
else if fm < 0 **then** a := m **else** b := m

A logically clearer and more concise way to write the statements that adjust the interval boundaries is

if fm <= 0 **then** a := m;
if fm >= 0 **then** b := m;

This pair of statements does not favor the unlikely case of *fm* = 0. When *fm* = 0, the interval is reduced to an empty interval by moving both boundaries to point *m*. (Note that mixed arithmetic of types integer and real is allowed in Pascal (PRM 149). The fact that variable *fm* is of type real does not force us to write fm = 0.0 instead of fm = 0.

The binary search is continued until the interval is less than *eps*. A useful control statement for this purpose is Pascal's repeat statement. Applied to the BISEARCH program, it takes the form:

repeat
                    <statements for computing m, f(m) and comparison>
until abs(a - b) < eps

Applying the Pascal rule that the result of a function is transmitted to the main program by assignment to the function variable, function BISEARCH in Pascal has the following structure:

function BISEARCH(**function** f : real; a, b, eps : real) : real;
       var m, fm : real;
begin
          <test for f(a) = 0, f(b) = 0 or swap(a,b) if necessary>
          repeat
                <Compute midpoint(a,b) and store f(midpoint) in fm>
                if fm <= 0 **then** <move lefthand boundary a to m>;
                if fm >= 0 **then** <move righthand boundary b to m>
          until abs(a - b) < eps;
          BISEARCH := m
end;

The complete program written in Pascal is found at the end of this chapter.

A Recursive Binary Search Program

Instead of using the repeat statement, BISEARCH can be written as a recursive procedure. The specification of the recursive function is the same as that of the iterative version. The biggest change is that the repeat statement is replaced by the recursive call in the alternatives of an if statement:

if (abs(a - b) < eps) **or** (fm = 0) **then** BISEARCH := m
else if fm < 0 **then** BISEARCH := BISEARCH(f, m, b, eps)
else BISEARCH := BISEARCH(f, a, m, eps)

The size of interval [a, b] and the case *fm* = 0 must be tested before the sign of *fm* is inspected or else the recursion will not terminate.

Placing the test f(a) ≤ 0 **and** f(b) ≥ 0 at the beginning makes the recursive version rather costly. At least one of the values f(a) or f(b) is computed at every recursive call,although these values are known in the preceding recursive call. This problem is solved by declaring a local function BISEARCH and by embedding it in an enclosing ZEROPOINT that performs the adjustment exactly once before calling BISEARCH. This leads to the following recursive version:

```
function ZEROPOINT(function f : real; a, b, eps : real) : real;

    function BISEARCH(a, b, eps : real) : real;
        var fm : real;
    begin
        m := (a+b)/2 ; fm := f(m);

        if (abs(a - b) < eps) or (fm = 0) then BISEARCH := m
        else if fm < 0 then BISEARCH := BISEARCH(m, b, eps)
        else BISEARCH := BISEARCH(a, m, eps)
    end;

begin
    if f(a) = 0 then b := a else if f(b) = 0 then a := b
    else if f(a) > 0 then swap(a,b);
    ZEROPOINT := BISEARCH(a, b, eps)
end;
```

It is not strictly necessary to declare BISEARCH as a function. It could be declared as a procedure and the first assignment to BISEARCH could be replaced by an assignment to the identifier ZEROPOINT, because the scope of BISEARCH is part of the scope of function ZEROPOINT. With such an arrangement, the other two assignments to BISEARCH and the last assignment to ZEROPOINT could then be replaced by the procedure call BISEARCH(a, b, eps).

Linear Regression in Pascal

Newton's algorithm needs two functions as input: function f whose zeropoint we are looking for and its derivative $g = $ f'. Thus, the heading of the ZEROPOINT function that uses Newton's algorithm is

```
function ZEROPOINT(function f, g : real; a, b, eps : real): real;
```

If $f(a) = 0$ or $f(b) = 0$, we start the algorithm in $x = a$ or $x = b$ so that it terminates immediately when it finds $f(x) = 0$. If the derivative is increasing on the interval [a, b], the maximum of $g(x)$ is found in b, if decreasing, then $\max(g(a .. b)) = g(a)$. Since the algorithm should start in the endpoint where the derivative g has its maximum, the computation is initialized by

```
    if (f(a) = 0) or (g(a) > g(b)) then x := a else x := b
```

An iterative version of Newton's algorithm computes the sequence

$$x_1 = p(x), x_2 = p(x_1), x_3 = p(x_2), \ldots$$

by repeated substitution of the result x in the formula for function p. The repetition should terminate when $f(x) < 1/2$ *eps*. Thus, the loop has the form:

    repeat
          <compute fx = f(x) and gx = g(x)>
          <compute p(x) = x - fx/gx and assign result to x>
    until abs(fx) < 0.5 * eps

Note that p(x) = x in case fx = f(x) is exactly zero.

Since *eps* does not change, there is no need to recompute the expression 0.5 * eps every time the termination condition is evaluated. Recomputation can be avoided by multiplying *eps* by 0.5 in the initialization. When the loop has terminated, the result is assigned to the function name. A recursive version of Newton's algorithm can be designed just as easily as for BISEARCH. This is left as an exercise to the reader (see Problem 3 below).

Numeric Integration in Pascal

In the discussion of the algorithm for computing a definite integral on a closed interval [a, b] with Simpson's Rule, we used the following variables.

n: for the number of subintervals. This number is multiplied by 2 at the end of an iteration, because an iteration makes use of the old number of subintervals (cf. equation 4).

h: for the length of the given interval [a, b]. The purpose of keeping that length in *h* is to avoid recomputing the difference b - a.

OldODD: for the sum of the function values in the odd dividing points of the preceding iteration.

NewODD: for the sum of the function values in the odd dividing points of the current iteration.

OldArea: for the area computed in the preceding iteration.

NewArea: for the area computed in the current iteration.
    The input of function SIMPSON consists of the function *f* to be integrated, the interval boundaries *a* and *b*, and the desired accuracy. Function SIMPSON has the form

```
function SIMPSON(function f : real; a, b, eps : real) : real;
        var    n : integer ;
        h, OldODD, NewODD, OldArea, NewArea : real;
begin
        <initialization>
        repeat
                <iteration>
        until abs(OldArea - NewArea) < (0.5 * eps);
        SIMPSON := NewArea
end;
```

Since the initialization depends on the iteration, we discuss the latter first. The identity of OldODD and OldArea changes at the start of each new iteration. What used to be new in the preceding iteration now becomes old. Thus an iteration starts with the following initialization.

OldODD := NewOdd ; OldArea := NewArea

The iteration continues with the computation of the function values in the new odd dividing points. Since there is a new odd dividing point in the middle of every old subinterval, there are as many new odd dividing points as there are old subintervals. This number is kept in variable n (which is still equal to the old number of subintervals). The first new dividing point is in $x_1 = a + (b - a)/(2 * n)$. If index i steps through the new odd dividing points, we have

$$x_i = x_1 + (i - 1) * (b - a)/n = \\ a - (b - a)/(2 * n) + i * (b - a)/n, \text{ for } i > 0 \tag{7}$$

Thus, the sum of the function values in the new odd dividing points is computed by the for statement:

NewODD := 0 ; c := a - h/(2*n);
for i := 1 **to** n **do** NewODD := NewODD + f(c + i * h/n)

The auxiliary variables c and i must be added to the local declarations.

The next step is to compute the NewArea by the formula of line 6.

NewArea := (2 * NewODD - OldODD)/(3*n) * h + 0.5 * OldArea

The last step of the iteration is the adjustment of variable n to the current number of subintervals. Putting the entire iteration together, we have

repeat
      OldODD := NewODD ; OldArea := NewArea;
      NewODD := 0 ; c := a - h/(2*n);
      for i := 1 **to** n **do** NewODD := NewODD + f(c + i * h/n);
      NewArea := (2*NewODD - OldODD)/(3*n)*h + 0.5*OldArea;
      n := n*2
until abs(NewArea - OldArea) < (0.5 * eps)

As in BISEARCH, *eps* can be replaced by 0.5 * eps in the initialization. Because of the way the iteration starts, the variables to be initialized are NewODD and NewArea rather than OldODD and OldArea. The initialization that corresponds to the one in the discussion is

h := (b - a) ; n := 1 ; NewODD := 0 ;
NewArea := h * (f(a) + f(b))/3 ; eps := 0.5 * eps

The complete program for SIMPSON is found at the end of this chapter.

A Recursive Integration Function in Pascal

A recursive version of the integration function SIMPSON must determine whether or not the desired accuracy has been reached. The body of a recursive function SIMPSON can be designed as follows.

<Compute NewArea>
if abs(NewArea - OldArea) < (0.5 * eps) **then** SIMPSON := NewArea
else SIMPSON := <recursive call with NewArea as one of the parameters>

The question arises whether SIMPSON should be written as a single function that calls itself recursively or as a function that calls a locally defined procedure (or function) recursively. If we decide the former, then SIMPSON must be specified with a parameter that corresponds to OldArea in order to be able to perform the termination test. This would force the user of SIMPSON to pass a value for this parameter at the initial call. The value of that parameter is essentially the initial value of NewArea as in the iterative version of SIMPSON. Since the initialization should not be left to the user, but performed by the function itself, we opt for a local procedure within SIMPSON. In retrospect, we see that in the recursive versions of both BISEARCH and SIMPSON a local recursive procedure or function is what we want. In BISEARCH, the local function serves the purpose of avoiding the recomputation of the initialization. In SIMPSON, it avoids the extension of the parameter list with parameters that should not be under user control. The resulting program is

```
function SIMPSON (function f : real; a, b, eps : real) : real;
       var h : real;
       procedure APPROX(ODD, AREA : real ; n : integer);
               var NewODD, NewArea, c : real ; i : integer;
       begin
               <Compute new approximation>
               <either assign to SIMPSON or call recursively>
       end;
begin
       <initialization>
       APPROX(0, InitArea, 1)
end;
```

The body of recursive procedure APPROX is practically the same as the iteration step in the repeat statement of the iterative version, but instead of the until clause, it has an if statement in which it determines whether to call itself recursively or to terminate.

if abs(NewArea - AREA) < (0.5 * eps) **then** SIMPSON := NewArea
else APPROX(NewODD, NewArea, 2 * n)

If the initialization in SIMPSON changes *eps* to 0.5 * eps, the test in the termination statement of APPROX can be simplified to

if abs(NewArea - AREA) < eps **then** . . .

It is remarkable how similar are both the iterative and the recursive versions of functions BISEARCH and SIMPSON. This similarity is caused by the fact that both functions build a sequence of approximations and terminate when the approximations are closer than half the required accuracy.

6.4 The Ada Programs

Generic Functions

Like Pascal, Ada has no call by name parameters that would allow us to pass an expression as a parameter with the intention that the corresponding actual parameter is computed each time the formal parameter is encountered. However, Ada is more restrictive than Pascal, because Ada does not even allow functions or procedures as parameters (ARM 6.1, 6-1).

In preceding chapters we saw that functions and procedures can be passed as generic parameters in Ada. Thus, instead of a function BISEARCH that takes a function *f* as parameter, as we wrote in Pascal, we now write a generic function BISEARCH that takes a function *f* as a generic parameter.

generic with function f(x : REAL) **return** REAL;
function BISEARCH(a, b, eps : REAL) **return** REAL;

The program piece called BISEARCH is in fact not a function, but a template for creating a function. One can declare a new function to be an instantiation of BISEARCH and use that function to perform the binary search. Unfortunately, one must fix the generic parameters in the instantiation. This means that a new instance of BISEARCH must be created for every function F that one would like to use as input. For example, the declarations

function F(x : REAL) **return** REAL **is** . . . **end**;
function G(x : REAL) **return** REAL **is** . . . **end**;
function FBSEARCH **is new** BISEARCH(F);
function GBSEARCH **is new** BISEARCH(G);

create two instances of BISEARCH: one for searching a zeropoint of F and one for searching a zeropoint of G.But FBSEARCH cannot be used for G nor GBSEARCH for F.FBSEARCH can, of course, be used many times, as any function can. Thus, if F has many zeropoints, FBSEARCH can be used to find each one of them. Assuming zeropoints of F are found in interval [a, b] and in [p, q], we can write the following statements.

zero1 := FBSEARCH(a, b, 0.1E-6) ; zero2 := FBSEARCH(p, q, 1.3E-8);

Return and Loop Statements

The body of the generic function BISEARCH starts out the same way as the corresponding Pascal program. If the condition $f(a) \leq 0$ **and** $f(b) \geq 0$ is not true at the beginning, the values of the interval boundaries are swapped so that the condition is true from then on. If by any chance $f(a) = 0$ or $f(b) = 0$, the zeropoint is found and the program should return the appropriate result.

if $f(a) = 0.0$ **then return** a ; **end if**;
if $f(b) = 0.0$ **then return** b ; **end if**;
if $f(a) > 0.0$ **then** swap(a,b) ; **end if**;

We could have accomplished the same thing as in Pascal and make the interval empty by assigning *a* to *b* or *b* to *a* if one of them is the zeropoint. But the use of the return statement is a clearer indication of what is intended.

Moving the boundary is done in Ada exactly as in Pascal (except for the slight differences in syntax).

<compute function value fm in midpoint of interval [a, b]>

if fm <= 0.0 **then** a := m ; **end if**;
if fm >= 0.0 **then** b := m ; **end if**;

There is a slight difference between the two languages with respect to iteration statements. Ada does not have a repeat statement as Pascal does. The Ada statement corresponding to the repeat statement in the Pascal version of function BISEARCH is

loop
        -- statements for computing m, fm, and comparison
        exit when ABS(a - b) < eps ;
end loop;

Since an acceptable approximation is found for the zeropoint of function F when ABS(a - b) has reached a value smaller than *eps*, the exit statement might as well be replaced by a return statement. This is indeed correct Ada: an exit statement leaves the scope of the closest surrounding loop statement (ARM 5.7, 5-10), while a return statement immediately terminates the execution of the procedure or function in which it occurs (ARM 5.8, 5-10). The loop statement is then

```
        loop
            <statements for computing m, fm and comparison>
            if ABS(a - b) < eps then return m ; end if;
        end loop;
```

The structure of BISEARCH is then as follows.

```
        generic  with function f(x : REAL) return REAL;
        function BISEARCH(a, b, eps : REAL) return REAL;

        function BISEARCH(a, b, eps : REAL) return REAL is
            m, fm : REAL;
        begin
            <test for f(a) = 0.0, f(b) = 0.0, or swap(a,b) if necessary>
        loop
            <compute midpoint (a,b) and store f(midpoint) in fm>
            if fm <= 0.0 then <move lefthand boundary a to m> ; end if;
            if fm >= 0.0 then <move righthand boundary b to m> ; end if;
            if ABS(a - b) < eps then return <m as approx. zeropoint> ; end if;
        end loop;
        end BISEARCH;
```

The termination test statement, if ABS(a-b) . . . , can be moved to another place in the loop statement. It would make sense, for instance, to move it in front of the other two if statements so that the boundaries are not moved when the termination point has already been reached. There is no great saving in this optimization, but, on the other hand, moving the termination test does not incur any extra computing.

Arithmetic Type Conversion

Note the use of the REAL literal 0.0 in the expression f(a) = 0.0. Ada is more restrictive than Pascal in that arithmetic operands must not be mixed in expressions. The types (not necessarily the subtypes) of the operands of arithmetic operators such as "+", "=", etc. must be the same arithmetic type: either both REAL or both INTEGER, but no mixture. However, for the specific case of REAL and INTEGER values, the Ada language provides conversion functions by the name of the type to be converted into (ARM 4.6, 4-21). For example, the statements

    u := 3.14 ; i := 2 ; x := u/REAL(i) ; k := INTEGER(u);

show how an INTEGER value can be converted to a REAL value and vice versa. Thus, instead of f(a) = 0.0 we could have written f(a) = REAL(0).

Floating Point Types

Pascal provides the type REAL as the only floating point type with the precision of the representation dependent entirely on the machine on which the program runs. In Ada, a user can declare different floating point types of the form

>**type** t **is digits** something;

where *something* is a small positive integer that indicates the number of significant digits in the floating point numbers of type *t* (ARM 3.5.7, 3-20). For example, numbers *p* and *q* declared of type *mil*, where

>**type** mil **is digits** 6;

are represented in six digits. The type REAL in Ada is just one example of these types.

>**type** REAL **is digits** 8;

The fact that BISEARCH was written as a generic function provides the opportunity to make it amenable to the specific precision desired by the user. Instead of fixing type REAL in the program, we can introduce a generic type parameter.

>**generic**
>>**type** Number **is digits** <>;
>>**with function** f(x : Number) **return** Number;
>>**function** BISEARCH(a, b, eps : Number) **return** Number;

The specification of *Number* as **digits** <> indicates that this generic parameter is one of the floating point types (ARM 12.1.2, 12-5). The user determines the specific precision he wants by fixing the specific floating point type at each instantiation of BISEARCH. For example,

>**function** F(x : REAL) **return** REAL **is begin** . . . **end**;
>**function** G(y : mil) **return** mil **is begin** . . . **end**;
>**function** FBSEARCH **is new** BISEARCH(REAL, F);
>**function** GBSEARCH **is new** BISEARCH(mil, G);

Floating Point Constants

One might ask whether the expression f(a) = 0.0 is independent of the particular floating point type. This is indeed the case. The various floating point types are all derived from a common parent type. When a type is derived, it inherits (among other things) the literals of that parent type (ARM 3.4, 3-10).

Therefore, the floating point literals belong to all floating point types. This makes the expression f(a) = 0.0 correct for any floating point type that will be substituted for *Number*.

A Recursive ZeroPoint Function in Ada

The argument for making BISEARCH a local function of ZEROPOINT (in order to avoid repeated initialization at every recursive call) is valid as much for the Ada program as for the Pascal program. A recursive version in Ada has the form

```
generic type Number is digits <>;
       with function f(x : Number) return Number;
function ZEROPOINT(a, b, eps : Number) return Number;

function ZEROPOINT(a, b, eps : Number) return Number is

       function BISEARCH(a, b, eps : Number) return Number is
              var m, fm : Number;
       begin
              <compute midpoint(a,b) and store f(midpoint) in fm>
              if <termination satisfied>  then return midpoint; end if;
              if sign(fm) < 0
                     then BISEARCH(a, m, eps);
                     else BISEARCH(m, b, eps);
              end if;
       end;

begin
       <test for f(a) = 0.0, f(b) = 0.0 or swap(a,b) if necessary>
       return BISEARCH(a, b, eps);
end;
```

A peculiar rule is that one must first give the generic function declaration and then separately the function body. One is not allowed to combine the two into a single unit as is allowed for local functions in package bodies. As a result, one must write the function heading twice!

The programmer does not have quite the same freedom in Ada as in Pascal when constructing nested subprograms. In Ada, a return statement in an inner procedure cannot act on behalf of the surrounding function, whereas in Pascal the programmer can use the name of the surrounding function (in this case ZEROPOINT) in an assignment statement in the inner procedure. A return statement in BISEARCH would just return to the body of the surrounding function ZEROPOINT. Another return statement in ZEROPOINT is needed to get the result out to the environment of the caller of ZEROPOINT.

A ZeroPoint Package

Instead of making BISEARCH a local function of ZEROPOINT, its existence can be hidden from the user by writing a package that exports ZEROPOINT and includes both ZEROPOINT and BISEARCH in its body. With this arrangement there is no need for nesting one function inside of the other. One might expect some improvement in efficiency because the declaration of BISEARCH is processed only when the package is elaborated instead of each time ZEROPOINT is called. The latter will inevitably be reprocessed if the two functions are nested. In fact, there is no need for nested procedures and functions in Ada, as there is in Pascal, because procedures and functions can share subprograms and data in package bodies and keep these objects hidden from the user.

A non-nested recursive version using packages has the form:

```
generic type Numeric is  . . . ;
        with function f( . . . ) return Numeric;
package ZP is
        function ZEROPOINT(a, b, eps : Numeric) return Numeric;
end ZP;

package body ZP is
        function BISEARCH( . . . ) return Numeric is
        begin   . . .  end BISEARCH;

        function ZEROPOINT(a, b, eps : Numeric) return Numeric is
        begin   . . .  end ZEROPOINT;
end ZP;
```

We made package ZP generic so that the two functions can share the generic type parameter. ZP is written out in full at the end of this chapter.

Newton's Algorithm in Ada

Newton's algorithm in Ada uses a loop very similar to the repeat statement in the corresponding Pascal program. Instead of pursuing the design of the iterative version of Newton's algorithm in Ada, we discuss the design of the recursive version which hides the auxiliary function in the body of a package. The visible part of this package consists of the following generic declaration.

```
generic type Numeric is digits <>;
        with function f(x : in Numeric) return Numeric;
        with function g(x : in Numeric) return Numeric;
package ZP is
        function ZEROPOINT(a, b, eps : Numeric) return Numeric;
end ZP;
```

As in the Pascal program, function ZEROPOINT chooses x = a or x = b as starting point depending on whether g(a) > g(b) or vice versa. If f(a) or f(b) is equal to zero, the program starts at that zeropoint (and will immediately terminate).

> **if** f(a) = 0.0 **or** g(a) > g(b) **then** x := a; **else** x := b; **end if**;

The auxiliary function NEWTON that ZEROPOINT calls in the statement

> **return** NEWTON(x, eps);

is the recursive function that performs the core of the computation after the initialization. Its body consists of the following statements.

> fx := f(x);
> **if** ABS(fx) < eps **then return** x; **end if**;
> **return** NEWTON(x - fx/g(x), eps);

NEWTON calls itself recursively replacing parameter x by the new value fx = x - f(x) / g(x). The form of the body of generic package ZP is

> **package body** ZP **is**
>
>> **function** NEWTON(x, eps : Numeric) **return** Numeric **is**
>>   <local declarations>
>> **begin**
>>   . . .
>> **end** NEWTON;
>>
>> **function** ZEROPOINT(a, b, eps : Numeric) **return** Numeric **is**
>>   <local declarations>
>> **begin**
>>   <initialization>
>>   **return** NEWTON(x, eps);
>> **end** ZEROPOINT;
>
> **end** ZP;

The form of this package is remarkably similar to the one for the Binary Search.

Simpson's Rule in Ada

The iterative version of Simpson Integration is basically the same as that in Pascal except for the use of a loop statement instead of a repeat statement. If the difference between the old and new areas is less than 0.5 * eps, the execution of SIMPSON can be terminated and the result can be returned.

```
  loop
        OldODD : = NewODD; OldArea : = NewArea;
        <compute NewODD>
        <compute NewArea>
        if ABS(NewArea - OldArea) < 0.5 * eps then return NewArea; end if;
        n := n * 2;
  end loop;
```

In Ada, one cannot replace *eps* by 0.5 * eps in the initialization, because input parameters are read-only. The same effect is obtained by declaring a local constant initialized to 0.5 * eps. NewODD and NewArea can be declared in the package body and can be used for communication between SIMPSON and a recursive function or procedure that replaces the iteration. It is then possible to implement the auxiliary subprogram as a procedure because the result is now stored in the shared variable NewArea (which remains hidden from the user). This leads to the following format of the package body.

package body SI **is**

```
        NewODD, NewArea : Number;

        procedure APPROX(a, b, eps : Number) is
              <local declarations>
        begin
              <compute NewODD, NewArea>
              if <old and NewAreas close enough, terminate>;
              else <call APPROX recursively>;
        end APPROX;

        function SIMPSON(a, b, eps : Number) return Number is
              <local declarations>
        begin
              <initialize NewODD, NewArea>
              <call APPROX which leaves its result in NewArea>
              return NewArea;
        end SIMPSON;
```

end SI;

Since the values of *a, b* and *eps* do not change, a slight optimization is obtained by adding the local variables *left, right* and *accur* to the package body. These variables cannot be declared as constants, because their values are set each time that SIMPSON is called. The initialization in SIMPSON is

```
        left := a; right := b; accur := 0.5 * eps;
        NewODD := 0;
        NewArea := (f(a) + f(b)) * (b - a) / 3;
```

Since procedure APPROX now operates within the package body that hides variables *left, right* and *accur* from the user, it is no longer necessary to include these variables as parameters in the heading of APPROX.

procedure APPROX **is**
        <local ODD and AREA, initialized to NewODD and NewArea>
begin
        <computation of NewODD and NewArea, using left and right>
        if <areas closer than accur, terminate> **else** <call APPROX again>
end APPROX;

6.5 The Complete Programs

The Iterative Pascal Program for Binary Search

```
function BISEARCH (function f : real; a, b, eps : real) : real;
     var m, fm : real;
begin
     eps := eps/2 ; fm := f(a);
     if fm = 0 then b := a else if f(b) = 0 then a := b
     else if fm > 0 then swap(a,b);

     repeat
          m := (a+b)/2 ; fm := f(m);
          if fm <= 0 then a := m;
          if fm >= 0 then b := m
     until abs(a - b) < eps;

     BISEARCH := m
end;
```

The Recursive ZeroPoint Program in Pascal

```
function ZEROPOINT(function f : real; a, b, eps : real) : real;

     procedure BISEARCH(a, b, eps : real);
          var m, fm : real;
     begin
          m := 0.5 * (a+b) ; fm := f(m);

          if(abs(a-b) < eps) or (fm=0) then ZEROPOINT := m else
          if fm < 0 then BISEARCH(m, b, eps) else BISEARCH(a, m, eps)
     end;

begin
     if f(a) = 0 then b := a else if f(b) = 0 then a := b;
     if f(a) > 0 then BISEARCH(b, a, 0.5*eps) else BISEARCH(a, b, 0.5*eps)
end;
```

The Iterative Ada Program for Binary Search

```
generic type Number is digits <>;
        with function f(x : Number) return Number;
function BISEARCH(a, b, eps : Number) return Number;

function BISEARCH(a, b, eps : Number) return Number is

        m, fm : Number;
        aa : Number := a;
        bb : Number := b;

begin

        fm := f(aa);
        if fm = 0.0 then return aa ; end if;
        if f(bb) = 0.0 then return bb ; end if;
        if fm > 0.0 then SWAP(aa, bb) ; end if;

        loop
                m := (aa + bb)/2.0 ; fm := f(m);
                if ABS(aa - bb) < 0.5 * eps then return m ; end if;
                if fm <= 0.0 then aa := m ; end if;
                if fm >= 0.0 then bb := m ; end if;
        end loop;

end BISEARCH;
```

The Recursive ZeroPoint in Ada

```ada
generic  type Number is digits <>;
        with function f(x : Number) return Number;
package ZP is
        function ZEROPOINT(a, b, eps : Number) return Number;
end ZP;

package body ZP is

        function BISEARCH(a, b, eps : Number) return Number is
                m, fm : Number;
        begin
                m := 0.5 * (a+b) ; fm := f(m);
                if ABS(a-b) < eps or else fm = 0.0 then return m ; end if;
                if fm < 0.0
                        then   return BISEARCH(m, b, eps) ;
                        else   return BISEARCH(a, m, eps) ;
                end if;
        end BISEARCH;

        function ZEROPOINT(a, b, eps : Number) return Number is
        begin
                if f(a) = 0.0 then return a ; elsif f(b) = 0 then return b ; end if;
                if f(a) > 0.0
                        then return BISEARCH(b, a, 0.5*eps) ;
                        else return BISEARCH(a, b, 0.5*eps) ;
                end if;
        end ZEROPOINT;

end ZP;
```

Newton's Algorithm in Pascal

```pascal
function ZEROPOINT ( function f, g : real; a, b, eps : real) : real;
     var fx, gx, x : real;
begin
     if (f(a) = 0) or (g(a) > g(b)) then x := a else x := b;
     eps := 0.5 * eps;
     repeat
          fx := f(x);  gx := g(x);
          x := x - fx/gx
     until abs(fx) < eps;
     ZEROPOINT := x
end;
```

Newton's Algorithm in Ada

```ada
generic  type Numeric is digits <>;
          with function f(x : in Numeric) return Numeric;
          with function g(x : in Numeric) return Numeric;
package ZP is
     function ZEROPOINT (a, b, eps : Numeric) return Numeric;
end ZP;

package body ZP is

     function NEWTON(x, eps : Numeric) return Numeric is
          fx : Numeric;
     begin
          fx := f(x);
          if ABS(fx) < eps then return x; end if;
          return NEWTON(x - fx/g(x), eps);
     end NEWTON;

     function ZEROPOINT (a, b, eps : Numeric) return Numeric is
          x: Numeric;
     begin
          if f(a) = 0.0 or g(a) > g(b) then x := a; else x := b; end if;
          return NEWTON(x, eps);
     end ZEROPOINT;

end ZP;
```

The Iterative Pascal Program SIMPSON

```pascal
function SIMPSON(function f: real ; a b, eps : real) : real;
    var i, n : integer ; c, h, OldODD, NewODD, OldArea, NewArea : real;
begin
    eps := 0.5 * eps ; h := (b - a) ; n := 1 ;
    NewODD := 0 ; NewArea := h * (f(a) + f(b))/3;

    repeat
        OldODD := NewODD ; OldArea := NewArea;
        NewODD := 0 ; c := a - h/(2*n);
        for i := 1 to n do NewODD := NewODD + f(c + i * h/n);
        NewArea := (2*NewODD - OldODD)/(3*n)*h + 0.5*OldArea;
        n := 2 * n
    until abs(NewArea - OldArea) < eps;

    SIMPSON := NewArea
end;
```

The Recursive Pascal Program SIMPSON

```pascal
function SIMPSON(function f : real; a, b, eps : real) : real;
    var h : real;
    procedure APPROX(ODD, AREA : real ; n : integer);
        var NewODD, NewArea, c : real ; i : integer;
    begin
        NewODD := 0 ; c := a - h/(2*n);
        for i := 1 to n do NewODD := NewODD + f(c + i * h/n);
        NewArea := (2 * NewODD - ODD)/(3*n) * h + 0.5 * AREA;
        if abs(NewArea - AREA) < eps then SIMPSON := NewArea
        else APPROX(NewODD, NewArea, 2*n)
    end;

begin
    h := (b - a) ; eps := 0.5 * eps;
    APPROX(0, h * (f(a) + f(b))/3, 1)
end;
```

The Iterative Ada Program SIMPSON

```
generic  type Number is digits <>;
         with function f(x : Number) return Number;
function SIMPSON(a, b, eps : Number) return Number;


function SIMPSON(a, b, eps : Number) return Number is

    n : INTEGER := 1 ; h : Number := b - a;
    c, OldODD, OldArea : Number; NewODD : Number := 0.0;
    NewArea : Number := h * (f(a) + f(b))/3.0;

begin

    loop
    OldODD := NewODD ; OldArea := NewArea;
    NewODD := 0.0 ; c := a - h/Number(2*n);
    for i in 1 . . n loop
        NewODD := NewODD + f(c + Number(i) * h/Number(n)) ;
    end loop;
    NewArea := (2.0*NewODD - OldODD)/Number(3*n)*h + 0.5*OldArea;
    if ABS(NewArea - OldArea) < 0.5 * eps then return NewArea ; end if;
    n := 2*n;

    end loop;
end SIMPSON;
```

The Recursive Ada Program SIMPSON

```ada
generic  type Number is digits <>;
        with function f(x : Number) return Number;
package SIM is
      function SIMPSON(a, b, esp : Number) return Number;
end SIM;


package body SIM is

   left, h, accur : Number;  n : INTEGER;

   function APPROX(ODD, AREA : Number) return Number is
      c, NewArea : Number ; NewODD : Number := 0.0;
   begin
      c := left - h/Number(2*n);
      for i in 1 . . n loop
         NewODD := NewODD + f(c + Number(i) * h/Number(n)) ;
      end loop;
      NewArea := (2.0*NewODD - ODD)/Number(3*n)*h + 0.5*AREA;
      if ABS(NewArea - AREA) < accur then return NewArea ; end if;
      n := 2 * n; return APPROX(NewODD, NewArea);
   end APPROX;

   function SIMPSON(a, b, eps : Number) return Number is
   begin
      left := a; h := b - a ; accur := ).5 * eps; n := 1;
      return APPROX(0.0, h * (f(a) + f(b))/3.0);
   end SIMPSON;

end SIM;
```

6.6 Reminders

1. In both Ada and Pascal, real numbers are approximated by rational numbers. The accuracy of the approximation depends upon the particular machine implementation.

2. Mixed arithmetic of integers and reals is allowed in Pascal (with automatic conversion of integers to reals). It is not allowed in Ada.

3. In neither language is the set of integer constants a subset of the set of real constants.

4. Reevaluation of expression parameters is not included in either language.

5. Subexpressions in Boolean expressions must be parenthesized in Pascal because of the unusual precedence rules that Pascal applies to arithmetic and Boolean operators.

6. In Pascal, a function value is transmitted to its calling environment by assignment to the function name as if this name were a local variable of the function body. Ada requires an explicit return statement.

7. In Pascal, a value parameter is treated as an initialized local variable and one can assign a new value to it. In Ada, one cannot assign a new value to an in parameter because it is treated as a constant.

8. In Pascal, functions and procedures can be passed as parameters. In Ada one must use generic definitions to pass procedures and functions as parameters.

9. Ada does not have a repeat statement with the test at the end as Pascal does. The effect of the repeat statement can be achieved in Ada by writing a loop statement and including a conditional exit statement at the end of the loop.

10. In Pascal, one must nest procedure declarations in order to obtain the effect of hiding. In Ada, one can achieve this effect without nesting procedures by using a package that exports only those procedures one does not want to hide.

6.7 Problems

1. Procedure TABULATE takes as input a function F, the endpoints of an interval [a, b] and a number n indicating the number of subintervals on [a, b]. Write a program in each language for procedure TABULATE that evaluates and lists the function values in the midpoints of each subinterval.

2. The trapezoid method for numeric integration of a smooth continuous function $f(x)$ approximates the integral by connecting successive function values by a straight line segment. The area associated with $[x_{i-1}, x_i]$ is

$$A_i = 0.5 * (f(x_{i-1}) + f(x_i)) * (x_i - x_{i-1}) .$$

The total area is

$$A = A_1 + A_2 + \ldots + A_n.$$

Let the interval $[a, b]$ be divided in n equal parts $h = (b - a) / n$. Since each function value $f(x_i)$ occurs in two successive subareas A_i and A_{i+1}, except for the first and the last, the total area is

$$A = 0.5 * h * [f(a) + f(b) + 2 * Sum(f(x_i))]$$
$$\text{for } i = 1, 2, \ldots , \text{n-1}$$

Design a formula for computing $A(2n)$ from $A(n)$. Define

$$A(1) = 0.5 * (b - a) * (f(a) + f(b))$$

and write a program in both Pascal and Ada that computes the integral of $f(x)$ on the interval $[a, b]$ within a given accuracy *eps* using this method.

3. Newton's algorithm has been implemented as an iterative program in Pascal and as a recursive program in Ada. Write a recursive version of Newton's algorithm in Pascal and an iterative version in Ada.

4. Integer string addition is defined for strings consisting of the digits $0, 1, \ldots , 9$. For instance,

    ”18” + ”25” = ”43”

is computed without converting the strings to integer numbers using the elementary rules

    ”8” + ”5” = ”3” plus carry
    ”1” + ”2” + carry = ”4”.

Write an iterative and a recursive program in each language for integer string addition. One may assume that the input strings are not longer than 36 characters each.

5. When a rational number is represented in six decimals, the desired number lies in the interval whose boundaries are $0.5*10^{-6}$ from the given number (e.g., the bounds of 38.1496 are 38.14955 and 38.14965). When two rational numbers are multiplied, the precision of the result depends not only on the precision of the input numbers, but also on their magnitude. The range of the result is found by multiplying the lower bounds and by multiplying the upper bounds. Write programs in Pascal and Ada that compute the product of two rational numbers with its range of precision.

Seven

Type Abstraction

Topics: composite record types, structured variables, initialization of record
            variables, with statement, exceptions, generic packages, generic
            data and type parameters, package initialization, anonymous types.

Issues: open types, abstraction and information hiding, initialization of data
            structures, functions and side effects, generalization of data
            structures.

7.1 Problem Statement

In many applications, the need arises to arrange elements in arrival time order
so that they can be processed on a first-come, first-serve basis. A *queue* is the
abstraction that has the required property: elements are inserted at one end and
removed from the other end. The problem for this chapter is to implement a
queue.

The approach in the Ada section emphasizes two features that provide advances
over Pascal. First, a queue will be implemented as a unique object where the
queue structure and its status variables are hidden. The only interface visible to
the user is that which exports the two queue operations ENQUEUE and DEQUEUE.
Then we will further generalize the solution with an implementation of queues as a
generic package that allows us to define the operations on queues without fixing
the particular type of element that is put into, or taken out of, a queue. The
additional power that generic units provide over common subprogram definitions
is the ability to pass data types as generic parameters. This feature, which we refer
to as *type abstraction*, enables us to define structures independent of the elements
they contain.

7.2 Problem Discussion

The two basic queue operations are ENQUEUE and DEQUEUE. ENQUEUE inserts an element at the end of a queue while DEQUEUE removes the first element of a queue. Two additional useful operations are the ones that determine whether or not a queue is full or empty.

The implementation of these operations depends on the representation we choose for queues. We have a choice between a list representation and an array representation. Both representations allow more flexibility than needed, because both allow access to their individual elements. Thus, the information hiding principle must be applied to restrict the operations to the front and the rear of a queue.

The advantage of a list representation is that the space requirement is proportional to the queue length. If the queue is short, the list needs only a few elements for storing the queue. A disadvantage, however, is that space management operations of garbage collection and space allocation are non-trivial and expensive.

The advantage of an array representation is the simplicity of the space management. A disadvantage is that the array space is allocated permanently, which is wasteful during times when the queue is short. An additional disadvantage is that the array may not be able to handle peak demands because of the fixed size. This problem does not arise with lists. Nevertheless, for this chapter the array representation was chosen because it facilitates a demonstration of Ada's support for information hiding and type abstraction.

Let us consider an array representation that keeps the head of the queue in a fixed place, say in the first component. The second element is then kept in the second array component, etc. This arrangement makes it very easy for DEQUEUE to locate the head of the queue. If we keep track of the queue length, ENQUEUE can also easily find the first unused array component. Moreover, the tests for empty and full simply compare the current queue length with the size of the array:

   EMPTY: current length = 0; FULL: current length = array size.

Unfortunately, fixing the position of the head causes considerable overhead in DEQUEUE because, after removing the head, all remaining queue elements must be shifted one position in order to get the new head in the correct position. A slight modification solves this problem: instead of keeping the head in a fixed position, we use a head pointer that is incremented to the next array component when the head element is dequeued. If the head is in the last array component, the pointer is reset to the first component after dequeuing. Thus, the DEQUEUE operation increments the head pointer modulo the array size:

   DEQUEUE: head: = (head + 1) **mod** array size.   (1)

The combination of head pointer and queue length can be used to locate the rear of the queue. Operation ENQUEUE computes the position for a new element by the formula

$$\text{ENQUEUE: rear} = (\text{head} + \text{length})\ \textbf{mod}\ \text{array size}. \tag{2}$$

For these formulae to be correct, the operations must update the queue length before terminating: DEQUEUE decrements the length and ENQUEUE increments it by one.

The type of the objects that are queued is irrelevant for our discussion. Since a particular choice is required by Pascal, we arbitrarily choose a type, say real.

7.3 A Pascal Solution

Record Types and Initialization

The upperbound for the length of the queues is fixed arbitrarily at 10.

const qsize = 10;

The index range for the array representing a queue is defined by range type *qindex*:

type qindex = 0 . . 9;

The queue type is represented by a record with an array component for the body of the queue, a head pointer and a length component. The array is indexed by the range type *qindex*. Since the head pointer points within the array, its type is also *qindex*. The length component, on the other hand, has a slightly more extended range: its value is zero when the queue is empty and *qsize* when it is full.

type queue = **record**
                    head   : qindex;
                    length : 0 . . qsize;
                    qbody : **array** [qindex] **of** real
            end;

The *length* field is defined by an anonymous range type. Since this range type is compatible with type integer, there is no need for an explicit type name because the *length* field can be treated as an integer with a restricted value range.

There are certain properties of queues that we want to keep invariant. The first property is that

empty slots + full slots = total slots.

In order to satisfy this invariant, the record fields must be initialized before ENQUEUE and DEQUEUE can be applied to a queue. It is of particular importance that the *length* field is initialized to zero.

The second invariant states that elements are removed in the same order in which they were inserted:

$$\text{value of the } k^{\text{th}} \text{ DEQUEUE} = \text{value of the } k^{\text{th}} \text{ ENQUEUE}$$

In order to ensure that this invariant holds, we must initialize the head pointer to a component of the array, say the first one. It is not necessary to initialize all array components, because the ENQUEUE and DEQUEUE procedures will make sure that elements are inserted and removed in the correct order.

In Pascal, the initialization is accomplished by a procedure:

```
procedure QUINIT (var q : queue);
begin
      q.length := 0;  q.head := 0
end;
```

Basic Queue Operations

The two auxiliary functions FULL and EMPTY return Boolean results that indicate whether the queue is full or empty. These functions simply check the conditions q.length = qsize and q.length = 0. (See the complete Pascal programs at the end of the chapter.)

The procedure to enqueue an element must determine the next available slot according to 2. Once the element has been queued, the length must be increased to reflect the new length of the queue

```
procedure ENQ(var q : queue ; x : real);
begin
      with q do
            begin
            qbody [(head + length) mod qsize] := x;
            length := length + 1
            end
   end;
```

The function to dequeue an element returns the element at the head of the queue. This function has the side effect of modifying the queue passed to it as a reference parameter. Although side effects are allowed, the Pascal Reference Manual strongly discourages their use (PRM 79). We believe that side effects are sometimes useful and this case is an example of a benign side effect similar to that of the GET and PUT operations.

The dequeue operation first removes the head and then changes the head pointer according to 1. The operation ends with decrementing the queue length.

```
function DEQ (var q : queue) : real;
begin
        with q do
                begin
                DEQ    := qbody[head];
                head   := (head + 1) mod qsize;
                length:= length - 1
                end
end;
```

Revision for Object Safety

The current implementation assumes that the queue will be used properly and that the user will not make mistakes such as dequeuing from an empty queue and enqueuing into a full queue. To prevent such mistakes, the user code should look something like:

```
if not EMPTY(q) then r := DEQ(q);
if not FULL(q)  then ENQ(q, r);
```

However, there is no guarantee that the user will maintain this discipline and thus, it is safer to embed checks in the routines themselves rather than in the user programs.

Maintaining a disciplined queue requires that elements can neither be queued when the queue is full nor be removed when the queue is empty. Even if the queue operations perform the checks, the user must be notified concerning the success or failure of the operation. This can be done in Pascal with a status parameter as shown in the following version of the enqueuing operation.

```
procedure ENQ (r : real ; var q : queue ; var success : boolean);
begin
        if FULL(q) then
                success := false
        else    begin
                success := true;
                with q do begin . . . end
                end
end;
```

The same status parameter can be added to DEQ because var parameters are allowed in Pascal functions. The internal structure of the operation is analogous to ENQ.

The designer can now be guaranteed that queues will be handled with integrity. The cost to the user, however, is the checking of the status after each operation.

```
ENQ(q,r,enqsuccess);
if enqsuccess then . . . ;
```

Thus, writing the code is no easier for the user, but the user can no longer do damage to queues.

7.4 An Ada Solution

A solution similar to that of the Pascal program will be presented first. Then the more powerful features of Ada supporting encapsulation and information hiding will be used to create a more rigorous and yet more flexible solution to the problem.

A Pascal-like Solution

The package mechanism, of course, is the appropriate means of defining the queue type and its attendant operations. Following the Pascal design, we would write:

```
package QueueManager is

        qsize    : constant INTEGER := 10;
        subtype qindex is INTEGER range 0 . . qsize - 1;

        type queue is record
                head   : qindex := 0;
                length : INTEGER range 0 . . qsize := 0;
                qbody  : array (qindex) of FLOAT;
        end record;

        function   FULL   (q : in queue) return BOOLEAN;
        function   EMPTY  (q : in queue) return BOOLEAN;
        procedure  ENQ    (q : in out queue ; r : in FLOAT;);
        procedure  DEQ    (q : in out queue ; r : out FLOAT;);

        overflow, underflow : exception;
end QueueManager;
```

Anonymous Types and Subtypes

The *length* component is declared to be of an anonymous subtype. For subtypes this causes no naming problems, because the underlying base type has a distinct name (in this case INTEGER). The length field is compatible with INTEGER expressions provided that assignments to it are within the specified range. The situation is slightly different for the *qbody* field. This field is declared to be of an anonymous type (rather than an anonymous subtype). The difficulty with an anonymous type is that there is no way of referring to it. Hence, it cannot be used in other declarations or parameter specifications which means that the *qbody* field cannot serve as an argument in any procedure or function call. Although there is no need to pass objects of this particular anonymous type as parameter, Ada forbids the use of anonymous types for record components entirely (ARM3.7, 3-33). No record component declaration can be of the form

```
x : array . . .
y : record . . .
z : access . . .
```

(The last two are never allowed for data objects, only for type definitions (ARM 3.2.1, 3-5).)

Since Ada forbids the use of anonymous types in record component declarations, one must always define the desired type explicitly before defining the the record type. For our particular example we introduce the type *bodies* and declare it to be

type bodies **is array** (qindex) **of** FLOAT;

The record field *qbody* can then be declared to be of type *bodies*.

Ada Functions and Side Effects

While in Pascal we were able to declare the dequeue operation as a function, in Ada we cannot because of restrictions concerning side effects. Functions in Ada may have side effects in global variables but not in formal parameters--the parameters must always be in parameters. Since the enqueue and dequeue operations change the internal values of the queue object, objects of type *queue* cannot prima facie be functional parameters. The parameter mode of type *queue* in the package above is both in and out, similar to a var parameter in Pascal. However, the semantics of in out parameters in Ada are hidden from the user. He cannot rely on a paticular interpretation such as value-result or the reference semantics of the var parameter in Pascal (ARM 6.2, 6-3).

Queue Initialization

While in Pascal there is only one way to initialize an object (through an assignment statement), in Ada there are three ways in which an object can be initialized. The first is like that of Pascal, that is, by explicit assignment before use. This approach is not very safe because the user may forget to call the initialization procedure. The second is that objects may be given initial values when they are declared. This is indeed more convenient and more likely to be used precisely because it is so convenient. However, there is still no guarantee that the user of a type will in fact provide an initial value even in as convenient a form as this. For record types, there is a third means of initializing the values of objects: provide default initial values for the components of the record. In this way, it can be guaranteed that all objects will be initialized properly because the initialization is implicit in the object's declaration. The components *head* and *length* are critical and must be initialized to the value zero. This has been guaranteed by the record type definition at the beginning of this section.

Exceptions

As the Pascal programs developed, it was clear that some means of guaranteeing the integrity of the queue objects was needed. For that reason we added the status parameter in which success or failure of each operation was reported. In Ada we do not use status variables but instead declare two exceptional conditions: *overflow* and *underflow* (ARM 11.1, 11-1). It is unfortunate that Ada's syntax is designed so that it is not clear from the package specification which exceptions are raised by which procedures. In our particular example it is obvious that ENQ raises *overflow* and DEQ *underflow*. In general, however, commenting on the part of the designer must supply the connections and the conditions under which particular exceptions occur.

Procedure ENQ raises exception *overflow* when the queue is full. When this situation is detected and the exception is raised, control is returned to the calling scope. The ENQ procedure appears as follows (the DEQ procedure is analogous).

```
procedure ENQ (q : in out queue ; r : in FLOAT;) is
begin
      if FULL(q) then raise overflow ; endif;
      q.qbody (q.head + q.length) mod qsize := r;
      q.length := q.length + 1;
end ENQ;
```

There is a distinct advantage for the user in having exceptions rather than status variables: the algorithm is not cluttered with all the attendant checks for the exceptional cases; instead, the sequence of statements for exceptional cases can be relegated to a separate exception handler (cf. Chapter 3).

Open Type Problems

The record type defined for queues is called an *open type* because its structure is visible to the user. While the operations necessary for proper use have been exported, the user is not forced to apply these operations on objects declared with that open type. A malicious user can undermine the discipline by simply ignoring the provided operations and by using the object components and status variables directly. For example, the queue can be summarily emptied by resetting the length of the queue to zero; or, an arbitrary number of elements can be removed from the head of the queue by resetting the head pointer; etc. Even where one is convinced that there are no malicious users, there exist cases where programmers are tempted by clever programming to short circuit the supplied operations and write implementation dependent code that makes use of the current structure of the type. While there exist cases (see Chapters 2 and 3) where open types are useful, structures such as stacks and queues that must be used in a disciplined manner are too prone to be abused if provided by an open type.

Packages as Unique Objects

The integrity of queues can be guaranteed by hiding their implementation in a package body. By implementing the queue as a package, the only access to the object is through the exported operations, while the actual object itself is not even visible to the user.

The visible part of a queue package might appear as

package RealQueue **is**

```
        function   FULL    return BOOLEAN;
        function   EMPTY  return BOOLEAN;
        procedure  ENQ     (r : in FLOAT);
        function   DEQ     return FLOAT;

        overflow, underflow : exception;
```

   end RealQueue;

Note that the operation DEQ is now a function rather than a procedure as it was in the preceding implementation. The side effect is now on a object that is global to the function's implementation and that is allowed in Ada. Remember, the rule in Ada is that side effects in functions are allowed only on global variables and are not allowed on functional parameters.

Anonymous Types Revisited

Since the body of a queue package will contain the queue object as a local variable, there is really no need to define a type *queue*. Instead, one would expect to be able to make the following object declaration with an anonymous record type.

```
q  : record      -- illegal Ada
            head   : qindex;
            length : INTEGER range 0 . . qsize;
            qbody  : bodies;
        end record;
```

Unfortunately, anonymous record types are not allowed in Ada (ARM 3.2, 3-5). The only anonymous types allowed are anonymous array types. (Anonymous subtypes are of course allowed in all cases.)

Two possibilities, then, are available as solutions. The first is to define the record type *queue* and then declare one object of that type. The second is to dispense entirely with the record packaging and declare the logical components of the queue as separate and independent objects. Since the implementation is completely hidden within the package body, there is no need to go beyond the second alternative. The first alternative is useful when the implementor needs to be protected from himself. There are cases where that is needed, but this is not one of them.

Since *qbody* is then no longer a record field, it can be declared with an anonymous array type. The explicit array type *bodies* is then no longer needed.

Unique Object Implementation

If we choose the loosely coupled implementation of the queue object, the implementation of the package appears in outline as follows.

```
package body RealQueue is
        qsize    : constant INTEGER : = 10;
        subtype qindex is INTEGER range 0 . . qsize - 1;

        head    : qindex;
        length  : INTEGER range 0 . . qsize;
        qbody   : array (qindex) of FLOAT;  -- anonymous type

        -- function and procedure implementations
    begin
        head : = 0;  length : = 0;
    end RealQueue;
```

The variables local to the package body are similar to Algol's own variables: They continue to exist throughout distinct invocations of the package's operations. They exist as long as the package exists.

Initialization of Packages

It is primarily for pedagogical reasons that we did not provide initial values for the objects that comprise the queue. This was a case where they could be initialized more appropriately at their declaration. There are, however, cases where it is combersome to initialize objects when they are declared. For example, suppose an array is to have each component initialized to its index value. For very small arrays, an aggregate could be used, but after a certain length, the aggregate method becomes tedious and cumbersome and a loop becomes very attractive. To facilitate this sort of initialization, an Ada package has an initialization part, denoted by keywords **begin** and **end**, that gets executed when the package is elaborated. Local variables can be initialized within this scope. Thus *head* and *length* obtain their initial values by assignment when the initialization part of the package is elaborated.

Return Revisited

The implementations of the operations are straightforward and analogous to their counterparts in the open type package. However, one must be careful in transforming the procedure DEQ into the function DEQ. In the open type procedure the head of the queue is extracted before the bookkeeping is done to determine the new head of the queue. A literal translation of this procedure into the function

```
function DEQ return FLOAT is
begin
        if EMPTY then raise underflow ; end if;
        return qbody (head);       -- this statement is in the wrong place
        head    : = head + 1 mod qsize;
        length  : = length - 1;
end DEQ;
```

would not produce a correct program because the bookkeeping would never get done. The return statement terminates the execution of the function and control is returned at that statement to the invoker.

There are two ways around this problem: either introduce a local variable in which the head is remembered, or move the return statement to the end and use *qbody*((*head* - 1) **mod** *qsize*) as argument. The first option is chosen here because it follows what is intuitively the algorithmic progression.

```
function DEQ return FLOAT is
        r : FLOAT := qbody(head);
begin
        if EMPTY then raise underflow ; end if;
        head   := (head + 1) mod qsize;
        length := length - 1;
        return r;
end DEQ;
```

Note that we take advantage of the object initialization feature to preset the value of the variable r. If the queue is empty, the value has no significance since it is not returned and the exception is raised instead.

Drawbacks of the Unique Object Implementation

There are three basic problems with the current implementation: first, there is only one queue; second, there is only one type of queue; third, there is only one length for the queue. In Chapter 4, the notion of generic packages was introduced to provide functions as parameters. Since generic parameters can also be types, declaring a generic package seems to be a step in the right direction for solving these three problems. A generic package does not define a single package, but can be instatiated as many times as required by the designer to provide the necessary number of queues. By making the element type of the queue a type parameter, queues of different types can then be instantiated as needed. By making the length of the queue a data parameter, the third problem is solved: the length of the queue can be as large as desired for a particular queue.

Generic Packages with Type and Data Parameters

A generic clause accepts the same kind of data parameters as functions and procedures do, but the parameter modes are restricted to in and in out. Just as for functions and procedures, an in parameter is treated as a constant within the package. To amend the current implementation to provide real queues of any length, the in parameter *qsize* is included in the generic clause (and, of course, the declaration of *qsize* is eliminated from the package body).

```
generic qsize : in POSITIVE;
package RealQueue is . . . end RealQueue;
```

An in out parameter, on the other hand, acts as an object name, renaming the argument given in the instantiation. The argument necessarily must be a variable name of a type for which assignment is available.

There are four kinds of generic type parameters: scalar types, array types, private types and access types. For the compiler to know which default operations apply to the generic formal type, the scalar types are denoted in a special way described in the following example.

```
generic type A is (<>);       -- a discrete type
        type B is range <>;   -- an INTEGER subtype
        type C is digits <>;  -- a floating point type
        type D is delta <>;   -- a fixed point type
```

The default operations defined for discrete types are the relational operations (such as "<", "=", etc.) and the attributes POS, VAL, PRED and SUCC. The default operations on the other three scalar types include the arithmetic operations and the specific attributes for those types (ARM appendix A).

However, since we do not want to unduly restrict the component type of the queue and since we are not concerned with the structure of the type but only with queueing objects of that type (for which only assignment is required), a private type parameter is exactly what is needed here. Assignment is available by default and, therefore, no explicit function parameters need to be added to the generic clause.

```
generic qsize : in POSITIVE;
        type element is private;
package Queue is

        function  FULL   return BOOLEAN;
        function  EMPTY  return BOOLEAN;
        procedure ENQ    (e : in element);
        function  DEQ    return element;

        overflow, underflow : exception;

end Queue;
```

The element of the queue was given the type name *element*. Note that it appears in the ENQ and DEQ operations as the type of object being queued and removed. When the package is instantiated the actual parameter, the element type, is systematically substituted for all occurrences of *element*. Thus, instantiating the package as an integer queue of 23 elements

package IntQ **is new** Queue (23, INTEGER) ;

results in a package that is the equivalent of

```
package IntQ is

    function   FULL    return BOOLEAN;
    function   EMPTY   return BOOLEAN;
    procedure ENQ      (e : in INTEGER);
    function   DEQ     return INTEGER;

    overflow, underflow : exception;

end IntQ;
```

Changes to the package body are relatively minor. The type name *element* is substituted wherever the type name FLOAT occurs. (As will be seen in the final program, the variable name *r* has been changed to *e* for obvious reasons.) The constant *qsize* is no longer needed because it has been replaced by the generic parameter *qsize*. However, all uses of *qsize* remain just as they are since the generic parameter functions exactly as a constant definition.

7.5 The Complete Programs

Pascal Program

```pascal
const qsize    = 10;
type  qindex   = 0 . . 9;
      queue    = record
                        head   : qindex;
                        length : 0 . . qsize;
                        qbody  : array [qindex] of real
                 end;
      . . .

var   u,v : queue;
      . . .

procedure QUINIT (var q : queue);
begin
      q.length := 0 ; q.head := 0
end;

function FULL (q : queue) : boolean;
begin
      FULL := (q.length = qsize)
end;

function EMPTY (q : queue) : boolean;
begin
      EMPTY := (q.length = 0)
end;

procedure ENQ (x : real ; var q : queue ; var success : boolean);
begin
      if FULL(q) then
            success := false
      else  begin
            success := true;
            with q do
                  begin
                  qbody [(head + length) mod qsize] := x;
                  length := length + 1
                  end
            end
end;
```

```
function DEQ(var q : queue ; var success : boolean) : real;
begin
        if EMPTY(q) then
                success : = false
        else    begin
                success : = true;
                with q do
                        begin
                        DEQ    : = qbody [head];
                        head   : = (head + 1) mod qsize;
                        length: = length - 1
                        end
                end
end;
. . .

quinit(u) ; quinit(v);

. . .
```

Ada Open Type Solution

```
package QueueManager is

        qsize : constant INTEGER := 10;
        subtype qindex is INTEGER range 0 . . qsize - 1;

        type bodies is array(qindex)of FLOAT;
        type queue is record
                head    : qindex := 0;
                length  : INTEGER range 0 . . qsize := 0;
                qbody   : array (qindex) of FLOAT;
        end record;

        function   FULL  (q : in queue) return BOOLEAN;
        function   EMPTY (q : in queue) return BOOLEAN;
        procedure  ENQ   (q : in out queue ; r : in FLOAT);
        procedure  DEQ   (q : in out queue ; r : out FLOAT);

        overflow, underflow : exception;

end QueueManager;


package body QueueManager is

        function FULL(q : in queue) return BOOLEAN is
        begin
                return q.length = qsize;
        end FULL;

        function EMPTY(q : in queue) return BOOLEAN is
        begin
                return q.length = 0;
        end EMPTY;

        procedure ENQ(q : in out queue ; r : in FLOAT) is
        begin
                if FULL(q) then raise overflow ; end if;
                q.qbody(q.head + q.length) mod qsize := r;
                q.length := q.length + 1;
        end ENQ;
```

```
procedure DEQ(q : in out queue ; r : out FLOAT) is
begin
        if EMPTY(q) then raise underflow ; end if;
        r:= q.qbody (q.head);
        q.head:= (q.head + 1) mod qsize;
        q.length:= q.length - 1;
end DEQ;

end QueueManager;
```

Ada Program for the Queue as a Unique Object

```
package RealQueue is

        function    FULL    return BOOLEAN;
        function    EMPTY   return BOOLEAN;
        procedure ENQ       (r : in FLOAT);
        function    DEQ     return FLOAT;

        overflow, underflow : exception;

end RealQueue;


package body RealQueue is

        qsize    : constant INTEGER := 10;
        subtype qindex is INTEGER range 0 . . qsize - 1;

        head    : qindex;
        length  : INTEGER range 0 . . qsize;
        qbody   : array (qindex) of FLOAT;

        function FULL return BOOLEAN is
        begin
                return length = qsize;
        end FULL;

        function EMPTY return BOOLEAN is
        begin
                return length = 0;
        end EMPTY;
```

```
procedure ENQ(r : in FLOAT) is
begin
        if FULL then raise overflow ; end if;
        qbody (head + length) mod qsize := r;
        length := length + 1;
end ENQ;

function DEQ return FLOAT is
        r : FLOAT := qbody (head);
begin
        if EMPTY then raise underflow ; end if;
        head   := (head + 1) mod qsize;
        length:= length - 1;
        return r;
end DEQ;

begin
        head   := 0;
        length := 0;
end RealQueue;
```

Generic Unique Object Package in Ada

```
generic qsize   : in POSITIVE;
        type    element is private;
package Queue is

        function   FULL    return BOOLEAN;
        function   EMPTY   return BOOLEAN;
        procedure ENQ      (e : in element);
        function   DEQ     return element;

        overflow, underflow : exception;

end Queue;


package body Queue is

        subtype qindex is INTEGER range 0 . . qsize - 1;

        head    : qindex;
        length  : INTEGER range 0 . . qsize;
        qbody   : array (qindex) of element;
```

```
function FULL        return BOOLEAN is . . . end FULL;
function EMPTY       return BOOLEAN is . . . end EMPTY;

procedure ENQ (e : in element) is
begin
        if FULL then raise overflow ; end if;
        qbody(head + length) mod qsize := e;
        length := length + 1;
end ENQ;

function DEQ return element is
        e : element := qbody(head);
begin
        if EMPTY then raise undeflow; end if;
        head    := (head + 1) mod qsize;
        length := length - 1;
        return e;
end DEQ;

begin
        head    := 0;
        length := 0;
end Queue;
```

7.6 Reminders

1. Functions in Pascal can have side effects on the formal parameters. In Ada, parameters of functions can only be in parameters and hence there cannot be side effects in the parameters. Side effects are allowed on global variables.

2. Exceptions provide a convenient way of handling truly exceptional conditions. While status parameters have their strong points, there are cases where exceptions provide a clean method of separating the exception handling statements from the algorithm itself.

3. Open type definitions are useful for some objects, such as vectors, etc. where the component elements may be safely accessed and used. Other objects, such as queues, need more protection to ensure their integrity. Unique objects and abstract types provide this safety.

4. The only anonymous types allowed in Ada are array types.

5. Initial values for objects can come in three ways: by assignment, by initialization at declaration time and, for records, initial value for the components in the type definition.

6. Exceptions are raised at the point of detection. At that point the current scope is exited and a handler is searched for. Handlers can be installed at the appropriate levels where knowlege is available to handle the exceptions.

7. Unique objects are suitable where the number of these occurrences is not very large.

8. Package Initialization is yet another way to initialize variables. This form of initialization applies to variables local to the package implementation. The initialization occurs when the package is elaborated.

9. Use the return statement carefully. The return terminates the execution of the function at that point and returns to the caller.

10. Data types can be generalized through the use of generic packages with data and type parameters. This enables the designer/programmer to construct a single maintainable sequence of code from which the other desired instances can be derived.

11. Data parameters to generic units can have modes in or in out. The former are constants and the latter renamed variables within the generic unit.

12. An Ada program may not rely on a particular interpretation of in out parameters. It is incorrect to assume reference semantics, as in Pascal, or to assume copy-result semantics.

13. Type parameters can be one of the scalar definitions, array types, access types and private types. Additional operations may be required with private type parameters.

7.7 Problems

1. In the first version of queues we let the head of the queue always be the first element of the array. Implement this version in Ada. Are there language facilities available to make it easy to write?

2. A double ended queue (a Dequeue, pronounced "deck") is an object that allows the addition of elements at both the head and the tail of the Dequeue and that allows the removal of elements from both the head and tail as well. Implement a generic package that provides a unique Dequeue object and then use it to implement generic packages of unique queue and stack objects.

3. Unique objects are useful when only a limited number of objects are needed. However, suppose that the queue is an object that is required in large numbers in a particular application. Queues of differing types of components are required and for a given type of Queue (i.e., for a queue with a given type of component) various length queues are required as well. For this kind of application, it makes more sense to define a queue type rather than a queue object (as has been done in this chapter). It is much easier and less expensive to declare objects to be of a given type than to instantiate a generic package when a new object is needed. There are several approaches possible. One is to define a queue type and export it with the operations on queues and to specify the component type and queue length as generic parameters (a hybrid of the first Ada example--with open types--and the last--with generic parameters). However, this does not give us quite the flexibility that is needed with respect to the lengths of the queues: a different package would have to be instantiated for each length of queue for each different component type. The second approach is to make the length of the queue a record parameter as done for *vstrings* in Chapter 4. However, we have now lost the safety that the unique object offered with its hidden implementation. A third approach, then, is to declare the parameterized queue type to be private and thus hide its structure from the user. Define and program a generic queue package that implements the third approach. Should the private type be limited?

4. Suppose that you need a queue of queues. In Pascal, of course, the queues will have to be of fixed length. Change the Pascal program to provide a queue of queues rather than a queue of reals. What will happen to the function DEQ? Given the model of *vstring* in Chapter 4, and the definition of the private type *queue* in Problem 3, define an open type *queue* such that objects need not be constrained at declaration and hence can assume

any length queue during its lifetime. Instantiate the Ada generic package for the unique queue object with that unconstrained queue type of variable length. What are the advantages of Ada generic packages over changing code in Pascal?

5. Given that a variable length queue can be constructed (cf. Problem 4) without using lists, modify the solution to Problem 3 so that objects can be declared to be of a variable length queue. Given this type of queue, a useful operation is the ability to increase the length of the queue (particularly when the queue overflows). Extend the revised package of Problem 3 to include the length increase operation. What is entailed by this increase length operation? Will you need an initialization operation? Further extend the package to supply the inverse operation: to decrease the length of a queue. Are there further problems encountered here?

Eight

Recursive Data Structures

Topics: access variables, recursive data structures, dynamic variables, initialization, pointer assignment, dereferencing, case statement, out and in out parameters, default generic subprogram parameters.

Issues: dangling pointers, garbage collection, structured object comparison, forward definitions, direct and indirect side effects.

8.1 Problem Statement

For many applications, the array and record structures are sufficient for describing the required data. For other applications, the data requirements are more dynamic and the fixed structures are too limiting. While the fixed structures can be used, they suffer from two problems: space inefficiency and space limitations. Dynamic structures that make use of pointers, on the other hand, can grow and shrink with the demands of the application.

One large class of dynamic data structures is that of recursive data structures: the element that is the building block of the structure points to elements of the same type as itself. Lists and trees are common examples of recursive data structures.

The problem discussed in this chapter is that of constructing a lexicon of strings using a recursively defined labeled binary tree. In this labeled binary tree, a new string is inserted (if it does not exist already in the tree) as a labeled node as a left descendant if it alphabetically precedes a given node's label and as a right descendant if it alphabetically succeeds that node's label.

8.2 Problem Discussion

An *n*-ary tree is a ordered collection of nodes and directed arcs satisfying the following three conditions. First, each node, except one, has exactly one parent: in other words, it has exactly one incoming arc that connects it to its parent node. Second, each node has at most *n* sons: that is, it has at most *n* outgoing arcs that connect to the son nodes. Finally, there is a unique node, called the root of the tree, that has no parent. Thus, in a binary tree, each node has at most two sons.

A labeled tree is a tree in which each node is labeled from some predefined set. For the lexicon example, the label set is {L-character set}* : that is, any string constructable in the character set of the language. For practical purposes, a length limitation may be imposed to restrict the size of the labeling set, say 32 characters. Therefore, the label set is the set of all strings composable from the language's character set whose length is less than or equal to 32.

The most natural representation of a labeled binary tree is that of a recursive data structure that uses pointers to point to the son nodes. The node in the labeled binary tree is a record with three components: the label, the pointer to the left son and the pointer to the right son. An actual tree is then constructed from the unique node: the root. Thus a variable is needed to point to the root of the tree. Obviously, an empty tree (a tree that has not yet grown) has no root: in other words, it has no pointer to a node. The unique name for no pointer is *null*.

The insertion procedure begins at the root. If there is no root node, then a root node is created whose label is the string to be inserted. If there is a root node, then the string is compared with the label of that root. If the string is less than the label (i.e., it alphabetically precedes the label) then the string is inserted in the left subtree; if the string is greater than the label (i.e., it alphabetically succeeds the node label) then the string is inserted in the right subtree; otherwise, it matches the node label and is already in the tree. (Note: a subtree is a tree that is created by taking a node from the tree and treating it as the root of the subtree.)

8.3 A Pascal Solution

Recursive Data Structures

The labeled binary tree node consists of three components: the label and two pointers to the node's two sons. The type *vstring* (cf. Chapter 4) is used for the node label for two reasons. First, *vstring* provides the necessary flexibility needed to represent the labels of the nodes. Second, we wish to re-enforce the idea of reusable software: that is, constructing new software from old pieces wherever possible.

The pointer components are indicated in Pascal by prefixing an up-arrow to the type of the component.

      left, right :   ↑ binarytreenode;

The up-arrow specifies that the components are pointer variables and can point only to objects of the type following the up-arrow.

The recursively defined labeled binary tree node appears as

```
type   btreeptr        =  ↑ binarytreenode;
       binarytreenode  = record
                            nlabel     : vstring;
                            left,right : btreeptr;
                         end;
```

in Pascal. The type is recursive because the components *left* and *right* point to the type being defined and, hence, are bound to it (cf. PRM 10, 62).

Dynamic Variables

There are three kinds of varibles in Pascal: static variables, pointer variables and dynamic variables. Static variables come into existence by declarations, exist for as long as the scope in which they are declared exists, and are referenced by the variable name. Pointer variables introduce one level of indirection into the scheme described above. The pointer variables are static variables but contain values that point to dynamic variables. A dynamic variable comes into existence by an explicit allocation operation and ceases to exists when they are no longer referenced by pointer variables or when explicitly deallocated.

The pointer to a dynamic variable may be set in one of two ways. First, by assignment from another pointer variable. If *root2* points to a *binarytreenode* dynamic variable, then the assignment

      root2 : = root1;

assigns the pointer in *root1* to *root2* so that they both point to the same dynamic variable of type *binarytreenode*. Second, a reference may be created by allocating space for the dynamic variable by means of the standard procedure NEW.

      NEW (root1);

A new dynamic variable is created and the reference to it is assigned to *root1*. The dynamic variable itself is a *binarytreenode* that has no initial values, that is, it is uninitialized. It begins existence at the moment of allocation and continues to exist until deallocated. The deallocation occurs when the DISPOSE procedure is invoked.

DISPOSE (root1);

At that point, the dynamic variable referenced by *root1* ceases to exist.

Another form of the allocation procedure is

NEW (p, t1, . . . , tn);

which allocates dynamic variables for variant records where *t1, . . . ,tn* are the tags defining which variant is being allocated. Caution must be exercised here as this allocation fixes the size of the object but does not constrain the programmer to assign only values appropriate to the allocated variant. No assignment to the tags has been done in this allocation--that must be done separately--but the appropriate size has been determined and allocated. Later assignments of different tags will not change the size that has been allocated but will undoubtedly cause unreliable results if the resulting record is bigger than the variant that was allocated. The analogous form of DISPOSE is available to deallocate variant records. The safety of the deallocation may depend upon the implementation, but care should be taken to deallocate exactly the variant that was allocated, otherwise, unpredictable results may occur.

Dereferencing Pointer Variables

The value of pointers lies in the   namic manner in which data structures can be built. The assignment of pointers to pointer variables was discussed in the preceding section. The second important aspect of pointer variables lies in the dynamic variables themselves. Getting from the pointer variable to the actual dynamic variable requires a *dereferencing* operation. In Pascal, this is accomplished by means of the up-arrow appended to the pointer variable name. Component reference is then accomplished by the familiar record dot notation.

root1 ↑ .nlabel

For example, given that the pointer variable *b* is of type *btreeptr*, the following statements dereference *b* and assign, respectively, the value *x*, NIL and NIL to the components of the dynamic variable denoted by *b*.

b ↑ .nlabel := x ; b ↑ .left := NIL ; b ↑ .right := NIL

Similarly, the dereferencing operation can be used to retrieve the value from a dynamic variable.

x := b ↑ .nlabel

Pointer Problems

There are two basic problems with pointer variables: lost dynamic variables and dangling pointers. Consider the following sequence of code:

```
NEW(root1) ; NEW(root2);
root1 : = root2;
  . . .
```

Two dynamic variables have been allocated but the first is lost due to the assignment of the reference in *root2* to *root1*. Generally, this is not a problem. If the garbage collection algorithm is good it may not even mean wasted space. But logically, it has not been deallocated by the DISPOSE operation and has, therefore, been lost. Care must be taken to ensure that data is not inadvertantly lost due to careless pointer assignment.

Dangling pointers are more serious because they are more insidious. Suppose we have the following sequence of code:

```
NEW(root1);
root1 ↑ .nlabel : = x ; { initialize various components, etc. }
root2 : = root1;
  . . .
DISPOSE(root1);
  . . .
x : = root2 ↑ .nlabel ; . . . root2 ↑ .nlabel : =  . . . ;
```

The dynamic variable denoted by *root1* is initialized and then *root2* is set to denote the same dynamic variable. The DISPOSE operation erases the dynamic variable referenced by both *root1* and *root2*. However, as seen here, *root2* continues to be used as though it still referenced the dynamic variable that has been deallocated. Unpredictable results invariably ensue (how unpredictable depends upon the particular implementation of dynamic variables).

Pointer-Valued Functions

Pointers may be returned as values from functions. However, certain care must be exercised inside the functions because of the nature of functions and pointers. For example, since the returned value is a reference to a dynamic variable, one might think that the following allocation to the function name would work:

```
NEW(NEWNODE);
```

where NEWENODE is a function that returns a reference to a new node. However, this statement does not have the intended effect; rather, the reference to NEWENODE is interpreted as a function call instead of as a function name which can be assigned to.

An auxiliary variable, then, is needed for the basic allocation activities. In the function that allocates and initializes a labeled *binarytreenode*, the variable *node* is used for allocation and initialization.

> **function** NEWNODE (l : vstring) : btreeptr;
>   **var** node : btreeptr;
> **begin**
>   NEW (node);
>   node ↑ .left : = NIL ;   node ↑ .right : = NIL;
>   node ↑ .nlabel.len : = l.len ;   node ↑ .nlabel.str : = l.str;
>   NEWNODE : = node
> **end**;

Alternatively, one might allocate the dynamic variable for *node*, assign the reference to the function name and then initialize the variable itself.

> NEW(node);
> NEWNODE : = node;
> node ↑ .left : = NIL ; . . . etc.

We choose the first method for stylistic reasons: the node is then completely initialized before the act of returning the value is performed.

Iteration versus Recursion

The insertion operation can be implemented in one of two ways: either iteratively or recursively. The tradeoff is between space efficiency and elegance. For purposes of illustration, we will implement the operation both ways.

The implementation of the insertion operation in both cases is a function that requires a label and a tree as input and that returns a pointer to the labeled node either inserted into the tree or already existing in the tree. In the iterative version, after the check for an empty tree, the program loops until the node is found which has the specified label. When the label is found it is either because it already existed in the tree or because it was just inserted into the tree.

The use of pointers introduces the notion of indirect side effects. At some point in the tree, a labeled node may be inserted into the tree, thereby affecting the tree as a structure but not affecting the pointer to the root node. These considerations might lead one to think that the function

> **function** INSERT (nlabel : vstring ; root : btreeptr) : btreeptr;

might be correct. However, the presence of indirect side effects should not be allowed to mask the fact that there may well be a direct side effect as well. When the tree is empty, the root node must be created and inserted. At that particular point, the value parameter is not sufficient, and a result parameter is required so that the pointer to the root node is properly set. Because of the reference parameter for the root of the tree, an auxiliary variable is required to traverse the tree iteratively. In the single case when the root does not exist, it will be created and the pointer to the tree set accordingly.

```
function INSERT(nlabel : vstring ; var r : btreeptr) : btreeptr;
    var root : btreeptr;
begin
    root := r;
    if root = NIL then begin root := NEWNODE(nlabel) ; r := root end;
    while not equal(root ↑ .nlabel, nlabel) do
        case less(nlabel, root ↑ .nlabel) of
        true :  begin
                    if root ↑ .left = NIL then root ↑ .left := NEWNODE(nlabel);
                    root := root ↑ .left
                end;
        false : begin
                    if root ↑ .right = NIL then root ↑ .right := NEWNODE(nlabel);
                    root := root ↑ .right
                end
        end;
    INSERT := root
end;
```

The case statement is used here, instead of the if statement, for comparison with Ada's case statement.

In the recursive version, the recursion stops when the tree (or subtree) passed is either empty or the tree's root contains the label that is to be inserted; otherwise, the left or right subtree is passed to the recursively called INSERT function.

```
function INSERT(nlabel : vstring ; var root : btreeptr) : btreeptr;
begin
        if root = NIL then
                begin
                root := NEWNODE(nlabel);
                INSERT := root
                end
        else if equal(nlabel, root ↑ .nlabel) then
                INSERT := root
        else if less(nlabel, root ↑ .nlabel) then
                INSERT := INSERT(nlabel, root ↑ .left)
        else INSERT := INSERT(nlabel, root ↑ .right)
end;
```

Note that the direct side effect on the root is not the singular case as in the former algorithm but one of the two normal terminating cases. If the label does not exist, there is a direct side effect on the root parameter. Note also, that because of the recursion, an auxiliary variable is not needed to traverse the tree.

8.4 An Ada Solution

Access Types

Ada separates the notion of the pointer type from the type of the object to which it points. Where in Pascal there is the single type modified by the pointer indication (an up arrow), there exists in Ada the concept of the *access* object and the *dynamic* object. A dynamic object may be of any type: scalar or structured. The *access* type determines a class of dynamic variables that may be created upon demand and destroyed when no longer referenced.

The *access* type is defined in the following form (ARM 3.8, 3-40):

> **type** name **is access** subtype indication;

The *subtype indication* specifies the kind of object that can be referenced by objects of the access type. For example, consider the type *string* and an access type *stringptr*.

> **type** string **is** . . . ;
> **type** stringptr **is access** string;

Variables of type *stringptr* may point to dynamic objects of type *string* and several *stringptr* variables may reference the same *string* object.

Recursive Data Structures

Access types may be used wherever any other type may be used: to define variables, to define the components of arrays, and to define the components of records. It is in this latter use that we find the capacity to define recursive data structures. In contrast to Pascal, the recursive data structure must be defined in three steps in Ada.

First, an incomplete type specification must be provided because names must be declared before they are used. The order of declaration is important here. The record type must be incompletely declared first. The access type can then be defined. Finally, once the access type has been defined, the record type can then be fully specified. This order is required because a record definition cannot be made using incompletely declared types; the compiler must be able to allocate the appropriate space in the record.

The incomplete declaration defines the type name only.

    type binarytreenode;

As the access type requirements are the same regardless of the dynamic variable type, we can use the incomplete definition to define the access type.

    type binarytree **is access** binarytreenode;

The recursion can now be completely specified.

```
type binarytreenode is record
        label  : vstring;
        left   : binarytree;
        right  : binarytree;
end record;
```

The node in the binary tree consists of the label and the pointers to the right and left sons. (We use the type *vstring* from Chapter 4 for the label.) The *right* and *left* sons are of the access type *binarytree* and point to, possibly empty, subtrees.

Initial Values for Access Variables

There exists a unique value that refers to no object: it is designated by the keyword **null**. When an access variable is declared, it automatically receives the value *null* so that there is no possibility of random references (ARM 3.8, 3-40). The only other values that an access variable may have are the designations provided by an allocation statement. As with other declarations, initial values may be given in the object declaration.

Dynamic Variables

There are restrictions placed upon access-type variables. They may reference only objects that are created dynamically using the allocation statement. For example, if *S1* is declared

    S1: STRING(1 . . 13) : = "sample string";

there is no way for an access type variable to reference *S1*. *S1* is a static object, not a dynamic object. Its existence is dependent upon the existence of its enclosing scope: it comes into existence when the scope in which it is declared is elaborated, and ceases to exist when the scope is terminated. The static object can be referenced only by its name, *S1*, and may not be referenced in any other way.

Dynamic objects, on the other hand, are created independently of the opening and closing of scopes. The allocation statement provides the mechanism for creating new dynamic objects (ARM 4.8, 4-24).

> **new** . . . ;

Functionally, the allocation statement is similar to Pascal's NEW procedure: a dynamic object is created and its name (address) returned to be kept in a pointer variable. There are, however, significant differences from the Pascal procedure. There are two forms of allocation for dynamic objects. The first allocates the dynamic object but provides no initial value. The second form allocates the dynamic object and also provides an initial value for that object.

In the first form of allocation, the object is created by the following clause.

> **new** subtype indication;

The subtype indication fixes the subtype of the dynamic object but provides no values other than the constraints required to fix the subtype. Array bounds must be fixed at allocation time if they are not constrained by the type definition. For example, in

> **new** typename indexconstraint;

the index constraint fixes the bounds of the array object. For objects of record types that have parameters, the parameters must be specified at the time of allocation. These discriminant constraints must be satisfied.

> **new** typename discriminant-constraint;

For example,

```
S  : = new STRING(1 . . 20);
D  : = new date;                -- for type date, see Chapter 2
V  : = new vstring(17);         -- for type vstring, see Chapter 4
```

The second form allocates the dynamic object and provides an initial value for the object. For scalar variables, the form is

> **new** typename'(expression);

where the expression is the value to be given to the new object. For structured variables, the form is

> **new** typename'aggregate;

where the aggregate specifies all of the values for the particular structured type. If the structured type is an array, the aggregate specifies all of the values of the array; if a record, it specifies all of the values of the record.

```
S  : = new STRING'("momentum");
I  : = new INTEGER'(73);
D  : = new date'(Apr, 10, 1982);
V  : = new vstring'(len => 9, str => "something");
```

S is an access variable that points to a dynamic string of eight characters, initialized to "momentum". I is an access variable that can reference integers and is allocated an integer whose initial value is 73. D is an access variable that references an initialized date record. V is an access variable that points to a vstring whose constraint is fixed by the complete aggregate that serves as initial value.

The form that we will use extensively in this problem is the aggregate initialization form. If *root* is an access variable (of type *btreeptr*) that references objects of type *binarytreenode*, then the allocation desired takes the form:

root := **new** binarytreenode'(somelabel, **null**, **null**);

The primary purpose of the index and discriminant constraint specifications is to fix the size of the object to be allocated. Where no constraints exist, the size is fixed by the type definition. Once the discriminant has been fixed, the object is constrained and the discriminants cannot be changed, not even by complete aggregate or record assignment (cf. Notes ARM 5.2, 5-3). The subtype of the dynamic object has been fixed and may not be changed. Of course, a new object with different constraints may be created to replace the other, but, once allocated, the size of the object and the subtype of the object are fixed.

Access Variable Assignment and Dereferencing

The references to dynamic objects may be shared among access variables. Assignment of the pointers to objects is identical to any other assignment statements: the two operands must be of the same subtype. If *root1* and *root2* are *btreeptr* variables, then the assignment

root1 := root2;

is legal and both variables now designate the same *binarytreenode* object.

The dynamic object designated by an access variable may be referenced by dereferencing the pointer and gaining access to the object itself. In Pascal, the variable had to have an up arrow appended to it to specify the dereferencing operation. In Ada, the dereferencing occurs in one of several ways. If the dynamic object is a record, the dereferencing operation is accomplished by the dot notation used to fetch the desired record component. For example,

root1.label, root1.left, and root1.right

all dereference the access variable *root1* and retrieve the values of the dynamic object's label, left son and right son, respectively. If the dynamic object is an array, the dereferencing is accomplished by subscripting the access variable.

S1(15)

retrieves the 15th character in the string designated by *S1*. For both this case and the record case, the dereferencing occurs implicitly by referencing a component of the dynamic object.

Scalar objects present a different problem. There is no component to reference that implicitly dereferences the access variable. The solution provided in Ada is not very satisfactory but is adequate. The qualification

> .all

may be applied to any access variable to reference the entire dynamic object regardless of whether it is scalar or structured. For a pointer to an integer, the phrase

> intobject.all

retrieves the integer value from the object designated by *intobject*. The all qualification may appear on the lefthand side of an assignment statement as well. In this case, the meaning of the phrase is: assign the value on the right of the assignment statement to the object designated by the access variable. Thus,

> intobject.all := 74;

inserts the value 74 into the dynamic integer object designated by *intobject*.

Note, however, that the assignment statements

> root1 := root2;   root1.all := root2.all;

are not identical. In the first case, the access variables both designate the same dynamic object. In the second case, the access variables designate distinct objects which have the same values.

Pointer Problems

In the discussion on Pascal, we noted two problems that might occur using pointers: dangling references and lost objects. Lost objects occur here as well, so that care must be taken not to lose the reference to an object until it is no longer needed. Dangling references, on the other hand, cannot, in normal circumstances, occur in Ada. There is no explicit deallocation in Ada, so no object is deallocated while references to it exist.

The non-normal circumstances in which dangling references can arise are those where UNCHECKED_DEALLOCATION is used. The generic procedure, UNCHECKED_DEALLOCATION, can be instantiated for a particular dynamic object and access type and used to deallocate dynamic objects explicitly (ARM 13.10.1, 13-16). If FREE is such an instantiation, then the invocation

> FREE (root1);

deallocates the dynamic object designated by *root1* and sets the value of *root1* to null. However, if *root2* designates the same object as *root1*, *root2* is now in error because it designates an object that no longer exists. Caveat Emptor !

Functions and Side Effects

Formal parameters for functions in Ada can have only the mode in (ARM 6.5, 6-10). Side effects are ostensibly limited to data global to the function. However, with access variables, there is a level of indirection such that the actual parameter itself cannot be changed but the object designated by the parameter can be changed. We call this an indirect side effect. Similarly, while access type constants always designate the same dynamic object, the value of the dynamic object is not necessarily constant and may change.

With this in mind, it might be thought that the specification of INSERT as a function would be correct.

function INSERT (label : **in** vstring; root : **in** binarytree) **return** binarytree;

Any insertion in the tree might be considered to be an indirect side effect. Unfortunately, there is the boundary case which requires a direct effect on *root*: when the tree is empty and the first label is inserted into the tree. A function similar to that in the Pascal solution is therefore not feasible. We must use a procedure instead and return the designator of the inserted or matched node in the parameter *node*.

In, Out and In Out Parameters

Ada provides three modes for formal parameters (ARM 6.2, 6-3) where Pascal provides only two. The mode *in* indicates that the parameter is a local constant whose value is provided by the argument. The mode *out* indicates that the parameter is a local variable whose value is assigned to the argument. The mode *in out* indicates that the parameter is a combination of the above two modes. The parameter mechanism used depends upon the type of the parameter. For scalar and access type parameters, the copy-result mechanism is used: values are copied into the formal parameters from the argument and then copied back when the subprogram completes. For structured parameters, the language does not define the mechanism and either the copy-result or the reference mechanism may be used. The programmer is warned not to depend on either one.

The procedure specification for INSERT contains one parameter for each mode. The parameter *label* has the mode in and provides the value for the labeled node. The parameter *root* has mode in out and provides the pointer to the tree which may be empty. It is precisely because the tree may be empty and a node set for the root that this mode is required. Once the *root* designates an object, all effects on the parameter are indirect. The parameter *node* is the returned designator of a new node (if the label was not found in the tree) or an existing node (if the label already exists in the tree).

> **procedure** INSERT
>   (label : **in** vstring; root : **in out** binarytree; node : **out** binarytree);

The Iterative INSERT

The iterative version is similar to the Pascal version. However, there are two points of difference. First, we can use the parameter *node* instead of a local variable to trayerse the binary tree. Second, we do not require a NEWNODE procedure. Initialized allocation serves this purpose. If the tree is empty, a binary tree node is created for the input label and inserted at the root. The tree is traversed according to the specification: if the input label is less than the current node's label, traverse the left subtree; if the input label is greater than the current node's label, traverse the right subtree. When a subtree is empty, create a node for the label and insert it in the tree at that point. The iteration stops when the labeled node is found (either because it was previously there or because it was just inserted). The pointer to the node is returned via the *node* parameter.

```
      procedure INSERT
             (label : in vstring; root : in out binarytree; node : out binarytree) is
      begin
             node := root;
             if node = null then
                   node := new binarytreenode'(label, null, null);
                   root := node;
             end if;
             while node.label = label loop
                   case label < node.label is
                   when true =>
                         if node.left = null then
                               node.left := new binarytreenode'(label, null, null);
                         end if;
                         node := node.left;
                   when false =>
                         if node.right := null then
                               node.right := new binarytreenode'(label, null, null);
                         end if;
                         node := node.right;
                   end case;
             end loop;
      end INSERT;
```

Note that we do not need an auxiliary variable as we did in the Pascal version. The *out* parameter serves this purpose here. At the end of the loop, *node* points to the desired binary tree node.

A Generalized Case Statement and a Recursive INSERT

Ada provides an extension of the if statement (ARM 5.3, 5-4) that functions as a generalized case statement. The form of the statement is

> **if**   expression **then** . . . ;
> **elsif** expression **then** . . . ;
> . . .
> **else** . . . ;

where the elsif . . . then clauses can occur as many times as are desired.

The recursive version is implemented entirely with this generalized case statement and the use of recursion. Four conditions must be considered in the case statement: the two terminating conditions where the root is null or the label is found; and the two recursive conditions that determine which subtree to traverse.

```
procedure INSERT ( label  : in vstring;
                   root   : in out binarytree;
                   node   : out binarytree) is
begin
   if    root = null then
         root  := new binarytreenode'(label, null, null);
         node := root;
   elsif root.label = label then
         node := root;
   elsif label < root.label then
         INSERT (label, root.left, node);
   else  INSERT (label, root.right, node);
   end if;
end INSERT;
```

A Generic Solution and Subprogram Parameters

Ada's generic facilities enable the programmer to generalize the labeled binary tree program to provide arbitrary labels. Thus, instead of having a particular solution for a *vstring* label, we can produce a program that can be instantiated for any kind of label. There are two restrictions, however, to the claim that it can be instantiated for any label. First, there must be assignment defined for the type, otherwise the node in the tree cannot be given the label value. This eliminates labels that are limited private. Second, ordering operations "=" and "<" must be defined for the label. For all types except limited private, the equality operation is automatically provided by the language. However, the operation "<" is not automatically provided. The user is required to provide this operation for the generic package instantiation.

The label type is the primary parameter for the generic package. We name this type *labeltype* to indicate its function within the package specification and implementation.

> **generic type** labeltype **is private**;
> **package** LabeledBinaryTree **is** . . . **end** LabeledBinaryTree;

The *labeltype* parameter is treated as private within the package. This implies that only the operations of assignment and equality are provided automatically with the actual parameter (ARM 12.1.2, 12-4). Any other operations required by the package must be specified in the generic parameter list. Since we require the ordering operation, "<" , we must indicate this with a parameter declaration.

> **generic type** labeltype **is private**;
>   **with function** "<" (l1, l2 : **in** labeltype) **return** BOOLEAN;
>   . . .

The with clauses specify the operations that must be provided in the package instantiation.

Generic subprogram parameters may have default values in a manner similar to default values for in parameters in subprograms. These default subprograms are specified in one of two ways. The first form of this default is the named specification.

> **with** subprogram specification **is** name;

Subprogram, entry and enumeration attributes may be used as the default *name* (ARM 12.3.6, 12-14). The parameter and result type profiles of the formal subprogram parameter and the default argument must match. If there exists a subprogram, in the scope of the generic instantiation whose type profiles match the default, then the argument for this parameter may be omitted in the instantiation. For example,

> **with function** "<" (l1,l2 : **in** labeltype) **return** BOOLEAN **is** "<" ;

specifies a default for the function "<" whose formal parameter type profile is *labeltype, labeltype* and whose result type profile is BOOLEAN.

The second form is used where the default subprogram has the same name, and the same parameter type and result type profiles.

> **with** subprogram specification **is** <>;

For example, the following two declarations are equivalent.

> **with function** ```"<"``` . . . **is** ```<>```;
> **with function** ```"<"``` . . . **is** ```"<"```;

The requirements for instantiation are the same as for the first form: the argument can be omitted if the appropriate subprogram is known in the scope of the instantiation.

Generic Instantiation with Subprogram Parameters

Assuming that the type *vstring* defined in the package VariableStrings has an ordering operation *lessthan* defined for it, we can instantiate the package for *vstrings* in one of the two following ways (ARM 12.3, 12-6).

> **package** VstringBTree **is new** LabeledBinaryTree (vstring);
> **package** VstringBTree **is new** LabeledBinaryTree (vstring, ```">"```);

In the first, we allow the compiler to locate the default operation by means of its specification. In the second we specifically select the desired ordering operation (which in this case is the opposite to the default and causes the labels to be stored in reverse alphabetical order.)

8.5 The Complete Programs

The Pascal Program

```
type   btreeptr          =  ↑ binarytreenode;
       binarytreenode    =  record
                                  nlabel      : vstring;
                                  left,right  : btreeptr;
                            end;

function NEWNODE (l : vstring) : btreeptr;
       var node : btreeptr;
begin
       new (node);
       node ↑ .left := NIL ;          node ↑ .right := NIL;
       node ↑ .nlabel.len := l.len ;  node ↑ .nlabel.str := l.str;
       NEWNODE  := node
end;

function INSERT(nlabel : vstring ; var r : btreeptr) :  btreeptr;
       var root : btreeptr;
begin
       root := r;
       if root = NIL then begin root := NEWNODE(nlabel) ; r := root end;
       while not equal(root ↑ .nlabel, nlabel) do
          case less(root ↑ .nlabel, nlabel) of
          true :  begin
                     if root ↑ .left = NIL then root ↑ .left := NEWNODE(nlabel);
                     root := root ↑ .left
                     end;
          false : begin
                     if root ↑ .right = NIL then root ↑ .right := NEWNODE(nlabel);
                     root := root ↑ .right
                     end
          end;
       INSERT := root
end;
```

{an alternative recursive solution}

```
function INSERT(nlabel : vstring ; var root : btreeptr) : btreeptr;
begin
        if root = NIL then
                begin
                root := NEWNODE(nlabel);
                INSERT := root
                end
        else if equal(nlabel, root ↑ .nlabel) then
                INSERT := root
        else if less(nlabel, root ↑ .nlabel) then
                INSERT := INSERT(nlabel, root ↑ .left)
        else    INSERT := INSERT(nlabel, root ↑ .right)

end;
```

The Non-Generic Ada Program

```
package VariableString is
      type vstring (len : NATURAL : = 32) is private;
      function "<"  (v1, v2 : in vstring) return BOOLEAN;
       . . .
end VariableString;

package LabeledBTree is
      type binarytreenode;
      type binarytree is access binarytreenode;
      type binarytreenode is record
            label        : vstring;
            left, right  : binarytree;
      end record;

      procedure INSERT
            (label: vstring; root: in out binarytree; node: out binarytree);

end LabeledBTree;

package body LabeledBTree is

      procedure INSERT
            (label: vstring; root: in out binarytree; node: out binarytree)   is
      begin
      node : = root;
      if node = null then
          node : = new binarytreenode'(label, null, null);
          root : = node;
      end if;
      while node.label / = label loop
          case label < node.label is
          when true   =>
              if node.left = null then
                  node.left : = new binarytreenode'(label, null, null);
              end if;
              node : = node.left;
          when false   =>
              if node.right = null then
                  node.right : = new binarytreenode'(label, null, null);
              end if;
              node : = node.right;
          end case;
      end loop;
      end INSERT;
```

-- an alternative recursive implementation

```
procedure INSERT ( label  : in vstring;
                    root   : in out binarytree;
                    node   : out binarytree)  is
begin
      if root = null then
              root  := new binarytreenode'(label, null, null);
              node := root;
      elsif  root.label = label then
              node := root;
      elsif  label < root.label then
              INSERT (label, root.left, node);
      else   INSERT (label, root.right, node);
      end if;
end INSERT;

end LabeledBTree;
```

The Generic Ada Program

```ada
generic type labeltype is private;
      with function "<" (l1, l2 : in labeltype) return boolean is <>;
package LabeledBinaryTree is

        type binarytreenode;
        type binarytree is access binarytreenode;
        type binarytreenode is record
                label   : labeltype;
                left, right    : binarytree;
        end record;

        procedure INSERT ( label  : in labeltype;
                           root   : in out binarytree;
                           node   : out binarytree);

end LabeledBinaryTree;

package body LabeledBinaryTree is

        procedure INSERT ( label   : in labeltype;
                           root    : in out binarytree;
                           node    : out binarytree)    is
        begin
                if root = null then
                        root := new binarytreenode'(label, null, null);
                        node := root;
                elsif root.label = label then
                        node := root;
                elsif label < root.label then
                        INSERT (label, root.left, node);
                else  INSERT (label, root.right, node);
                end if;

        end INSERT;
end LabeledBinaryTree;
```

8.6 Reminders

1. Where Pascal provides recursive data structures by self reference and a pointer indicator (the up arrow), Ada distinguishes the notions of the access type and the dynamic object type.

2. An incomplete type definition is required in Ada in order to declare recursive or mutually dependent data structures, making the declaration a three step process rather than a single step process.

3. The value null is automatically provided as an initial value for all access type objects. In Pascal, the initial value is undefined and must be set before use.

4. In both languages, pointers may only reference dynamic objects created by allocation. Ada, however, provides a language mechanism that allows initial value specification.

5. Once the subtype constraints have been fixed at allocation, Ada does not allow the constraints to change whereas Pascal does. In this way Ada avoids a class of dereferencing problems.

6. Dereferencing an access variable does not require any special symbols. Component selection and indexing automatically dereference the pointer. Scalar objects and structured objects as a whole can be obtained by the .all qualification.

7. Dangling references are not a problem in Ada unless UNCHECKED_DEALLOCATION is used.

8. Functions in Ada can have no direct side effects on the formal parameters. Indirect side effects and side effects on global data are allowed.

9. Ada provides three parameter nodes, in, in out and in where Pascal provides only two. However, in Ada no specific semantics such as call by reference or copy-result are specified.

10. Ada's case statement differs only in syntactic details from Pascal's. However, **when others** => provides a catch all condition for unreferenced values.

11. An extension to the if statement in Ada provides a generalized case statement, where in Pascal, nested if statements must be used.

12. Where Ada's generic type parameters are private, operations may have to be supplied with the type. Generic subprogram parameters provide this mechanism. Default subprograms may be specified.

8.7 Problems

1. The binary tree implementation is rather incomplete--only an INSERT operation has been defined. Extend the package to include the operations FIND and LIST labels. The first locates a specified label and the second provides a list of the labels in alphabetical order.

2. The current implementation provides an open type. This enables the user to gain access to the tree and do arbitrary, and possibly unsafe, things with it. Rewrite the package to provide the type *binarytree* as a private type. What effect does this have on the interface subprogram specifications? Are status variables and exceptions necessary?

3. Add a new operation to the private type implementation of the previous exercise: a PRUNE operation that removes the subtree that emanates from label provided as a parameter and returns it.

4. A binary tree created by the original INSERT will often be rather lopsided and irregular in shape. Write a tree balancing operation that returns a tree where the distance (number of links) from the root to the leaves (nodes with no descendants) never differs by more than 1 for all the leaves.

5. Consider the problem of providing a generic package for an *n*-ary labeled tree. Is it possible? What kind of ordering relation is required? What kind of implementation is required for the INSERT operation? Try to construct the package with only the INSERT operation.

Nine

Sets

Topics: sets, subtypes, constants, address specifications, pragmas, based numbers, use statement, standard system packages.

Issues: overloading operations, set literals and aggregates, low level detail.

9.1 Problem Statement

Some problems are naturally describable in terms of sets and operations on sets. An example is the way the *program status register* is handled to control a machine's interrupt mechanism. Typically, the program status register has a bit for each device or fault that indicates whether the corresponding interrupt is *enabled* (bit = 0) or *disabled* (bit = 1). By setting these bits, the program status register acts as a *mask* for the interrupt processor. An operating system designer can write programs that manipulate these bits and that dynamically control which interrupts will be accepted and which ones will be ignored.

An example of a Program Status Register is the following: the PSR consists of 16 bits (one word in a typical minicomputer) which have the following interpretation (bit 15 is the most significant bit).

bit	interrupt
15	cardreader
14	paper tape reader
13	paper tape punch
12	communications interface (asynchronous)
11	line printer
10	binary synchronous communications interface
9	magnetic tape
8	disc

211

7	realtime clock
6	console
5	cycle counter
4	protection
3	parity error
2	auto start
1	program flag
0	overflow

In addition to the mask bits that can be manipulated by the programmer, the hardware typically defines a fixed number of *priority interrupt levels* that are used by the devices and faults to cause an interrupt. The number of levels is for most machines far less than the number of devices and potential faults. It is therefore necessary to allocate each device and each fault to a particular interrupt level. For most operating systems this allocation is done under program control once and for all when the system is started. The priority of the levels decreases with increasing level number: level 0 has a higher priority than level 1, etc. If contention occurs among the interrupts enabled, the interrupt with the highest priority occurs first.

The task we discuss in this chapter is the design of an interrupt manager that allows nesting of interrupts so that an interrupt occurring at a higher priority will be accepted even if an interrupt at a lower priority is being serviced. We assume that the hardware recognizes six priority interrupt levels for the following purposes:

level 0	auto start;
level 1	realtime clock and cycle counter;
level 2	protection, parity, program flag and overflow;
level 3	disc and magnetic tape;
level 4	binary synchronous communications and line printer;
level 5	communications interface, paper tape reader and punch, and cardreader.

Assume, for purposes of the example, that the PSR is physically located at 100_8.

9.2 Problem Discussion

The task consists of two subtasks: the allocation of devices and faults to priority levels and the design of the interrupt handler. If the collection of devices and faults is represented by a set, allocation to priority levels is a matter of assigning subsets to data objects that represent the levels. The program status register is an object of the same type as the levels: at each moment its content is a subset of the set of devices and faults. The difference between the levels and status register PSR is that the former are initialized when the operating system starts up and remain constant at runtime, while the PSR is modified each time the Interrupt Handler is activated.

For the purpose of this discussion we assume that the Interrupt Handler is activated automatically by the hardware when an interrupt occurs. The hardware also identifies the particular device or fault that caused the interrupt. We represent this piece of information in our programs by a parameter to the procedure that implements the Interrupt Handler.

An interrupt from a device or fault x will occur if and only if the corresponding bit in the PSR is enabled (i.e. x does not belong to the subset currently in the PSR) and no interrupt of a higher priority level is being serviced. Keeping in mind that interrupts of higher levels must be allowed to occur, the Interrupt Handler proceeds as follows. It begins by saving the current value of the PSR in order to restore that value when the interrupt has been processed. It then disables all interrupts by setting the PSR to the entire set of devices and faults so that it can determine which device caused the interrupt and at which priority level the interrupt occurred. Once that level has been determined, the Interrupt Handler prepares a new value for the PSR which enables interrupts for all higher levels and disables interrupts for the others. This is done by taking the union of the subsets associated with the disabled levels. After placing this new value in the PSR, the Interrupt Handler calls the specific operating system routine that has been written to handle an interrupt for a particular level. Since these routines have no bearing on the problem, we omit their programs from our presentation. When that specific handler has finished, the Interrupt Handler terminates after restoring the old value of the PSR.

9.3 Sets in Pascal and Ada

Pascal (PRM 8, 50-51) provides a set type generator for constructing set literals, and six operations on sets. Such a facility is lacking in Ada. Before proceeding with a discussion of the Pascal and Ada programs, we first consider an implementation of sets in Ada and compare that implementation with Pascal's set facility.

The Type Set

In Pascal, a set type is the powerset of the values of a base type. The base type is either a scalar type or a subrange type. The syntax is

type identifier = **set of** basetype;

To define set types in Ada similar to sets in Pascal, we wish to introduce a type that takes an arbitrary scalar type as parameter. We want to be able to define sets of integers, of characters, etc. Since generic units are the only ones that accept types as parameters, it is obvious that the set type must be defined in a generic package. The desired base type of a set can then be defined as a generic parameter and can be used in the representation of a set. For example, if a set is represented by a Boolean array that uses the given base type as array index, then the following generic definition will suffice.

```
generic type setelement is (<>); -- cf. Chapter 7
package SetManager is
        type set is array (setelement) of BOOLEAN;
            . . .
    end SetManager;
```

The problem with this approach is that the open type definition is liable to misuse. The set type should be declared private so that the representation of sets remains hidden from the user. The actual representation of the type *set* must then be declared in the private part of the package.

```
generic type setelement is (<>);
package SetManager is
        type set is private;
            . . .
    private
        type set is array (setelement) of BOOLEAN;
    end SetManager;
```

Unfortunately, one cannot initialize an array type. (One can initialize an array in a data declaration, but not in a type declaration.) The only place where initial values can be given in a type definition is in a record declaration: the component parts of records may be assigned initial values. For this reason, we modify the definition slightly so that an initial value for the array structure can be included.

```
    private
        type setarray is  array (setelement) of BOOLEAN;
        type set is  record e : setarray : = (others  => FALSE); end record;
    end SetManager;
```

The price for the initial value is an extra (but hidden) type definition and the dot notation required to access the array now that it is part of a record. By setting all values to FALSE, the initial value represents the empty set. The auxiliary type *setarray* is needed because a record field must be a named type and cannot be an anonymous array type (ARM 3.7, 3-33).

Deferred Constants

When a new type is introduced, one often needs constants of that type. For sets, an obvious candidate to include in package SetManager is the empty set. However, a slight difficulty arises with private types. On the one hand, a constant cannot be completely defined in the visible part of the package, because the structure of the private type is still unknown at that point. On the other hand, defining a constant solely in the private type does not help, because it then remains hidden from the user. The problem is solved by the use of a *deferred constant* whose declaration is included in the visible part preceding the private part and whose elaboration is then placed in the private part.

```
generic type  setelement is (< >);
package SetManager is
        type set is private;
        nullset : constant set;

        . . .
private
        type setarray  . . . ;
        type set  . . . ;
        nullset : constant set := (e => (others => FALSE));
end SetManager;
```

It would seem that the assignment to constant *nullset* is superfluous, because the type definition already initializes all objects of type *set*. This is not so, because the declaration of a constant always requires an explicit assignment (ARM 3.2.1.2, 3-3).

Pragmas and Size Specifications

Pascal's set representation is chosen to be space efficient and to exploit the boolean operations of the underlying machine. We would like to make Ada's implementation as near to Pascal's as possible and ensure two characteristics: the representation must use a packed bit array, and the size of the representation must match the word size of the underlying machine.

The Ada concept that allows a programmer to express such specific requirements is that of *pragmas* which are compiler directives (ARM 2.8, 2-7 and appendix B). In our case, we wish to instruct the compiler to pack the array as tightly as possible. This is achieved by the PACK pragma which selects the best fit for the bit array. The pragma for packing is located with the representation specifications (if any) after all the declarations have been made (ARM 13.1.5, 13-1). The form of this pragma (and generally the form of all pragmas) is

```
pragma PACK (set);
```

where the parenthesized expression specifies the structures to be packed.

Ada provides representation specifications that allow the programmer to specify various low level details about types and objects such as sizes and addresses. These specifications occur in the declarative part after all the declarative items but before the program components (ARM E.2). The size of any type can be specified in the length specification

for typename 'SIZE **use** expression;

where the expression evaluates to an integer that specifies the number of bits to be used for objects of that type (ARM 13.2.5, 13-3). (There are other size specifications that can be made with this form as well: the amount of storage for dynamic variables of a particular type; the amount of storage space to be reserved for an activation of a task type; and the actual delta for fixed point types. See Chapter 14 for a more complete discussion.) The size specified must be sufficient to contain the type; otherwise, a compilation error results.

The desired size can be specified in one of two ways. The first possibility is by a generic parameter so that the size can be whatever is desired.

```
generic type setelement is (<>);
        setsize : POSITIVE := 32;
package SetManager is
        . . .
private
        . . .
        pragma PACK (set);
        for set'SIZE use setsize;
end SetManager;
```

When a new set type is created, the programmer has the option of using the default size (of 32 bits) or of specifying a particular desired value. The generic size parameter provides maximum flexibility in instantiating set types of different sizes. But the programmer must use this flexibility wisely, because the efficiency of the machine instructions can easily be lost if the specified size is not in accordance with the hardware characteristics. Therefore, it may be better to restrict the flexibility and not provide a generic parameter for the size. Another way of specifying the size is by using the standard system package (ARM appendix C) where implementation dependencies such as the word size of the machine are defined. The length specification, then, is removed from the generic parameter list and the length is specified only in the private part.

```
private
        type setarray is . . . ;
        type set is  . . . ;
        nullset : . . . ;
        pragma PACK (set);
        for set'SIZE use SYSTEM.STORAGE_UNIT;
end SetManager;
```

Set Literals

Initial values for objects of any type are constructed from literal values. Pascal provides a set constructor for set literals: a list of the set elements enclosed by square brackets.

[1, 5, 10, 11], ['a' . . 'd', 'q'], [ ], [Monday]

Obviously there is no set constructor in Ada since there is no language supplied set type. However, Ada's array and record aggregates provide the necessary tools for constructing set literals.

Since we made *set* a private type, all operations on sets (except for the default operations assignment and equality) must be explicitly exported from the set package. Thus, to create set literals, the package must export a function, called MAKESET, that generates a subset out of a collection of values of the base type. For instance, if the base type is *day*, function MAKESET must be able to create literals that represent subsets such as

workdays = {Monday . . Friday},
weekend = {Saturday, Sunday}.

In the powerset corresponding to *workdays* the bits of the range (Monday . . Friday) are set to TRUE and the other two to FALSE; *weekend* is the bit-wise complement of *workdays*.

The type of MAKESET's parameter should be chosen so that we can pass aggregates such as *workdays* and *weekend* to function MAKESET. In order to allow for variable size aggregates, we make the set literal type an unconstrained array type. The size of a parameter of that type is derived from the actual parameter each time the function is called (ARM 6.4.1.10).

Next we decide whether to use the base type of the set elements as the component type or as the index type of the array type.

choice 1: **type** setliteral **is array** (POSITIVE **range** <>) **of** setelement;
choice 2: **type** setliteral **is array** (setelement **range** <>) **of** BOOLEAN;

Each of these choices has its pros and cons. The first does not permit the use of ranges and the second requires an irrelevant BOOLEAN value. For example, instead of the range (Monday . . Friday) we must write

choice 1: (Monday, Tuesday, Wednesday, Thursday, Friday)
choice 2: (Monday . . Friday => TRUE). -- named notation

The first cannot be written as a range, because component values cannot be represented by a range (but index values can, ARM 4.3.2, 4-10). The second choice clearly requires named index notation for selecting the desired set elements. A particular problem with the first choice is that we cannot represent the empty literal. Ada requires that aggregates have at least one element, which rules out the aggregate of the form "( )". Although this notation is not valid for the second choice either, here there is another way of representing the empty literal by using FALSE as the component value:

> choice 2: empty set = (Sunday . . Saturday $\Rightarrow$ FALSE).

This representation is not nearly as nice as in Pascal where the empty literal is the same as the empty set and is denoted by "[ ]".

Although the first choice lacks the range and empty literal notations, we prefer it over the second choice, because the notation is closer to the customary set notation and Pascal's notation. Instead of calling MAKESET for creating an empty set, we assign the constant *nullset* to a set variable. With the addition of the type *setliteral*, the revised form of the generic set package is:

```
generic type setelement is (< >);
packageSetManager is

        type  set is private;
        nullset : constant set;
        type  setliteral is array (POSITIVE range <>) of setelement;

        function  MAKESET (u : in setliteral)  return set;
            . . .
    private
            . . .
    end SetManager;
```

Note that *setliteral* is an unconstrained array type, while *set* is a constrained array type. We did this on purpose so that set literals can be of various sizes and so that sets are of fixed size and can be implemented efficiently.

The MAKESET function translates the input set literal into a powerset of base type *setelement*. If local variable *s* is declared of type *set* (which implies its initialization to the empty set), MAKESET uses its input set literal to set the individual bits in variable *s* by the following statement.

```
for i in u'FIRST . . u'LAST loop  s(u(i)) := TRUE; end loop;
```

Set Operations

Pascal provides three set operations and three relational operations on sets. The set operations are set union " + ", set intersection "*" and set difference "-". The relational operations are set inclusion (<= and >=) and set membership (**in**).

In Ada, it is possible to overload all of these infix operators, except **in**, and give them set interpretations. In place of the infix set membership operation, a function, MEM, will return the boolean value indicating whether the first parameter value is an element of the set specified by the second parameter. In addition set union and set difference have been overloaded further to allow the union of an element with a set and subtract an element from a set. The implementations are rather straightforward and are left until the complete program solution. (It should be noted, however, that their implementation is not as efficient as the language supplied operations of Pascal. To provide that sort of efficiency, the programmer would need to provide machine code implementations.)

```
generic type setelement is (< >);
package SetManager is

    type  set  is  private;
    nullset : constant set;
    type  setliteral  is  array (POSITIVE range < >) of setelement;

    function MAKESET   (u : in setliteral) return set;

    function "+"        (S1, S2 : in set) return set;
    function "+"        (S1 : in set; Se : in setelement) return set;
    function "-"        (S1, S2 : in set) return set;
    function "-"        (S1 : in set; Se : in setelement) return set;
    function "*"        (S1, S2 : in set) return set;
    function "<="       (S1, S2 : in set) return BOOLEAN;
    function ">="       (S1, S2 : in set) return BOOLEAN;
    function MEMBER     (Se : in setelement; S2 : in set) return BOOLEAN;

    private
        . . .
    end SetManager;
```

Comparison of Sets in Pascal and Ada

When we compare sets in Pascal and Ada, we discover two main differences: declaring set types is slightly more convenient in Pascal than in Ada; and set literals are easier to construct in Pascal than in Ada. It would appear that Pascal has the advantage because of the slightly better constructs included in the language. However, Ada is rich enough to enable the programmer to design set facilities that are almost as easy to use as those in Pascal. In one respect Ada has the advantage over Pascal, because its overloading feature allows us to use the normal symbolic representation for the standard set operations.

9.4 A Pascal Solution

Set Definitions

The Pascal program begins with the definition of the *programstatus*, which is a list of possible interrupts for both devices and faults.

> **type** programstatus = (cardreader, ptapereader, ptapepunch, asynch,
>   lineprinter, bisynch, mtapereader, disc,
>   rtclock, console, cyclecounter, protection,
>   parity, autostart, programflag, overflow);

This enumeration defines the scalar type for which we can define the appropriately sized set, *programstatusset*.

> programstatusset = **set of** programstatus;

The set has 16 elements, precisely the number of bits in our typical minicomputer word.

A number of set objects are needed to provide the appropriate interrupt and interrupt priority level control. The PSR is the actual program status register of the machine (located at 100_8). Unfortunately, we have no mechanism to specify the exact address of a declared variable in Pascal, so for purposes of proceeding, we assume that in some way the PSR gets assigned to the correct location.

> **var**   PSR : programstatusset;

If we assume that the priorities are assigned once and for all when the operating system starts, we could represent the priority levels by set literals that represent the devices and faults associated with the various levels. Since these literals are rather verbose (and cannot be named in Pascal because of the restriction that constants must be scalar), we decide to represent the priority levels by variables that are initialized to these set literals. Thus, we introduce the following set variables to contain the specifications of the required priority levels ranging from "all devices are allowed to interrupt" through "no devices are allowed to interrupt."

> **var**   disableall, level0, level1, level2, level3, level4, level5,
>   enableall : programstatusset;

The various data objects must be initialized to their appropriate values. An initialization procedure provides this necessary processing and must be invoked during the system's warm start up. For our purposes, we may assume that the system interrupt mechanism is disabled until it is explicitly enabled.

```
procedure SYSTEMINITIALIZATION;
begin
    enableall   := [ ];
    level0      := [autostart];
    level1      := [rtclock, cyclecounter];
    level2      := [protection, parity, programflag, overflow];
    level3      := [disc, mtapereader];
    level4      := [bisynch, lineprinter];
    level5      := [cardreader . . asynch];
    disableall  := level0 + level1 + level2 + level3 + level4 + level5;
    PSR         := enableall    {set the system going}
end;
```

The Interrupt Handler

The Interrupt Handler operation is invoked with the interrupting device as its input parameter. The current PSR is saved and the entire interrupt mechanism temporarily disabled. The level of the interrupting device is then determined, the new PSR is set to allow higher priority levels to interrupt the current processing, and the appropriate level handler is invoked. When the interrupt has been serviced, the old PSR is restored, returning the machine to the previous level of priority.

```
procedure INTERRUPTHANDLER (intdevice : programstatus);
        var oldPSR : programstatusset;
begin
        oldPSR := PSR;
        PSR := disableall ;
        if intdevice in level0 then
                AUTOSTARTPROCESSOR
        else if intdevice in level1 then
                begin
                PSR := PSR - level0;
                LEVEL1PROCESSOR (intdevice)
                end
        else if intdevice in level2 then
                begin
                PSR := PSR - (level0 + level1);
                LEVEL2PROCESSOR (intdevice)
                end
        else if intdevice in level3 then
                . . .
        PSR := oldPSR   {restore to previous level of service}
end;
```

9.5 An Ada Solution

The Program Status

One use of packages in Ada is to collect related items of information to indicate their logical relationship. We collect all the definitions and declarations related to the Program Status together in one package, PSManager. This package consists only of a visible part because it contains only type and data declarations and no procedures or functions.

```
with SetManager;
package PSManager is

    type ProgramStatus is
        (CardReader, PTapeReader, PTapePunch, Asynch, LinePrinter,
        MTapeReader, Bisynch, Disc, RTClock, Console, CycleCounter,
        Protection, Parity, Autostart, ProgramFlag, Overflow);

    subtype interrupt is ProgramStatus;
    subtype device    is ProgramStatus range Cardreader . . Cyclecounter;
    subtype fault      is ProgramStatus range Protection . . Overflow;

    package PS is new SetManager (ProgramStatus);

    PSR : PS.set;
    for PSR use at 8#100#;

end PSManager;
```

The subtypes *interrupt*, *device* and *fault* are introduced for reasons of self-documentation. They describe in a natural way that the program status is also a list of interrupts that may be divided into two classes: device interrupts and fault interrupts. This provides the user with helpful additional information.

The SetManager package has been instantiated to provide sets of program status. Objects of type *PS.set* can now be declared and all the set operations performed on them. The PSR is one such set. It is, in fact, the most important piece of data in the package. There were two primary aims for this package: to define the program status word as a set type and to define and declare the program status register as an instance of that type.

Address Specifications and Based Numbers

Recall that the PSR was to be located at a specific address. Ada provides an address specification mechanism to enable the system programmer to do just that (ARM 13.5, 13-8). The general form is

for name **use at** address-specification;

The address specification provided here, "8#100#", is the based form of integer representation. The address is 100_8, i.e., 100 in base 8. The general form is (ARM 2.4.2, 2-5)

base # integer number #

This is a particularly convenient form of representation when dealing with machine dependent details.

The Interrupt Handler Interface

The Interrupt Handler is constructed as a package with a single procedure, INTERRUPTHANDLER, in its visible part, because initialization can be done, unlike Pascal, in the package body. The elaboration of the declaration of the Interrupt Handler package body sets the interrupt mechanism in its initial system state.

with PSManager; **use** PSManager;
package InterruptManager **is**

   procedure INTERRUPTHANDLER (intdevice : **in** interrupt);

end InterruptManager;

The use statement opens the visible part of the package PSManager so that the declarations are directly visible to the declarations here. Hence, the use of the subtype *interrupt* is legal. Without the use statement, one would have to write *PSManager.interrupt*. The subtype rather than the type is used here because it is more explicit and declares the desired intent of the parameter.

Set Variables

Package PSManager defines the program status set which we need to control the levels of priority within the interrupt handler. The use clause in the visible part has already made the contents visible in this package's visible part and hence it is also visible in the body as well. However, we wish to use the package PS which is within that package and add it to the use clause. The variables are declared and initialized for the various levels of priority. As we have noted in several of the preceding chapters, this initialization feature at declaration time is a distinct advantage over Pascal. We include these priority variables within the package body since their existence is not required outside and, thus far, their structure is needed only within the interrupt handler package.

```
package body InterruptManager is
    use PS;
    level0      : constant set := MAKESET ((Autostart));
    level1      : constant set := MAKESET ((Rtclock, CycleCounter));
    level2      : . . . ;
    . . .
    Enableall   : constant set := nullset;
    Disableall  : constant set := Level0 + Level1 + Level2 +
                                   Level3 + Level4 + Level5;
    . . .
end InterruptManager;
```

The variables here have all been declared as constants. Should a dynamically changing priority system be desired, the variables *level0* through *level5* would have to be changed from constants to ordinary initialized variables.

Interrupt Initialization and Handling

In the Pascal program, the initialization was rather extensive because of the variable initializations. Here in the Ada program, the only initialization required is the enabling of the interrupts. This is done in the body of the Interrupt Manager by setting the program status register to *EnableAll*.

The implementation of the procedure INTERRUPTHANDLER is quite similar to the Pascal implementation with minor differences in syntactic details.

```
procedure INTERRUPTHANDLER (intdevice : in interrupt) is
    oldPSR : PS.set := PSR;
begin
    PSR := DisableAll ;
    if MEMBER (intdevice, level0) then
        AUTOSTARTPROCESSOR;
    elseif MEMBER (intdevice, level1) then
        PSR := PSR - level0;
        LEVEL1PROCESSOR (intdevice);
    . . .
    end if;
    PSR := oldPSR;
end INTERRUPTHANDLER;
```

9.6 The Complete Programs

The Ada Program for Sets

```
generic type setelement is (<>);
package SetManager is

   type set is private;
   type setliteral is array (POSITIVE range < >) of setelement;
   nullset : constant set;   -- a deferred constant

   function  MAKESET (u : in setliteral) return set;
   function  "+"      (S1, S2 : in set) return set;
   function  "+"      (S1 : in set; Se : in setelement) return set;
   function  "-"      (S1,S2 : in set) return set;
   function  "-"      (S1 : in set; Se : in setelement) return set;
   function  "*"      (S1, S2 : in set) return set;

   function  "<="     (S1, S2 : in set) return BOOLEAN;
   function  ">="     (S1, S2 : in set) return BOOLEAN;
   function  MEMBER   (Se : in setelement; S2 : in set) return BOOLEAN;

private

   type setarray is  array (setelement) of BOOLEAN;
   type set is record e : setarray := (others => FALSE); end record;

   nullset : constant := (e => (others => FALSE));

   pragma PACK (set);
   for set'SIZE use SYSTEM.STORAGE_UNIT;

end SetManager;
```

```
package body SetManager is

      first   : constant INTEGEF := setelement'FIRST;
      last    : constant INTEGEF := setelement'LAST;

      function MAKESET (u : in s tliteral) return set is
            s : set;
      begin
            for i in u'FIRST . . u LAST loop  s.e (u(i)) := TRUE;  end loop;
            return s;
      end MAKESET;

      function  "+" (S1, S2 : in set) return set is
            S : set;
      begin
            for i in first . . last l op  S.e(i) := S1.e(i) or S2.e(i);  end loop;
            return S;
      end "+";

      function "+" (S1 : in set; e : in setelement) return set is
            S : set := S1;
      begin
            S.e(se) := TRUE;
            return S;
      end "+";

      function "-" (S1, S2 : in se :) return set is
            S : set := S1;
      begin
            for i in first . . last l op
                  if S2.e(i) ther  S.e(i) := FALSE; end if;
            end loop;
            return S;
      end "-";

      function "-" (S1 : in set ; S e : in setelement) return set is
            S : set := S1;
      begin
            S.e(Se) := FALSE;
            return S;
      end "-";
```

```
function "*" (S1, S2 : in set) return set is
      S : set;
begin
      for i in first . . last loop  S.e(i) := S1.e(i) and S2.e(i);  end loop;
      return S;
end "*";

function "<=" (S1, S2 : in set) return boolean is
begin
      return S1 * S2 = S1 ;
end "<=";

function ">=" (S1, S2 : in set) return boolean is
begin
      return S2 <= S1 ;
end ">=";

function MEMBER (Se : in setelement ; S2 : in set) return boolean is
begin
      return S2.e(Se) ;
end MEMBER;

end SetManager;
```

The Pascal Program

```
type programstatus =        (cardreader, ptapereader, ptapepunch, asynch,
                            lineprinter, bisynch, mtapereader, disc,
                            rtclock, console, cyclecounter, protection,
                            parity, autostart, program flag, overflow);

     programstatusset = set of programstatus;

var PSR,
    level0, level1, level2, level3, level4, level5,
    enableall, disableall : programstatusset;

procedure INITIALIZE;
begin
        level0      := [autostart]
        level1      := [rtclock, cyclecounter]
        level2      := [protection, parity, program flag, overflow];
        level3      := [disc, mtapereader];
        level4      := [bisynch, lineprinter];
        level5      := [cardreader . . asynch];
        disableall  := level0 + level1 + level2 + level3 + level4 + level5;
        enableall   := [ ];
        PSR := enableall
end;

procedure INTERRUPTHANDLER(intdevice : programstatus);
        var oldPSR : programstatusset;
begin
        oldPSR := PSR;
        PSR := disableall;
        if intdevice in level0 then
                AUTOSTARTPROCESSOR
        else if intdevice in level1 then
                begin
                PSR := PSR - level0;
                LEVEL1PROCESSOR (intdevice)
                end
        else if intdevice in level2 then
                begin
                PSR := PSR - (level0 + level1);
                PROCESSFAULTS (intdevice)
                end
```

```
else if intdevice in level3 then
        begin
        PSR := level3 + level4 + level5;
        LEVEL3PROCESSOR (intdevice)
        end
else if intdevice in level4 then
        begin
        PSR := level4 + level5;
        LEVEL4PROCESSOR (intdevice)
        end
else if intdevice in level5 then
        begin
        PSR := level5;
        LEVEL5PROCESSOR (intdevice)
        end;
    PSR := oldPSR
end;
```

The Ada Program

with SetManager;
package PSManager **is**

      type ProgramStatus **is**
          (CardReader, PTapeReader, PTapePunch, Asynch, LinePrinter,
          Bisynch, MTapeReader, Disc, RTClock, Console, CycleCounter,
          Protection, Parity, AutoStart, Program Flag, Overflow);
      subtype interrupt **is** ProgramStatus;
      subtype device **is** ProgramStatus **range** CardReader . . CycleCounter;
      subtype fault **is** ProgramStatus **range** Protection . . Overflow;

      package PS **is new** SetManager (ProgramStatus);

      PSR : PS.set;
      for PSR **use at** 8#100#;

end PSManager;

with PSManager;
package InterruptManager **is**

      use PSManager;
      procedure INTERRUPTHANDLER(intdevice : **in** interrupt);

end InterruptManager;

package body InterruptManager **is**
      use PS;

      level0 : **constant** set := MAKESET ((Autostart));
      level1 : **constant** set := MAKESET ((Rtclock, CycleCounter));
      level2 : **constant** set := MAKESET ((Protection, Parity,
                            Program Flag, Overflow));
      level3 : **constant** set := MAKESET ((Disc, MTapeReader));
      level4 : **constant** set := MAKESET (Bisynch, LinePrinter));
      level5 : **constant** set := MAKESET ((CardReader, PTapeReader,
                            PTapePunch, Asynch));
      EnableAll : **constant** set := nullset;
      DisableAll : **constant** set := level0 + level1 + level2 +
                           level3 + level4 + level5;

    -- interrupt processors defined here

```
procedure INTERRUPTHANDLER(intdevice : in interrupt) is
      oldPSR : PS.set := PSR;
begin
      PSR := DisableAll;   -- turn off all interrupts

      if MEMBER(intdevice, level0) then
            AUTOSTARTPROCESSOR;
      elseif MEMBER(intdevice, level1) then
            PSR := PSR - level0;
            LEVEL1PROCESSOR(intdevice);
      elseif MEMBER(intdevice, level2) then
            PSR := PSR - (level0 + level1);
            PROCESSFAULTS(intdevice);
      elseif MEMBER(intdevice, level3) then
            PSR := level3 + level4 + level5;
            LEVEL3PROCESSOR(intdevice);
      elseif MEMBER(intdevice, level4) then
            PSR := level4 + level5;
            LEVEL4PROCESSOR(intdevice);
      elseif MEMBER(intdevice, level5)
            PSR := level5;
            LEVEL5PROCESSOR(intdevice);
      end if;

      PSR := oldPSR;

   end INTERRUPTHANDLER;

begin

      PSR := EnableAll;

end InterruptManager;
```

9.7 Reminders

1. The set type generator, set constructor and basic set operations are provided as language constructs in Pascal but not in Ada. However, generic packages with type parameters, array aggregates and overloading of operations provide the necessary tools to build essentially the same facilities in Ada.

2. Type parameters are available only in generic units in Ada. They are not allowed in Pascal at all.

3. For types, initial values can be specified only for the components of a record type.

4. Pragmas provide special information to the compiler. PACK, for example, indicates that space efficiency is the most important characteristic in determining the representation of the packed type.

5. The actual size (with respect to the number of bits used) to represent a given type can be specified by the statement

   for typename 'SIZE **use** expression;

   Representation specifications occur after all declarations but before implementations.

6. Certain kinds of system implementation dependent information is available from the standard SYSTEM package.

7. Ada does not allow the use of anonymous types for parameters. In declarations anonymous array types are allowed, but anonymous record types are not.

8. Aggregates can be constructed in two ways, by positional notation in which the values are listed in the order of the components or by named notation where the component is named in the form "name ⇒ value". Ranges, list and the keyword **others** are allowed in the named specifications. The others clause cannot be used for unconstrained arrays.

9. The attributes LENGTH, FIRST and LAST are very useful for parameters specified as unconstrained arrays because their value depends on the actual parameter which may have different size and bounds for each subprogram call.

10. **In** parameters may have default values.

11. Related type, subtype and object declarations can be conveniently packaged together in the visible part of a package for which no corresponding body is needed.

12. Objects may be assigned specific addresses in Ada.

13. Based numbers provide an alternative means of specifying integer values. The Base is specified first and the based value is bracketed by "#", e.g., 8#100#. This provides a convenient means of writing binary, octal and hexidecimal numbers.

14. The use statement *opens* a package visible part and makes its content immediately visible within the scope of the statement.

9.8 Problems

1. Extend the SetManager Package to provide two further operations: *properly includes* and *is properly included in*.

2. The logical operations (**and, or,** and **xor**) are defined for one dimensional arrays of boolean values as well as for simple boolean values. Rewrite the implementations of the set operations to operate on the set representation as a unit rather than on a component by component basis.

3. A set literal is constructed from an array aggregate passed as an actual parameter to the MAKESET routine. One way of determining what elements are currently in a set is by testing each element by the membership operation. For large sets this can be rather cumbersome. Write an operation that returns an array of set element values that occur in the input set. The array should only contain the exact number of components equal to the number of elements acutally in the set.

4. Pascal's set capabilities are limited by the size of the implementation's machine word. Ada does not have this limitation. However, for very large sets, say sets of integers, the bit array representation may be inappropriate. An alternative representation is to list the elements that currently exist in a set of this type. Write a generic package for sets whose elements are represented in a list.

5. The concept of a subset might be likened to that of a subtype: that is, the object is declared to be restricted to a certain subset of values by restricting the range of values in the scalar range that may occur in the subset object. Thus if the set type is the scalar range 1 . . 10, then objects of the subset 2 . . 4 can have only the following values: {}. {2}, {3}, {4}, {2,3}, {2,4}, {3,4}, {2,3,4}. Replace the type definition

type set **is private**;

with

      type subset(lb : setelem := setelem'FIRST;
                  ub : setelem := setelem'LAST) **is private**;.

(Call the package SET instead of SetManager.) Should exceptions be introduced? What is the result of subset + element if the element is not in the subset? What is the result of $subset_1$ + $subset_2$ if the ranges only partially overlap? What if they are completely disjoint? Delineate the semantics very carefully for the set operations.

Ten

Variant Records

Topics: variant records, discriminants, subtypes, exceptions, case statements, file handling.

Issues: type unions, nesting of records, naming of variants, file buffers, creation of files.

10.1 Problem Statement

Sometimes one needs data structures that can hold objects of different types. An example is a Symbol Table used by a compiler to store descriptors for scalar variables, arrays, functions, etc. These descriptors are of different types, because they contain different information. An array descriptor, for instance, includes information about the array bounds, a function descriptor information about the parameters and the result, while none of this information is included in descriptors for scalar variables. The point is that these objects, although they are of different types, are stored in one Symbol Table.

Storing objects of different types in a data structure is not possible for any of the structures discussed in preceding chapters. For instance, the vectors of Chapter 3 and the queues of Chapter 7 each have elements of a single uniform type. The generic mechanism permits only a single uniform parameter type.

In this chapter we discuss how objects of heterogeneous types can be stored in a single data structure with the use of *variant records*. The example we have chosen is that of code generation for arithmetic expressions. The input for the code generator is a sequence of lexical units, called *lexemes*, which are produced by the parser of a compiler. The output of the code generator is a sequence of machine instructions. The details of lexeme formats and machine instruction fields are included in the subsequent problem discussion.

235

10.2 Problem Discussion

Postfix Notation

Pascal and Ada require arithmetic computations to be expressed in *infix* notation and to conform to certain rules which govern the order of expression evaluation. For example, the expressions

$$E_1 : a + b * c, \quad E_2 : (a+b) * c$$

differ in the order of applying the operations: in E_1 the multiplication is applied before addition and in E_2 addition is applied before multiplication. Evaluation is from left to right (so that 12 - 4 - 3 = 5 and not 11, which would be the result working from right to left), but that multiplication and division take precedence over addition and subtraction. If need be, the normal order of evaluation can be changed by the use of parentheses as shown in example E_2.

The Syntax Analyzer transforms the infix form of arithmetic expressions into a *postfix* form because it is a more convenient notation for the code generator. In postfix notation, the operator of a dyadic expression (an expression with one operator and two operands) is written following both operands and not between its operands as is in infix notation. The general form of a dyadic expression in infix and postfix notation is, respectively,

INFIX : opnd$_1$ optr opnd$_2$ POSTFIX : opnd$_1$ opnd$_2$ optr.

The postfix representation of expressions E_1 and E_2 is

$$E_1 : a\ b\ c * +, \quad E_2 : a\ b + c *$$

An important property of the postfix notation is that expressions are free of parentheses and consist merely of operands and operators. In a BNF notation one can describe postfix expressions by the production rules:

$$
\begin{aligned}
\text{postfixexpr} &\Rightarrow \text{monadicpfexpr} \mid \text{dyadicpfexpr} \\
\text{monadicpfexpr} &\Rightarrow \text{operand\{monadicoperator\}} \\
\text{dyadicpfexpr} &\Rightarrow \text{operand operand dyadicoperator} \\
\text{operand} &\Rightarrow \text{variable} \mid \text{constant} \mid \text{postfixexpr}
\end{aligned}
$$

where "{ . . . }" indicates an optional part.

The Intermediate Representation

The Lexical Analyzer of a compiler assembles character strings into lexical units that represent identifiers, numbers and other language objects, while the Syntax Analyzer performs the task of building the structure of the intermediate representation by producing the generated lexemes in the correct order. For arithmetic expressions, this order is the postfix form. Thus, the intermediate representation generated by the Front-End for the expressions E_1 and E_2 of the earlier example is:

Expression E_1

lexeme(a)
lexeme(b)
lexeme(c)
lexeme(*)
lexeme(+)

Expression E_2

lexeme(a)
lexeme(b)
lexeme(+)
lexeme(c)
lexeme(*)

The intermediate representation of a program is the output of the compiler's front-end and is used as input for the compiler's code generating procedures. Since we have chosen code generation as our problem for this chapter, it is not our task to design the parser that transforms the input text for arithmetic expressions into the intermediate form. Instead, we will design code generator procedures that take the intermediate form (i.e., a sequence of lexemes) as input and produce machine code sequences.

For the sake of simplifying the problem, we restrict ourselves to operands and operators of certain kinds and ignore others. The operands we consider are simple arithmetic variables and constants, while we disregard operands such as function calls or subscripted variables. The operators we consider are "+", "-", "*" and "/", while we ignore operators such as exponentiation, assignment and comparison.

Operand Lexemes

We distinguish two classes of operands: variables and constants. With respect to variables, it is useful to distinguish between global and local variables: global variables exist throughout the execution of a program, whereas local variables are created and deleted when procedures, functions or blocks are entered and exited. With respect to constants it is useful to distinguish between small constants and other constants: small constants are used more frequently than large constants and can often be used directly in machine instructions while the values of large constants must be retrieved from memory. For example, a machine instruction set will typically contain instructions of the form

(Op, Reg, constvalue) and (Op, Reg, MemAddress)

which have the effect of performing the operation and leaving the result in the specified register.

Reg := Op(Reg, constvalue) and Reg := Op(Reg, Mem[MemAddress])

The operand *constvalue* is a small constant that is directly given in the instruction. The second instruction is more costly than the first because it includes a memory reference which is not needed for a small constant. In our example, we assume that a small constant is an integer number in the range [-2047 . . 2047]. We will use the term *constant* for small constant and *literal* for long constant.

Each class of operand has a number of attributes. The first attribute is the type of the operand, which is either an integer operand or a floating point operand (we call it a real operand). The second attribute is an address which indicates the location of the operand relative to other objects in the same scope. These addresses are generated by the Syntax Analyzer. For instance, if procedure P has the local variables a, b, c declared by

> **procedure** P(. . .);
>   **var** a, b, c : int;
> **begin** . . . **end**;

then the local address of a is 0, that of b is 1 and that of c is 2. The third attribute is the index into either the Symbol Table or the literal table. This index selects the entry which contains all the necessary information concerning the operand. For example, the Symbol Table entry of a variable includes its source name. This information is useful for a compiler procedure that detects an error, retrieves the original name of a variable from the Symbol Table and represents the object in user-readable form in an error message.

Operand lexemes have four fields: the operand class, the operand type, the operand address, and operand reference index. The complete layout for operand lexemes and their allowed values is shown below.

class	type	address	reference
global var	int/real	global address	SymbolTable index
local var	int/real	local address	SymbolTable index
constant	int	value	None
literal	int/real	global address	Literal Table index

Operator Lexemes

Operators have two attributes: their type and their identifier. An operator is either *monadic* in type (if the operator takes a single operand) or *dyadic* (if it takes two operands). An operator identifier is its numerical representation (in this case a mapping from operators to integers). Note that there is no particular attribute indicating the precedence of the operator relative to other operators. There is no need for such a field since the Syntax Analyzer has already translated precedence rules into a unique order expressed in the postfix form.

class	type	identifier
operator	monadic/dyadic	operator number

Result Lexemes

The table for operand lexemes should be extended with one additional entry representing *subexpressions*. The need for subexpression lexemes is best illustrated by the following example. When the code generator encounters the lexeme sequence

lexeme(a); lexeme(b); lexeme(c); lexeme(∗); lexeme(+)

for the expression E_1 : a + b ∗ c $\Rightarrow$ a b c ∗ + it will start with generating code for subexpression S : b ∗ c. By the time code is to be generated for the addition operator, the lexeme sequence is

lexeme(a); lexeme(S = subexpr(b ∗ c)); lexeme(+),

indicating that the second operand of the addition operator is the result of computing a subexpression.

Result operands have two attributes: the type of the result and the register specification. The value of the type attribute depends upon the type of the subexpression. (For instance, if *b* and *c* are integers, the type of *b* ∗ *c* is also an integer, but if one of the operands is of type real, the result is also of type real.) The register attribute specifies the index of one of the fast registers which is in our example an integer in the range 0 . . 15.

class	type	address
result	int/real	regindex

The complete table for the operands and operators is summarized below.

class	type	address/ident	reference
globalvar	int/real	global address	Symbol Table index
localvar	int/real	local address	Symbol Table index
constant	int	value	None
literal	int/real	global address	Literal Table index
result	int/real	regindex	None
optr	mon/dyad	optr number	None

Machine Instructions

The Code Generator accepts a sequence of lexemes as input and produces a sequence of machine instructions. The machine instructions in our example are represented by symbolic instructions that have the following form:

(Operation, Register, Mode, Address)

The Operation field describes which operation the machine should execute: addition, multiplication, load into register, store into memory, convert from integer to real, etc. The Register field indicates which fast register is used in the operation. The Mode field describes the nature of the address field used in the operation. For the particular machine model we have in mind, the Mode can have one of four values:

1. An absolute address which represents a memory location or a Register (if the address value is in the range 0 . . 15);

2. A relative address which represents a pair (Reg, offset) where Reg is one of the registers and offset a small constant in the range 0 . . 255;

3. An immediate address which represents an integer number in the range -2047 . . 2047;

4. An indirect address which represents a memory location or a register that contains the address of the second operand.

The mode and address fields together determine the second operand of an instruction. The interpretation of the instructions is as follows.

Monadic Operation	(Op, Reg, Opnd2)	means Reg := Op(Opnd2)
Dyadic Operation	(Op, Reg, Opnd2)	means Reg := Reg Op Opnd2
Load Operation	(Ld, Reg, Opnd)	means Reg := Opnd2
Store Operation	(St, Reg, Opnd2)	means Opnd2 := Reg

Our machine has no other operations on memory locations than store. All other operations leave their results in a fast register. For example the following sequence of instructions computes the expression a b c + * d + .

Symbolic Instruction	**Meaning**
(Load, Reg(0), Location(a))	$R_0 := a$
(Load, Reg(1), Location(b))	$R_1 := b$
(Add, Reg(1), Location(c))	$R_1 := R_1 + c$
(Mul, Reg(0), Reg(1))	$R_0 := R_0 * R_1$
(Add, Reg(0), Location(d))	$R_0 := R_0 + d$

The Code Generation Driver Routine

At the heart of the Code Generator is the driver routine that reads the lexemes from the input sequence,recognizes monadic and dyadic operators, and calls the appropriate code generator procedure for the specified operator. A lexeme stack is used by the driver to store the operands for later use by the code generating procedures. In terms of the stack operations PUSH and POP, the driver operates as follows:

> **loop**
> > **if** input empty, quit
> > read(input lexeme)
> > **if** input lexeme is an operand, PUSH(input lexeme)
> > **if** input lexeme is an operator, call code generator (operator)
> **end loop**

When it encounters an operator, the driver calls the procedure that generates code for that specific operator. If it is a monadic operator, the code generating procedure removes the top of the stack and replaces it by a lexeme representing the result of the monadic operation. If the operator encountered in the input sequence is a dyadic operator, the code generating routine for that operator removes the top two items from the stack and replaces them by a single lexeme representing the result of the dyadic operation. The way the driver handles the expression a b c + * d + is listed in the following table

read	call	stack	result
a		a	
b		a b	
c		a b c	
+	+	a x	x := b + c
*	*	y	y := a * x
d		y d	
+	+	z	z := y + d
done		z	

By the time the driver has finished reading the input sequence, the result lexeme representing the entire expression is the only item in the stack.

Processing Subexpressions

The code generated for a subexpression depends on the types of the operands and on the type of the operator. In most cases a single instruction is emitted for every call to a code generating procedure. However, there are two cases of dyadic operations in which the code generator must produce an additional instruction: if neither operand is the result of a subexpression; and if one of the operands is of type real and the other is not. The first case makes it necessary to generate an extra load instruction, because our machine does not provide memory-to-memory operations. In case of a dyadic operator there are two subcases in which the additional load instruction is generated: if the operator is commutative and neither operand is a result; and if the operator is not commutative and the left operand is not a result. Generating the additional load instruction assures that for commutative dyadic operators at least one of the operands is a result and that for non-commutative operators the left operand is a result. For instance, the code generated for subexpressions a + b, where both *a* and *b* are memory operands is

Reg := a; Reg + b.

In the second case, an additional instruction is generated to convert one of the operands because there are no instructions for mixed types: both types must be either real or integer. The extra instruction generated in this case is the one that converts the integer operand into an operand of type real. If *q* is an integer operand, the conversion is accomplished by the monadic operation

Reg := Conv(q).

The translation scheme is listed below in two tables, the first for monadic operations and the second for dyadic operations.

Operand lexeme	destination register	generated code
global variable	select one	(Op, Reg, Abs Address)
local variable	select one	(Op, Reg, Rel Address)
constant	select one	(Op, Reg, Imm Address)
literal	select one	(Op, Reg, Abs Address)
result	take same	(Op, Reg, Abs Address)

left operand	right operand	generated code	operator
result	global variable	(Op, Reg, Abs Address)	
result	local variable	(Op, Reg, Rel Address)	
result	constant	(Op, Reg, Imm Address)	
result	literal	(Op, Reg, Abs Address)	
result	result	(Op, Reg, Abs Address)	
global variable	result	(Op, Reg, Abs Address)	commutative
local variable	result	(Op, Reg, Rel Address)	commutative
constant	result	(Op, Reg, Imm Address)	commutative
literal	result	(Op, Reg, Abs Address)	commutative

A result lexeme has the form (result, <type>, Reg) and is created when a subexpression is processed. The program for handling dyadic subexpressions has the following structure:

-- check for conversion
>   **if type**(leftopnd) is real **and** type(rightopnd) is integer **then**
>   call monad procedure for rightopnd with opcode(Conv)
>   **else if** type(leftopnd) is integer **and** type(rightopnd) is real **then**
>   call MONAD procedure for leftopnd with opcode(Conv)

-- check for conditions requiring a load instruction
>   **if** (operator non-commutative **and** left operand **not** a result) **or**
>   (both operands **not** a result)
>   **then** generate (Load, SELECT(reg), Address(left operand))
>   generate instruction according to the appropriate table above

-- clean up
>   **if** both input operands are results, free register of right operand

In this example we will not pay attention to register optimization. We assume that enough registers are available and we do not try to keep intermediate results in registers as long as possible. Also, matters of common subexpressions and reordering of subexpressions are totally ignored.

We use a stack that initially lists all registers, except special registers, as available Selecting a free register amounts to popping the top element from the free stack. If no free register is available when one is needed, the code generator produces an error message. Releasing a register amounts to pushing its index onto the free stack. A register is released when it has been used as a second operand, because the register of the first operand can be used for the result.

Summary of the Problem Discussion

At this point all the ingredients for a code generator for arithmetic expressions have been developed.

- Input to the arithmetic code generator is a sequence of lexemes in postfix order produced by the front-end of the compiler.
- The code generator driver stacks the operand lexemes and calls the appropriate code generating procedure when it encounters an operator lexeme.
- The code generation procedures translate the operand and operator lexemes into machine instructions, making use of the various facts about the operands, and produce result lexemes which are put on the stack for subsequent use.

Design the data structures to be used for lexemes and machine instructions and write the procedures for the driver and code generations for monadic and dyadic expressions. The usual stack operations may be assumed to exist for the lexeme and register stacks.

10.3 A Pascal Solution

Representation of Lexemes

The DRIVER routine of the Code Generator reads the lexemes from the input sequence, one at a time, and, if the lexeme is an operand, places it on top of the lexeme stack. Since a natural implementation for the stack is an array and in Pascal all elements of an array must be of the same type, we must introduce a single type *lexeme* that can be used for the various kinds of lexemes such as global variable, constant, result, etc. Separate type declarations for each kind of lexeme will not work because of Pascal's typing rules: the variable and the expression must be of the same type. It should be clear that there is no way of predicting the class of the lexeme when reading it from the input sequence and, hence, no way of supplying the desired variable to store it.

The flexibility needed for lexemes is obtained by representing lexemes as variant records. A collection of variant records has a unique type, but individual objects of that type may have different layouts. These layouts are determined by the tag field of the variant record (PRM 141). For example, we can use the tag field to distinguish between the various classes of lexemes:

```
type lexeme =  record
                 case class : lexclass of
                     glob  : ( . . . );
                     loc   : ( . . . );
                     cons  : ( . . . );
                     lit   : ( . . . );
                     res   : ( . . . );
                     optr  : ( . . . )
               end;
```

The case structure of the record lists a layout for each different class: for variables and literals we need fields for their *type*, *address* and *reference*; for constants, results and operators we need fields for their *type* and *value* (representing, respectively, their value, register and identity). This structure for each class is as follows.

```
glob  : (type : arith; loc : address; ref : integer);
loc   : (type : arith; loc : address; ref : integer);
cons  : (type : arith; val : integer);
lit   : (type : arith; loc : address; ref : integer);
res   : (type : arith; val : reg);
optr  : (type : optype; val : optrid)
```

There are several problems with this approach. First, the name *type* cannot be used for a record field name, because this name conflicts with the predefined delimiter **type** that is part of the Pascal language. Second, the names of fields in variants must be different. We are not allowed to use the same name (such as *ref* or *loc* or *val*) for fields in different variants.

The design can be simplified considerably (although with some loss of logical clarity) if we partition the lexemes into two subgroups: *reflex* and *valex*. The first group consists of the lexemes that possess address and reference fields (global variables, local variables, literals) and the second group of the lexemes that have no descriptor in a Symbol or Literal table (constants, results, operators). An additional simplification is obtained by taking the type field out of the variants and replacing it by a Boolean *nature* field indicating whether or not an operand lexeme is integer and whether or not an operator lexeme is monadic. Although the partitioning into two subgroups simplifies the design, the class information is still relevant for the procedures operating on lexemes. It is therefore necessary to add a global *class* field which specifies the class of a particular lexeme. The modified design leads to the following record structure for lexemes:

```
type lexeme =   record
                        class    :  lexclass;
                        nature   :  Boolean;
                case    group    :  lexgroup of
                        reflex   :  (loc : address;  ref : reference);
                        valex    :  (val : integer)
                end;
```

Pascal's enumerated types enable us to define the types *lexclass* and *lexgroup* according to our interpretation:

```
type   lexclass   =   (glob, loc, cons, lit, res, optr);
       lexgroup   =   (reflex, valex);
```

The types *address* and *reference* can be defined as subrange types (PRM 140) assuming we know the size of the address space and of the tables.

```
const   addressspace   = 65535;
        tablesize      = 192;                    {an arbitrary choice}

type    address        = 0 . . addressspace;
        reference      = 0 . . 191;
```

Not being able to initialize objects in Pascal makes it impossible to specify in a declaration which kind of lexeme a new variable is going to represent. It is not possible to declare objects x and y by declarations such as

x : lexeme(reflex); y : lexeme(valex); {incorrect Pascal}.

The tag field cannot be set in a declaration. Instead, one must write

    x, y : lexeme;
    x.group : = reflex; y.group : = valex

As a result, the compiler must always allocate space sufficient for storing the
largest variant. Since the programmer is able to change the value of a tag field by
a simple assignment statement, it is legal to write

    x.group : = valex

further on in a program with the effect that the content of record x is interpreted
according to a different variant. Clearly, unpredictable results occur (although one
can do very clever things that way). We recommend that a programmer be very
cautious with assigning to tag fields and use this feature only in conjunction with
assigning values to the entire record (as, for example, at the point of
initialization).

Representation of Instructions

The Mode field of a machine instruction determines the interpretation of the
address field. If the Mode is absolute, the address field represents a memory
address or a register; if immediate, it represents an integer constant; if relative, it
represents a register with an offset; and if indirect, it represents the location that
contains the address of the operand. These address interpretations are nicely
implemented by a variant record of the form

```
type machaddress =
    record
    case   mode  : addressmode of
           abs   : (loc : address);
           rel   : (base : register; offset : 0 . . 255);
           imm   : (val : integer);
           ind   : (container : address)
    end;
```

Addressmode is an enumerated type containing the values *abs, rel, imm*, and
ind. The type defining the operations of the machine instruction is another
candidate for an enumerated type, whereas defining the register can be most
clearly expressed as a subrange type.

```
type   addressmode   = (abs,rel,imm,ind);
       operation     = ( load, store, convert,
                          add, sub, mul, div,
                          radd, rsub, rmul, rdiv);
       register      = 0 . . 15;
```

Machine instructions can now be defined as a record type.

```
type machinstruction =
    record
            op     : operation;
            reg    : register;
            opnd  : machaddress
    end;
```

This design can be improved slightly by changing instructions into variant records, using their mode as tag field.   The separate type declaration for machaddress can then be omitted, which leads to the revised declaration:

```
type machinstruction =
    record
            op     : operation;
            reg    : register;
        case mode : addressmode of
              . . .
    end;
```

The types of the four alternative address fields are the same as previously defined in type machaddress.

Input-Output

The code generator gets its input from a file of lexemes and places its output in a file of machine instructions. These files are represented in Pascal by two file variables (PRM 145) declared by

input : **file of** lexeme; output : **file of** machinstruction;

A side effect of the file declarations is that the files are opened automatically for both input and output. We cannot make use of the standard procedures READ and WRITE for handling input and output because these procedures require that the elements in the files are of predefined type integer, real, char or Boolean (PRM 162). The operation GET(input) gets the next lexeme of the input sequence in the buffer variable, denoted by *input* ↑ . The sequence of instructions

output ↑ := some machinstruction; PUT(output)

places a machine instruction in the output file. Note that the produced machine instruction cannot be used directly as argument of procedure PUT. The data must be transmitted through the buffer variable *output* ↑ because procedure PUT identifies the output file by the buffer name. The Pascal library contains a standard procedure EOF(filename) that returns TRUE if and only if the end of file *filename* has been reached (PRM 158).

The Driver Routine

In the problem discussion we designed the DRIVER routine as a loop that terminates when the end of the input file is reached. The routine reads the next item from the input file and processes the input item depending on whether this item is an operand or an operator: operands are pushed onto the lexeme stack; operators are used for calling the appropriate code generator procedure. The DRIVER routine has access to the new input item through the buffer variable *input* ↑ which has the record structure of lexemes. A Pascal implementation of the DRIVER routine is as follows:

```
while not EOF(input) do
  begin
    GET(input);
    if input ↑ .class / = optr then PUSH(input ↑ )
    else
      if input ↑ .nature then MONAD(args)
      else
        begin
          {get the lexemes from the stack}
          DYAD(args)
        end
  end
```

Note that the use of the buffer variable *input* ↑ does not imply reading from the input. The value of the buffer does not change until the next call to procedure GET.

The arguments passed in the call to procedures MONAD and DYAD are the opcode that should be put in the output instruction and the operand lexemes from the lexeme stack. The mapping from the operator code in lexemes to machine opcodes is somewhat tedious in Pascal because there is no function that maps an index into a value of an enumerated type. Thus, the *opcode* argument should be the result of a mapping function specified as follows.

function MAP(op : integer) : operation;

The mapping function consists of a case statement that maps the various operator representations into the operations load, store, convert, add, sub, mul and div. Given this mapping function, argument *arg* can be replaced by the following expression.

arg := MAP(input ↑ .val)

If this argument expression is passed when the DRIVER routine calls one of the code generating procedures, these procedures can directly copy the argument value into the opcode field of the output instruction.

Code Generation

The task of the code generator procedures consists of emitting the machine instruction sequences for subexpressions and of updating the lexeme stack. We separate these tasks in two procedures for manipulating the lexemes, procedures MONAD and DYAD, and a subprogram GENERATE that actually assembles instructions and writes them out onto the output file. Procedure GENERATE is called by MONAD and DYAD when all the parts of an instruction have been determined. The specifications of the procedures are

> **procedure** MONAD   (op : operation; opnd : lexeme);
> **procedure** DYAD   (op : operation; opnd1, opnd2 : lexeme);
> **procedure** GENERATE (op : operation; reg : register; lex : lexeme);

The MONAD procedure operates on a single operand, whereas the DYAD procedure operates on the two top elements from the stack.

Generating a Machine Instruction

Procedure GENERATE constructs a machine instruction out of its parameters and writes this instruction to the output file. It copies the operation and register fields from its first two parameters and obtains the mode and address field from the input lexeme. The mode and address depend on the class of the lexeme: if the class is global, literal or register, the address mode must be set to absolute; if constant, the mode must be set to immediate; and if local, the result mode must be set to relative. (Mode indirect is irrelevant for our example as we are not supporting subscripted variables.)

```
with output ↑ do
    case lex.class of
        glob : begin mode : = abs;    loc  : = lex.loc end;
        loc  : begin mode : = rel;    base : = AR; offset : = lex.loc end;
        cons : begin mode : = imm;    val  : = lex.val end;
        lit  : begin mode : = abs;    loc  : = lex.loc end;
        res  : begin mode : = abs;    loc  : = lex.val end
    end
```

We assume that one of the registers has been permanently reserved for pointing to the current set of local variables. This is set as part of the activation record of the most recent subprogram invocation. The variable AR contains the value of this register.

One might consider the statement

> offset : = lex.loc

to be incorrect altogether because the lefthand side is of type 0 . . 255 and the righthand side is of type *address*: that is, the types do not match. Although there is no explicit statement in the Report that allows assignment between objects of different subrange types derived from the same base type, we assume that this case was intended to be covered by statement 2 of PRM 9.1.1, on page 149.

When the operation and register parameters have been copied into the output buffer *output* ↑ , GENERATE emits the actual machine instruction by the statement PUT(output) (PRM 158).

Monadic Subexpressions

If the operand is not a register operand, a register must be selected in which the monadic operation can be performed. On the other hand, if the operand is a register operand, that register can also be used as the destination register. Thus, the destination register *reg* is determined by the following statement.

    if opnd.class = res **then** reg : = opnd.val **else** reg : = SELECT

The code for the monadic operation is then generated by the call

    GENERATE(opcode, reg, opnd)

where *opcode* and *opnd* are the same parameters that were passed to MONAD.

The last task of MONAD is to update the stack: The result lexeme must be pushed onto the top of the stack, which is accomplished by:

```
with opnd do
    begin
    group : = valex;
    class : = res;
    nature : = nature and (opcode / = convert);
    val : = reg
    end;
PUSH (opnd)
```

Dyadic Subexpressions

Processing dyadic expressions is complicated by the fact that extra instructions must be generated if the types of the operands do not match or if neither one of the operands is a register operand. In the case of non-matching types, the integer operand must be converted into a real operand. The conversion is achieved by calling MONAD and passing the integer operand. The result of the conversion is then popped into the appropriate lexeme variable. The following statement that takes care of the conversion (if necessary).

> **if** opnd1.nature **and not** opnd2.nature
> >   **then**   **begin** MONAD(convert, opnd1); POP(opnd1) **end**
> **else if** opnd2.nature **and not** opnd1.nature
> >   **then**   **begin** MONAD(convert, opnd2); POP(opnd2) **end**

Another instruction must be generated if neither operand is a register operand or if the operation is not commutative and the lefthand operand is not a register operand. Creating the register operand is accomplished by the call to MONAD.

> **if** opnd1.class /= res **then**
> >   **if** (opcode = div) **or** (opcode = sub) **or** (opnd2.class /= res)
> >   >   **then**   MONAD(load, opnd1)
> >   >   **else**   SWAP(opnd1, opnd2)

When the right operand is a result, and the operation is commutative, the two operands can be exchanged. The lefthand operand is then a result.

Before calling GENERATE, the dyadic subexpression handler must reconsider the operation it received as a parameter. The DRIVER routine always passes an integer operation as input parameter, while the operands may be of type real. If they are of type real, the operation must be converted to the corresponding floating point operation, which can be done by stepping through the enumerated type with the Pascal library routine *succ* (PRM 161):

> **if not** opnd1.nature **then**
> >   **begin**
> >   >   opcode := succ(opcode); opcode := succ(opcode);
> >   >   opcode := succ(opcode); opcode := succ(opcode)
> >   **end**

After the operation has been adjusted, the machine instruction for the subexpression is generated by the statement

> GENERATE(opcode, opnd1.val, opnd2).

The mode and address field are obtained from the righthand operand, in the same manner as that in which the monadic procedure obtains these from its single operand.

The dyadic procedure ends the same way as the monadic procedure by placing the result lexeme on the stack. It then checks whether the righthand operand is also a register operand. If so, and if its register is not the same as that of the lefthand operand, that register is released by the statement

> **if** opnd2.class = res **then**
> **if** opnd1.val /= opnd2.val **then** RELEASE (opnd2.val)

10.4 An Ada Solution

The principle of the Ada solution is the same as that in Pascal: the concept on which the solution is based is that of variant records. The main difference between the Pascal and Ada programs is the program organization and the use of information hiding. In our Ada solution, we design three packages: one for lexemes, one for machine instructions and one for generating symbolic machine code. The first two packages collect together related types, constant and data declarations, while the last hides the actual implementation of the code generator. In this section, we first discuss the packages for the lexemes and machine instructions. Before discussing the code generator, we consider first the problems with variant record assignment and then the problem of typed I/O.

Lexemes

The lexeme package exports the data type *lexeme* and the supporting types for lexeme groups and classes.

> **package** LEXEMES **is**
>
> > **type**   lexclass   **is**   (glob, loc, cons, lit, res, optr);
> > **type**   lexgroup   **is**   (reflex, valex);
> > **subtype** address   **is**   INTEGER **range** 0 . . MEMORY_SIZE;
> >
> > **type** lexeme **is** . . . ;
>
> **end** LEXEMES;

The discrete types *lexclass* and *lexgroup* are the same as the corresponding enumerated types in Pascal. In Ada, *address* is a subtype rather than a type as in Pascal with the maximum value specified by the constant MEMORY_SIZE, a system dependent quantity known to the Ada system (ARM 13.7, 13-9).

Type *lexeme* is implemented as a variant record (ARM 3.7.3, 3-38). Unlike Pascal, the discriminant (corresponding to the tag in Pascal) is explicitly stated as a parameter of the type.

> **type** lexeme(group : lexgroup) **is** . . .

The discriminant behaves as an in parameter which implies that its value is a constant within the record definition. This also implies that assignments to the discriminant such as

> x : lexeme; x.group : = valex;   -- incorrect Ada

are not allowed. One can use the discriminant as a record field, one can read its value, but one cannot assign to it, except in complete record assignment.

The actual record definition for type *lexeme* is semantically the same as in Pascal. The syntax is slightly different, but self explanatory (ARM 3.7.3, 3-38).

```
type lexeme (group : lexgroup : = reflex) is
    record
            class       : lexclass;
            nature      : Boolean;
            case group is
                    when reflex  = > loc : address; ref : Tables.reference;
                    when valex   = > val : INTEGER;
            end case;
    end record;
```

The default initialization of the discriminant is discussed in a subsequent subsection on assignment to variant records. Because of the delimiter **when**, it is not necessary to enclose the fields of a variant, such as the reflex variant, in a pair of parentheses. The type of the reference field is defined in some package for creating and manipulating Tables. We assume that this package is used elsewhere in the compiler for creating a Symbol Table and a Literal Table. The Table package is of no further relevance to our problem and therefore remains unspecified here.

Machine Instructions

The package for machine instructions exports the type *machinstruction* and its supporting types. As in Pascal, it is implemented by a variant record whose discriminant is the address mode.

```
package INSTRUCTIONS is
        maxreg : constant : = 15;
        type operation        is (load, store, convert,
                                  add, sub, mul, div,
                                  radd, rsb, rmul, rdiv);
        type addressmode    is (abs, rel, imm, ind);
        subtype register      is INTEGER range 0 . . maxreg;
        AR : constant register : = maxreg;
        type machinstruction (mode : addressmode : = abs) is  . . . ;
end INSTRUCTIONS;
```

Again, the type definitions are almost the same as in Pascal. The major difference is their grouping into packages. The constant AR is the register pointing to the activation record of a subprogram. Its value is the base for a set of local variables.

The variant record implementation of type *machinstruction* is semantically the same as in Pascal (except for the restrictions on assignment to the discriminant).

```
type machinstruction (mode : addressmode : = abs) is
    record
            op    : operation;
            reg   : register;
            case mode is
                when abs   = > loc : address;
                when rel   = > base : register : = AR;
                                offset : INTEGER range 0 . . 255;
                when imm  = > val : INTEGER;
                when ind   = > container : address;
            end case;
    end record;
```

The need for initialization of the discriminant is explained in the next subsection.

Assignment to Variant Records

In Ada one can declare a variable of a variant record type either as an object that can be any one of the variants or as an object that has a specific variant. The distinction is made in the declaration by specifying the discriminant value or by omitting it. For example,

```
x, y : lexeme;
p : lexeme(reflex);
q : lexeme(valex);
m : machinstruction(rel);
```

introduces variables x and y that can take the shape of any variant of lexemes, whereas p and q are specific variants of lexemes and m is a specific variant of a machine instruction. However, one should be aware of the (rather strange) rule that unconstrained record declarations such as

```
x, y : lexeme;
```

are allowed only if the discriminant in the type declaration of lexemes has a default value(ARM 3.7.2, 3-37)! If no default discriminant value is supplied in the type declaration, then all object declarations using that type must be constrained: in other words, declared with a discriminant value. This limitation would rule out the declarations for x and y, but allow those for p and q.

There is a significant difference between the declarations of x and y on the one hand and the declarations of p and q on the other hand. When the discriminant is given in the object declaration, as is the case in the declaration of p and q, the discriminant of these objects is fixed once and for all and can never be changed. This implies that p and q are of a specific subtype of type *lexeme* and each object is a fixed lexeme variant. The subtype of p and q is fixed in the declaration and can never be changed. However, this is not the case for variables x and y.

Although their discriminant value is set by the default value included in the type definition, the language rules do not exclude a complete record assignment to such record variables (ARM 3.7.1, 3-35). In other words, the subtype of x and y is not fixed in their declaration, although their discriminant is initialized. Thus, in order to obtain the ability of assigning different variant values to variant record objects, these objects must be declared without giving the discriminant a value. Such object declarations are allowed only if the discriminant has a default value. It is therefore necessary to initialize the discriminant value in the original variant record type definition so that the discriminant has a default value.

Since we wish to have the flexibility of assigning different variant values to a particular variable of type *lexeme* or *machinstruction*, the discriminants in both type declarations have been initialized to default values. The declarations of x and y are now legitimate and assignments such as

```
x := (valex, res, TRUE, 5);
y := p; y := q; q := x;
```

are permissible. Note that variable y is first of variant *reflex* and then of variant *valex*. The last assignment is correct because the subtypes match. Assignments such as

```
p := x;
q := p; p := q;
```

are incorrect because the subtypes do not match in any of these assignments . In the first case, the current variant does not match the subtype of p. In the second, the subtypes conflict because of their definition.

If a literal value (an aggregate) is assigned to a variant record, its first component must correspond to the discriminant (ARM 4.3.1, 4-8). This rule was obeyed in the assignment to record x. The rule extends naturally to the case of more than one discriminant: the order of appearance in an aggregate is governed by the order of appearance in the record's parameter list.

The flexibility of using unconstrained variant record variables is seemingly lost when one operates with access variables to dynamic variant records (ARM 5.2, 5-3). The object pointed to by an access variable can be created only by an allocator (ARM 4.8, 4-24) which must include a value for the discriminant. The discriminant value fixes the size, as well as the subtype, of the dynamic variable when it is allocated.

The flexibility is only seemingly lost because, while the discriminant of the dynamic variable cannot be changed, the access variable itself can refer to any record variant. Allocating a new variant with its values is no more difficult than assigning new aggregate values to static variables. The access variables can be viewed as unconstrained objects while the dynamic variables are considered as constrained objects.

Input Output

In Ada a file contains typed objects as it does in Pascal. However, there are a number of important differences (ARM 14, 14-1). For example, in Ada,
- file variables are associated with external files through file names;
- two modes of access are defined: sequential and direct access;
- files are explicitly opened and closed;
- the generic I/O packages must be instantiated for each file element type -- thereby creating a set of operations for each file element type;
- specific packages are defined for text I/O, integer, real and enumeration types -- the last three are generic and instantiable for any desired specific integer, real or enumeration type.

As we are accessing both the lexeme and instruction files strictly sequentially, we instantiate the two files from the generic SEQUENTIAL_IO package.

> **package** Lexinput **is new** SEQUENTIAL_IO(lexeme);
> **package** Objcode **is new** SEQUENTIAL_IO(machinstruction);

The natural place for these instantiations is at the end of the packages for lexemes and machine instructions. Each package gives us a complete set of type definitions for files and of file operations such as OPEN, READ, etc. A variable of the type FILE_TYPE must be used in the file operations to coordinate them. The declarations that we need in our example are

> input   : Lexinput.FILE_TYPE;
> output   : Objcode .FILE_TYPE;

These declarations occur in the scope of the code generating subprograms because they are used by the DRIVER program for reading the input and by the subprogram that emits the code for storing the generated machine instructions.

Ada distinguishes between a file and its name and requires that a file must be explicitly opened or created before use. For our specific example we may assume that the input exists in some file *source* and that the output file should be created by the program. If we chose the name *destination* for the output file, the use of the file variables *input* and *output* must be preceded by the statements

> Lexinput.OPEN(input, IN_FILE, source);
> Objcode.CREATE(output, OUT_FILE, destination);

Where Pascal distinguishes between a file and its buffer by augmenting the file name by the symbol " ↑ ", Ada provides only the file. The user of the file must supply the buffer.

After the files have been opened and created, they can be used for reading and writing in statements such as

Lexinput.READ(input, x); Objcode.WRITE(output, m);

where *x* is a lexeme and *m* a machine instruction. Since *input* is opened as an input file, one cannot apply procedure WRITE to it. Likewise, procedure READ cannot be applied to file *output*. The READ statements will be used in the DRIVER program and the WRITE statements in the subprogram emitting the machine instructions. By proper use of the scoping facilities (in particular the use clause (ARM 8.4, 8-6) we can avoid having to use the prefixes Lexinput and Objcode for every READ or WRITE statement.

The Code Generator

All the user of the Code Generator needs to know is the existence of the DRIVER routine. The fact that it calls the procedures for processing monadic and dyadic subexpressions is immaterial to the users. In order for the code generator to have access to its input and output files, the names of these files are required as parameters of the DRIVER routine. This leads to the following design of the code generator package.

```
package CODEGEN is

    subtype filename is STRING(1 . . 24);
    procedure DRIVER(source, destination : filename);
    regallocation, exprnesting : exception;


end CODEGEN;
```

The exceptions are included so that the subprograms that process subexpressions can signal that there is a shortage of fast registers and that the nesting of subexpressions is too deep.

The Package Bodies

The packages LEXEMES and INSTRUCTIONS consist primarily of type and subtype definitions. The visible parts do not contain specifications of subprograms that must be elaborated in the package body. Therefore, in such a case as we have here, there is no need for a separate body; the packages are completely defined by their visible part.

CODEGEN, on the other hand, specifies a procedure whose code must be elaborated in the package body. The latter will also contain the auxiliary subprograms for processing subexpressions and for emitting code. The data objects shared by these subprograms are the lexeme stack, the stack of free registers and their status variables. The structure of the body is given as follows.

```
with LEXEMES, INSTRUCTIONS, STACK;
use  LEXEMES, INSTRUCTIONS;
package body CODEGEN is

        input   : Lexinput.FILE_TYPE;
        output  : Objcode.FILE_TYPE;

        exprdepth   : constant := 12;
        stackindex  : INTEGER range 1 . . exprdepth;
        package lexstk is new STACK(lexeme);
        package regstk is new STACK(register);

        procedure GENERATE
            (opcode: in operation; REG: in register; opnd: in lexeme)
        is separate;

        procedure MONAD(opcode: in operation; opnd: in lexeme)
        is separate;

        procedure DYAD
            (opcode: in operation; opnd1, opnd2: in lexeme)
        is separate;

        procedure DRIVER(source, destination : filename) is
            . . .
        end DRIVER;

    end CODEGEN;
```

The package STACK defines an abstract stack object and is used to define the lexeme and register stacks.

Separate Compilation

In Chapter 3 we discussed briefly Ada's STANDARD library which contains predefined types, such as INTEGER, CHARACTER, etc, predefined packages for I/O processing and all user defined program units that are not defined inside program bodies. We saw in Chapter 3 that a library unit Q that uses a library unit P includes the name of the latter in a with clause preceding its declaration:

```
with P;
package Q is . . . end Q;
```

A library unit R that depends on unit Q lists Q in its with clause, but not P. For with clauses, Ada uses the non-inheritance rule that excludes units on which the declared unit depends indirectly (ARM 10.1.1.9, 10-3).

In large programs, one often wants to declare a unit within another unit without including its entire implementation. An example of such a situation is the body of CODEGEN that includes the declarations of the procedures GENERATE, MONAD and DYAD, but not their bodies. Each of the three bodies is represented by the keyword **separate**, indicating that the implementation is described elsewhere. In fact, a separate unit is described as a secondary library unit, distinct from a primary library unit that has an independent scope. These secondary library units do not have an independent scope, but have a scope that is defined by the position of their declaration inside another unit.

When the compiler encounters a secondary library unit, it must have a way of locating the scope of that unit. The relationship between a secondary library unit and its definition scope is expressed by a *separate* clause of the form:

> **separate**(CODEGEN)
> **procedure** MONAD(. . .) **is**
>   . . .
> **end** MONAD;

and likewise for procedures GENERATE and DYAD.

Suppose that the body of MONAD contained a program unit X that is also marked separate. The proper prefix for unit X is then the full path name CODEGEN.MONAD that describes the entire nested scope up to the top level of a primary library unit. Thus, the implementation of the separate unit X is:

> **separate** (CODEGEN.MONAD)
> **procedure** X **is** . . . **end** X;

In other words, for separately compilable units, Ada applies the full inheritance rule that requires the declaration of the complete path describing the nested scope in which the unit is defined (ARM 10.2.1.3, 10-8).

One should not confuse the separate clause with the with clause or the use clause. The separate clause describes the nesting of scopes, the with clause describes the dependency on units not defined in that scope and the use clause opens an external scope so that names can be written without name qualification. For the declaration of secondary library units the question arises whether or not the separate clause must be extended using a with clause equal to that of its nested parent scope in which it is logically defined. In our particular example, the question is whether the implementation of MONAD should have a with clause listing the packages LEXEMES, INSTRUCTIONS and STACK that are used by its parent scope CODEGEN. The answer is: NO, a secondary unit inherits all the with clauses from its parent scope (ARM 10.2[6], 10-6). Thus, the separate clause of MONAD automatically imports the with clause of package CODEGEN. The same is true of the use clauses attached to the parent scope. There is no need to repeat the use clause for the implementation of MONAD.

Although not necessary, attaching a with clause (and a use clause) to a secondary library unit is certainly permitted. The effect is that the unit has access to the union of all the external units listed in its own with clause and those attached to units of its parent scope. Duplication of names in with clauses is allowed. The Ada programs at the end of this chapter reflect these separate compilation rules.

The Driver Routine in Ada

The DRIVER routine starts with initializing the register stack by the statement

> **for** k **in** 0 . . (maxreg - 1) **loop** PUSH(k); **end loop**;

The last register is not released because it is permanently reserved for the activation record pointer, AR.

Since the DRIVER routine does all the reading from the input file, its program should start with

> **use** Lexinput;

so that the procedures OPEN and READ can be used without package name prefix. After opening the input file, the DRIVER starts its reading loop which is terminated when the end of the input file has been read. After reading the next input lexeme, the DRIVER checks for an operator lexeme. If it finds one, it must convert the numeric representation of an operator into an operation representation that is passed to the subexpression program. This mapping can easily be implemented in Ada by using the VAL attribute of discrete types (ARM 3.5.5, 3-16). The operator test is implemented by the following statement.

```
if lex.class = optr
    then   opcode : = operation 'VAL(lex.val);
           if lex.nature
                 then   MONAD(opcode, lexstk.POP);
                 else   right : = lexstk.POP;
                        left  : = lexstk.POP;
                        DYAD(opcode, left, right);
           end if;
    else   lexstk.PUSH (lex);
end if;
```

If the lexeme is not an operator, it is pushed onto the stack to be used later. The DRIVER program ends with closing the input and output files.

Code Emission in Ada

Subprogram GENERATE which writes out the code and assembles the result lexeme can be written as:

procedure GENERATE
        (opcode : operation; REG : register; opnd : lexeme);

If the operand pointed to by parameter *opnd* is a global variable, a literal or a register, the address mode of the machine instruction must be set to *abs*, if constant, to *imm* and if local, to *rel*. The case statement that emits the correct machine instruction depending on the class of the input lexeme is as follows.

```
case opnd.class is
    when glob  = > WRITE(output, (abs, REG, opnd.loc));
    when loc   = > WRITE(output, (rel, REG, AR, opnd.loc));
    when cons  = > WRITE(output, (imm, REG, opnd.val));
    when lit   = > WRITE(output, (abs, REG, opnd.loc));
    when res   = > WRITE(output, (abs, REG, opnd.val));
    when others = > null;

end case;
```

Note that the write statement can remain without prefix if the output package Objcode is included in a use clause at the beginning of GENERATE. Note also that Ada requires that all values of a discrete type must be included in the alternatives of a case statement (ARM 5.4, 5-5). If several alternatives remain and are treated the same, they can be put together in an alternative labelled **others**. In our particular case the remaining alternative is that of lexeme class *optr* even though this case cannot occur because operators are spotted in the DRIVER routine and removed from the stack. The null statement is just a place holder to achieve the correct syntax and semantics required by Ada. Finally, GENERATE creates the result lexeme for the register containing the result of the subexpression evaluation and puts in on the lexeme stack.

        lexstk.PUSH((valex, res, opnd.nature **and** opcode / = convert, REG));

Processing Subexpressions in Ada

MONAD must select a register if the operand is not a register already.

```
if opnd.class = res
    then   GENERATE(opcode, opnd.val, opnd);
    else   GENERATE(opcode, regstk.POP, opnd);
end if;
```

The program for dyadic subexpessions consists of three parts: generating a conversion instruction if necessary; generating a load instruction if necessary; generating the instruction that implements the dyadic expression. The type conversion is achieved by the following fragment.

```
if left.nature and not right.nature then
        MONAD(opcode, left); left : = lexstk.POP;
elsif right.nature and not left.nature then
        MONAD(opcode, right); right : = lexstk.POP;
end if;
```

The goal of the next fragment is to guarantee that a result lexeme occurs as the left hand operand. If the left operand is already a result, no action is necessary. If it is not, and either the operator is not commutative or the right operand is not a result, then invoke MONAD to load the value represented by the left operand. Otherwise, the right operand represents a result, the operation is commutative, and the operands can be exchanged, leaving a result in the left operand.

```
if left.class / = res then
        if right.class / = res or opcode = div or opcode = sub
                then   MONAD(load, left);
                       left : = lexstk.POP;
                else   SWAP(left, right);
        end if;
end if;
```

In generating the machine instruction, the operation code may have to be converted from an integer operation to a real operation. The correction and machine instruction generation are accomplished by the statements

```
if left.nature then
        GENERATE(opcode, left.val, right);
else   opcode : = operation'VAL(operation'POS + 4);
        GENERATE(opcode, left.val, right);
end if;
```

At the end of the DYAD program the register of the righthand operand is released, provided it is not the same register as that of the lefthand operand. This is done by the statement

```
if right.class = res and then left.val / = right.val
then regstk.PUSH(right.val); end if;
```

Remember that the delimiter sequence **and then** permits the evaluation of the second expression only when the first expression results in the value TRUE. In the statement above the short-circuit operation is required because the reference to *right.val* may raise an exception unless the lexeme is a result lexeme.

10.5 The Complete Programs

The Pascal Program

```
const  tablesize      = 192;
       exprdepth      = 12;
       maxreg         = 12;
       addressspace   = 65535;
       AR             = maxreg;

type   lexclass       = (glob, loc, cons, lit, res, optr);
       lexgroup       = (reflex, valex);
       address        = 0 . . address space;
       reference      = 0 . . 191;
       operation      = (load, store, convert, add, sub, mul, div,
                            radd, rsub, rmul, rdiv);
       register       = 0 . . maxreg;
       addressmode    = (abs, rel, imm, ind);
       lexeme         = record
                                class  : lexclass;
                                nature : boolean;
                          case group : lexgroup of
                                reflex  : (loc : address; ref : reference);
                                valex   : (val : integer)
                          end;
       machinstruction = record
                                op   : operation;
                                reg  : register;
                          case mode : addressmode of
                                abs  : (loc : address);
                                rel  : (base : register; offset : 0 . . 255);
                                imm  : (val : integer);
                                ind  : (container : address)
                          end;
       stackindex     = 1 . . exprdepth;

var    stack      : array[stackindex] of lexeme;
       top        : 0 . . exprdepth;
       free       : array[register] of register;
       freetop    : -1 . . maxreg;
       input      : file of lexeme;
       output     : file of machinstruction;
```

```pascal
procedure INIT;
begin
      top := 0;
      freetop := 0;
      while freetop < maxreg do
            begin
            free[freetop] := freetop; freetop := freetop + 1
            end;
      freetop := maxreg - 1                    {Reg[maxreg] is AR}
end;


procedure PUSH(lex : lexeme);  . . .  end;
function POP : lexeme;  . . .  end;
function SELECT : register;  . . .  end;
procedure RELEASE(r : register);  . . .  end;

procedure DRIVER;
      var   opcode : operation;
            opnd1, opnd2 : lexeme;
begin
      INIT;
      while not EOF(input) do
            begin
            GET(input);
            if input ↑ .class /= optr then PUSH(input ↑ )
            else    begin
                  case input ↑ .val of
                        0 : opcode := add;
                        1 : opcode := sub;
                        2 : opcode := mul;
                        3 : opcode := div
                        end;
                  if input ↑ .nature
                        then   begin
                              POP(opnd1);
                              MONAD(opcode, opnd1)
                              end
                        else   begin
                              POP(opnd2); POP(opnd1);
                              DYAD(opcode, opnd1, opnd2)
                              end
                  end
            end
end;
```

```
procedure GENERATE(opcode : operation; inreg : register; opnd : lexeme);

begin
    with output ↑ do
        begin
        op := opcode; reg := inreg;
        case stack[q].class of
            glob : begin mode := abs;   loc   := opnd.loc end;
            loc  : begin mode := rel;   base  := AR; offset := opnd.loc end;
            cons : begin mode := imm;   val   := opnd.val end;
            lit  : begin mode := abs;   loc   := opnd.loc end;
            res  : begin mode := abs;   loc   := opnd.val end
        end   {case}
        end;  {with}
    PUT(output);
    with opnd do
        begin
        group := valex; class := res; val := inreg;
        nature := nature and (opcode /= convert)
        end;
    PUSH(opnd)
end;

procedure MONAD(opcode : operation; opnd : lexeme);
        var reg : register;
begin
        with opnd do
                begin
                if class = res then reg := val else reg := SELECT;
                GENERATE(opcode, reg, opnd)
                end
end;
```

```
procedure DYAD(opcode : operation; opnd1, opnd2 : lexeme);
begin
      if opnd1.nature and not opnd2.nature then
            begin
            MONAD(convert, opnd1) ;
            POP (opnd1)
            end
      else if opnd2.nature and not opnd1.nature then
            begin
            MONAD(convert, opnd2);
            POP (opnd2)
            end;

      if (opnd1.class /= res) then
            if (opnd2.class /= res) or (opcode = sub) or (opcode = div)
            then   begin
                  MONAD(load, opnd1);
                  POP (opnd1)
                  end
            else   swap (opnd1, opnd2);

      if not opnd1.nature then
            begin
            opcode := succ(opcode); opcode := succ(opcode);
            opcode := succ(opcode); opcode := succ(opcode)
            end;

      GENERATE(opcode, opnd1.val, opnd2);

      if opnd2.class = res then
            if opnd1.val /= opnd2.val then RELEASE(opnd2.val)

end
```

The Ada Program

```
with Tables;
package LEXEMES is

        type      lexclass   is  (glob, loc, cons, lit, res, optr);
        type      lexgroup   is  (reflex, valex);
        subtype   address    is  INTEGER range 0 . . MEMORY_SIZE;

        type lexeme (group : lexgroup := reflex) is
            record
                    class    : lexclass;
                    nature   : BOOLEAN;
            case group is
                when reflex  => loc : address; ref : Tables.reference;
                when valex   => }val : INTEGER;
            end case;
            end record;
        package Lexinput is new SEQUENTIAL_IO(lexeme);

end LEXEMES;

package INSTRUCTIONS is

        maxreg : constant      := 15;
        type     operation     is  (load, store, convert, add, sub, mul, div,
                                          radd, rsub, rmul, rdiv);
        type     addressmode   is  (abs, rel, imm, ind);
        subtype register       is  INTEGER range 0 . . maxreg;
        AR     : constant      := maxreg;

        type machinstruction(mode : addressmode := abs). is
            record
                    op  : operation;
                    reg : register;
            case mode is
                when abs  => loc : address;
                when rel  => base : register := AR;
                             offset : INTEGER range 0 . . 255;
                when imm  => val : INTEGER;
                when ind  => container : address;
            end case;
            end record;
        package Objcode is new SEQUENTIAL_IO(machinstruction);

end INSTRUCTIONS;
```

```
package CODEGEN is

        subtype filename is STRING(1 . . 16);

        procedure DRIVER(source, destination : in filename);

        regallocation, exprnesting : exception;

end CODEGEN;

with LEXEMES, INSTRUCTIONS, STACK;
use  LEXEMES, INSTRUCTIONS;
package body CODEGEN is

        input      : Lexinput.FILE_TYPE;
        output     : Objectcode.FILE_TYPE;

        exprdepth  : constant := 12;
        AR         : constant register := register'LAST;

        package lexstk is new STACK(lexeme, exprdepth);
        package regstk is new STACK(register, register'LAST - 1);

        procedure GENERATE
                (opcode: operation; REG: register; opnd: lexeme)
        is separate;

        procedure MONAD(opcode : in operation; opnd : in lexeme)
        is separate;

        procedure DYAD
                (opcode : in operation; opnd1, opnd2 : in lexeme)
        is separate;
```

```
procedure DRIVER(source, destination : in filename) is
        use LEXEMES.Lexinput;
        lex, left, right : lexeme;
begin
        for k in 0 . . (maxreg-1) loop PUSH(k); end loop;
        OPEN(input, IN_FILE, source);
        Objcode.CREATE(output, OUT_FILE, destination);

        while not END_OF_FILE(input) loop
                READ(input, lex);
                if lex.class = optr then
                        if lex.nature then
                                MONAD(operation'VAL(lex.val), lexstk.POP);
                        else    right := lexstk.POP;
                                left := lexstk.POP;
                                DYAD(operation'VAL(lex.val), left, right);
                        end if;
                else    lexstk.PUSH (lex);
                end if;
        end loop;
        CLOSE(input); Objcode.CLOSE(output);

exception
        when STACK.overflow =>
                CLOSE(input); Objcode.CLOSE(output);
                raise exprnesting;
        when others =>
                CLOSE(input); Objcode.CLOSE(output);
end DRIVER;

end CODEGEN;
```

```
separate (CODEGEN)
procedure GENERATE
       (opcode : in operation; REG : in register; opnd : in lexeme)
is
       use INSTRUCTIONS.Objcode;
begin
    case opnd.class is
       when glob => WRITE(output, (abs, opcode, REG, opnd.loc));
       when loc  => WRITE(output, (rel, opcode, REG, AR, opnd.loc));
       when cons => WRITE(output, (imm, opcode, REG, opnd.val));
       when lit  => WRITE(output, (abs, opcode, REG, opnd.loc));
       when res  => WRITE(output, (abs, opcode, REG, opnd.val));
       when optr => null;
    end case;

    if opcode = convert
       then lexstk.PUSH ((valex, res, false, REG));
       else lexstk.PUSH ((valex, res, opnd.nature, REG));
    end if;
end GENERATE;



separate (CODEGEN)
procedure MONAD(opcode : in operation; opnd : in lexeme) is
begin
       if opnd.class = res
              then   GENERATE(opcode, opnd.val, opnd);
              else   GENERATE(opcode, regstk.POP, opnd);
       end if;
exception
       when regstk.underflow => raise regallocation;
end MONAD;
```

```
separate (CODEGEN)
procedure DYAD(opcode : in operation; opnd1, opnd2 : in lexeme) is
        left    : lexeme := opnd1;
        right   : lexeme := opnd2;
begin
        if left.nature and not right.nature then
                MONAD(convert, left);
                left := lexstk.POP;
        elsif right.nature and not left.nature then
                MONAD(convert, right);
                right := lexstk.POP;
        end if;

        if left.class /= res then
                if right.class /= res or opcode = div or opcode = sub
                        then    MONAD(load, left);
                                left := lexstk.POP;
                        else    swap (left, right);
                end if;
        end if;

        if left.nature then
                GENERATE(opcode, left.val, right) ;
        else GENERATE
                (operation'VAL(operation'POS(opcode) + 4), left.val, right);
        end if;

        if right.class = res and then left.val /= right.val then
                regstk.PUSH (right.val);
        end if;

end DYAD;
```

10.6 Reminders

1. In Pascal one can assign to the tag field of a variant record. In doing so, the shape of a record variable may change. Therefore, in Pascal the amount of space needed by the largest variant must be reserved for every variant of a record.

2. In Ada one cannot arbitrarily assign to the discriminant of a variant record. The discriminant is an **in** parameter of the variant record type definition. Assignment is only allowed in complete record assignment.

3. It is not clear whether assignment of variables of different subrange types derived from a single base type is allowed in Pascal. Many implementors of Pascal systems assume that this is the case.

4. In Pascal it is not possible to fix the variant subtype of a variable in its declaration. In Ada this can be done by passing the desired discriminant value as actual parameter of the type specification.

5. In Pascal I/O operations are applied to a file buffer which is denoted by the file name postfixed by the symbol " ↑ ". In Ada I/O operations are applied to a file object that has been associated with a file name in a CREATE or OPEN statement.

6. In Pascal a file is opened for both reading and writing at the declaration of a file (which implies the creation of a file buffer). In Ada a file is explicitly opened as input file, output file or read-write file.

7. In both languages files are composed of elements of a specified type. For structured types, Pascal's read and write operations cannot be used, because their operands must be of a predefined type. Such a restriction does not exist in Ada. Pascal provides the operations GET and PUT for structured type file buffers.

8. Mapping of an integer type or an enumerated type into another enumerated type is cumbersome in Pascal because there exists no inverse function of function ORD. Ada provides this function as the VAL attribute of a discrete type.

9. It is possible in Ada to assign an entire record aggregate to a record variable. This is allowed under two conditions: (1) the variable must have been declared of that record type without constraints (i.e., not of a subtype of that record type) and (2) if the record type has discriminants, the discriminants must have default values that are defined in the original type definition. In case these conditions are satisfied for a variant record type, an unconstraint variable of that type can change shape (and discriminant value) by a record aggregate assignment which changes the entire record object.

10. A case statement or case layout of a record must include all alternatives of a discrete type in Ada. In Pascal no similar requirement is imposed for the corresponding enumerated types.

11. If an access variable points to a variant record (in Ada), the record object pointed to cannot change its variant. Its discriminants are fixed because the type definition of an access type requires that the component be of a specific *sub*type.

12. Files are handled in Pascal in two stages: the declaration of a file with its buffer and the read/write operations on that buffer. Ada requires four stages: (1) the creation of a new instantiation of one of the standard I/O packages; (2) opening or creating files that are instantiations of the file type defined by the new I/O package; (3) READ or WRITE operations on the declared file; (4) closing the file. All operations OPEN, READ, CLOSE, etc. are specific versions of the standard operations defined by the new I/O package.

13. Auxiliary subprograms and shared data objects are hidden in package bodies so that users cannot interfer with the maintenance of the representation.

10.7 Problems

1. The DRIVER routine uses a stack in which the input lexemes for operands are stored. Since the local variables of a recursive procedure adher to a stack discipline, the restriction on the subexpression depth can be removed from the programs by replacing the loop of the DRIVER routine by a recursive procedure. Write such a recursive procedure for both languages.

2. The address mode *indirect* is relevant if subscripted variables are included in expressions. The code generated for an expression such as

$$a + b[i + 1] * c \Rightarrow a\ b\ i\ 1\ +\ [\ ]\ c\ *\ +$$

is

$$R := i;\ R + 1;\ R + b;\ R := \uparrow R;\ R * c;\ R + a$$

where "[ ]" represents the subscripting operation and " $\uparrow$ R" the indirect operation that extracts the value of the memory cell whose address is in register R.Modify both the Pascal and Ada programs to handle subscripted variables.

3. The current design does not allow the assignment of expressions to variables. Extend the Ada code generator to provide assignment to simple variables. If assignment is considered a dyadic operation, does this affect

the processing of either the DRIVER, the dyadic code generator, or the actual generation of code?

4. In some electronic mail systems, messages are identified by descriptors that come in one of two flavors. If a message is sent from one user to another, its descriptor consists of an identification of the sender and of the receiver, a pointer to the text and a unique number that is attached by the mailing system. If a message is a response to another message, its descriptor consists of four fields: an identification of the sender, the unique message number, a pointer to the actual text and the message number of the message to which it is responding. We assume the existence of an array of mailboxes whose elements are selected by using the identification of a receiver as subscript value. A message is placed in a mailbox by the statement

   deposit(m, u);

where *m* is a message descriptor and *u* is the user id of a receiver. The mail system provides to its users a procedure SEND which takes a message descriptor as single parameter. Design suitable data structures for both kinds of message descriptors and write programs in both Pascal and Ada for procedure SEND that internally uses procedure DEPOSIT. It is assumed that the DEPOSIT procedure is given.

5. Family relationships are recorded in data objects that indicate a person's father and next sibling. A person who is the youngest in a family has no sibling indication. The record of a male person indicates his wife (if any) and for a female person it indicates her husband and her oldest child (if any). Design a suitable type for *person* in both languages such that variables of type *person* point to objects of type *persondescriptor*. The latter type consists of the fields that hold the family information of a male or female person. Write a program in both languages that records the birth of a son or a daughter and a program for counting the number of brothers and sisters of a given person.

Eleven

Parallel Computations

Topics: parallel programs, concurrent computations, Ada tasks, rendezvous, task entries, accept statements, select statements.

Issues: synchronization, parallel processes, wait state, reactivation.

11.1 Problem Statement

A collection of Producer processes generates jobs to be performed by a collection of Consumer processes. The processes are running concurrently, each at its own speed independent of the others. Job descriptions are written and forwarded as messages. Producer processes put messages into a mailbox and Consumer processes take these messages out of a mailbox. The programming task of this chapter is the design and implementation of mailbox management so that no race conditions arise and so that messages are taken out in FIFO (first in-first out) order. A race condition arises if two concurrent processes operate on a mailbox slot in overlapping time intervals. A typical situation giving rise to a race condition is that of two Producers each trying to write a message in one and the same slot or of a Consumer removing a message from the mailbox that is still being delivered by a Producer.

If a mailbox is full, Producers must wait until there is room in the mailbox. When an empty slot becomes available, it does not matter which Producer gets the first free slot. Similarly, Consumers must wait if a mailbox is empty. It is immaterial which Consumer removes the first message when that arrives.

11.2 Problem Discussion

Solution Requirements

Producer processes apply the operation DEPOSIT to deliver a message to a mailbox, while Consumer processes apply the operation REMOVE to take a message out of a mailbox. The problem statement implies the following requirements:
- concurrent operations must not be applied to the same mailbox slot;
- if a mailbox is full, Producer processes must wait until an empty slot becomes available;
- if a mailbox is empty, Consumer processes must wait until a new message arrives;
- messages must be removed from a mailbox in the same order in which they were deposited.

The first requirement can easily be satisfied by writing procedures DEPOSIT and REMOVE as *critical sections*. A critical section is one of a collection of programs of which only one can be executed at a time. We denote a critical section s for the sake of this discussion by the scheme

>   **begin** critsec(s)
>   code of critical section
>   **end** critsec(s)

The letter *s* denotes a class of critical sections that mutually exclude each other. The implementation of critical sections will be discussed separately for each of the two languages. Taking into account the requirements for handling overflow and underflow, the basic structure of the subprograms DEPOSIT and REMOVE is

>   **procedure** DEPOSIT(msg : message, mb : mailbox)
>   **begin** critsec(d)
>   **while** mb has no empty slots, wait
>   select an empty slot
>   copy(msg into mb[slot])
>   update state of mailbox mb
>   **end** critsec(d)

>   **function** REMOVE(mb : mailbox) **return** message
>   **begin** critsec(r)
>   **while** no messages in mb, wait
>   select a slot that contains a message
>   update state of mailbox mb
>   return selected message
>   **end** critsec(r)

Synchronization

It is essential in this representation that the while loops, which may cause a wait, are included in the critical sections. Suppose the while loop in the last program was placed before the beginning of critsec(r), and suppose there is exactly one message in the mailbox. In this situation the two concurrent Consumer processes both could execute the while loop (because the while loop is not part of the critical section) and both could find that the mailbox is not empty. Both processes would then proceed and execute the critical section (although not simultaneously, of course). The first Consumer to execute the critical section would successfully remove the single message from the mailbox. The second Consumer, having passed the while loop, would enter the critical section believing there is a message in the mailbox while there is none. Obviously, such a situation should not be allowed to occur.

Another problem is that Producers and Consumers may run into a *deadlock*. Deadlock occurs when processes are waiting and prevent each other from proceeding. A deadlock problem would have arisen in our programs if the critical sections for DEPOSIT and REMOVE would have been in the same class. In this case, execution of DEPOSIT would exclude not only executions of other simultaneous deposits, but also of all REMOVE operations. Alternatively, that a Consumer could wait in subprogram REMOVE because the mailbox is empty. Since the Consumer has entered the critical section, no execution of REMOVE or DEPOSIT is possible. This implies that the redeeming Producer that is willing to deposit a message will not be able to do so, because the Consumer waiting for the arrival of that message is precisely the one that makes the delivery impossible by holding the critical section. In order to prevent this occurrence, the subprograms DEPOSIT and REMOVE should be in different critical section classes and should be allowed to execute simultaneously. This is expressed in the subprograms by the use of the two distinct names in the phrases *critsec(d)* and *critsec(r)*.

A Queue Implementation

If DEPOSIT and REMOVE can operate on a mailbox concurrently, it remains to be seen how the requirement is satisfied that simultaneous execution of these operations does not involve the same mailbox slot. We solve this problem as part of implementing the required FIFO scheme which guarantees that messages are removed from a mailbox in the same order in which they were delivered.

The FIFO scheme can easily be implemented by treating a mailbox as a queue (cf. Chapter 7). We introduce the variable *head* to keep track of the first available empty slot and the variable *tail* to keep track of the oldest message in the mailbox. If the capacity of the mailbox is N, the slots can be numbered from 0 to N-1 and the variables *head* and *tail* can both be initialized to zero. When a new message is delivered, it will be placed in mailbox[head **mod** N] and *head* is incremented by one. When a message is removed, it is taken from mailbox[tail **mod** N] and *tail* is incremented by one. Delivery of a message is not permitted when the mailbox is full. This situation is characterized by

full : head - tail = capacity(mailbox)

No message can be taken out when the mailbox is empty. This situation is characterized by

empty : head = tail

Including these refinements, procedures DEPOSIT and REMOVE look like this:

initialize head and tail to zero

procedure DEPOSIT(msg : message, mb : mailbox)
begin critsec(d)
        while mailbox full, wait
        copy(msg into mb[head **mod** capacity(mb)])
        increment(head)
end critsec(d)

function REMOVE(mb : mailbox) **return** message
begin critsec(r)
        while mailbox empty, wait
        copy(mb[tail **mod** capacity(mb)] into temp)
        increment(tail)
        return temp
end critsec(r)

The explicit selection of a slot or message in the mailbox has been omitted because of the trivial choice determined by the variables *head* and *tail*. The wait statements in both subprograms guarantee that

$0 \le$ head - tail $\le$ capacity

is always true.

Race Conditions and FIFO Order

One can easily check that at a time when neither DEPOSIT nor REMOVE is being executed

mesnum = head - tail = #deposit - #remove

where *mesnum* represents the number of messages in the mailbox, #deposit the number of completed DEPOSIT operations and #remove the number of completed REMOVE operations. Emphasizing the adjective *completed*, this relation is also true at a time when some Producer executes DEPOSIT and is in the process of copying its message into mailbox[head **mod** capacity], while some Consumer is executing remove and is in the process of copying a message from mailbox[tail **mod** capacity]. However, when this happens, we can be sure that

head - tail $<$ capacity(mailbox) and head - tail > 0

otherwise the Producer would still be waiting in deposit's while statement and the Consumer would still be waiting in remove's while loop. The fact that in this particular situation

$0 <$ head - tail $<$ capacity(mailbox)

implies that the relation

head $=$ tail **mod** capacity(mailbox)

cannot be true. This in turn implies that the Producer and the Consumer that are simultaneously copying into and from the mailbox cannot be operating on one and the same slot of the mailbox. This proves that the requirement that no race conditions occur is satisfied even though the critical sections for DEPOSIT and REMOVE are not mutually exclusive.

The FIFO order is determined by the particular way in which the variables *head* and *tail* are updated in the subprograms DEPOSIT and REMOVE. Which slot is to be filled next depends on DEPOSIT, but not on REMOVE because the former uses variable *head* and changes its value whereas subprogram REMOVE does not use variable *head* at all. The next message to be selected for removal depends on subprogram REMOVE, but not on subprogram DEPOSIT because the selected slot depends on the value of variable *tail* which is used and updated exclusively by subprogram REMOVE. The subprograms process the mailbox slots in circular order and in the same direction.

Comparison with Chapter 7

The major distinction between the queue operations of Chapter 7 and the management of mailboxes described in this chapter is that in the former underflow or overflow of queues is considered as an exception (and is treated as an error) while here underflow and overflow of mailboxes is prevented by having Producers and Consumers wait if necessary until the state of the mailbox changes. This is a typical distinction between the execution of a single program and a collection of concurrent processes executing in parallel. There is no sense in letting an isolated single program wait, because there is no concurrent program that can get the waiting program started again. For concurrent processes, however, it does make sense to have a process wait, because the processes that run may change the state and enable a waiting process to start again at some later time.

Another distinction is the exclusive execution of mailbox operations. No special facilities are needed if only one program is running at a time, because the execution order of programs results in exclusive execution. Except for the synchronization, the programs for DEPOSIT and REMOVE resemble very closely those for enqueue and dequeue in Chapter 7. There is a slight difference in the use of state variables: in Chapter 7 we used the pair *(head, qsize)* instead of the pair *(head, tail)* and incremented *head* modulo the capacity. Although we could do the same here as in Chapter 7, we have a slight preference for using variable *tail* in order to clarify the point that each of the subprograms DEPOSIT and REMOVE operates on its own state variable independently of the other.

11.3 A Pascal Solution

Pascal has no constructs for process synchronization built into the language. To solve the problem in Pascal, we assume the existence of a data type *semaphore* (invented by E.W. Dijkstra) and the operations P and V on semaphores. Of the many kinds of semaphores that exist we use the so called counting semaphores. Such a semaphore is initialized to some positive integer value. The effect of P(sem) is that the semaphore parameter is decremented (by one) and the effect of V(sem) is the opposite. Execution of P(sem) has a special effect if the value of parameter sem is negative after decrementing. If so, the process executing the P operation is put on a waiting list associated with semaphore sem and is not allowed to proceed with the execution of its program. Alternatively, if the value of the semaphore parameter is non-negative after decrementing, the process executing the P operation is allowed to proceed immediately without waiting. The operation V(sem) has a special effect if the semaphore parameter has a negative value before incrementing. If so, one of the processes on the waiting list is removed and reactivated. The reactivated process has now completed its P operation and is allowed to proceed with executing the program following the call P(sem). If the V operation finds a non-negative semaphore value, the operation V(sem) amounts to no more than "increment(sem)". One can easily see that the scheme

    P(sem);
    critical section code;
    V(sem)

implements a critical section that can be executed by only one process at a time if and only if semaphore sem is initialized to one. Note that the fact that there are n processes on waitinglist(sem) is expressed by the fact that Val(sem) = -n.

Record Implementation of Mailboxes

Following the design of the queue programs in Chapter 7, we declare in Pascal

```
const capacity  = 24; {a completely arbitrary choice}
type  mbindex   = 0 . . (capacity-1);
      mailbox   = record
                        head  : mbindex;
                        tail  : mbindex;
                        body  : array[mbindex] of message;
                        . . . {to be filled in}
                  end;
```

The type *message* remains unspecified here. All we assume is the existence of a Pascal procedure

```
copy(msg1 : message; var msg2 : message)
```

which copies *msg1* into *msg2*. It is clear that such a procedure can easily be written when the representation of messages is determined.

The initialization of mailboxes is crucial. We argued in Chapter 7 that in particular the variables *head* and *tail* must be correctly initialized, while initialization of the mailbox body is unimportant because messages are deposited in the proper slots before they are removed.

```
procedure MBINIT(var mb : mailbox);
begin
      with mb do
            begin
            head  := 0;
            tail  := 0
            end
end;
```

The semaphores for exclusive execution of deposits and removes should be defined as part of a mailbox so that operations on different mailboxes can be applied simultaneously. (Definition of a global semaphore for Consumers would allow for only one single DEPOSIT operation at a time on the total collection of all existing mailboxes.) The extended definition of mailboxes is:

```
type mailbox = record
                    head  : mbindex;
                    tail  : mbindex;
                    body  : array[mbindex] of message;
                    dsem  : semaphore;
                    rsem  : semaphore
               end;
```

The semaphores must both be initialized to one so that the first Producer and the first Consumer can start executing DEPOSIT and REMOVE respectively. Assuming a semaphore is a record consisting of a value field and a waiting list, the mailbox initialization procedure must be extended with the assignment statements

> dsem.val := 1;
> rsem.val := 1

The remaining synchronization problem is that of overflow and underflow expressed by the while statements in the problem discussion. The obvious way to implement a potential wait is by substituting a P operation for these while statements. To achieve the desired result, we need two additional semaphores, one for stopping Producers when the mailbox is full and one for stopping Consumers when the mailbox is empty. In terms of production, one might say that Producers produce messages and Consumers produce empty slots. In terms of consumption, Producers consume empty slots and Consumers messages. Therefore, we introduce the semaphores *mesnum* and *slotnum*, respectively counting the number of messages and the number of empty slots.

The while statement in procedure DEPOSIT is replaced by P(slotnum) and the while statement in procedure REMOVE by P(mesnum). If a Producer must wait in P(slotnum), reactivation must come from a Consumer creating an empty slot by removing a message. Likewise, if a Consumer must wait in P(mesnum) because of an empty mailbox, reactivation must come from a Producer depositing a message in the mailbox. Thus, P(slotnum) is performed in deposit to prevent overflow, while V(slotnum) is performed in REMOVE when an empty slot becomes available. Likewise, P(mesnum) is performed in REMOVE to prevent underflow, while V(mesnum) is performed in deposit when a new message has been delivered. These two additional semaphores must also be included in the type definition of *mailbox*, because the number of messages and empty slots must be separately counted for each mailbox. The initialization procedure must be extended with two assignment statements that initialize semaphores *mesnum* and *slotnum* respectively to zero and capacity(mailbox), assuming that a mailbox is initially empty.

Basic Mailbox Operations

Instead of incrementing both variables *head* and *tail* and using these values modulo the mailbox capacity as indices, the increment might as well be computed modulo the mailbox capacity. This guarantees that the value of both variables is in the range [0 . . (capacity-1)]. It is clear that this change does not alter the reasoning about the absence of race conditions. With this little modification in mind the subprogram bodies are:

DEPOSIT: REMOVE:

```
with mb do                          with mb do
   begin                               begin
   P(dsem) ;                           P(rsem);
   P(slotnum) ;                        P(mesnum);
   copy(msg, body[head]) ;             copy(body[tail], msg);
   head := (head + 1) mod capacity ;   tail := (tail + 1) mod capacity;
   V(mesnum) ;                         V(slotnum);
   V(dsem)                             V(rsem)
   end                                 end
```

Note that the relation

$$slotnum + mesnum = capacity$$

is true when no execution of DEPOSIT or REMOVE is in progress, but not necessarily when one or both subprograms are being executed. By executing P(slotnum) the number of empty slots is decremented before the slot is actually used. This is done to make sure that there will be an empty slot available and also to make sure that a process coming along next will find the number of slots already decreased. Thus, the relation is temporarily invalid after execution of P(slotnum), but is restored when *mesnum* is increased in V(mesnum). Likewise, the relation is invalid between the execution of P(mesnum) and V(slotnum) in subprogram REMOVE. These intermediate states of the mailbox reflect the action of putting a message into a slot and of extracting one from a slot.

11.4 An Ada Solution

The solution in Ada is very different from that in Pascal, primarily because Ada contains powerful constructs for implementing concurrency and synchronization. The basic construct for concurrent processes is the Ada *task*. A task resembles an Ada package in that it consists of a visible part and a separate implementation body. However, instead of exporting types, constants, variables, procedures and functions, a task exports only *task entries* that correspond most closely to procedures with in, out or in-out parameters. Entries are not like functions, because entries can not return a value.

Task Objects and Task Types

A unique mailbox for messages of a given type, say type *message*, can be implemented by a task. The visible part of the mailbox task exports two entries, one for DEPOSIT and one for REMOVE.

```
task Mailbox is
    entry DEPOSIT(msg : in message);
    entry REMOVE(msg : out message);
end Mailbox;
```

If *x* and *y* are variables of type *message*, a user can operate on the mailbox by statements such as

DEPOSIT(x) ; REMOVE(y) ; . . .

At this point, the Pascal solution to the Producer-Consumer problem is more general than the Ada solution, because in Pascal we were able to declare mailboxes as a record type instead of as a unique object. The Pascal program leaves room for the declaration of an arbitrary number of mailboxes that have the same structure and that can be manipulated in the same manner by applying the procedures DEPOSIT and REMOVE.

A similar generality can be obtained in Ada by declaring a task type instead of a task. A task type is a template for a task just as a data type is a template for a data object. Specific instances of a task type are created by task variable declarations, analogous to data variable declarations (ARM 9.2.2, 9-4).

```
task type TT is
    entry P( . . . );
    entry Q( . . . );
end TT;

x, y : TT;
```

Variables *x* and *y* are two separate tasks whose structure is defined by type TT. It makes no sense to call TT.P(. . .) or TT.Q(. . .), because TT is not a task (but a task template). Entry calls that do make sense are x.P(. . .), x.Q(. . .), y.P(. . .) and y.Q(. . .), because *x* and *y* are tasks. Tasks *x* and *y* have the same structure, but run independently. Each has its own set of state variables and its own locus of control. Although their structures are the same, it is unlikely that at any given time their states will be the same.

To get the same effect as in the Pascal programs, we declare *mailbox* as a task type.

```
task type Mailbox is
    entry DEPOSIT (msg : in message);
    entry REMOVE (msg : out message);
end Mailbox;
```

The task type declaration can be used to declare an arbitrary number of mailboxes. We may declare for instance

A, B : Mailbox;

and use these mailboxes for storing and retrieving messages by statements such as

```
A.DEPOSIT(x);
B.REMOVE(x);
B.DEPOSIT(y);  . . .
```

The declaration of A and B creates two independent instances of task type Mailbox, each essentially having its own copy of the entries DEPOSIT and REMOVE. These copies are distinguished from one another by prefixing their application with the name of the task object to which the operation is applied.

Although this version is equivalent to the Pascal solution for mailboxes, both solutions are fairly rigid in being defined only for a specific type of message and in creating mailboxes all of the same size. Such restrictions cannot be removed from Pascal programs, but Ada is much more flexible in that regard. Further on in this chapter we will generalize the mailbox concept to one that allows mailboxes of various sizes and that can be defined for arbitrary types of messages. Before discussing these generalizations, we first complete the solution equivalent to the Pascal programs and look at the implementation of task type Mailbox.

Task Bodies

A task body implements the task entries that are visible to the user. The implementation itself is hidden from the user in the same manner as in a package body. The major distinction between package bodies and task bodies is that the latter describe the necessary synchronization of the implemented entries whereas the former contain no synchronization information. Thus, a task body not only defines the implementation of its entries, but also specifies the order of execution for these entries.

The first and most important characteristic of task bodies is that only one entry can be executed at a time. This makes every entry in a task behave like a critical section with respect to itself and to all other entries of the task in which it is defined. As a consequence, it would not be possible to place subprograms DEPOSIT and REMOVE into two different classes of critical sections (as we did for the Pascal programs) if these subprograms are included as entries of a single task (or task type). If one wants the concurrent execution of DEPOSIT and REMOVE, it will be necessary to define these subprograms as entries of two separate tasks.

The basic language constructs for defining the order of execution are sequencing and selection. Sequencing allows a programmer to specify that entries E_1 and E_2 must be executed in a particular order. Selection allows a programmer to specify that the next entry to be executed may be one of a collection of entries.

Accept Statements

The basic structure of an entry implementation is

accept E(formal parameters) **do** body of E **end** E;

The entry specification between the keywords **accept** and **do** is a replication of the entry specification in the visible part. Sequencing is specified by writing a succession of **accept** statements. For instance,

accept E_1(formal parameters) **do** body of E_1 **end** E_1;
accept E_2(formal parameters) **do** body of E_2 **end** E_2;
accept E_3(formal parameters) **do** body of E_3 **end** E_3;

specifies that the first entry to be executed is E_1, which can be followed by the execution of no other entry than E_2, which in turn is followed by an execution of E_3.

One often finds a sequence of accept statements embedded in a loop so that it can be processed repeatedly. For instance,

while Boolexpr **loop**
    accept E_1(. . .) **do** . . . **end** E_1;
    accept E_2(. . .) **do** . . . **end** E_2;
    accept E_3(. . .) **do** . . . **end** E_3;
end loop;

specifies that the sequence E_1, E_2, E_3, E_1, E_2, E_3, . . . is executed as long as the Boolexpr is true after performing E_3.

Applied to our example, an implementation such as

loop
    accept DEPOSIT (msg : **in** message) **do** . . . **end** DEPOSIT;
    accept REMOVE (msg : **out** message) **do** . . . **end** REMOVE;
end loop;

specifies that DEPOSIT and REMOVE are executed alternatingly. Every DEPOSIT is followed by a REMOVE and every execution of REMOVE is followed by a DEPOSIT. This works fine for a mailbox consisting of a single slot, but not for mailboxes with more than one slot, because the reason for having more than one slot is to allow for some fluctuation in the number of DEPOSIT and REMOVE operations.

Before discussing the Ada construct that provides the desired flexibility of choosing which entry to execute next, it is worth mentioning that a task may contain private code of its own in between accept statements. This code is executed in the normal sequence of instructions, after the preceding accept statement and before the subsequent accept statement.

Select Statements

A **select** statement allows for a choice between entries. The format is

select A_1; B_1; . . . **or** A_2; B_2; . . . **or** . . . **end select**;

where A_1, A_2, . . . are accept statements as described above and B_1, B_2, . . . are accept statements, select statements or private statements that the task executes in between accept statements. For our example we write

```
loop
      select
            accept DEPOSIT(msg : in message) do  . . .  end DEPOSIT;
      or
            accept REMOVE(msg : out message) do  . . .  end REMOVE;
      end select;
end loop;
```

The effect of this statement is that either DEPOSIT or REMOVE is executed so that DEPOSIT and REMOVE behave as critical sections with respect to one another.

This implementation is closer to what we really want. The only thing missing is the control of underflow and overflow: it should not be possible to execute DEPOSIT when the mailbox is full or REMOVE when the mailbox is empty. These restrictions can be implemented by qualified accept statements. Qualified accept statements may be used in select statements and have the form

when Boolexpr $=>$ **accept** Entry(. . .) **do** . . . **end** Entry;

The Boolexpr of the when clause is called the *guard* of the accept statement. Only those entries of a select statement are eligible for execution whose guards are true. Guards may depend on local variables, but not on entry parameters.

A mailbox task maintains its state in some local variables. Following the design of the mailbox type in Pascal, *box* is an array of *capacity* elements numbered from 0 through (capacity-1), *head* indicates the first empty slot and *tail* the oldest message. If we introduce a counter *mesnum* for the number of messages in a mailbox, we can modify the select statement to include the necessary guards:

```
loop
      select
            when mesnum < capacity =>
            accept DEPOSIT(msg : in message) do  . . .  end DEPOSIT;
      or
            when mesnum > 0 =>
            accept REMOVE(msg : out message) do  . . .  end REMOVE;
      end select;
end loop;
```

As long as the relation

$$0 < \text{mesnum} < \text{capacity}$$

is true, either one of the two entries may be selected. But when mesnum = 0, DEPOSIT is eligible, while REMOVE is not. Alternatively, when mesnum = capacity, DEPOSIT is not eligible, but REMOVE is. Note that we have guaranteed that at least one guard is always true. If no alternative is selectable, the select statement is in error. An else clause as the last alternative can always guarantee that a selectable alternative exists.

Task Rendezvous

Suppose several concurrent Ada tasks A, B, C, . . . , call the entries DEPOSIT and REMOVE of a Mailbox task M.The event caused by these tasks is called a *rendezvous* (which essentially means a task encounter). Suppose task A calls entry DEPOSIT. It is possible that task M is still busy executing either DEPOSIT or REMOVE on behalf of another task. If so, task A must wait until task M is done and control in M returns to the top of the loop. At that time M may select entry DEPOSIT and execute it on behalf of task A.When the execution is completed, task A may continue and control in M returns to the top of the loop again. If there is no task calling either DEPOSIT or REMOVE, task M waits at the beginning of the select statement until that situation changes. Task M is reactivated and selects an entry as soon as one of the other tasks calls one of M's entries. So, the essential characteristic of a rendezvous is the fact that the calling task and the called task are coupled for the duration of the execution of an entry. After completion of the execution caller and callee both go their own way independent of one another.

Ada programs need no semaphores, nor does a user have to write P and V operations to achieve the necessary synchronization. The combination of accept statements, select statements and guards provides a convenient set of language constructs to express the order of execution (and restrictions on the execution) of task entries. The presentation in this chapter is deliberately limited to the major task concepts. More complicated forms of task bodies that include nested accept statements or alternative accept statements for a single entry are discussed in subsequent chapters. In general, we recommend that programmers stick to simple structures for task bodies consisting of accept and select statements with the necessary guards, interspersed with the task's own statements in between accept statements. In our particular example, we can implement the accept bodies in one of two ways: either by including the action of updating variable *mesnum* in the accept bodies, or by updating this variable in between the accept statements. The two alternative implementations are:

```
select
  when mesnum < capacity = >
  accept DEPOSIT(m: in message) do
    box(head) : = m;
    mesnum : = mesnum + 1;
    head : = (head + 1) mod capacity;
  end DEPOSIT;
or
  when mesnum > 0 = >
  accept REMOVE(m: out message) do
    m : = box(tail);
    mesnum : = mesnum-1;
    tail : = (tail + 1) mod capacity;
  end REMOVE;
end select;
```

```
select
  when mesnum < capacity = >
  accept DEPOSIT(m: in message) do
    box(head) : = m;
  end DEPOSIT;
  mesnum : = mesnum-1;
  head : = (head + 1) mod capacity;
or
  when mesnum > 0 = >
  accept REMOVE(m: out message) do
    m : = box(tail);
  end REMOVE;
  mesnum : = mesnum-1;
  tail : = (tail + 1) mod capacity;
end select;
```

In the lefthand version the statements for updating the mailbox state variables are included in the accept bodies, in the righthand version these statements are placed outside of the accept bodies. In this particular example there is no great difference between the two versions. The righthand version has the slight advantage of allowing for a higher degree of concurrency: the calling task on whose behalf the mailbox manager executes one of the entries is reactivated as soon as the execution of the entry is completed. This implies for the righthand version that the caller is already proceeding when the mailbox manager updates the mailbox status variables, while in the lefthand version the caller is not reactivated until all the updating is completed. In case the statements outside of accept statements are fairly elaborate or contain calls on other tasks, the higher degree of concurrency provided by the righthand version is desirable.

Mailboxes of Various Size and Message Type

In preceding chapters we have seen examples of lifting type and size restrictions by the use of generic packages (cf. Section 6.4). It seems that one should be able to generalize the original mailbox object in a similar manner and write

```
generic type message is private;
         capacity : in NATURAL : = 24;
task Mailbox is                           -- this is not legal Ada

        . . .
end Mailbox;
```

Mailboxes would then be created by instantiating this task. Unfortunately, the similarity between tasks and packages does not go as far as suggested here. Generic units can be written for packages and subprograms, but not for types or tasks (ARM 12.1, 12-1).

Although the restriction is a little awkward, it can easily be circumvented by embedding the task definition in a generic package. This idea leads to the declaration

```
generic type message is private
        capacity : in NATURAL : = 24;   -- default initialization
package Mailbox is
    task Manager is
        entry DEPOSIT(msg : in message);
        entry REMOVE(msg : out message);
    end Manager;
end Mailbox;
```

Mailboxes are now created by instantiating the generic Mailbox package in declarations such as

```
package LMB is new Mailbox(linemsg);
package RMB is new Mailbox(FLOAT, 13);
```

Mailbox LMB has the default capacity of 24 slots and can handle messages of type *linemsg*; Mailbox RMB has 13 slots and handles real numbers. If *u* is a variable of type *linemsg* and *x* is a FLOAT variable, the mailboxes can be used in statements such as

```
LMB.Manager.DEPOSIT(u); RMB.Manager.REMOVE(x);
```

These names can be shortened by including a use clause or by renaming (cf. Chapters 3 and 5).

Note that the visible part of package Mailbox contains a task declaration and not a task type declaration. There is no need for a task type because of the fact that the package is generic. Each time the package is instantiated, a new mailbox is created which includes the creation of its own manager. So, the ability to create an arbitrary number of mailboxes is already achieved by the generic nature of the mailbox package. We saw in Chapter 7 that generic packages essentially implement limited private objects for which no other operations are defined than the ones included in the definition of that object. Default operations such as assignment or array access are not applicable to limited private objects or packages.)

Hidden Tasks

Another variation on the generalized mailbox is obtained by hiding the manager task in the body of the mailbox package. In that case the visible part does not export entries, but ordinary procedures. If we call these procedures SEND and RECEIVE, the structure of the generic mailbox package is

```
generic type message is private;
        capacity : in NATURAL := 24;
package Mailbox is
        procedure SEND     (msg : in message);
        procedure RECEIVE (msg : out message);
end Mailbox;
```

The implementation of the procedures SEND and RECEIVE is included in the body of the mailbox package together with a complete declaration of the Manager task (both its visible part and its body). The structure of the package body is then

```
package body Mailbox is
        <visible part of Manager task>
        <implementation of procedure send>
        <implementation of procedure receive>
        <implementation body of Manager task>
end Mailbox;
```

The implementation of procedures SEND and RECEIVE is just a call to the entries of the Manager task. For instance,

```
procedure SEND(msg : in msg) is
begin
        Manager.DEPOSIT(msg);
end SEND;
```

The Manager task body contains the declarations of the mailbox state variables *head*, *tail* and *mesnum*, the mailbox object and the necessary select and accept statements as described earlier in this chapter.

The user of this version of mailboxes is not aware of the synchronization and the task communication defined by the manager. User programs are entirely written in terms of the visible part of the generic mailbox package. Thus, after declaring

```
package LMB is new Mailbox(linemsg);
package RMB is new Mailbox(REAL, 13);
```

messages are stored into and retrieved from these mailboxes by statements such as

```
LMB.SEND(u);  RMB.SEND(3.14);  LMB.RECEIVE(u);  . . .
```

where *u* is a variable of type *linemsg*. Note the additional advantage of losing one extra level of naming which is obtained by hiding the manager task in the mailbox package body.

11.5 The Complete Programs

The Pascal Program

```
const  capacity  = 24;     {a completely arbitrary choice}
type   mbindex   = 0 . . (capacity-1);
       mailbox   = record
                         head      : mbindex;
                         tail      : mbindex;
                         dsem      : semaphore;
                         rsem      : semaphore;
                         mesnum    : semaphore;
                         slotnum   : semaphore;
                         body      : array[mbindex] of message
                   end;

procedure MBINIT(var mb : mailbox);
begin
       with mb do
              begin
              head := 0;
              tail := 0;
              dsem.val := 1;
              rsem.val := 1;
              mesnum.val := 0;
              slotnum.val := capacity
              end
end;
```

```
procedure DEPOSIT                          procedure REMOVE
    (m: message; var mb: mailbox);             (var m: message; var mb: mailbox);
begin                                      begin
    with mb do                                 with mb do
       begin                                     begin
       P(dsem);                                  P(rsem);
       P(slotnum);                               P(mesnum);
       copy(m, body[head]);                      copy(body[tail], m);
       head := (head + 1) mod capacity;          tail := (tail + 1) mod capacity;
       V(mesnum);                                V(slotnum);
       V(dsem)                                   V(rsem)
       end                                       end
end;                                       end;
```

The Ada Task Type Version

task type Mailbox **is**

      entry DEPOSIT(msg : **in** message);
      entry REMOVE(msg : **out** message);

end Mailbox;

task body Mailbox **is**

      capacity : **constant** := 24;
      subtype slotindex **is** INTEGER **range** 0 . . (capacity - 1);
      head, tail : slotindex := 0;
      mesnum : INTEGER **range** 0 . . capacity := 0;
      box : **array**(slotindex) **of** message;

begin
    loop
        select
            when mesnum < capacity =>
            accept DEPOSIT(msg : **in** message) **do**
                box(head) := msg;
                head := (head + 1) **mod** capacity;
                mesnum := mesnum + 1;
            end DEPOSIT;
        or
            when mesnum > 0 =>
            accept REMOVE(msg : **out** message) **do**
                msg := box(tail);
                tail := (tail + 1) **mod** capacity;
                mesnum := mesnum - 1;
            end REMOVE;
        end select;
    end loop;

end Mailbox;

For this program to be valid Ada, we assume that it is part of a scope in which type *message* is defined.

The Ada Hidden Task Version

```
generic type message is private;
          capacity : in NATURAL := 24;
package Mailbox is

          procedure SEND      (msg : in message);
          procedure RECEIVE (msg : out message);

end Mailbox;


package body Mailbox is

          task Manager is
                  entry DEPOSIT(msg : in message);
                  entry REMOVE(msg : out message);
          end Manager;

          procedure SEND(msg : in message) is
          begin
                  Manager.DEPOSIT(msg);
          end SEND;

          procedure RECEIVE(msg : out message) is
          begin
                  Manager.REMOVE(msg);
          end RECEIVE;

          task body Manager is

                  -- identical to body of preceding program,
                  -- after omitting the first line defining capacity

          end Manager;

end Mailbox;
```

Since type *message* is here a generic parameter, there is no need to assume that this package is defined in a scope that defines that type.

11.6 Reminders

1. Pascal has no built-in support for concurrent processes. The Ada language provides the concept of tasks that run independently and concurrently.

2. Synchronization of concurrent processes can be implemented by extending Pascal with P and V operations on semaphores. In Ada, synchronization is accomplished by the rendezvous mechanism of Ada tasks.

3. A critical section is a piece of program belonging to a class of program sections of which only one can be executed at a time. In Pascal critical sections can be constructed with P and V operations. In Ada all entries of tasks are by definition implemented as critical sections.

4. Signalling and waiting for events can be implemented in Pascal by P and V operations. In Ada, no explicit signal is needed. A task calling the entry of a server task waits until a rendez-vous has taken place and continues when the requested entry has been executed.

5. The order of execution for task entries is determined by the control structure of a task body. Sequential execution is specified by successive accept statements, selective execution by select statements.

6. An accept statement that is part of a select statement may be guarded by a condition that determines the eligibility of that accept statement at each specific moment.

7. The Boolean expression representing a guard may use constants and variables visible in the scope of the task body. It cannot use parameters passed to it by entry calls.

8. A task type is a template for a task of which many instances can be created. It plays the same role for creating task objects as data types do for creating data objects.

9. In Pascal one has to write different types and procedures for every mailbox (or queue) that has a specific size and handles a particular message type. In Ada one can write a generic package that handles mailboxes of all sizes and of different message types.

10. A task can be completely hidden in the body of a package so that the synchronization of concurrent operations on common data objects remains invisible to the user.

11.7 Problems

1. In the problem discussion it was argued that the while wait statement should be included in the critical sections of DEPOSIT and REMOVE or else a process might get incorrect information about the state of the mailbox. Investigate whether or not the state information may also be erroneous if the order of the statements P(dsem) and P(slotnum) is reversed. Argue that one can reverse the order of the V operations in both programs for DEPOSIT and REMOVE.

2. A fixed set of N Producer processes put messages in a mailbox of N slots. Process P_i always places its messages in the ith slot. A single Consumer process removes the messages in Round Robin fashion (which means, if the mailbox is viewed as a circular buffer, the Consumer process goes around taking messages out of non-empty slots moving in a fixed direction, either clockwise or counterclockwise.) A Producer should not overwrite its own messages and the Consumer should not try to remove a message before it has been delivered. Write Pascal and Ada programs for a Producer process and for the Consumer process.

3. In the Ada programs a mailbox is represented first as a task type and then as a generic package. A third alternative is a representation as explicit type mailbox. Assuming we wish to declare mailboxes of various sizes for a specific type of message, a suitable package declaration is

    package MBMANAGEMENT **is**

    type mailbox(size : **in** NATURAL := 18) **is limited private**;

    procedure DEPOSIT(m : **in** msg; mb : **in out** mailbox);
    procedure REMOVE(m : **out** msg; mb : **in out** mailbox);

    private

    task type MBmanager **is**
        entry SEND(m : **in** msg; mb : **in out** mailbox);
        entry RECEIVE(m : **out** msg; mb : **in out** mailbox);
    end manager;

    type mailbox(size : **in** NATURAL := 18) **is**
    record
        head, tail : INTEGER **range** 0 . . (size - 1) := 0;
        manager : MBmanager;
        box : **array**(0 . . (size - 1)) **of** message;
    end record;

    end MBMANAGEMENT;

The mailbox type is marked limited private in order to disable assignments to mailboxes. It is necessary to include the task type in the private part because of the use of this type in the record field *manager* and Ada's requirement that declarations precede usage. The idea of including an instance of the task type as a record field in type mailbox is that every mailbox when it is created will get its own task that manages its mailbox operations. Write the package body for MBMANAGEMENT. Watch out when writing the guards of send and receive in the task body for MBmanager.

4. Suppose all mailboxes we are interested in consist of only one single message slot. Write the Pascal and Ada programs for many Producer and many Consumer processes communicating via a one slot mailbox. Check whether your programs are completely different from the many slot mailbox solution or just special cases of the programs presented in this chapter.

5. In very special cases it may be desirable to treat the messages of a mailbox in Last-in First-out (LIFO) order. (This may be so if deactivating and reactivating a process is fairly costly in terms of space or time and if there is a chance to keep a Producer process active if its message is processed quickly.) Write the Pascal and Ada programs for multi-slot mailbox management applying the LIFO discipline. Indicate the simplifications with respect to the programs that use the FIFO scheduling rule.

Twelve

Classical Scheduling Problems

Topics: task types, entry attributes, guarded accept statements, the else
            alternative, nested accept statements, initializing task entries,
            procedural form of entries.

Issues: resource scheduling, cooperating processes, processor configuration
            independence, task parameterization.

12.1 Problem Statement

When a number of concurrent processes share resources, a number of problems
arise about scheduling the use of these resources. While trying to maximize
concurrency, considerations such as *fairness* in scheduling arise. Does each
process have an equal chance at using a particular resource or does the scheduling
algorithm discriminate against certain processes? Is it possible for a process to
starve, while waiting for a particular resource because the other processes are
scheduled instead? Is it possible for *deadlock* to develop because of contentive
use of resources by several processes?

A number of programming problems have become classics in the field of
concurrent computation and are as ubiquitous here as stacks in abstraction
discussions. Among these are the following two problems.
- The Readers/Writers problem.
- The Dining Philosophers problem.

The Readers/Writers problem is concerned with the disciplined access to a
shared database and the strategies that allow safe access, and that maintain
database consistencies despite seemingly concurrent modifications. The primary
scheduling concern here is that of fairness between reading processes, where
concurrency can be maximized, and writing processes which must have exclusive

299

access to the database in order to maintain consistency. A secondary concern is that of starvation: insuring that readers do not starve writers or that writers do starve readers.

The Dining Philosophers problem is concerned with the sharing of resources such that concurrency is maximized while process starvation and deadlock are prevented. The philosophers must share resources (the eating utensils) or they will (literally) starve. Solutions must guarantee that no two philosophers can collude and starve a third and that deadlock, where no philosopher can eat, will not occur.

12.2 The Readers/Writers Problem

An arbitrary number of processes share a database. At any given point, a number of processes may wish to read the database and some may wish to modify it. In order to maintain the consistency of the database, only one modifying process is allowed access to the database and no readers are allowed (again, for reasons of consistency). Reading the database, on the other hand, can be performed safely by any number of processes.

The tension in the scheduling of readers and writers exists between the exclusivity required by the writers and the concurrency possible by the readers. In maximizing the concurrency of readers, the scheduler should not starve the writers. On the other hand, the desire for a database reflecting the most current information should not give rise to a scheduler that starves the readers. The scheduler should provide some sense of fairness.

For both languages, we shall program the strategy of C.A. R.Hoare in "Monitors: An Operating Systems Structuring Concept," **Communications of the ACM,** 17:10, October 1974 (on page 556): ". . . a new reader should not be permitted to start if there is a writer waiting. Similarly, to avoid the danger of indefinite exclusion of readers, all readers waiting at the end of a write should have priority over the next writer." For the Ada discussion, we shall also present an alternative strategy -- first come, first serve -- to further the discussion of Ada's capabilities.

State Representation in Pascal

The Pascal solution is constructed using a number of counting variables and semaphores (cf. Chapter 11). The latter provide the wait and signalling mechanisms as well as exclusive access to the counting variables.

The variable *nrreaders* keeps track of the readers currently accessing the database. Variable *waitwrite* maintains the count of processes wishing to modify the database; it may also indicate that one process has current access to the database and *waitwrite* - 1 processes are waiting for access. Variable *waitread* specifies the number of processes waiting to gain reading access as soon as the current modification completes.

> **var**   nrreaders   : integer;
>   waitwrite   : integer;
>   waitread   : integer;

We assume that in the initial state no reading or writing is in progress. This is reflected in the state variables by initializing all three to zero.

In addition to the counting variables, we need three semaphores: *mutex*, *oktoread* and *oktowrite*. The *mutex* semaphore is used as a mutual exclusion semaphore for the operations on the three counters. The semaphores *oktoread* and *oktowrite* are used as signals to indicate that conditions have changed and either reading or writing may take place. If a writer has completed its modification, it will signal the processes waiting to read that it is *oktoread*. Or, if no processes are waiting to read, the writer signals the next writer (if any) that it is *oktowrite*.

> **var**   mutex : semaphore;
>   oktoread   : semaphore;
>   oktowrite   : semaphore;

A semaphore is automatically initialized to zero when it is declared. Since semaphore *mutex* must start with value one (so that the first process can enter the critical section protected by *mutex*), we include a V operation on *mutex* in the initialization procedure.

> **procedure** initialize;
> **begin**
>   nrreaders   : = 0;
>   waitread   : = 0;
>   waitwrite : = 0;
>   V (mutex)
> **end**;

Readers

Readers gain access to the database by performing a STARTREAD operation and signal their access completion by a STOPREAD operation. The main requirement of readers is that they may not proceed if writing is in progress or if a writer is waiting for access. If this is the case, *waitwrite* will be non-zero and *waitread* will be incremented. The process must then wait until it is safe to proceed. If the operation can proceed, the operation increments the current reader count *nrreaders*.

```
procedure STARTREAD;
begin
        P(mutex);
        if waitwrite > 0
        then    begin
                waitread : =  waitread  +  1;
                V (mutex);
                P (oktoread)
                end
        else    begin
                nrreaders : =  nrreaders  +  1;
                V (mutex)
                end
    end;
```

Note that the operation releases the semaphore *mutex* before it waits on the *oktoread* signal. Once this signal is received, the operation completes without entering the critical section again and without updating the state variables. We will see shortly how the state variables are updated when a reader must wait for a writer.

The STOPREAD operation decrements the current reader count and signals a waiting writer process (if any) after all readers have completed reading the database.

```
procedure STOPREAD;
begin
        P (mutex);
        nrreaders : =  nrreaders - 1;
        if nrreaders = 0 and waitwrite > 0 then  V (oktowrite);
        V (mutex)
    end;
```

Writers

The STARTWRITE operation is similar to STARTREAD. The writer can proceed if there are no readers and no one is writing. If there are readers or if there is a writer, then the process wanting to write must wait until it receives a signal that it can safely proceed.

The STOPWRITE operation is the most complicated of the four. The *waitwrite* count is decremented to indicate that the writing process has completed. Then, if there are readers waiting, the leaving writer signals all of them to go ahead. If no readers are waiting, but a writer is waiting, then that writer is signalled to go ahead.

```
    procedure STARTWRITE;
    begin
        P (mutex);
        waitwrite : =  waitwrite +  1;
        if nrreaders > 0 or waitwrite > 1 then
                begin
                    V (mutex);  P (oktowrite)
                end
        else V (mutex)
    end;

    procedure STOPWRITE;
    begin
        P (mutex);
        waitwrite : =  waitwrite -1;
        if waitread > 0 then
                for i = 1 to waitread do
                        begin
                        V (oktoread);
                        nrreaders : =  nrreaders +  1;
                        waitread : =  waitread - 1
                        end
        else if waitwrite > 0 then V (oktowrite);
        V (mutex)
    end;
```

Note that the current readers count is incremented here rather than in STARTREAD. Putting the increment here in STOPWRITE seems somewhat unnatural, because one would expect readers to update variable *nrreaders* in STARTREAD, and not a writer that is done writing. Let us consider, however, what may go wrong if *nrreaders* is incremented in STARTREAD instead of in STOPWRITE when a writer completes writing and readers are waiting. In that arrangement, a reader goes through the following steps:

```
    . . .
    P (oktoread);        {wait until reading is permitted}
    . . .                {problem can occur here}
    P (mutex);           {enter critical section}
    nrreaders : =  nrreaders +  1;
    V (mutex)            {leave critical section}
```

After having received the *oktoread* signal, the reader must enter the critical section guarded by semaphore *mutex* in order to increment the reader count. It is at the point between the two P operations that the problem occurs. All the waiting readers have received the signal that they can go ahead, but the reader count is still zero. If in the meantime a writer process performs a STARTWRITE, it can gain access to *mutex* before the first awakened reader and begin writing. It is possible, therefore, for reading and writing to occur simultaneously. This situation should not be allowed to occur. Indeed, the problem is avoided by incrementing *nrreaders* in STOPWRITE, because then the next process wanting to write will find the number of readers already incremented when it calls STARTWRITE.

State Representation in Ada

Ada's tasking facility (entries and accept statements in particular) provides a natural mechanism for implementing Hoare's readers/writers strategy. First, the entry mechanism, with its implicit queueing, provides a language-supplied means of keeping track of readers and writers. Second, the accept statement provides a means of allowing readers and writers to proceed. We will exploit these facilities in constructing the scheduling of readers and writers.

There are several ways in which a scheduling mechanism for readers and writers can be designed in Ada. First, we can supply a package with procedural interfaces to allow the user to gain access to the database.

```
package RWScheduler is
        procedure STARTREAD;
        procedure STOPREAD;
        procedure STARTWRITE;
        procedure STOPWRITE;
end RWScheduler;
```

However, since we may have several databases as resources, this does not provide fine enough control over database management. This can be solved by making the package generic and instantiating as many schedulers as are needed. The means of associating the scheduler with the resource (by convention), however, is not quite as elegant as we would like it to be.

Alternatively, we can define the scheduler as a task type. Because objects can be declared to be of task types, we can declare the scheduler to be a part of the database itself. This method provides a very strong association between the scheduler and the resource. In fact, we can then carefully define the grain of control over the database by associating schedulers with the desired partitions of the database.

```
task type RWScheduler is
        entry STARTREAD;
        entry STOPREAD;
        entry STARTWRITE;
        entry STOPWRITE;
end RWScheduler;
```

Entries and Accept Statements

The strategy calls for preventing readers from gaining access to the database as soon as a writer wishes to modify it. Furthermore, readers waiting to access the database should get access before the next writer is scheduled. The implementation of these rules require the use of counters similar to those in the Pascal program. However, Ada provides some language support for our problem by giving the programmer access to the length of the waiting queues attached to task entries. Each task entry possess an attribute COUNT that represents the current length of the waiting queue of that entry (ARM 9.9, 9-14). COUNT supplies exactly the information that we desire: it can give us the number of readers waiting on an entry WAITREAD and the number of writers waiting on entry WAITWRITE. At least one reader is waiting to gain access to the database if

> STARTREAD'COUNT $>$ 0.

Attributes can be used in the guards of accept statements to control whether or not an accept statement is eligible for execution. Use of the guards to accept statements can cause problems if the programmer does not choose them with care. At least one selection alternative must be open or the exception SELECT_ERROR will be raised (ARM 9.7.1, 9-10). This can be avoided by including an else clause as the last alternative, thereby guaranteeing that one option, at least, is always open. However, with careful selection of Boolean conditions the else clause can be safely omitted.

The two primary alternatives to be considered are whether to allow a read to start or whether to allow a write to start. As we have noted, a read can always start when there are no writers waiting.

> **when** STARTWRITE'COUNT $=$ 0 $=>$
> **accept** STARTREAD **do**
>   nrreaders := nrreaders + 1;
> **end** STARTREAD;

Note that we maintain a count of the number of readers accessing the database. We used this information to determine when to allow a writer access for modifications. We must, of course, allow the reader to indicate that access is no longer needed to the resource. This introduces a second selection alternative:

> **accept** STOPREAD **do** nrreaders := nrreaders - 1; **end** STOPREAD;

Since unguarded alternatives are always open, no else clause is needed.

Whether to allow a writer access to the resource, depends on the number of readers currently using it. Once a writer issues a call to the entry STARTWRITE, readers cannot gain access to the resource. As soon as the number of readers using the resource is zero, the writer can proceed.

> **when** nrreaders $=$ 0 $=>$ **accept** STARTWRITE;

A writer has now gained access to the resources and no other process is to be allowed access. This is assured by waiting for the writer to signal completion on the entry STOPWRITE.

>   **accept** STOPWRITE;

One might think that the strict sequencing of writers can be implemented by a construct of nested accept statements:

>   **when** nrreaders = 0 =>
>   **accept** STARTWRITE **do accept** STOPWRITE; **end** STARTWRITE;

However, the semantics of the rendezvous mechanism are such that the writer that calls entry STARTWRITE is supended until the accept statement has been completed. The only writer who is allowed at this point to call the nested entry is the one currently suspended. With this arrangement, clearly everything will come to an abrupt halt.   Since the writer must be allowed to continue when it receives permission to go ahead and write, we leave the STARTWRITE accept statement as it is (making the entry call a purely synchronizing call) and accept the STOPWRITE separately.

>   **when** nrreaders = 0 => **accept** STARTWRITE;
>   **accept** STOPWRITE;

Note that the statement sequence for the selection alternative is not a single accept statement, but a sequence of two such statements.   While many select statements for resource management tasks consist entirely of alternative accept statements, this need not be the case.   Any sequence of statements can appear after the initial accept statement and function together as a selection alternative. In fact, we extend this sequence even further in this implementation.   Waiting readers need to be given access to the resource.

>   **while** STARTREAD'COUNT /= 0 **loop**
>   **accept** STARTREAD **do**
>   nrreaders = nrreaders + 1;
>   **end** STARTREAD;
>   **end loop**;

As long as readers are queued to the STARTREAD entry, they will be given access. But what about readers that ask for permission while the waiting readers are granted their access? With this program sequence, they will be allowed as well. This seems to indicate that we could inadvertently starve the writers if readers ask for permission as fast as it can be given. Let us, therefore, replace the while statement with a much safer one.

>   **for** i **in** 1 . . STARTREAD'COUNT **loop** . . .

Because the discrete range is evaluated only once (ARM 5.5, 5-6), only a fixed number of readers will be granted access. A few extra processes may sneak in just before the range evaluation, but we have removed the possibility of starving the writers (assuming, of course, that the allowed readers stop reading).

```
task body RWScheduler is
        nrreaders : INTEGER := 0;
begin
    loop
            select when STARTWRITE'COUNT = 0 =>
                    accept STARTREAD do
                            nrreaders := nrreaders + 1;
                    end STARTREAD;
            or      accept STOPREAD do
                            nrreaders := nrreaders - 1;
                    end STOPREAD;
            or      when nrreaders = 0  => accept STARTWRITE;
                    accept STOPWRITE;
                    for i in 1 . . STARTREAD'COUNT loop
                            accept STARTREAD do
                                    nrreaders := nrreaders + 1;
                            end STARTREAD;
                    end loop;
            end select;
    end loop;
end RWScheduler;
```

FIFO Readers/Writers

We have exploited the properties of entry queue counts to implement the previous example. There are other properties that can be exploited as well. The fact that entry calls are queued (ARM 9.5, 9-7) can be used to implement a FIFO (first-come, first-serve) strategy for a readers/writers scheduler.

The interface must be slightly different from the preceding example because we want a single queue of processes asking permission to access the resources. Assuming that there is an enumerated type

```
type request is (read, write);
```

we can define the task type interface as a start operation and the appropriate stop operations.

```
task type FCFSScheduler is
        entry START(r : in request);
        entry STOPREAD;
        entry STOPWRITE;
end FCFSScheduler;
```

Note that we still distinguish explicitly between the completion of reading and writing. We will see shortly that the reason for this distinction is the use of different guards.

Since we no longer have a separate writers queue, we need to know when we are reading and when we are writing. The Boolean variable *writing* provides this indication and is set to TRUE when a write request is accepted from the START entry queue.

> writing : BOOLEAN : = FALSE;

When a request for read access is encountered, *nrreaders* is incremented. When a request for write access is encountered, the readers currently accessing the database must finish before writing can begin. This logical description is identical to the first part of the previous example. However, the implementation is quite different:

```
select
        when not writing  =>
        accept START(r : in request) do
            if r  =  read then
                    nrreaders : = nrreaders +  1;
            else
                    for i in 1  . .  nrreaders loop
                        accept STOPREAD;
                    end loop;
                    nrreaders : =  0;
                    writing : =  TRUE;
            end if;
        end START;
or
        when writing  =>
        accept STOPWRITE do
            writing : =  FALSE
        end STOPWRITE;
or
        when not writing  = .
        accept STOPREAD do
            nrreaders : =  nrreaders - 1;
        end STOPREAD;
end select;
```

Once a writer has asked for access, all further request entries are suspended until a STOPWRITE signal is received. Before actual writing can start, all readers currently using the resource must issue a STOPREAD. Note that this is indicated by the nested accept statement. We cannot allow the rendezvous of the write request to complete until all the readers are finished; otherwise readers might get inconsistent data. Nesting the accept statement allows us to wait on the current readers and keep the writer waiting at the same time. Once all the readers have finished, the readers count is reset to zero, the writers flag set to TRUE, and the rendezvous is completed, allowing the writer to modify the resource. Only a STOPWRITE operation can then be selected. Once the writer has finished the modification, access requests can again be processed, because the writing flag has been reset to FALSE.

Comparison of the Solutions

The two solutions are constructed using widely disparate mechanisms. We have already alluded to the problem encountered in constructing the Pascal solution. The construction of a solution such as ours is susceptible to other problems as well, particularly to the problems of semaphores. For example, in both STARTREAD and STARTWRITE, there are two V operations but only one P operation. It would be fairly easy to omit one of the V operations.

Where the Pascal solution is rather complicated in its interactions between the different operations, the Ada solution is uncomplicated and straightforward. The use of the language facilities simplifies the interactions between the operations. The support provided by the language makes it easier to determine that the Ada solution works correctly than it is for the Pascal solution.

12.3 The Dining Philosophers Problem

The dining philosophers problem has become a paradigm in the discussions of deadlock and starvation. Its primary concern is the sharing of resources among concurrent processes. The philosophers in the problem (there are usually 5 philosophers) alternate between eating and thinking. Each philosopher has a place at the table and one fork. However, two forks are needed to eat from the platter of tangled spaghetti in the center of the table, which magically is always full. The goal is to define an algorithm for a philosopher in such a way that concurrency in the use of the resources is achieved, and deadlock and starvation are avoided.

The typical first solution to this problem is for each philosopher to pick up his fork and then try to pick up his right neighbor's fork. Clearly, if everyone picks up his fork simultaneously, no fork on the right is available and deadlock occurs.

A solution to this deadlocked arrangement is to pick up two forks at once. This requires a guarantee that two philosophers cannot pick up a single fork simultaneously: one of two contending philosophers must always get there first. In this way, deadlock is prevented from occurring. But, two philosophers can work in collusion and starve the philosopher between them by alternately eating, so that two forks are never available to the middle philosopher.

In order to prevent starvation, some sort of status must be provided to indicate that a philosopher is hungry. When this occurs, the algorithm should guarantee that he will eventually get to eat. The solution presented here is derived from deBruijn's solution to the problem of critical sections without special instructions in **Communications of the ACM**, 10:3 (March 1967), pages 137-138.

The solution requires a status variable for each philosopher, indicating whether he is hungry or not, and a status variable for each fork, indicating who has the current rights to it. If neither neighbor is hungry, the hungry philosopher can immediately begin to eat. If either neighbor is hungry, one of four states will occur. In state one the philosopher in question has the right to both his own fork and his right neighbor's fork. He will be able to proceed, because each neighbor will defer since they do not have rights to both of the forks that they need and he never stops claiming to be hungry. In state two the philosopher has rights to neither fork. In this case, he must wait to claim that he is hungry until given the right to at least one of the forks. If both neighbors are hungry, he will have to wait for the rights to both of the forks. In state three the philosopher has a right to only one of the forks and the neighbor with whom the philosopher is contending for the other has rights to both his forks. In this case, the philosopher will defer. In state four each contending philosopher has the right only to one fork. A sequence of deferring to each other occurs until finally one philosopher remains claiming to be hungry. At that point, he succeeds and begins to eat. When finished eating, the philosopher confers the rights to his forks to his two neighbors and returns to his philosophical quest.

```
        claim to be hungry

        while either neighbor is hungry loop
            while either
                1)      the left neighbor is hungry and the fork shared
                        is his by right
        or
                2)      the right neighbor is hungry and the fork shared
                        is his by right
            withdraw the claim to be hungry
            otherwise maintain the claim to be hungry
        end loop

        EAT

        give the rights to the forks to the neighbors
        withdraw the claim to be hungry
```

State Representation in Pascal

In addition to the semaphores required for the Readers/Writers problem, we shall require the notion of a process. A process is syntactically identical to a procedure except for the keyword **process** instead of the keyword **procedure**. Semantically, the process is initiated by the process invocation, which is identical to a procedure invocation, and proceeds independently of the initiating process. Communication between processes is possible only through shared variables, i.e., there is no direct communication mechanism defined in the programming language.

Each philosopher has a status variable to indicate whether or not he is hungry and each fork has a status variable to indicate the philosopher who has the right to the fork. Before defining these variables, we first define the number of philosophers the program will have and the notion of philosopher identity.

> **const** maxphilosophers : 5;
> **var** philid = 1 . . maxphilosophers;

The states of philosophers and forks are represented by arrays, indexed by the philosopher's identity. For the philosopher status, the element is a Boolean variable: if it is TRUE, the philosopher is hungry; if FALSE, he is not hungry. The state of the fork is determined by a philosopher identifier.

> hstat : **array** [philid] **of** boolean;
> fstat : **array** [philid] **of** philid;

In the initial state, no philosopher is hungry ($hstat_i$ = FALSE for all i) and each philosopher has the right to his own fork ($fstat_i$ = i for all i).

The modification of the state variables is protected by a mutual exclusion semaphore, *mutex*, guarding a critical section. The semantics of semaphores are such that an initial V operation is needed before access to that critical section is possible. If this initial V operation is included in an initialization procedure that sets the state variables to their initial values, we can guarantee that the critical section cannot be entered for the first time without having initialized the state variables.

> mutex : semaphore;

The SETHUNGER and SETRIGHT operations implement the means of claiming to be hungry and conferring rights to a fork, respectively.

> **procedure** SETHUNGER (p : philid; h : boolean);
> **begin**
> > P (mutex);
> > hstat [p] := h;
> > V (mutex)
> **end**;

```
procedure SETRIGHT (f : philid; r : philid);
begin
        P (mutex);
        fstat [f] : = r;
        V (mutex)
end;
```

We provide a small amount of abstraction for accessing the two state variables: HUNGRY returns TRUE if hstat[philosopher] is TRUE and RIGHT returns the identity of the philosopher having the right to it (forks are identified by the philosopher who has the fork in front of him).

```
function HUNGRY (p : philid) : boolean;
begin
        HUNGRY : = hstat [p]
end;

function RIGHT (f : philid) : philid;
begin
        RIGHT : = fstat [f]
end;
```

Philosophers in Pascal

We define a philosopher as a process and then instantiate a process for each philosopher. Required at each instantiation is the identity of the philosopher.

```
process philosopher (me : philid); begin  . . .  end;
philosopher(1);  . . .
```

The philosopher then initializes its local variables to identify his left philosopher, right philosopher, his own fork and the fork of his right neighbor.

```
var left, right, mf, rf : philid;
. . .
mf      : = me;
right   : = me mod maxphilosophers + 1;
rf      : = right;
if me > 1
        then left : = m-1
        else  left : = maxphilosophers;
```

Gaining access to the forks required for eating can be viewed as entering the critical section. As noted in the discussion, the philosopher claims to be hungry and defers only if there is contention for forks for which he has no rights.

```
    while true do {forever}
        begin
        SETHUNGER (me, true);
        while HUNGRY(left) or HUNGRY(right) do
                begin
                while (HUNGRY(left) and RIGHT(mf) /= me) or
                      (HUNGRY(right) and RIGHT(rf) /= me)
                        do    SETHUNGER(me, false);
                SETHUNGER(me, true)
                end;
        . . .
        end;
```

After eating, the philosopher puts down his forks (confering the rights to them to his neighbors) and indicates that his appetite has been satisfied.

```
    SETRIGHT     (mf, left);
    SETRIGHT     (rf, right);
    SETHUNGER    (me, false);
```

Philosophers in Ada

The Ada solution differs from the Pascal solution in one significant respect: it can be implemented in a distributed system. Each philosopher has sufficient knowledge to maintain the state and interactions between philosophers are restricted to neighbors.

There are two task types: a status manager and a philosopher. The first manages the state of the philosopher and the state of his fork. This task provides the functional interface between tasks: the philosophers do not communicate directly with each other, but indirectly through the intermediary status manager task. The general structure of the solution is:

```
    package body DiningPhilosophers is
        subtype philid . . . ;
        task type StatusManager . . . ;
        task type Philosopher . . . ;

        -- arrays of StatusManagers and Philosophers

        task body StatusManager . . . ;
        task body Philosopher . . . ;
    begin
        -- initialization
    end DiningPhilosophers;
```

The package DiningPhilosophers has no interface to the outside world. It is a self-contained system in that all the interactions are between components within the package and depend on nothing outside the package. (In this sense, it might be considered a main program.) We have defined the package in such a way that it is configurable for any number of philosophers.

> **generic** maxphilosophers : POSITIVE;
> **package** DiningPhilosophers **is end** DiningPhilosophers;

Note that we still must use the keywords **is end** in the declaration even though the visible part is completely empty.

The most natural way of expressing the concurrent processes, such as the status managers and the philosophers, is as task types. One might ask why we did not define generic packages that embody tasks and instantiate one for each status manager and one for each philosopher. The reason is that there is no way for the one instantiated task to communicate with another in this kind of implementation. With task types, however, arrays of task objects can be constructed in such a way that process identities are associated with the array index. In an instantiated package, there is no way to pass the names of the other instantiated packages into a package so that these can be referenced.

Arrays of task objects, then, provide a convenient means of instantiating groups of identical tasks, and provide a useful way of distinguishing between them for communication purposes.

> **subtype** philid **is** INTEGER **range** 1 . . maxphilosophers;

> **task type** StatusManager **is**
>   **entry** SETHUNGER   (h : **in** BOOLEAN)
>   **entry** SETRIGHT   (r : **in** philid)
>   **entry** GETHUNGER (h : **out** BOOLEAN);
>   **entry** GETRIGHT   (r : **out** philid);
> **end** StatusManager;

> **task type** Philosopher **is**
>   **entry** INIT(id : philid);
> **end** Philosopher;

> stat   : **array** (philid) **of** StatusManager;
> phil   : **array** (philid) **of** Philosopher;

Note that we have used anonymous array types for the arrays of tasks. Since we do nothing but refer to these tasks by name, this works out well.

Task Parameters and Initialization

In our Pascal solution, a process declaration was allowed to have formal parameters which could be set at the time of instantiation with actual parameters. Ada does not allow parameters for task types (although it does allow parameters for array, record, and private types). Therefore, some means must be found to provide each task with parametric information.

In the preceding example we saw that generic packages provide parametric information, but we also found that packages are not the right construct for our example. The only solution left to us is that of an initializing entry which must be called first before any other use of the task is meaningful. While this may seem to introduce the problem that initialization cannot be guaranteed, we observe that the sequencing of accept statements assures that no harm can be done. In contrast to the unpredictable results that are caused by the use of an uninitialized variable, quite predictable results are obtained from the use of an uninitialized task: nothing (literally) happens; the task waits for a rendezvous on the initializing entry.

Clearly, this approach is not as elegant and clean as that of parameterized tasks, but it is not as unsafe as that of uninitialized variables. Basically, it is just rather clumsy. Where parameterization is required, such as establishing identities and correlating tasks with components in the array structure, initializing entries must be used. Their placement in the task bodies must occur near the beginning of the body and before any other accept statements. Parameterization of the tasks, then, occurs in the initialization portion of the package body.

```
     begin  -- initialization of the package body
          for i in philid loop
                stat(i).SETRIGHT(i);
                phil(i).INIT(i);
          end loop;
     end DiningPhilosophers;
```

Each philosopher is given the rights to his own fork, and given his own identity. Note that entry invocations select first the array component by index and then entry name by dot notation. Entries are referenced as though they were components of a record.

Tasks are similar to subprograms in that initialization of local variables can occur at the point of declaration or at the beginning of the computation. Because of the parameterizing problems, we must initialize at the beginning of the computation. In the task body of StatusManager, initialization is a combination of both declarative and computational initialization. The status variable indicating whether the philosopher is hungry, *hstat*, is declared to have the initial value FALSE. The right to the fork, on the other hand, is assigned as a result of an initializing entry, which in this case is a standard entry as well.

```
task body StatusManager is
      hstat   : BOOLEAN := FALSE;
      fstat   : philid;
begin
      accept SETRIGHT (r : in philid) do fstat := r end SETRIGHT;
      . . .
end StatusManager;
```

Task type Philosopher, on the other hand, has a specific initializing entry, INIT, through which the philosopher's identity is established. From this identity, the identities of the *right* and *left* philosophers, and the identity of *mf* (my fork) and *rf* (right neighbor's fork) are established.

```
task body Philosopher is

      me, left, right, mf, rf : philid;

begin

      accept INIT(id : in philid) do me := id; end INIT;

      mf      := me
      right   := me mod maxphilosophers + 1;
      rf      := right;
      if me > 1
            then left := me - 1;
            else  left := maxphilosophers;
      end if;
      . . .
end Philosopher;
```

Note that we included only the minimum of computation in the body of the accept statement. In general, this is a good rule to follow.

Because the status values are used in Boolean expressions for determining the terminating conditions of while loops, it would be useful to be able to write

```
while stat(left).HUNGRY or . . .
```

thereby invoking a functional form of an entry call to determine if a particular philosopher is hungry. Unfortunately, this form is not allowed, because Ada treats entries as procedures and not as functions (ARM 9.5, 9-6). The declarations and invocations are like those of procedures. We must, therefore, find a way to transform the procedural invocations into functional subprograms. The invocations of the StatusManager entries GETHUNGER and GETRIGHT are encased in the functions HUNGRY and RIGHT. The former returns a Boolean value and the latter a *philid* value.

```
function HUNGRY (p : in philid) return BOOLEAN is
      b : BOOLEAN;
begin
      stat(p).GETHUNGER(b);
      return b;
end HUNGRY;

function RIGHT (p : in philid) return philid is
      r : philid;
begin
      stat(p).GETRIGHT(r);
      return r;
end RIGHT;
```

Since tasks have a structure similar to packages, we are able to hide the modification and inspection of status variables in the task body. In addition, the fact that a task is an independent activity makes it possible for us to separate the maintenance of state variables from the philosophers operating on these variables. The implementation of the state variables and their operations is confined to the StatusManager that runs concurrently with the philosophers. The interaction between philosophers and the StateManager takes place through entry calls only.

The basic service loop of the StatusManager is straightforward. No entry has priority over any other.

```
select
      accept SETHUNGER(h : in BOOLEAN) do
            hstat : = h;
      end SETHUNGER;
or
      accept SETRIGHT(r : in philid) do
            fstat : = r;
      end SETRIGHT;
or
      accept GETHUNGER(h : out BOOLEAN) do
            h : = hstat;
      end GETHUNGER;
or
      accept GETRIGHT(r : out philid) do
            r : = fstat;
      end GETRIGHT;
end select;
```

Critical Sections in Ada

The philosopher claims to be hungry. If neither neighbor is hungry, the philosopher proceeds immediately to eating. If there is contention, then passage into the critical section depends upon the combination of fork rights and claims to be hungry. The logic of the Ada and Pascal programs are identical. The difference is in the implementation of the logical functions of each statement.

```
stat(me).SETHUNGER(TRUE);
while HUNGRY(left) or else HUNGRY(right) loop
    while  (HUNGRY(left) and then FRIGHT(mf) /= me)
    or else(HUNGRY(right) and then FRIGHT(rf) /= me)
    loop
            stat(me).SETHUNGER(FALSE);
    end loop;
    stat(me).SETHUNGER(TRUE);
end loop;
```

Note that we have used the short-circuit boolean operations to minimize the amount of intertask communication. It is a good general rule to use these operators whenever possible. No difference in logical results are obtained and it is much more efficient. The only justification for not using them is the presence of side-effects in the expression evaluation.

In leaving the critical section, the two programs are functionally identical.

```
stat(mf).SETRIGHT (left);
stat(rf).SETRIGHT (right);
stat(me).SETHUNGER (FALSE);
```

The rights to the forks are passed to the neighbors and the philosopher indicates that he has finished eating.

Comparison of the Solutions

The logic and apparent form of the two solutions are quite similar. Ada requires extra structural details but gains information hiding and logical independence from a single processor configuration. The lack of task parameterization and a functional form for entries is bothersome but not critical. The ability to describe a problem in a processor-configuration-independent manner is a strong recommendation for Ada and its tasking mechanism.

12.4 The Complete Programs

The Pascal Readers/Writers Program

```
var    waitread   : integer;
       waitwrite  : integer;
       nrreaders  : integer;
       i          : integer;

       mutex      : semaphore;
       oktoread   : semaphore;
       oktowrite  : semaphore;


procedure STARTREAD;
begin  P(mutex);
       if waitwrite > 0 then
               begin
               waitread := waitread + 1;
               V (mutex);
               P (oktoread)
               end
       else    begin
               nrreaders := nrreaders + 1;
               V (mutex)
               end
end;


procedure STOPREAD;
begin
       P (mutex);
       nrreaders := nrreaders - 1;
       if nrreaders = 0 and waitwrite > 0 then V (oktowrite);
       V (mutex)
end;
```

```
procedure STARTWRITE;
begin
        P (mutex);
        if nrreaders > 0 or waitwrite > 0 then
                begin
                waitwrite : = waitwrite + 1;
                V (mutex);
                P (oktowrite)
                end
        else    begin
                waitwrite : = waitwrite + 1;
                V (mutex)
                end;
end;


procedure STOPWRITE;
begin
        P(mutex);
        waitwrite : = waitwrite - 1;
        if waitread > 0 then
                for i = 1 to waitread do
                        begin
                        V (oktoread);
                        nrreaders : = nrreaders + 1;
                        waitread : = waitread - 1
                        end
        else if waitwrite > 0 then V (oktowrite);
        V (mutex)
end;


procedure INITIALIZE;
begin
        waitread      : = 0;
        waitwrite     : = 0;
        nrreaders     : = 0;
        writing       : = FALSE;
        V (mutex)
end;
```

The Ada Readers/Writers Program

```
task type RWScheduler is
      entry STARTREAD;
      entry STOPREAD;
      entry STARTWRITE;
      entry STOPWRITE;
end RWScheduler;


task body RWScheduler is
      nrreaders : INTEGER := 0;
begin
      loop
            select
                  when STARTWRITE'COUNT = 0 =>
                  accept STARTREAD do
                        nrreaders := nrreaders + 1;
                  end STARTREAD;
            or
                  accept STOPREAD do
                        nrreaders := nrreaders - 1;
                  end STOPREAD;
            or
                  when nrreaders = 0 =>
                  accept STARTWRITE;
                  accept STOPWRITE;
                  for i in 1 .. STARTREAD'COUNT loop
                        accept STARTREAD do
                              nrreaders := nrreaders + 1;
                        end STARTREAD;
                  end loop;
            end select;
      end loop;
end RWScheduler;
```

```
task type FCFSScheduler is
          -- Assume  type request is (read, write);
          entry START(r : in request);
          entry STOPREAD;
          entry STOPWRITE;
end FCFSScheduler;


task body FCFSScheduler is
      nrreaders    : NATURAL := 0;
      writing      : BOOLEAN := FALSE;
begin
      loop
            select
                  when not writing =>
                  accept START(r : in request) do
                        if r = read then
                              nrreaders := nrreaders + 1;
                        else
                              for i in 1 . . nrreaders loop
                                    accept STOPREAD;
                              end loop;
                              nrreaders := 0;
                              writing := TRUE;
                        end if;
                  end START;
            or
                  when writing =>
                  accept STOPWRITE do
                        writing := FALSE;
                  end STOPWRITE;
            or
                  when not writing =>
                  accept STOPREAD do
                        nrreaders := nrreaders - 1;
                  end STOPREAD;
            end select;
      end loop;
end FCFSScheduler;
```

The Pascal Dining Philosophers Program

```
const maxphilosophers = 5;

type  philid = 1 . . maxphilosophers;

var   hstat  : array [philid] of boolean;
      fstat  : array [philid] of philid;
      mutex : semaphore;

. . .

procedure SETHUNGER (p : philid; h : boolean);
begin
      P (mutex);
      hstat [p] := h;
      V (mutex)
end

procedure SETRIGHT (f : philid; r : philid);
begin
      P (mutex);
      fstat [f] := r;
      V (mutex)
end;

function HUNGRY (p : philid) : boolean;
begin
      HUNGRY := hstat [p]
end;

function RIGHT (f : philid) : philid;
begin
      RIGHT := fstat [f]
end;
```

```
process philosopher (me : philid);
      var left, right, mf, rf : philid;
begin
      mf     := me;
      right  := me mod maxphilosophers + 1;
      rf     := right;
      if me > 1 then left := me - 1 else left := maxphilosophers;

      while true do
      begin SETHUNGER(me, true);
            while HUNGRY(left) or HUNGRY(right) do
            begin
                  while  (HUNGRY(left) and RIGHT(mf) /= me) or
                         (HUNGRY(right) and RIGHT(rf) /= me)
                         do SETHUNGER(me, false);
                  SETHUNGER(me, true)
            end;

            {EAT}

            SETRIGHT (mf, left);
            SETRIGHT (rf, right);
            SETHUNGER (me, false)

            {THINK}
      end
end;


procedure INITIALIZE;
      i : integer;
begin
      for i = 1 to maxphilosophers do
            begin
                  SETHUNGER(i, false);
                  SETRIGHT(i, i);
                  philosopher(i)
            end;
      V(mutex)
end;
```

The Ada Dining Philosophers Solution

```
generic  maxphilosophers : POSITIVE;
package DiningPhilosophers is
end DiningPhilosophers;


package body DiningPhilosophers is

        subtype philid is INTEGER range 1 . . maxphilosophers;


        task type StatusManager is

                entry SETHUNGER    (h : in BOOLEAN);
                entry SETRIGHT     (r : in philid);
                entry GETHUNGER    (h : out BOOLEAN);
                entry GETRIGHT     (r : out philid);

        end StatusManager;


        task type Philosopher is

                entry INIT(id : philid);

        end Philosopher;



        stat : array (philid) of StatusManager;
        phil : array (philid) of Philosopher;
```

```
task body StatusManager is
        hstat   : BOOLEAN := FALSE;
        fstat   : philid;
begin
        accept SETRIGHT (r : in philid) do
                fstat := r;
        end SETRIGHT;
        loop
                select
                        accept SETHUNGER(h: in BOOLEAN) do
                                hstat := h;
                        end SETHUNGER;
                or
                        accept SETRIGHT(r: in philid) do
                                fstat := r;
                        end SETRIGHT;
                or
                        accept GETHUNGER(h: out BOOLEAN) do
                                h := hstat;
                        end GETHUNGER;
                or
                        accept GETRIGHT(r: out philid) do
                                r := priority;
                        end GETRIGHT;
                end select;
        end loop;
end StatusManager;

task body Philosopher is

        me, left, right, mf, rf : philid;

        function HUNGRY (p : in philid) return BOOLEAN is
                b : BOOLEAN;
        begin
                stat(p).GETHUNGER(b);
                return b;
        end HUNGRY;

        function FRIGHT (p : in philid) return philid is
                r : philid;
        begin
                stat(p).GETRIGHT (r);
                return r;
        end FRIGHT;
```

```
begin   -- of task body Philosopher
       accept INIT(id : in philid) do me := id end INIT;
       mf    := me;
       right := me mod maxphilosophers + 1;
       rf := right;
       if me > 1
              then left := me - 1;
              else left := maxphilosophers;
       end if;

       loop
           stat(me).SETHUNGER(TRUE);
           while HUNGRY(left) or else HUNGRY(right) loop
              while (HUNGRY(left) and then FRIGHT(mf) /= me)
              or else (HUNGRY(right) and then FRIGHT(rf) /= me)
              loop
                  stat(me).SETHUNGER(FALSE);
              end loop;

                  stat(me).SETHUNGER(TRUE);
           end loop;

           -- EAT

           stat(mf).SETRIGHT(left);
           stat(rf).SETRIGHT(right);
           stat(me).SETHUNGER(FALSE);

           -- THINK

       end loop;

   end Philosopher;

begin   -- initialization of package DiningPhilosophers

   for i in philid loop
          stat(i).SETRIGHT(i); phil(i).INIT(i);
   end loop;

end DiningPhilosophers;
```

12.5 Reminders

1. Task types can be used to associate schedulers with the resources to be scheduled.

2. Ada's entry mechanism provides queueing of entry calls.

3. The entry attribute COUNT enables the programmer to determine the length of an entry's queue.

4. When clauses with their boolean expressions provide a means of opening and closing accept statements, i.e., making them selectable in a select statement.

5. At least one alternative must be open in a select statement or else the exception SELECT_ERROR is raised. An alternative that is always open can be programmed as an else extension of a select statement.

6. A select statement alternative may have any sequence of code following an initial accept statement.

7. Nested accept statements are allowed, but should be used with care in order to prevent deadlock.

8. Empty package specifications are allowed. Typically, these indicate closed systems.

9. Task types provide a means of creating collections of identical objects that can be array elements or record fields. This cannot be done with packages.

10. Task types do not have parameters. Parameterization can be accomplished through an initialization entry.

11. Entries are analogous to procedures. The functional form is not allowed for entries.

12. Tasks (and task types) can be used to protect structures, hide information about their structure, and guarantee exclusive access to them.

12.6 Problems

1. Write a Readers/Writers Scheduler in both languages that gives priority to readers. Write another one in both languages that gives priority to writers.

2. Consider two types of readers: the first corresponds to the reader in the example who wants only consistent information; the second is a reader in a hurry who is willing to accept the risk of inconsistent data as long as immediate access is granted. Modify the first readers/ writers example to

provide this service. Why can't the second example (FCFS) be modified easily to provide this service?

3. Imagine two classes of writers: the first corresponds to the writer in the example who may have extensive modification and who requires exclusive access; the second is a writer that makes a single modification and can execute safely along with the readers (assuming for the moment that assignment is an indivisible action). Modify the first example to provide this service. Can it be provided in the second example? If so, do it.

4. Write a program for the Dining Philosophers that allows starvation (it is possible that a philosopher never gets a chance to eat because his neighbors happen to beat him at picking up the forks he needs all the time). In this version it is necessary that philosophers pick up the two forks at once, otherwise a deadlock may occur. Why can't this solution be used for distributed systems?

5. A different solution of the Dining Philosophers problem uses a host who receives requests from hungry philosophers and determines the order in which philosophers may eat. The entire state, including which forks are in use and who has the priority for using forks, is maintained by the host. Write a program in both languages that solves the Dining Philosophers problem in this spirit of central control.

Thirteen

Resource Allocation

Topics: manager and server tasks, task bodies, select and accept
                 statements, guarded accept statements, priority scheduling

Issues: process identity, resource allocation, protection, capabilities.

13.1 Problem Statement

Resources constitute a basic part of any programmed system. Some may be
shared by several processes, others may be used only by one process at a time;
some may be plentiful, others may be scarce and in demand among many
processes. When a resource is nonsharable, some form of scheduling is required
to manage its use. Further, when a resource is scarce and there is contention for
it, some form of priority is required to separate levels of importance and urgency
with respect to resource use.   Because of these scheduling and priority
considerations, it is important that the resources be protected against arbitrary and
unwarranted use.

The problem for this chapter is to design and implement a resource management
program that provides request priorities and protects the resources from arbitrary
and unwarranted use. Assume that there is a pool of resources (the nature of the
resource and its use is immaterial -- the management of the resource is the
important aspect) that may be requested, allocated and released. Two forms of
allocation should be provided. The first waits, if necessary, until a resource is
available and allocated before completing; the second allocates a resource if it is
immediately available (and if allowed according to scheduling considerations) but
returns immediately if no resource can be allocated. In allocating the resources,
the manager gives the available resource to the highest priority request and, if
there are several requests within the same level of priority, to the oldest request.

13.2 Problem Discussion

Let the resource pool be represented by pool[1 . . N], where N is the total number of resources. The number of available resources is remembered in a variable *free* which is decremented when a resource is allocated and incremented when a resource is released; the number of resources in use is N - free. The standard operations on resources are ALLOC, USAGE and DEALLOC.

The priority of a process is a cardinal number in the range [0 . . *maxprior*], where 0 is the lowest priority and *maxprior* the highest. In a first attempt at designing the resource management procedures, we write the following specifications

> **function**   ALLOC   (p : **in** priority) **return** resourceindex;
> **procedure** USAGE   (r : **in** resourceindex);
> **procedure** DEALLOC (r : **in** resourceindex);

The caller C of ALLOC transmits its priority through parameter *p* and receives in return the index of an available resource that will be reserved from now on for C.This process can now use the allocated resource by calling USAGE(pool[i]), where *i* is the value returned by ALLOC. When C is done using the resource, the latter is released by the procedure DEALLOC.

Implementation of the Resource Management Procedures

We have already mentioned the variable *free* which indicates the number of resources available. When ALLOC allocates a resource to some process, it decrements the count; when DEALLOC frees a resource, it increments the count. Clearly, the two operations must not access *free* at the same time or a race condition (cf. Chapter 11) will occur and result in an incorrect count.

The means of determining whether a resource is free is provided by the array *alloctable* indexed by the *resourceindex* and whose elements are boolean values.

> allocatable : **array** (1 . . N) **of** BOOLEAN;

When all resources are free, each element in the array has the value FALSE.

ALLOC searches the array to find a resource that is available. When such a resource is found, ALLOC sets this component to TRUE and returns the index for the allocated resource. DEALLOC, on the other hand, resets the indexed component to FALSE. This latter action occurs only to resources previously allocated and so does not interfere with ALLOC searching for and allocating a resource, nor does it interfere with other deallocations. Several searches executing concurrently, however, do interfere with each other and must be executed serially.

Given the constraints necessary to avoid race conditions and to maintain the integrity of the bookkeeping data, ALLOC should be implemented as an indivisible operation. For DEALLOC, the only necessary indivisible action is the decrementing of *free*. The general implementations of the resource manager's operations can be described as follows. (We use curly brackets to indicate the indivisible actions.)

```
ALLOC       :   {
                wait for a free resource
                decrement free
                r : = select a free resource
                allocable(r) : = TRUE
                }


DEALLOC     :   allocable(r) : = FALSE
                {increment free}


GRAB        :   {
                if there is no contention for resources and free / = 0 then
                        decrement free
                        r : = select a free resource
                        allocable(r) : = TRUE
                else return no allocation
                }
```

It is essential to increment *free* after the resource has been released. Otherwise a process requesting a resource may pass the wait statement in ALLOC (or the Boolean expression in GRAB) and start looking for an available resource before one has been marked as free.

We must be careful and make sure that we don't introduce deadlocks in the implementation of the indivisible actions in ALLOC, DEALLOC and GRAB. For example, ALLOC is waiting for the variable *free* to be incremented. The indivisibility of ALLOC should not preclude DEALLOC from executing and thereby incrementing *free*. If DEALLOC cannot increment *free*, ALLOC will never proceed.

Protecting the use of Resources

In the previous section we addressed the problems encountered when several processes interact with the bookkeeping data required in managing the resources. Here we discuss the problems of guaranteeing that resources are used only by the processes that have observed the prescribed rules.

The most appropriate way to guarantee that the resources are used only as prescribed is to require that some kind of identification be used in conjuction with the resources. One way to implement this is to use a process identifier. These identifiers are unique within a system and are provided by the underlying operating system. This requires that a correspondence be made between the user (i.e., the process) and the resource, and this correspondence must be verified at each use of a resource management operation. A severe disadvantage of this approach is that it may be possible to manufacture process identifiers arbitrarily and thereby subvert the protection system.

A safer implementation is that which provides an unforgeable token at the time of allocation. The token itself is the key to the use of the resource. By submitting the token with each operation, access is automatically granted to the resource. The token is a capability for the resource: possession of the capability is sufficient to guarantee the safety and integrity of the use of the resource. To maintain this safety and integrity, the capability must not be copiable in any way, nor be creatable except by the resource management routines, specifically ALLOC and GRAB. The obvious choice is to make *resourceindex* a capability. It then provides both the protection required and the identification of the protected resource.

13.3 An Ada Solution

Our Ada solution consists of three packages: one for managing process descriptors, one for resource management, and a third package that defines resources. The visible part of the latter is:

> **package** Resources **is**
>
>> NrResources : **constant** INTEGER := ... ;
>> **type** resource **is limited private**;
>>
>> **procedure** USAGE(res : **in out** resource);
>
> **private**
>
>> **type** resource **is** ... ;
>
> **end** Resources;

Since the nature of resources is here irrelevant, the type definition is not expanded further. All the resource management package needs to know is the existence of the type *resource*, the procedure USAGE, and the number of resources available.

We envision that the system uses process identifiers to contain basic information about processes. The only one that we are interested in is the processes' priority. It is static in nature and asigned when the process object is created. For purposes of clarity, we restrict the package declaration to the minimum amount of information.

```
package ProcManagement is

    maxprior : constant INTEGER : = 7;    -- an arbitrary choice
    subtype priority is INTEGER range 0 . . maxprior;
    type procid(x : priority) is limited private;

    function PRTY(pid : procid) return priority;

private

    type procid (x : priority) is  . . .  ;

end ProcManagement;
```

In Ada a programmer can state much more precisely than in Pascal how data objects should be handled. The declaration of *procid* as a limited private type enables a user to declare *procids*, but prohibits him from operating on them in any other way than through the function PRTY which is the only function that takes a *procid* as parameter. This results in far greater safety than is available in Pascal, because *procid* objects cannot be assigned to or manipulated in any way. In fact, in the implementation, a *procid* object behaves like a capability.

It should be noted that declaring a type limited private excludes not only assignment for objects of such a type, but also the test for equality (ARM 4-12, 4.5.2). However, the user can introduce an equality test as a Boolean function and can even represent this function by the symbol "=" (ARM 6-9, 6.7), so nothing is really lost with the restriction on limited private types. In the Ada programs that follow, *procid* objects will be used exclusively for obtaining the priority of a process and not for comparison. It is therefore not necessary to add an equality function to the visible part of package ProcManagement in addition to the function PRTY. This observation leads to the following declaration in the private part of package ProcManagement.

```
    type procid(x : priority) is record prior : priority : = x; end record;
```

Note that this elaboration of type *procid* remains hidden from the user because it is placed in a private part of the package (ARM 7.4.1, 7-5).

When a *procid* object is declared as in the declaration

```
    process : procid(4);
```

the priority field is initialized to the value of the actual parameter (in this case to 4). Since type *procid* is limited private, it is impossible for the priority value can be changed by the user. The user is not even able to access the priority field by the field designator process.prior (ARM 7.4.2, 7-6). The only way for a user to get the priority associated with a *procid* object is through a call to the function PRTY.

Resource Management

Resource management should also be based on the capability concept. When a resource is allocated, the user should receive an unalterable token that gives access to the allocated resource. In Pascal, the language mechanisms are incapable of supporting this kind of object. However, in Ada, resource identifications can be made into capabilities by declaring the type *resid* as limited private. Such a declaration excludes assignments and all other modifications of *resid* objects.

The only way users can operate on *resid* capabilities is by passing these objects as arguments to the procedures ALLOC, TRY, APPLY and DEALLOC. A small price one has to pay for excluding assignment to *resid* objects is that subprograms ALLOC and TRY must be written as procedures rather than as functions, because the return values of functions would not be assignable to such objects. (Note also that limited private objects cannot be initialized in their declaration (ARM 7.4.2, 7-6).)

In the problem discussion, we indicated that for protection of resources it is necessary to check that an allocated resource is used by no other process than the one it had been allocated to. Since Ada programs cannot alter a *resid* object, the scope rules suffice for guaranteeing that a process has access to no other *resid* objects than its own. Suitable specifications of the four resource management procedures are as follows.

```
procedure  ALLOC    (p : in procid; r : in out resid);
procedure  GRAB     (ok : out BOOLEAN; r : in out resid);
procedure  APPLY    (r : in resid);
procedure  DEALLOC  (r : in out resid);
```

It is still possible for a process to make a mistake and, for example, try to deallocate a *resid* object that has not been allocated or try to allocate twice in a row without an intermediate deallocation. The possibility of such an error is reflected in the visible part of ResourceManagement by including the declaration of an exception *improperindex*. The visible part of ResourceManagement is as follows.

```
with ProcManagement; use ProcManagement;
package ResourceManagement is
        type resid is limited private;
        -- procedures ALLOC, GRAB, APPLY, DEALLOC
        improperindex : exception;
private
        subtype resindex is INTEGER range 0 . . N;
        type resid is . . . ;
    end ResourceManagement;
```

It would be very useful if Ada allowed initialization in scalar and array type declarations, as for example in

        type resid **is new** INTEGER **range** 0 . . N : = 0; --improper Ada

where *N* is the total number of resources. The meaning of this initialization would be that every object declared of this type would be initialized to the given value. Such an initialization would be particularly useful for limited private types, because objects of such a type cannot be initialized in their declaration. Unfortunately, initialization of scalar and array types is not allowed in Ada.

The desirable default initialization can be obtained by implementing the resid type as a record (ARM 3.7, 3-23). The declaration of a record field may include an initial value which, by virtue of its occuring in a type definition, is automatically used for all objects declared of that type. Thus, an adequate type definition that prescribes a default initial value for all objects of type *resid* is

        type resid **is record** index : resindex : = 0; **end record**;

Declarations such as

        u, v : resid; w : resid;

introduce variables all of the same type and all with initial value 0. Note that the record structure of *resid* objects remains hidden outside of package ResourceManagement and its body because the complete definition occurs in the private part (ARM 7.4.1, 7-5). Note also the similarity in the relationship between type *resid* and subtype *resindex* and that between type *procid* and subtype *priority*. Both types are records consisting of a single field of the corresponding subtype, and both subtypes are ranges starting at zero.

Revised Resource Management Specification

The approach above assumes that the package Resources is used in the body of the resource management package. One disadvantage of this approach is that the management package is then defined only for a single specific resource, since Ada does not allow identical package names with different implementations. The best way around this problem is to generalize the package by means of generic parameters.

        with ProcManagement; **use** ProcManagement;
        generic type resource **is limited private**;
            with procedure USERESOURCE (res : **in out** resource);
        package ResourceManagement **is**

          . . .

        end ResourceManagement;

The package can now be instantiated for any type of resource as long as it has an associated operation that uses the resources.

The Package Bodies

The body of package ProcManagement is very simple and contains no more than the implementation of function PRTY. The body of that function consists of a single return statement that accesses the priority field of the record named by the actual parameter. The exact implementation is found in the complete set of programs at the end of this chapter.

The body of package ResourceManagement consists of an implementation of the four procedures and of several tasks that collaborate in maintaining the status of the resource pool and in scheduling the user processes according to priority. Since user processes must receive their resources in request arrival-time order per priority class, we introduce a manager task for each priority class and let user processes line up their requests by calls to a manager corresponding to their priority. The scheduler task provides the coordination between the user requests for resources and the priority managers. The entries are provided for the user to REQUEST and RELEASE resources. The priority manager acts as the conduit between the scheduler and the user whereby the available resources are delivered to the appropriate user according to the priority scheme. A resource is passed to the priority manager who then satisfies the first waiting reservation on its queue. This design leads to the following structure for the body of ResourceManagement:

```
with ProcManagement; use ProcManagement;
package body ResourceManagement is
        task Scheduler is  . . .  end Scheduler;
        task type PriorClassManager is  . . .  end PriorClassManager;
        manager : array(priority) of PriorClassManager;
        -- procedures ALLOC, TRY, APPLY, DEALLOC
        task body Scheduler is  . . .  end Scheduler;
        task body PriorClassManager is  . . .  end PriorClassManager;
end ResourceManagement;
```

Package ResourceManagement makes use of *priority* and *procid*, exported by package ProcManagement. These facilities can be used in the body of ResourceManagement without prefixing their names if a USAGE clause is included as is done here (ARM 8.4, 8-6). The implementation of the four procedures is preceded by the creation of the scheduler and of M manager tasks numbered from 0 through *maxprior*.

The resource management procedures, the Scheduler and the manager tasks operate on a common data base which consists of the resource pool. The common data base is created by the declaration

```
pool : array(1 . . N) of resource;
```

where N is the total number of resources.

The priority scheme is implemented as follows. Procedure ALLOC consists of two calls: a request to the Scheduler and a reservation requested from *manager(p)* where *p* is the caller's priority. The first provides the Scheduler with the necessary information about which managers can do something and which of those is the one with the highest priority index. The second arranges the reservation request in arrival time order within the priority class.

A user's call to the scheduler's entry REQUEST enters that user U_i into the schedule. A call to entry RESERVE lines U_i up in the queue of $manager_i$. $manager_i$ does not let U_i proceed until the scheduler passes it a resource index. At that time $manager_i$ can accept the first reservation request on his queue. With this scheme in mind, the body of ALLOC consists basically of

> Scheduler.REQUEST(p);
> manager(PRTY(p)).RESERVE(r);

On behalf of procedure GRAB, the scheduler task must be extended to include one more entry that allows GRAB to obtain a resource directly bypassing the managers. The GRAB is allowed only if a resource is available and there are no contending processes. Since this additional entry has the role of grabbing a resource it is appropriate to call it SEIZE.

> **task** Scheduler **is**
>   **entry** REQUEST (pr : **in** priority);
>   **entry** SEIZE   (r : **out** resindex);
>   **entry** RELEASE (r : **in** resindex);
> **end** Scheduler;

> **task type** PriorClassManager **is**
>   **entry** PASS   (r : **in** resindex);
>   **entry** RESERVE (r : **out** resindex);
> **end** PriorClassManager;

A resource must not be allocated to a *resid* object that already points to an allocated resource. Thus, procedures ALLOC and TRY begin with checking for a non-zero index (zero means no resource).

> **if** r.index /= 0 **then raise** improperindex; **end if**;

Procedures APPLY and DEALLOC do just the opposite and require that the resource to be operated upon has been allocated:

> **if** r.index = 0 **then raise** improperindex; **end if**;

After the test for a proper index, ALLOC calls the Scheduler and manager(p), where *p* is the priority of the caller. Procedure APPLY calls USAGE after the test and DEALLOC calls entry Scheduler.RELEASE(ri), where *ri* is the resource index of the resource to be released. The resource argument passed to DEALLOC is reset to the initial value zero to indicate that it is no longer pointing to a resource.

The construction of the immediate request, GRAB, poses an interesting problem. It is impossible to know whether any resources are available because the bookkeeping data is hidden inside the task Scheduler. Moving the variable *free* so that it is outside the task and global to the body of ResourceManagement does not help, because the resources may be allocated between the time the variable is checked and the time the entry call is accepted.

One very interesting solution to this problem is the following.

```
if r.index / = 0 then raise improperindex; end if;
select
        Scheduler.RESERVE(r.index);
else
        -- indicate no allocation was made
end select;
```

This new form of the select statement is called a conditional entry call. It does not occur in the body of a server task (such as Scheduler or a manager), but in the calling task (such as the user processes). The effect of this kind of select statement is that the caller will select the first alternative only if an immediate rendezvous with the server task is possible. If not, then the else part will be executed instead (ARM 9.7.2, 9-11). In this particular case, GRAB will go through with the call to the scheduler only if the latter is ready for executing its entry SEIZE. If not, the else part is selected and GRAB returns an indication of allocation failure. In any case, GRAB will not wait until the scheduler is done with serving other entries and ready to execute entry SEIZE.

Unfortunately, there are a number of reasons why the entry call might not immediately complete. First, the task might not be at a point where it can accept the entry call, either because it is elsewhere or because it is already in the midst of a rendezvous. Second, the task may be able to select the entry call, but choose not to do so; it might accept a call on the entry RELEASE instead. Third, there may be no resources available. The first two have nothing to do with the availability of resources, but with whether the task can, and in fact does, accept the entry call.

The first case is not really a deterent to using this construct because it actually captures part of the semantics of GRAB: only allow a resource to be seized if there is no contention. Obviously, if the scheduler is executing elsewhere, there is contention. The second case is different from the first. The scheduler may be at the point of selecting which entry to accept. If the choice is between a REQUEST call and a SEIZE call, the choice should go to the REQUEST accept statement in order to provide the desired semantics. However, if the the choice is between a process releasing a resource and another attempting to seize a resource, then the SEIZE accept statement should be chosen because there is no contention for the resource, only contention for entry into the task.

The conditional entry call used in GRAB can also be used to improve the performance of ALLOC if it is normally the case that some free resoures are available when allocation is requested. If there is no contention and free resources are available, there is in fact no need for a user process to line up in the queue of its manager (the one corresponding to its priority). Making processes wait in their manager's queues is necessary only when there is contention for resources. Therefore, when a user process requests a resource in the case where there are free resources available, the user process could bypass its manager altogether. This is achieved by including a conditional entry call to Scheduler.SEIZE in ALLOC.

```
select
        Scheduler.SEIZE(r.index);
else
        Scheduler.REQUEST(PRTY(p));
        manager(PRTY(p)).RESERVE(r.index);
end select;
```

Just as in GRAB, the call to Scheduler.SEIZE is successful only if an immediate rendezvous is possible. It is up to the Scheduler to make sure that an immediate rendezvous is possible only if some free resources are available. If the Scheduler is still serving a request or if no free resources are available, procedure ALLOC will proceed with the else part and use its manager as explained before. With this revised design, procedures ALLOC and GRAB will both immediately grab a resource if one is available, while in case no resource is available, or there is contention, ALLOC lets its caller wait in a manager queue whereas GRAB returns failure.

The Scheduler

The Scheduler is responsible for the bulk of the pool maintenance work. If this maintenance were distributed over the scheduler and the manager tasks, additional synchronization would be needed in order to prevent race conditions between the concurrent tasks. As it is, the manager tasks are designed primarily for implementing the FIFO queue for each priority class.

The Scheduler operates on a local data base that consists of a table recording the available resources, a table recording for each manager the number of user processes that are waiting for resources to become available, and a pair of state variables.

```
    free: resindex := N;
    avail: array(1 . . N) of BOOLEAN := (others => TRUE);
availindex: INTEGER range 1 . . N := 1;
    waitnum: array(priority) of INTEGER := (others => 0):
```

The table *avail* corresponds to the object *alloctable* in the problem discussion and its initialization reflects the fact that initially all resources are available. Variable *free* indicates the number of resources available for allocation. At times that the Scheduler is not updating the data base the following relationholds.

$$\text{free} = \text{Sum}_k(\text{avail}(k) = \text{TRUE})$$

Variable *availindex* is used for traversing table *avail*. The elements of table *waitnum* are numbered from 0 through maxprior, corresponding to the priority classes. All of its elements are initialized to zero because in the initial state no user processes are waiting for resources to become available.

The body of the Scheduler is a loop in which the Scheduler selects one of its three entries REQUEST, RELEASE and SEIZE. A REQUEST call should be honored at all times. The calling user process will then be placed on its corresponding manager queue to wait for a free resource. Thus, calls on entry REQUEST should be accepted both in the case where free = 0 and in the case where free > 0.

Unconditional acceptance of entry REQUEST can simply be implemented by a single accept statement without a guard. However, more interesting is an implementation that distinguishes between the cases *free = 0* and *free > 0* and that treats these cases in two separate accept statements for the single entry REQUEST. Ada specifically allows the inclusion of several accept statements for a single entry in a task body (ARM 9.5, 9-7). The distinction between the two cases will be useful because requests must clearly be handled differently depending on whether or not free resources are available. This is also true for entry RELEASE, but not for entry SEIZE, because the latter is acceptable only if there are free resources available and there are no requests.

```
loop
    select
            when free > 0  =>
            accept REQUEST(p : in priority) do  . . .  end REQUEST;
    or
            when free = 0  =>
            accept REQUEST(p : in priority) do  . . .  end REQUEST;
    or
            when free > 0 and SEIZE'COUNT = 0  =>
            accept RELEASE(r : in resindex) do  . . .  end RELEASE;
    or
            when free = 0  =>
            accept RELEASE(r : in resindex) do  . . .  end RELEASE;
    or
            when free > 0 and REQUEST'COUNT = 0  =>
            accept SEIZE(r : out resindex) do  . . .  end SEIZE;
    end select;
end loop;
```

Note that we have several boolean conditions guarding the accept statements for the entries RELEASE and SEIZE. The second boolean expression makes use of the attribute COUNT to determine if any processes are queued on the entries. In the case of RELEASE, we do not want to interfere with an attempted SEIZE, whereas in the case of SEIZE, we do not want to allow the entry call if there is any contention.

Resource Management

In the case that free resources are available, the Scheduler will select one, update the status of the resource pool and pass the designated resource on to the manager in whose queue the requesting process will enter.

> **while not** avail(availindex)
> **loop** availindex : = availindex **mod** N + 1; **end loop**;
> free : = free - 1; avail(availindex) : = FALSE;
> manager(p).PASS(availindex);

It is certain that the while statement will terminate successfully because of the facts that free > 0 and that the number of TRUE entries in table *avail* is equal to the value of variable *free*. The allocation state is updated in the third line and the designated resource is passed on to the proper manager in the fourth. Note that variable *availindex* is local to the body of the Scheduler and exists as long as the Scheduler exists. Each time a resource is requested, *availindex* contains the value assigned to it in the previous resource allocation (ARM 7.3, 7-4).

In the case that no free resources are available the Scheduler can do no more than take notice of the fact that there will be one more user process waiting until resources become available. The Scheduler remembers the number of user processes on a particular manager's queue for which no resource was available when requested in variable *waitnum(p)*. Variable *waitnum(p)* reflects the obligation of the Scheduler towards *manager(p)* to send that many *pass* signals in the future when resources become available. Thus, in case *free* $= 0$, acceptance of a request simply amounts to

> waitnum(p) : = waitnum(p) + 1;

In the case where *free* $= 0$, there are two possibilities to be considered: it may be that there are some user processes waiting in manager queues that could not get a resource when requested; alternatively, it may be the case that, although no free resources are available, no process is waiting for one to become available. The cases are distinguished by the fact that in the former case at least one of the numbers *waitnum(k)* is greater than zero, while in the latter case they are all equal to zero. If there are user processes waiting for a resource to become available, then the Scheduler will allocate the newly released resource to the first candidate on the non-empty manager queue which has the highest priority and is non-empty. Since an accept statement is in fact a procedure body, this inspection can be implemented using a return statement (ARM 5.8, 5-9).

```
declare
    pr : priority : = maxprior;
begin
    loop
        if waitnum(pr) > 0 then manager(pr).PASS(r); return; end if;
        if pr = 0 then avail(r) : = TRUE; free : = free + 1; return; end if;
        pr : = pr - 1;
    end loop
end;
```

The first exit is taken if there is a user process waiting on one of the manager queues. By decrementing the local variable *pr* and starting it at *maxprior*, it is assured that the manager queue which has the highest priority and is non-empty is chosen. The second exit is chosen if and only if all numbers *waitnum(k)* are zero. In this case the released resource is added to the collection of free resources.

In the case where *free* > 0, releasing a resource is the simple action of recording this fact in table *avail* and incrementing variable *free*.

```
    avail(r) : = TRUE; free : = free + 1;
```

Because the value of *free* is greater than zero, no processes can be waiting for a resource. The logic provided in the case where *free* = 0 guarantees that *free* > 0 occurs only when no processes are waiting for resources.

The Scheduler will allow seizure of a resource that bypasses the managers only if there are free resources available and there is no contention. A resource index is returned to the requesting user process. The basic mechanism is identical to that in the accept statement for REQUEST but the resource is returned directly.

```
    while not avail(availindex)
    loop availindex : = availindex mod N + 1; end loop;
    avail(availindex) : = FALSE; free : = free - 1; r : = availindex;
```

Again, it is certain that the while loop terminates since

$$free > 0 \text{ and } free = Sum_k(avail(k) = TRUE).$$

The managers are implemented by task type PriorClassManager which provides the two entries PASS and RESERVE. The first entry is called by the Scheduler and serves the purpose of signalling to a manager that it can dequeue a waiting user process. The user processes call entry RESERVE and wait in the appropriate manager queue until a resource becomes available. Hence, each reservation must be preceded by a signal from the Scheduler.

```
    loop
            accept PASS        (r : in resindex)  do  . . .  end PASS;
            accept RESERVE  (r : out resindex) do  . . .  end RESERVE;
    end loop;
```

The sequence of accept statements assures that a manager will RESERVE exactly once for each PASS it receives from the Scheduler.

The parameter of entry PASS is the resource index selected by the Scheduler. This is the index that the manager is going to use in the subsequent reservation. Since the Scheduler has already taken care of updating the status variables of the collection of free resources, all the manager has to do is to pass the selected resource to the requesting user process. Earlier we made the observation that the task of the managers is not to update the status variables, but to control the priority queueing when no resources are available. Thus, all a manager has to do is to transmit the resource index received from the Scheduler to the requesting user process. For this purpose, the body of task type PriorClassManager contains an own variable *temp* of type *resindex*. The implementation for entries PASS and RESERVE are simply:

```
pass : temp := r;
reserve : r := temp;
```

13.4 The Complete Ada Program

package ProcManagement **is**

      maxprior : **constant** INTEGER : = 7;   -- an arbitrary choice
      subtype priority **is** INTEGER **range** 0 . . maxprior;
      type procid(x : priority) **is limited private**;

      function PRTY(pid : **in** procid) **return** priority;

private
      type procid(x : priority) **is record** prior : priority : = x; **end record**;
end ProcManagement;

package body ProcManagement **is**

      function PRTY(pid : **in** procid) **return** priority **is**
      begin return pid.prior; **end** PRTY;

end ProcManagement;

with ProcManagement; **use** Procmanagement;
generic N : **in** POSITIVE;
      type resource **is limited private**;
      with procedure USAGE (r : **in** resource);
package ResourceManagement **is**

      type resid **is limited private**;

      procedure ALLOC   (p : **in** procid; r : **in out** resid);
      procedure GRAB   (ok : **out** BOOLEAN; r : **in out** resid);
      procedure APPLY   (r : **in** resid);
      procedure DEALLOC (r : **in out** resid);

      improperindex : **exception**;

private
      subtype resindex **is** INTEGER **range** 0 . . N;
      type   resid **is record** index : resindex : = 0; **end record**;
end ResourceManagement;

```
with ProcManagement; use ProcManagement;
package body ResourceManagement is

     pool : array(1 . . N) of resource;

     task Scheduler is
          entry REQUEST   (pr : in priority);
          entry RELEASE   (r : in resindex);
          entry SEIZE     (r : out resindex);
     end Scheduler;

     task type PriorClassManager is
          entry PASS      (r : in resindex);
          entry RESERVE   (r : out resindex);
     end PriorClassManager;

     manager : array(priority) of PriorClassManager;

     procedure ALLOC(p : in procid; r : in out resid) is
     begin
          if r.index /= 0 then raise improperindex; end if;
          select  Scheduler.SEIZE(r.index);
          else    Scheduler.REQUEST(PRTY(p));
                  manager(PRTY(p)).RESERVE(r.index);
          end select;
     end ALLOC;

     procedure GRAB(ok : out BOOLEAN; r : in out resid) is
     begin
          if r.index /= 0 then raise improperindex; end if;
          ok := TRUE;
          select  Scheduler.SEIZE(r.index);
          else    ok := FALSE;
          end select;
     end GRAB;

     procedure APPLY(r : in resid) is
     begin
          if r.index = 0 then raise improperindex; end if;
          USAGE(pool(r.index));
     end APPLY;
```

```
procedure DEALLOC(r : in out resid) is
begin
     if r.index = 0 then raise improperindex; end if;
     Scheduler.RELEASE(r.index); r.index := 0;
end DEALLOC;

task body Scheduler is separate;                    -- cf. Chapter 10

task body PriorClassManager is
     res : resindex;
begin
     loop
          accept PASS(r : in resindex) do res := r; end PASS;
          accept RESERVE(r : out resindex) do r := res; end RESERVE;
     end loop;
end PriorClassManager;

end ResourceManagement;
```

```
separate(ResourceManagement)
task body Scheduler is
      free         : resindex := N;
      avail        : array(1 . . N) of BOOLEAN := (others => TRUE);
      availindex   : INTEGER range 1 . . N := 1;
      waitnum      : array (priority) of INTEGER := (others => 0);
begin
   loop select
      when free = 0  =>
      accept REQUEST(pr : in priority) do
         waitnum(pr) := waitnum(pr) + 1;
      end REQUEST;
   or
      when free > 0  =>
      accept REQUEST(pr : in priority) do
         while not avail(availindex)
         loop availindex := availindex mod N + 1; end loop;
         avail(availindex) := FALSE; free := free - 1;
         manager(pr).PASS(availindex);
      end REQUEST;
   or
      when free = 0  =>
      accept RELEASE(r : in resindex) do
         declare
            pr : priority := maxprior;
         begin loop
            if waitnum(pr) > 0 then manager(pr).PASS(r); return; end if;
            if pr = 0 then free := free + 1; avail(r) := TRUE; return; end if;
            pr := pr - 1;
         end loop;
         end; -- end block
      end RELEASE;
   or
      when free > 0 and SEIZE'COUNT = 0  =>
      accept RELEASE(r : in resindex) do
         free := free + 1; avail(r) := TRUE;
      end RELEASE;
   or
      when free > 0 and REQUEST'COUNT = 0  =>
      accept SEIZE(r : out resindex) do
         while not avail(availindex)
         loop availindex := availindex mod N + 1; end loop;
         avail(availindex) := FALSE; free := free - 1;
         r := availindex;
      end SEIZE;
   end select;
   end loop;

end Scheduler;
```

13.5 Reminders

1. Process waitinglists are implemented in Ada by accept statements in task bodies.

2. Pascal does not allow initialization in declarations.   Ada allows initialization in object declarations, but in no other type declarations than record type declarations.

3. Pascal does not allow parameterization of declarations.   Ada allows parameterization of array types (in the definition part) and of records (in the naming part of a declaration).

4. Pascal provides no facilities for hiding internal structures of types, nor for hiding own data objects. Ada provides both.

5. Ada's limited private types can be used for the implementation of capabilities.

6. Assignment and equality tests are not available for objects of a limited private type.   Such objects cannot be initialized in declarations and parameters of such a type cannot have default values.

7. A programmer can define his own version of an equality test for objects of a limited private type.   This function can be represented by the symbol "="

8. Private types must be elaborated in the private part of a package.   The declarations in the private part are not visible to the user of a package. (The information is there for an Ada compiler.)

9. An Ada program can be split into separately compilable parts. The body of a subprogram can be replaced by a stub and can be defined elsewhere with an indication of the environment in which it belongs.

13.6 Problems

1. In the developed programs the tables *alloctable* and *avail* must be searched for a free resource when a resource can be allocated. An alternative design uses the table *freestack* which has as many entries as there are resources. The table is used as follows. When a resource is allocated, the one in freestack[top] is selected and the top pointer is decremented by one; when a resource is released, the top pointer is incremented by one and the released resource is recorded in freestack[top] (where *top* already has the incremented value).   Each element of *freestack* is initialized to its own index and *top* is initialized to the number of resources.   Rewrite the Scheduler task in Ada using table *freestack*.

2. Suppose an environment for concurrent processes has two kinds of resources that can be substituted for one another, but one kind is much nicer than the other. (Examples are: hard-copy and screen terminals, primary and secondary memory, a lineprinter and a laser printer, etc.) Suppose there are only a few copies of the nice resources, but plenty of the others. Concurrent processes have three ways of requesting resources: (1) ask for a nice resource and wait until one is available; (2) ask for a nice resource, but if none is available ask for a resource of the other kind; if none is available, wait until a resource of either kind becomes available; (3) ask for a second class resource, but don't wait if none is available. Write the necessary programs for the two kinds of resources and three kinds of requests in Ada. Note that there is no priority classification of the concurrent processes involved.

3. In order to minimize the time that resources are kept by user processes, the cost of using a resource is computed for each process by counting the total number of resource allocations that took place while a process was using a particular resource. The period of use is determined by the time of allocation and the instant of the matching deallocation. (We assume that the concurrent processes cannot conspire to hold all resources.) Write a revised version of the Scheduler in Ada that computes the cost of resource usage. Does the priority scheme have an affect on the cost computation?

Fourteen

Representation Specifications

Topics: delay statement, data representation, exceptions, priorities, based numbers, limited private types, and encapsulation of constants.

Issues: task initialization, task interaction, multi-layered systems, task communication.

14.1 Problem Statement

Device handlers constitute a large class of systems programs. In dealing with programs in this class, there are two basic issues that arise. First, there is natural concurrency that exists between the device and the processor as well as between devices. Second, there is a low level interface, presented by both the processor and the devices, that typically consists of tightly packed data structures, special instructions, and dedicated memory locations and registers. (While interrupts constitute a basic part of this interface, the discussion of this issue is deferred until the next chapter.) The problem in this chapter is to write a device handler for keyboard input that exploits Ada's features of concurrency and data representation.

The device in this problem is an asynchronous communications interface (ACI) used for keyboard input in a keyboard/CRT configuration (the CRT is handled separately and is not part of the problem). There can be up to 12 keyboards handled by a single ACI. The input characters are stored by the ACI into a dedicated memory buffer located at memory location 500_8 (the addressable units are words, although bytes are addressable through special instructions). This buffer is used cyclically (i.e., as a circular buffer) with the new data stored at the beginning of the buffer after the end of the buffer has been reached. The hardwired structure consists of a head index, a tail index (each one word in length and whose values are 1 to 64) and a 64 word buffer. Each element in the buffer consists of two bytes: the input character and the input device identifier, in the

353

most and least significant bytes respectively. When the head index has the same value as the tail index, the buffer is empty. When tail index **mod** 64 + 1 is equal to the head index, the buffer is full. If the buffer is full and data is not removed quickly enough, data may be lost. Rather than increment the tail pointer to create a *buffer empty* condition (and thereby losing 64 characters), incoming characters may be overwritten in the ACI itself if they cannot be added to the buffer. Clearly, the handler should be written in such a way that the buffer is never allowed to become full. The maximum input rate is 15 characters per second (using the repeat key) for each keyboard.

14.2 Problem Discussion

The keyboard handler functionally interfaces in two directions. On the one hand, it interfaces with the machine through the hardwired ACI buffer. The handler's primary purpose is to empty the ACI buffer as quickly as possible and to ensure that the buffer does not become full and that characters input from the keyboards are not lost. On the other hand, the handler provides the interface to the user processes to supply characters on demand if any are present. (What the handler should do if there are not any characters is a design decision that will be left for later discussion.)

The ACI handler should be structured so that there is as little interference with its processing as possible. The only processes that should be able to interfere with its operation are higher priority device and system processes. If there are a number of processes within the handler, the user interface processes should not impede the device process. For instance, the device process should not have to wait on the user interface process if the latter is busy. This implies that the interface between the two processes must be chosen with care.

The user interface processes should smooth out the asynchrony of the actual input and should buffer characters if the input gets ahead of the user process. Two sorts of interface procedures might be provided: read and wait if no characters are available; and second, read and return if no characters are available. The first is probably the more typical for this kind of application.

A means of passing incoming characters from the device handler to the interface process is needed that satisfies the constraints mentioned above. The hardware interface itself provides a suggestion. A circular buffer can be used independently and without interference by a single producer process and a single consumer process since the head pointer is used by the consumer process independently of the producer process which uses the tail. Of course, the customary critical section problems arise if there are two consumer processes trying to access the buffer simultaneously. So, intuitively, a circular buffer appears to be an ideal interface between the two processes, at least from the device handler standpoint. The ACI handler can work independently of the user interface process.

From the standpoint of the user interface process, however, the configuration of a single circular buffer interface is not quite what is needed. When a user process asks for a character, the interface process has to search through the buffer to find such a character. This search is time consuming and there are problems extracting the character from within the buffer. The typical rigor for a circular buffer is that of a queue: insert at the tail, remove from the head. The circular buffer concept is a useful one but its use has not been correctly determined. There should be a circular buffer for each keyboard, an intermediate buffer, that smooths out the differences between production and consumption. In this way, the queue discipline is observed, the appropriate character is readily at hand and the two processes are completely independent and non-interfering.

The intermediate buffer should be large enough to provide the necessary buffering, but small enough to be space efficient. A suggested size is 2 seconds of input: 30 characters. This implies that a *buffer full* condition may arise and a policy must be established for this condition. One option is to *push* the oldest character off the end of the buffer. However, this does not seem to be as reasonable a solution as that which discards the most recent input: that is, the system goes so far and then effectively ignores all new input. From a keyboard user's point of view, there is nothing more frustrating than randomly losing characters. It is probably more noticeable and less frustrating that the most recent characters are lost than characters input quite a bit earlier. The policy, then, is to ignore any characters once the intermediate buffer is full. In a well balanced system, there should be no problem, but in a heavily loaded system, losses may occur. When losses do occur , the user process should be notified of the number of characters lost before the current character was successfully input into the intermediate buffer.

A user interface process, then, retrieves a character and a count from the intermediate buffer for the appropriate keyboard and returns them to the caller. The device process, on the other hand, removes characters from the ACI buffer and parcels them out to the appropriate intermediate buffers. If the buffer is full, the device process keeps a count of the number of characters lost for that keyboard and inserts the lost count with the first character that can be inserted into the buffer. If no characters have been lost, the lost count is obviously zero.

An important question remains: how should the device process be structured so that the characters are removed in a timely way without letting the buffer get full? Clearly, the process should be driven from a timer since there is no interrupt to indicate when a character has been entered into the ACI buffer. At the maximum speed of 15 characters per second, 12 keyboards could have a maximum of 180 characters per second, or 18 characters per 100 milliseconds. Quite likely, the input will be less than that, so a time period of 100 milliseconds seems a reasonable solution.

14.3 An Ada Solution

The general organization of the Ada solution is similar to that described in the discussion of the problem but with two differences. First, in order to hide the structure of the solution (i.e., the composition in terms of tasks and packages) a single user interface procedure, READKEYBOARD, is presented to the user. The interface procedure is called identifying the desired keyboard as one of its parameters. The semantics of the user procedure are as follows: if a character is available, it will be returned immediately; if a character is not available, the procedure will wait until a character is input from the keyboard and will then return it. Second, an array of tasks will provide the actual user interfaces to the intermediate buffers. We make use of the entry/accept mechanism within each task to provide the wait mechanism and to guarantee safe and exclusive use of the individual intermediate buffers. The remainder of the organization is fundamentally the same.

The organization of the ensuing discussion will follow the development of the Ada program. We will first discuss the components that are external to the keyboard handler itself but used in its implementation. These pieces would most likely reside in general and system libraries. We will present the overall structure of the body of the keyboard interface package and then discuss the individual pieces. The emphasis is divided between program solutions and Ada constructs.

Constant Encapsulation and Priorities

Because of the low level nature of device handlers, there are certain related pieces of information that may be conveniently grouped together in individual packages. These represent one of the simplest uses of the package mechanism: to collect related constants and encapsulate them. The advantage of collecting these constants together is that they then reside in one location and changes, additions, and deletions are easily and safely performed. For our purposes here, we illustrate two such packages: one for system representation specifications and one for priority specifications. Among other constants contained in the system representation specification package are the location and size of the ACI's hardware buffer.

```
package SysRepSpecs is
    . . .
    acblocation    : constant INTEGER := 8#500#;
    acbsize        : constant INTEGER := 64;
    . . .
end SysRepSpecs;
```

Note the use of the based integers to initialize the constants. The general form for based numbers is *base#number#*. The utility of using the based integers should be obvious: no conversion has to be made to check that the locations match those given in the specifications. If the specifications are in octal notation, the initial values should be in octal as well.

The system priority specification package contains the constants that indicate the priority for the various processes. We shall see below how these are used with pragmas to direct the compiler to supply the priority information to the run-time support system.

> **package** SysPrioritySpecs **is**
>
>   . . .
>   acipriority   : **constant** INTEGER : = 5;
>   kbipriority   : **constant** INTEGER : = 4;
>
>   . . .
> **end** SysPrioritySpecs;

The values given as priorities represent relative degrees of urgency (ARM 9.8, 9-16) that are statically determined at compile time. The effect of priorities on the run-time scheduling mechanism is expressed by the following rule:

> If two tasks with different priorities are both eligible for execution and could sensibly be executed using the same processing resources then it cannot be the case that the task with the lower priority is executing while the task with the higher priority is not.

In the case illustrated here, we want the hardware handler to have a higher priority than the interface tasks. While the numbers themselves have been chosen arbitrarily, they do reflect the relative ordering of the tasks. Where the priorities of the tasks are the same (as for all the interface tasks described below), there is no scheduling defined. The priority is associated with a particular task by the specification of a pragma in the task specification.

> **pragma** PRIORITY (static expression);

At most, one such pragma may appear in any task specification. For a main program, the pragma must appear in the outermost declarative part.

A Generic Circular Buffer and Limited Private Types

In Chapter 7 we introduced the *queue* data structure implemented by means of a circular buffer. We wish to use that implementation here but because of the peculiarities of the hardware buffer, we require a small change: a head and tail index instead of a head index and a length specification. (Of course, a different solution would be to use the existing queue structure where we can and devise a new structure especially for the hardware buffer. However, we wish to solve the problem so as to include the special requirements of hardware buffer.)

We introduce two generic parameters: the head and tail index type and the element type. The head and tail indices implicitly specify the size of the circular buffer. The element type specifies the type of the element in the buffer. The type of the index rather than the length of the buffer is the first parameter primarily because it allows us later to provide detailed representation specifications for the actual parameters of the hardware buffer and thus closely control the actual structure that is instantiated. Secondarily, this approach is slightly more general in that any index type can be used in instantiating a buffer. The index type specification takes the form

    type indextype **is** $(< >)$;

where the box "$< >$" means that any discrete range or discrete type can be used as an actual parameter. The element type is specified by

    type elementtype **is private**;

and requires only that assignment and equality be defined for the actual parameter. While the structure of the type is of no importance to the buffering mechanism, objects of the type must be assignable for the buffer to work.

```
generic  type indextype is (< >);
         type elementtype is private;
package Buffer Module is

    type buffer is limited private;

    procedure GET    (b : in out buffer; e : out elementtype);
    procedure PUT    (b : in out buffer; e : in elementtype);
    function    EMPTY(b : in buffer) return BOOLEAN;
    function    FULL  (b : in buffer) return BOOLEAN;

    underflow, overflow : exception;

private

    type buffer is record
        head   : indextype := indextype 'FIRST;
        tail    : indextype := indextype 'FIRST;
        buf     : array (indextype) of elementtype;
    end record;

end Buffer Module;
```

The buffer itself is a private type: that is, an abstract type. The type name is given and the operations that can operate on that type are defined. Further, the buffer type is limited private. In other words, assignment and tests for equality or inequality are not available for objects of this type (ARM 7.4.4, 7-9). These restrictions have a number of important consequences: initialization at object declaration is not possible; constants cannot be declared outside the defining package; initial values cannot be specified in access type allocation; and default values for parameters are not allowed. Because of these restrictions and consequences, it is usually worthwhile to ensure that limited private types have initial values from their private definition. A record structure is implied by this, as the only type declarations that allow the specification of initial values are record components. The only alternative solution is an initialization procedure. However, there is no way of guaranteeing that it will be used properly. In the example above, the head and tail indices are critical--they must be initialized correctly or it would appear that the buffer contained some arbitrary number of values.

The Keyboard Interface Package

The user interface and the actual keyboard handler are packaged together in the KeyboardInterface package. The only interface presented by the package is that of a subtype *kbindex*, which indicates the range of keyboard identifiers, and the procedure READKEYBOARD, which enables the user to obtain a character from a specified keyboard.

```
generic nrofkeyboards : NATURAL;
package KeyboardInterface is

    subtype kbindex; NATURAL range 1 . . nrofkeyboards;

    procedure READKEYBOARD
        (k : in kbindex; c : out character; l : out POSITIVE);

end KeyboardInterface;
```

Note that the system builder can tailor the package to his requirements by instantiating the package for the number of keyboards actually in existence. The generic parameter *nrofkeyboards* is an example of a generic parameter that is identical with function and procedure parameters: it specifies an identifier, implicitly of mode in, and the type of the identifier. Its function is to specify parameters whose values are important within the generic unit -- in this case, the upper bound of the keyboard index. Parameters of this sort may have default values given. For example, if the standard keyboard configuration is always 12 keyboards, the generic parameter can be structured to indicate that fact, thereby enabling the system builder to instantiate the package without providing an actual parameter.

Organization of the Package Body

The declarative parts of local procedures, packages and tasks must precede their implementations. Within this constraint, declarations must occur before use. Thus, for example, the declarations of the keyboard interface task type must precede the declaration of the array of tasks, *kitasks*.

The units local to the package body are concerned with one of two things: the user interface or the ACI interface. For the user interface we have the following components: the package InterfaceBuffers, which defines the input; the task type *IfbHandler*, which defines the interface for the actual implementation of the interface procedure READKEYBOARD; the array of tasks *kitasks*, which provides a handler for each intermediate buffer; and the implementation of READKEYBOARD. For the ACI interface, we have the task ACIHandler which provides all the necessary mechanisms to handle the actual hardware interface.

```
with SysRepSpecs, SysPriority, BufferModule;
package body KeyboardInterface is

        package Interface Buffers is  .  .  . ;

        task type IfbHandler is  .  .  . ;
        kitasks; array (kbindex) of IfbHandler;

        task ACIHandler is  .  .  . ;
        procedure READKEYBOARD  .  .  . ;

        task body IfbHandler is  .  .  . ;
        task body ACIHandler is  .  .  . ;
begin
        -- package initialization
end KeyboardInterface;
```

Generic Instantiation

The purpose of the package InterfaceBuffers is to define the intermediate buffers for characters removed from the hardware buffer by ACIHandler and which are thus available to the consumer programs. This is accomplished by using the generic package BufferModule discussed above. The index type and buffer element type are first defined and then the package IFB (abbreviation for interface buffer) is instantiated using these types.

Instantiation requires the keywords **package** and **is new**, the name of the new package and the name of the generic package and parameters. The form is (ARM 12.3, 12-8)

package name **is new** generic package name (parameters);

where the parameters may be optional if default values have been given. The form is similar for functions and procedures.

```
with BufferModule;
package InterfaceBuffers is

        ifbsize : constant INTEGER := 30;
        type ifbindex is INTEGER range 1 .. ifbsize;
        type ifbelement is record
               char   : character;
               lost   : POSITIVE;
        end record;

        package IFB is new BufferModule (ifbindex, ifbelement);

        ifbarray : array (kbindex) of IFB.buffer;

end InterfaceBuffers;
```

The package IFB has been instantiated from the generic package BufferModule using the types *ifbindex* and *ifbelement*. The new package thus provides an interface analogous to that of BufferModule except that *ifbindex* and *ifbelement* have been substituted for *indextype* and *elementtype*. Thus we have a buffer of *ifbelement* elements, indexed by *ifbindex*, and operations appropriate to that definition.

Using a Package Interface

In the preceding example, the array of buffers is defined using the type *buffer* from the newly instantiated package IFB. The method used here to refer to components within the package interface is the dot notation. The package component is prefaced with the package name. This provides, in all cases, an unambiguous specification of component names. However, it may also generate some very long names. For example, to a user of the package InterfaceBuffers who wants to put something into the buffer, the reference would be

```
InterfaceBuffers.IFB.PUT( ... );
```

The use clause provides a means of shortening package component references where no ambiguity exists concerning the component names. The use clause *opens* the package interface and makes its components immediately accessible. If we open the InterfaceBuffers package by

```
use InterfaceBuffers;
```

we can then shorten the reference and perform the put operation by invoking IFB.PUT(. . .); instead of the longer name. The only constraint is that IFB.PUT must be unique at that point in the elaboration. Thus the declaration in the previous example of the intermediate buffers could be written alternatively as

> **use** IFB;
> ifbarray : **array** (kbindex) **of** buffer;

Task Types

An Ada task is not a program unit that may be generically defined. However, it is possible to replicate and instantiate tasks by means of task type definitions and task object declarations. The keyword **type** is included in the task interface declaration (ARM 9.1, 9-1).

> **task type** name **is** . . . **end** name;

The interface for a task type is the same as for a task: entry specifications and representation specifications. However, task objects may be declared using these task types (ARM 9.2, 9-3). Task objects may be singular objects similar to simple variables or part of compound objects such as records or arrays. The value of a task variable is a task of the task type. These task objects are treated in a manner similar to a limited private type: no assignment is possible and no check for equality or inequality is allowed. In addition, task objects behave as constants: their values cannot change. Thus, a task object can only be passed in subprogram calls and generic instantiations as an in argument. Should assignment of tasks be desired, access types that refer to the task type can be defined thus enabling the user to assign tasks and compare the equality of tasks (albeit indirectly through access values).

The task type needed here is that which governs the user's access to the intermediate buffers defined in the package InterfaceBuffers. As task types do not allow parameterization of the type, it is often the case that a task type will require an initialization entry to initialize local variables and establish initial conditions. Here it is required in order to provide the task object with its identity--that is, which keyboard it is controlling. The other entry enables the interface procedure to access the character buffer for that keyboard.

> **task type** IfbHandler **is**
>
> > **entry** INIT   (id : **in** kbindex);
> > **entry** READ (c : **out** character; l : **out** POSITIVE);
>
> **end** IfbHandler;

The task object defined here is an array of tasks, one for each keyboard. Each keyboard and corresponding intermediate buffer has a task associated with it. The association is made explicit by means of the INIT entry and corresponds to the implicit association provided by the index into the array

    kitasks : **array** (kbindex) **of** IfbHandler;

Using Task Interfaces

Unlike packages, task interfaces cannot be opened by means of the use clause. Name qualification must always be used in the form of the dot notation. For tasks, the task name must always be specified, while for task objects, the object name must always be specified. In the case under consideration here, the array name must be specified, the appropriate array component selected by means of an index and then the entry name given to select the appropriate action.

```
procedure READKEYBOARD
        (k : in kbindex; c : out character; l : out POSITIVE)
is
begin
        kitasks(k).READ(c, l);
end READKEYBOARD;
```

The interface procedure masks the fact that there is a task involved in retrieving a character. By hiding the implementation, a minimum amount of dependence is created upon the actual structure of the implementation. Here the task entry provides the wait mechanism should there be no character available.

Task Initialization

Packages may have generic parameters to tailor a particular package to individual use. Types may be parameterized to select the desired discriminants and thus fix the appropriate subtype. Task types, on the other hand, have neither of these facilities. Initialization of internal data can be accomplished, as in packages, by a sequence of statements. However, any desired parameter values can only be passed by means of some initializing accept statement. For example, the interface buffer handler tasks, defined in the array of tasks *kitasks*, need to know which keyboard they are guarding. The entry INIT provides the means of specifying this value:

    accept INIT(id : **in** kbindex) **do** myid : = id; **end** init;

Note that we have a local variable *myid* to hold the particular keyboard identifier.

This approach is functionally equivalent to that of parameterized types, although it is not nearly as elegant and certainly not as safe. With respect to the latter, there is no guarantee that the user will perform the appropriate initialization procedure. Alternatively, the power of generic packages can be used by packaging the task within the body of the task and renaming the entries as procedures. However, the ease of declaring task objects is lost by having to instantiate each package when the parameterized task is needed. Clearly, this cannot be done to create arrays, only to create particular objects.

Guarded Accept Statements

The READKEYBOARD semantics have been defined to include a wait if no data is present for that keyboard. Ada's accept mechanism provides facilities that can be used to implement this approach: the accept statement can have a boolean guard which will disallow the activation of the accept statement if the guard is not true. Include this within a loop and select statement combination and the desired semantics will occur.

```
loop
      select
            when not EMPTY(ifbarray(myid)) = >
            accept READ(c : out character; l : out POSITIVE) do
                  GET(ifbarray(myid), ifbdata);
                  c := ifbdata.data;
                  l := ifbdata.lost;
            end READ;
                  . . .
      end select;
end loop;
```

Note that we select the READ accept statement only if the appropriate keyboard buffer is not empty. Thus, the read entry will not be accepted until there is something in the buffer. Any calls on the READ entry will be queued until there is data in the buffer. When the boolean guard evaluates TRUE, the accept statement will be honored and a read will occur immediately or as soon as a READ operation is invoked by some user.

The Delay Statement

The program segment above has one severe disadvantage: it will busy wait until data is put into the buffer. This is a very inefficient use of the processor. One solution to this problem is to check periodically to see if there is data in the buffer. This can be accomplished by using a delay statement as an alternative in the looped select statement (ARM 9.6, 9.7.1). The delay statement has the form

```
delay simple-expression;
```

where the argument is of the predefined fixed point type *duration* (which is given in seconds). The type *duration* allows the specification of both positive and negative values up to 86400 seconds -- one days worth of seconds.

In this case, a wait of approximately 200 milliseconds seems to be a good first choice (the fastest input is 15 characters per second using the repeat key). Should this cause noticeable delay between the pressing of the key and the appearance of the character on the screen, the delay time can be decreased.

delay 0.2;

The Structure of the Body of ACIHandler

The implementation of the hardware handler consists of a package defining the hardware buffer, an array to maintain the counts of lost characters for each keyboard, a procedure to process characters out of the hardware buffer and into the appropriate intermediate buffers, and the actual body of the task itself.

```
task ACIHandler;

task body ACIHandler is
        package ACIBuffer is . . . ;
        lost : . . . ;
        procedure PROCESSCHAR is . . . ;
begin
        . . .
end ACIHandler;
```

Note that the interface specification is empty: if there are no entries for the task, only the name is required in the task specification.

Data Representation Specifications

The hardware provides a particular interface to be used by the handlers in processing the keyboard input. Often the format of hardware interface is very compact, providing as much data in as little space as possible. The problem confronting the programmer is to define a logical structure that adequately describes the data and its types and then to map that logical structure into the fixed physical structure required by the hardware interface.

Representation specifications provide the means of mapping the logical structure of the data onto the required physical structure. Four representation facilities are provided: length, enumeration type, record type, and address specifications (ARM 13, 13-1). These specifications must appear at the end of the declarative part, following all the declarations but preceding any sequence of statements.

Length specifications (ARM 13.2, 13-3) enable the programmer to define four different size requirements: the size, in bits, to be allocated for a particular type; the size of a collection, such as the amount of storage space to be allocated for an access type; the amount of space to be allocated for an activation of a task or task type; and the size of the actual delta for fixed point types. The form of the length specification is as follows.

for name'attribute **use** expression;

The attributes are SIZE, STORAGE_SIZE, STORAGE_SIZE, and DELTA respectively. For example, we want to specify that the length of any variable of type *acbindex* (the index into the ACI buffer) is to be one word, or 16 bits,

for acbindex'SIZE **use** 16;

even though its range of values requires far fewer bits to be properly represented.

Enumeration type representation specifications (ARM 13.3, 13-5) enable the programmer to define the internal representation for the enumerated values. Instead of automatically inheriting the internal codes 0 . . N for some enumeration, the internal codes can be specified as desired, either as contiguous or noncontiguous values. However, the ordering relation must be maintained and satisfied.

Record type representations allow the programmer to specify in detail the physical structure of a record. Each component in the record is described by a location clause that specifies which word in the record the component occurs in and its bit positions within that word. The record itself may optionally be aligned to begin the record at a particular bit boundary, such as at the byte, word, double word, boundary. The form of the record specification is as follows:

for typename **use record**

[**at mod** static simple expression]

component name **at** location specification **range** bit location range
. . .

end record;

The first storage unit of a record is numbered 0 and, within that, the first storage bit is numbered 0 as well. The specific machine dependent details can be found in the SYSTEM package (ARM 13.4, 13-6). Assuming that there is a constant *word* defined in terms of SYSTEM.STORAGE_UNIT, the programmer can use the expression N * word to define the appropriate word within a record structure. Within a particular word, the bit locations are specified from n to m where $n < m$, and $m \leq$ bitsize(machineword).

The logical structure of the components of the hardware buffer is as follows:

> **type** acbindex **is** INTEGER **range** 1 . . acbsize;
> **type** acbelement **is record**
>   char   : character;
>   kbnr : kbindex;
> **end record**;

The representation specification for the record structure guarantees that the element begins on a word boundary and that the two components each occupy one byte. The size specification indicates that the index object will require a full word of storage.

> **for** acbindex'SIZE **use** 16;
> **for** acbelement **use record**
>   **at mod** 16;
>   char   **at** 0 $*$ word **range** 0 . . 7;
>   kbnr **at** 0 $*$ word **range** 8 . . 15;
> **end record**;

Address specifications are the fourth kind of specifications that the programmer can control. One such specification we shall defer to the next chapter: the interrupt location. In this chapter, we have the requirement to specify the location of the hardware buffer. The address specification is of the form

> **for** name **use at** location;

The name is the name of the data structure and the location is a static simple expression. The structure for the hardware buffer elements have been carefully specified in the preceding paragraphs. To declare the buffer and its desired location, we first instantiate the appropriate form of the circular buffer, declare an object of the new buffer type, and then define its location.

> **package** ACB **is new** BufferModule (acbindex, acbelement);
> **use** ACB;
> acbuffer : buffer;
> **use** SysRepSpecs;
> **for** acbuffer **use** at acblocation;

PROCESSCHAR and Exceptions

The heart of the device handler is the operation PROCESSCHAR: characters are removed from the hardware buffer and parceled into the appropriate interface buffer; lost counts are maintained for each intermediate buffer when they are full, and passed in with the appropriate character when insertion becomes possible. The largest possible value is maintained if the lost count overflows.

```
lost : array (kbindex) of POSITIVE := (others => 0);

procedure PROCESSCHAR is
        use InterfaceBuffers, ACIBuffers;
        input : acbelement;
begin
        if not ACB.EMPTY(acbuffer) then
                ACB.GET (acbuffer, input);
                if IFB.FULL (ifbarray(input.kbnr))
                        then if lost(input.kbnr) /= POSITIVE'LAST then
                                lost (input.kbnr) := lost (input.kbnr) + 1;
                        end if;
                        else  IFB.PUT(ifbarray(input.kbnr),
                                        (input.char, lost (input.kbnr)));
                                lost (input.kbnr) := 0;
                end if;
        end if;
end PROCESSCHAR;
```

Note that a record aggregate is used as the second argument to IFB.PUT. Note also that even though the two buffer packages have been opened by the use statement, the GET and PUT operations must be distinguished from each other with name qualification to prevent any ambiguity.

The body of PROCESSCHAR provides a good example of the complexity that can arise in handling errors when successive operations depend upon the success of the previous operations. The levels of nesting are normal byproducts and serve primarily to obscure the normal algorithm. In fact, the normal algorithm is so completely enmeshed in the error handling algorithm that it is difficult to determine which is which.

```
procedure PROCESSCHAR is
        . . .
begin
        ACB.GET (acbuffer, input);
        IFB.PUT (ifbarray(input.kbnr), (input.char, lost (input.kbnr)));
        lost (input.kbnr) := 0;
exception
        when ACB.underflow => null;
        when IFB.overflow =>
                begin
                        lost (input.kbnr) := lost (input.kbnr) + 1;
                exception
                        when NUMERIC_ERROR =>
                                lost (input.kbnr) := POSITIVE'LAST;
                end;
end PROCESSCHAR;
```

Ada's exception mechanism enables the programmer to separate the normal algorithm from the error handling algorithm. Two benefits are drived from this. First, the normal algorithm is quite clear and the errors are explicitly enumerated as exceptions and are subordinated to the normal part. Second, the error handling algorithms are executed only when needed, and not constantly as in the first example.

The logic of the procedure itself is clarified and the complexity is reduced. If the hardware buffer is empty, nothing is to be done (hence the keyword **null** representing the empty statement) because not handling the exception would propagate the exception out to the calling scope. Here we do not want to do that. A block is required to handle the IFB.overflow exception in order to provide the necessary enclosing scope to catch the arithmetic overflow which is handled by maintaining the largest possible value for the lost count.

The ACI Handler

The body of statements for the device handling task is a loop that either delays, if the buffer is empty, or calls PROCESSCHAR.

```
begin -- body of ACIHandler
        loop
                if ACB.EMPTY(acbuffer) then
                        delay 0.1;
                end if;
                PROCESSCHAR;
        end loop;
end ACIHandler;
```

Package Initialization

The initialization part of the package occurs at the lexical end of the package and is enclosed by the keywords **begin** and **end**. Any initialization that is required which cannot be, or has not been, done by declaration initialization clauses can be done here. In this example, the keyboard buffer processes need to be given their identities. We have , therefore, a loop within which we call the entry INIT to provide each task with its keyboard identifier.

```
begin -- initialization of KeyboardInterface
        for i in kbindex loop
                kitasks(i).INIT(i);
        end loop;
end KeyboardInterface;
```

Comments

Ada provides mechanisms to enable the system programmer to solve machine dependent representation problems and to structure the solution in a naturally concurrent way. However, some of the mechanisms are by no means ideal. The specification of bit positions in record type representations as 0 to N may be counter to hardware documentation which is often presented as N to 0 within a word or even groups of words. This can be an irritating source of errors. On the whole, however, the mechanisms are quite adequate and provide for a good implementation.

14.4 The Complete Ada Program

```
package SysRepSpecs is
        . . .
        acblocation    : constant INTEGER := 8#500#;
        acbsize        : constant INTEGER := 64;
        . . .
end SysRepSpecs;



package SysPrioritySpecs is
        . . .
        acipriority    : constant INTEGER := 5;
        kbipriority    : constant INTEGER := 4;
        . . .
end SysPrioritySpecs;



generic    type indextype is (< >);
           type elementtype is private;
package BufferModule is

        type buffer is limited private;

        procedure GET      (b : in out buffer; e : out elementtype);
        procedure PUT      (b : in out buffer; e : in elementtype);
        function   EMPTY (b : in buffer) return BOOLEAN;
        function   FULL   (b : in buffer) return BOOLEAN;
        underflow, overflow : exception;

private

        type buffer is record
                head : indextype := indextype'FIRST;
                tail : indextype := indextype'FIRST;
                buf  : array (indextype) of elementtype;
        end record;

end BufferModule;

package body BufferModule is  . . .  end;
```

```
generic nrofkeyboards : NATURAL;
package KeyboardInterface is

        subtype kbindex is NATURAL range 1  . .  nrofkeyboards;

        procedure READKEYBOARD
            (k : in kbindex; c : out character; l : out POSITIVE);

end KeyboardInterface;


with SysRepSpecs, SysPrioritySpecs, BufferModule;
package body KeyboardInterface is

        package InterfaceBuffers is

            ifbsize : constant INTEGER : =  30;
            type ifbindex is new INTEGER range 1  . .  ifbsize;
            type ifbelement is record
                char : character;
                lost  : POSITIVE;
            end record;

            package IFB is new BufferModule(ifbindex, ifbelement);

            use IFB;
            ifbarray : array (kbindex) of buffer;

        end InterfaceBuffers;


        task type IfbHandler is

            entry INIT    (id : in kbindex);
            entry READ (c : out character; l : out POSITIVE);

            pragma PRIORITY (SysPrioritySpecs.kbipriority);

        end IfbHandler;

        kitasks : array (kbindex) of ifbHandler;

        task ACIHandler is
            pragma PRIORITY (SysPrioritySpecs.acipriority);
        end ACIHandler;
```

```
procedure READKEYBOARD
     (k : in kbindex; c : out character; l : out POSITIVE)
is
begin
     kitasks(k).READ(c, l);
end READKEYBOARD;



task body IfbHandler is

     use InterfaceBuffers;
     use IFB;

     myid    : kbindex;
     ifbdata : ifbelement;

begin

     accept INIT(id : in kbindex) do myid := id; end init;

     loop
          select
               when not EMPTY(ifbarray(myid)) =>
               accept READ(c : out character; l : out POSITIVE) do
                    GET(ifbarray(myid), ifbdata);
                    c := ifbdata.char;
                    l := ifbdata.lost;
               end READ;
          or
               delay 0.2;
          end select;
     end loop;

end IfbHandler;

task body ACIHandler is

     package ACIBuffer is
          use SysRepSpecs;

          type acbelement is record
               char : character;
               kbnr : kbindex;
          end record;
          type acbindex is new INTEGER range 1 . . acbsize;
```

```ada
        package ACB is new BufferModule (acbindex, acbelement);
        use ACB;
        acbuffer : buffer;

private
        for acbindex'SIZE use 16;
        for acbelement use record
            at mod 16;
            char at 0 * word range 0 . . 7;
            kbnr at 0 * word range 8 . . 15;
        end record;
        for acbuffer use at acblocation;

end ACIBuffer;


lost : array (kbindex) of POSITIVE := (others => 0);


procedure PROCESSCHAR is
        use InterfaceBuffers, ACIBuffer;
        input : acbelement;
begin
        ACB.GET(acbuffer, input);
        IFB.PUT(ifbarray(input.kbnr),(input.char,lost(input.kbnr)));
        lost (input.kbnr) := 0;

exception
        when ACB.underflow => null;
        when IFB.overflow =>
            begin
                lost (input.kbnr) := lost (input.kbnr) + 1;
            exception
                when NUMERIC_ERROR =>
                    lost (input.kbnr) := POSITIVE'LAST;
            end;

end PROCESSCHAR;
```

```
        use ACIBuffer;
        begin -- body of ACIHandler
            loop
                if ACB.EMPTY(acbuffer) then
                    delay 0.1;
                end if;
                PROCESSCHAR;
            end loop;
        end ACIHandler;


begin -- initialization of KeyboardInterface

        for i in kbindex loop
            kitasks(i).INIT(i);        -- initialize identity of task
        end loop;

end KeyboardInterface;
```

14.5 Reminders

The following reminders refer to Ada only.

1. Packages in Ada may be used to provide several levels of encapsulation: data collection, related types and operations, and abstract data types.

2. Ada's pragmas provide the means of giving different kinds of instructions to the compiler. One such instruction concerns the relative priority of tasks.

3. Ada's generic packages provide the means of tailoring various kinds of resource packages to individual use. Parameters may be values, objects, types or operations.

4. Discrete range types can be specified as generic parameters by means of a box, that is, "$(< >)$".

5. Other generic type parameters may be either private or limited private. Functions and procedures may be required with these types for operations other than assignment and tests for equality.

6. Private types inherit only assignment and tests for equality/inequality. Limited private types do not inherit even these operations.

7. Declarations must occur before use and declarative parts must precede implementation parts.

8. The use statement opens the contents of a package. However, where names conflict and create an ambiguity, the dot notation form of name qualification must be used to differentiate these ambiguous names.

9. The main purpose of the use statement is to reduce the size of names. Dot notation to qualify names is always proper.

10. References to task entries must always use the dot notation for name qualification.

11. Task types provide one means of replicating task objects. These objects are treated as limited private type objects.

12. The interface specifications of tasks and task types consist solely of entry specifications and representation specifications.

13. Tasks and task types have no parameters as do types and generic units (packages, procedures and functions). External initialization must be accomplished by means of an initialization entry.

14. Select alternatives may have boolean guards, If the boolean guard is FALSE, the alternative is not selectable.

15. The else clause in a select statement guarantees that at least one alternative will be selected.

16. Processing within a task may be suspended by means of the delay statement. This provides one means of avoiding busy waiting.

17. Four representations facilities are provided: length specifications, enumerated type specifications, record type specifications and address specifications.

18. Length specifications enable the programmer to specify the length, in bits, of objects of a particular type, the amount of storage for collections and task activations, and the size of the actual delta in fixed point numbers.

19. Enumeration specifications enable the programmer to specify either contiguous values other than 0 to N for enumerated type values or non-contiguous values that retain the ordering relation.

20. Record type specifications permit the exact layout of the record to be specified such that components can be organized at the bit level of storage. Records can also be aligned to any modulo base.

21. Data objects may be assigned particular locations by the address specification mechanism.

22. Record aggregates may be used as arguments for in parameters that require record types.

23. The exception mechanism provides a means of clarifying the logic of an algorithm by moving the error handling algorithms to the exception portion of the program unit. This leaves the normal algorithm completely separate.

24. Data local to a package and not amenable to declaration initialization can be initialized in the package initialization section at the end of the package. Tasks may be initialized here as well.

14.6 Problems

1. Program the body for the generic package BufferModule. Be careful about the incrementation of the indices. Why will modular arithmetic not work for this implementation? Are there more general arithmetic problems in allowing any discrete type as an index?

2. The cost of having N intermediate buffer tasks may be more than is acceptable (for argument's sake assume that it is, even though it probably is not). Reprogram the intermediate buffer handling and the READKEYBOARD routine such that there is only one task that controls the

use of the interface buffers. What kinds of problems might be encountered in such a solution when keyboard traffic is heavy and program consumption of keyboard characters is heavy as well?

3. Assume that it is desired that no characters should be lost. What problems must be solved to guarantee this as far as possible: in the hardware handler? in the intermediate buffering? Change the examples to incorporate this strategy. What problems result from this new strategy? How should these be handled?

4. Some computers, such as the PDP-11, have dedicated memory locations set aside for the handling of devices. Assume that the memory interface is as follows: a one character buffer is located at 77500_8; the status word is at 77501_8 and is comprised of a flag (bit 0) to indicate that a new character has been put in the data buffer, a keyboard number (bits 1 - 4), and an error flag (bit 5) to indicate that data has been lost; accessing the data buffer resets the new character and error flags. Reprogram the device handler to handle this new ACI device. Can the delay statement be used? If so, what should be the unit of delay?

Fifteen

Low Level I/O

Topics: hardware interrupts, data representation, derived types, type conversion, private types, limited private types, pragmas PACK and INLINE, access types, renaming, access type exceptions, derived types, anonymous subtypes, generic procedures.

Issues: abstraction, cooperating tasks, synchronization, Interrupt handling, device handling.

15.1 Problem Statement

The disc represents one of the primary hardware resources for information storage and retrieval in most computer systems. It offers a fairly large amount of storage space directly accessible in a reasonably short time. The mechanical structure of these devices varies in a few respects but basically consists of one or more *platters* rotating around a spindle with *read/write heads* that access the information on the platter *surfaces*. Each surface that is used contains concentric *tracks* which are in turn divided into the smallest addressable units called *sectors*. The storage space is dependent upon the number of platters, the number of surfaces, the number of tracks and the number and size of the sectors. The speed of access is dependent upon two factors: the rotation speed and the speed with which the read/write heads can be positioned over the desired track. This latter characteristic leads to one of the basic variations in disc units: the fixed head disc and the movable head disc. In the former, there is a read/write head positioned over each track on each surface while in the latter, there is one read/write head for each surface that can move to any track on that surface. Where there are several surfaces, it is usually the case that the heads move in concert, that is, together and not independently. Further, only one read/write head can be activated at a given time so that only one read or write operation can be performed at any given moment.

The basic problem to be solved is to write a handler for the disc that provides read and write operations to user processes but that performs all of the actual interface details itself. The problem is really more that of a basic disc manager rather than just a disc handler.

15.2 Problem Discussion

The basic components in addressing a piece of information in the disc unit are: (1) the particular platter, (2) the surface on the desired platter, (3) the track on the desired surface and (4) the sector within the desired track. This is a rather complex address that requires a level of detail far below that which should be required of users of the disc. A change in disc units could easily change the address structure, e.g., the number of sectors, tracks and surfaces could be different. It is important to hide this level of detail and create an abstraction which simplifies the addressing structure for the user.

A useful abstraction with respect to information is that of a *page*. The actual size of a page often depends on the requirements of the particular system but should be some multiple of the sector size for ease of conversion from page to platter/surface/track/sector. The virtue of the paged disc is that it hides these details that might change and maps the hardware device into a simple hardware-independent structure. Where the pages actually reside on the disc is a matter for the actual disc handler to determine. Should additional discs be added, or a different disc be used, the superstructure built upon the disc manager remains unaffected, though the number of available pages may differ.

Given the paged disc abstraction, some discipline must be imposed on its use. Users should not be able to claim arbitrary pages that may be already in use by some other user. To this end, a page manager is appropriate that services claims for the use of the disc pages and allows their return from use. The two operations are RESERVE and RELEASE: for purposes of simplicity, RESERVE will return a single available page and RELEASE will return the specified page to the free page list. Two exceptional conditions arise with respect to RESERVE and RELEASE: there may be no space available for the reserve and the released page may already be free.

Actual access to pages is through READ and WRITE operations provided by the disc I/O manager. For every READ or WRITE, the Disc I/O manager transfers the content of an entire page to or from the disc. Since transferring a page takes a relatively long time, the process requesting the tranfer should not wait all that time and remain idle, but proceed doing other useful work. If we treat READ and WRITE as requests, we can have the calling process continue while the disc I/O manager transfers a page. The calling process must then check at some later time whether or not the transfer has completed and may have to wait if it has not completed.

Checking the status of a transfer and waiting for its completion is implemented by a pair of operations STATUS and WAIT. In order to make sure that a calling process checks the correct transfer, READ and WRITE must return a token, a receipt one might say, that identifies the particular transfer request. (Note that the receipt cannot just be the page identity, because several processes may concurrently ask for the same page.)

When a receipt is passed as parameter to STATUS, the calling process receives in return the current status of the transfer identified by the receipt. The status may indicate that the transfer has been completed, that it has not been completed or that an error occurred. The calling process can act according to the information it receives and, for instance, continue its own work if the transfer is not completed and come back later. The STATUS operation is very useful in addition to WAIT, because it enables the program to monitor the progress of the request.

15.3 An Ada Solution

The Ada programs capitalize on the separation of interfaces from implementation. This facilitates the design and promotes the division of the solution into manageable parts. Further, it promotes the reusability of programs. We use four external packages (DiscCharacteristcs, LOW_LEVEL_IO, Semaphores, and DynamicQueue) to implement our disc manager. The implementations of the packages are separated from their interfaces in order to provide manageable chunks of programs.

Disc Characteristics and Encapsulation

There are a number of constants and types that describe various aspects of the disc interface and the disc's physical characteristics. The question before the designer is how to organize this information. On the one hand, there is the desire to encapsulate all the related information into a single package. There are several virtues of this approach: the facts about the disc can be easily located because they are isolated in a single place; and, dependencies upon this information are more easily traced if these facts are collected in a single place rather than dispersed in several places. On the other hand, there is the desire to hide as much implementation detail as possible from the rest of the system. Several advantages result from this latter approach: users are not aware of the actual structure of the disc but are aware only of the exported disc abstraction; and the abstraction cannot be subverted since no facts are available to the users.

Ideally, the designer can combine these two approaches and thus accrue all the advantages of both. However, in this case, there are factors that prevent this combined approach. The system low level I/O package requires knowledge of certain aspects of the disc interface in order to implement the low level routines

SEND_CONTROL and RECEIVE_CONTROL. This fact raises a conflict between the desires for encapsulation and information hiding. First, there is no way to encapsulate all the facts about the disc and hide the implementation in two distinct packages. Second, the low level I/O package is public and thus available for use by any package. Restrictions on the use of the low level I/O package occur only by conventions within the system. Because of the latter, there is no possibility of completely hiding the implementation details of the disc within a DiscManager package. We have, therefore, elected to follow the desires for encapsulation and collect the facts about the disc in a package DiscCharacteristics.

This package contains a description of the physical characteristics of the disc, the definitions of a disc buffer, a disc address, a disc request, a status returned from the disc unit, a disc command and the specification of the disc interrupt location. The disc requests, disc status and disc commands are defined as follows:

```
type discrequest     is (seek, read, write);
type discstatus       is (busy, done, seekerror, readerror, writerror);
type disccommand is record
        dreq   : discrequest;
        addr   : discaddress;
        bptr   : discbufferptr;
end record;
```

Packing Arrays

Ada has no syntactic notion of a packed array but has a means of specifying that an array should be packed as efficiently as possible. Pragma PACK indicates to the compiler that it is to select the representation which minimizes the amount of storage (cf. Chapter 9). Note that packing does not affect the components of an object, but does affect the space between components in that it instructs the compiler to minimize the gaps between components. Recall that a pragma must be placed after the declarations and before any use of representation attributes.

The disc buffer is a packed array of bytes (which is presumably defined in a system package providing the basic facts about the system). The buffer is the size of a sector on the disc, 512 bytes. In order to minimize copying of data, we pass around pointers to the disc buffer.

```
sectorlength : constant INTEGER := 512;
type discbuffer is array (1 . . sectorlength) of byte;
type discbufferptr is access discbuffer;
pragma PACK (discbuffer);
```

Anonymous Subtypes

The physical characteristics of the disc (the number of platters, surfaces per platter, tracks per surface and sectors per track) are defined by a set of constants.

```
platters  : constant INTEGER := 2;
surfaces  : constant INTEGER := 2;        --  per platter
tracks    : constant INTEGER := 203;      --  per surface
sectors   : constant INTEGER := 12;       --  per track
```

These constants are used to provide the underlying interpretation of the disc page abstraction. They provide the means of mapping a page onto the particular platter, surface, track, and sector. In addition, we use them to define the components of the record type *discaddress*.

```
type discaddress is record
      pl  : INTEGER range 0 . . platters - 1;
      tr  : INTEGER range 0 . . tracks - 1;
      su  : INTEGER range 0 . . surfaces - 1;
      se  : INTEGER range 0 . . sectors - 1;
end record;
```

Note that we defined the components in terms of anonymous subtypes rather than explicit subtypes. Given the definition of the basic facts about the disc as constants, we do this for several reasons. First, there is no loss of understanding and there is only a minimal effect upon readability. Second, we avoid excessive naming. The names of the subtypes would have to be quite similar to the constants in order to be self-documenting and this could be a source of programmer error and confusion. Third, the subtypes are used only for the fields of record *discaddress*. We are not going to declare variables of those subtypes.

One may ask, however, why we don't use subtypes instead of constant declarations. For example, given the definitions

```
subtype platter  is INTEGER range 0 . . 1;
subtype surface  is INTEGER range 0 . . 1;
subtype track    is INTEGER range 0 . . 202;
subtype sector   is INTEGER range 0 . . 11;
```

we can define the record type *discaddress* as

```
type discaddress is record
      pl  : platter;
      tr  : track;
      su  : surface;
      se  : sector;
end record;
```

The primary reason for not using this approach is the loss of readability in the conversion from a page to the disc address. The conversion uses modulo arithmetic to determine the mapping from the page to the appropriate sector. Instead of determining the surface address by the formula

p **mod** (sectors ∗ surfaces) / sectors

one would have to use the attribute *LAST* and add 1 to provide the desired divisor.

p **mod** ((sector'LAST + 1) ∗ (surface'LAST + 1)) / (sector'LAST + 1)

This loss of clarity in the conversion process is considered more important than the small loss of clarity in the record declaration.

Interrupt Representations

The disc unit indicates that an operation is completed by raising an interrupt. The disc handler fields the interrupt and proceeds with the next request. In order to do this properly we must associate the DISCINTERRUPT entry in the task *dh* with the actual interrupt. We do this in two steps. First, in the package DiscCharacteristics, we define a constant that describes the location of the disc interrupt.

discinterruptloc : **constant** address := . . . ;

where *address* is an integer subtype. Second, we define the representation (ARM 13.5, 13-7) of the entry DISCINTERRUPT in task *dh*.

```
task dh is
        entry DISCINTERRUPT;
        for DISCINTERRUPT use at DiscCharacteristics.discinterruptloc;
end dh;
```

The expression following the keywords **use at** must be an integer expression that specifies the location of the desired interrupt. Note that we have used the fully qualified name to designate the constant *discinterruptloc*. Alternatively we could have opened the scope of the package interface with **use** DiscCharacteristics; and dropped the package qualification.

Low Level I/O

The low level I/O facilities are not explicitly defined in the reference manual but a template of the package LOW_LEVEL_IO is given instead (ARM 14.6, 14-24). The actual implementation is system dependent and therefore unlikely to be entirely uniform across different systems and compiler implementations. The general scheme calls for two operations SEND_CONTROL and RECEIVE_CONTROL. SEND_CONTROL provides the means of commanding the device while RECEIVE_CONTROL provides the means of determining the current condition of the device and its operations. These two operations are overloaded for each device. The schema for SEND_CONTROL calls for two parameters: an in parameter that determines the device type and an in-out parameter that provides the command to the device. The schema for RECEIVE_CONTROL is identical to the preceding one except that the second parameter receives control information from the device.

> SEND_CONTROL   (device : *devicetype*; data : **in out** *datatype*);
> RECEIVE_CONTROL (device : *devicetype*; data : **in out** *datatype*);

For purposes of our example, we will define these two operations for the disc device defined in DiscCharacteristics. There are two types defined there that provide the second parameters to the two overloaded operations: the record type *disccommand* and the enumerated type *discstatus*. We provide an incomplete definition of the type *devicetype* since we are interested only in the disc.

> **package** LOW_LEVEL_IO **is**
>   **type** devicetype **is** (. . ., disc, . . .);
>   . . .
>   **use** DiscCharacteristics;
>   SEND_CONTROL   (d : devicetype; c : **in out** disccommand);
>   RECEIVE_CONTROL (d : devicetype; s : **in out** discstatus);
>   . . .
> **end** LOW_LEVEL_IO;

Disposable Semaphores

The disc manager provides a service to user processes that allows them to proceed independently and concurrently with their requested I/O. Central to the coordination between the user processes and disc manager is the concept of a receipt that can be used to determine the status and completion of the I/O request. A synchronization mechanism is necessary to the implementation of this receipt. Semaphores provide such a mechanism: a semaphore task type can be used to instantiate the necessary synchronizing task when it is needed. In order to ensure safety in the use of the semaphore, we will use a type that provides the maximum functionality that we need and no more: a *disposable* semaphore. This semaphore can have exactly one P and one V operation, thus guaranteeing that it can be used for exactly one I/O request. Misuse of the semaphore will have glaring consequences: a tasking error. With suitable encapsulation, we can guarantee that the semaphore is used correctly, but it does give us a secondary protection mechanism.

The Semaphore as a Limited Private Type

The limited private type *disposablesemaphore* is defined within a package Semaphores that supplies various other kinds of semaphores as well (such as counting semaphores). The underlying tasking mechanism is hidden within the package. This approach was taken in order to provide a uniform interface for all the different semaphores. The counting semaphore, for instance, is implemented as a limited private type with a parameter to set the count.

      type countingsemaphore (C : INTEGER) **is limited private**;

The operations P and V are overloaded for all semaphores.

      type disposablesemaphore **is limited private**;
      procedure P (s : **in out** disposablesemaphore);
      procedure V (s : **in out** disposablesemaphore);

Note that the parameters are of the mode in out. Functionally the parameter is changed and hence is specified as in out. However, it is not clear that this mode is strictly required because of the indirection inherent in objects of task types. The mode in would probably be acceptable because nothing is actually changed in the parameter representation of the semaphore. In these cases we recommend using the mode that describes functionally the action on the parameter.

The limited private type definition means that assignment and the test for equality are not defined or allowed for semaphores. This captures exactly the semantics that we want for semaphores: it does not make sense to copy semaphores nor does it make sense to determine if two semaphores are identical. Of course, semaphores can be shared by defining *access* types that point to semaphores, but that is quite acceptable and indeed what we do want to do.

Task Types as Limited Private Types

The implementation of the limited private type must be specified in the private part of the package. In this case, we wish to have a task type as the underlying representation. While this may seem unusual, it is a natural underlying implementation that eliminates the excess baggage of an enclosing record. (ARM 7.4.2, 7-7).

     private
         task type disposablesemaphore **is**
            entry P;
            entry V;
         end disposablesemaphore;
         . . .
     end Semaphores;

The task body is extremely simple: an accept statement for the V entry followed by an accept statement for the P entry. The order is important because it implements the semantics that we desire: the process performing the P operation must wait until after the V operation has been performed. The process performing the V should not have to wait at all.

```
task body disposablesemaphore is
begin
        accept V;
        accept P;
end disposablesemaphore;
```

Inline P and V Operations

The operations P and V are simply entry calls to the respective entry of the parameter. It seems that the overhead of a procedure call is rather excessive for a one statement body. Ada provides a pragma that enables the programmer to specify the subprograms that are desired to be expanded in line (ARM 6.3, 6-4). The pragma INLINE must appear in the same declarative part as the named subprograms. Since the procedures are declared in the package Semaphores specification, the pragma must appear in the specification also.

```
pragma INLINE (P, V);
```

The Context of DiscManager

The context of our compilation unit DiscManager consists of three packages. The first is DiscCharacteristics which supplies the basic facts about the disc. The second is LOW_LEVEL_IO which supplies the operations needed to handle the disc I/O. The third is a package that defines various kinds of semaphores.

```
with DiscCharacteristics, LOW_LEVEL_IO, Semaphores;
package DiscManager is  . . .  end DiscManager;
```

We may append a use clause following the with clause and thereby open the interfaces of the packages to the entire compilation unit.

```
with    DiscCharacteristics, LOW_LEVEL_IO, Semaphores;
use     DiscCharacteristics, LOW_LEVEL_IO, Semaphores;
package DiscManager is  . . .  end DiscManager;
```

However, we prefer not to do this but rather prefer to *use* the packages only at the most local scope in which they are required. This *need to know* approach is useful in that it helps to document the dependencies in the context as closely as possible.

DiscManager Specification

The DiscManager provides the abstraction of a paged disc and two distinct aspects of managing the disc. The first is that which manages the space and the second is that which manages the I/O requests. DiscSpaceManager provides two operations, RESERVE and RELEASE and two exceptions, *unreservedpage* which occurs when releasing a free page and *outofpages* which occurs when no pages are available. DiscIOManager provides the definition of a *receipt*, I/O status, I/O buffers, the READ, WRITE, WAIT and STATUS operations, and an exception *receiptmisuse*.

> **with** . . .
> **package** DiscManager **is**
>   -- page abstraction
>   **package** SpaceManager **is** . . . **end** SpaceManager;
>   **package** DiscIOManager **is** . . . **end** DiscIOManager;
> **private**
>   -- implementation of the page abstraction
> **end** DiscManager;

Derived Types and Type Conversions

The page abstraction is provided by two items: the private type *page* and the constant defining the length of the page, *pagelength*. The length of the page is identical to the length of a sector. The private type *page* is implemented as a derived integer type.

> **package** DiscManager **is**
>
>   **type** page **is private**;
>   **use** DiscCharacteristics;
>   pagelength : **constant** INTEGER : = sectorlength;
>   . . .
> **private**
>   **type** page **is new** INTEGER
>   **range** 1 . . platters * tracks * surfaces * sectors;
> **end** DiscManager;

The representation of the page abstraction as an integer is a natural choice. However, the situation is not quite so straightforward. Instead of being able to treat a page as an integer within the implementation, it must be treated as a completely distinct type because it is a derived type (ARM 3.4, 3-6). It is not an integer subtype, although that is really what we would like it to be. It is not possible to define a private type as a subtype unless it is encased in a record. For instance, we could have declared the type *page* as

type page **is record**
        p : INTEGER **range** 1 . . platters * tracks * surfaces * sectors;
end record;

However, every reference to a page object would have to be qualified to select the record component.

The derived type, on the other hand, when used in expressions with the disc constants to convert the page to the platter, surface, track, and sector address will have to be converted to an integer. Explicit conversion is allowed between derived types and their base type (ARM 4.6, 4-20). Consider the case where *p* is a page and *i* is an integer:

        INTEGER(p) . . . ; page(i) . . . ;

In any arithmetic expressions that involve pages with integer constants, the page object must be converted into an integer. For example, in the conversion of a page into a track, the page object is used in an expression with the integer constant *track*. So either one of the two expressions below must be used in order to perform the modulo arithmetic properly.

        INTEGER(p) **mod** tracks;
        P **mod** page(tracks);

In the first case, the result is an integer value; in the second the result is a page value. Note that the derived type *page* has inherited all of the predefined operations defined for the type INTEGER (ARM 3.4, 3-7) as well as all the values of that type. For types derived from user defined types, the operations inherited are those which are defined in the package specifications where the type is defined. These derived operations are implicitly overloaded at the place of the derived type definition.

Derived types themselves may be further derived. For example, we might define two new types of pages, directory pages and text pages.

        type dirpage **is new** page;
        type textpage **is new** page;

The expressions illustrating the type conversion must now express the lineage of derivation. Consider the cases where *t* is a text page and *d* is a directory page.

        INTEGER(page(t)) **mod** tracks;
        d **mod** dirpage(page(tracks));

Note that *dirpage* and *textpage* have both inherited the literals and operations of the type *page*. The expression INTEGER(t) is incorrect, because the base type of *textpage* is not INTEGER, but *page*. It is important to remember this lineage, especially if a conversion from a directory page to a text page is desired.

        textpage(page(d))

The directory page must first be converted to its base type before being converted to a text page.

Derived types provide one of the simplest means of guaranteeing the meaningfulness and validity of operands in expressions and operations that define an appropriate abstraction. Literals and basic operations are inherited from the base type. Ada's strong typing guarantees that only values of the specified type can be assigned to objects of that type or used in expressions of that type. It is interesting to note, however, that we have found subtypes and abstract types to be much more useful than derived types.

Derived Types, Subtypes and Renaming

The DiscIOManager package exports the types necessary to use the basic I/O operations that are encapsulated within the package. The types required by the I/O routines are the *receipt*, the read/write status *rwstatus*, a data buffer and a pointer to the buffer, *bufptr*.

The last two types have been defined for us in the package DiscCharacteristics. However, we want to export these two types explicitly from the package so that everything necessary for the application is defined in the package interface. Three options appear to be open to us. The first is to define *buffer* and *bufptr* as derived types based on *discbuffer* and *discbufferptr*. In doing this, we run into the problem that the pointer type *bufptr* must reference objects of type *buffer*, not objects of type *discbuffer*. This defect can be repaired by properly defining the pointer type. But now the buffers are entirely distinct and must be copied from one to the other. That is precisely the problem we wanted to avoid in using pointers.

The second option is to rename *discbuffer* and *discbufferptr* as *buffer* and *bufptr*. This would solve the problem nicely.

```
type buffer renames DiscCharacteristics.discbuffer;  -- illegal
type bufptr renames DiscCharacteristics.discbufferptr;
```

Unfortunately Ada does not allow the renaming of types. The programmer may rename objects, exceptions, packages, tasks and subprograms, but not types (ARM 8.5, 8-9).

The third option is to define *buffer* and *bufptr* as subtypes of *discbuffer* and *discbufferptr*, respectively. In a sense this is a renaming of the types because we do not restrict the subtypes in any way. Thus the subtypes are coextensive with the original types. This enables us to explicitly declare all of the types needed to use the exported operations.

```
subtype buffer is DiscCharacteristics.discbuffer;
subtype bufptr is DiscCharacteristics.discbufferptr;
```

Limited Private Types

The coordination of the request and completion of the request is of supreme importance. In order to promote as much concurrency as possible, we decided that READ and WRITE are treated as requests and that a calling process will wait at some later time (if necessary) until the request is completed. We saw that READ and WRITE must return a receipt so that the calling process can identify the particular transfer it is waiting for.

The semantics of the type *receipt* are entirely hidden within the confines of a limited private type. This guarantees that receipts cannot be counterfeited and that assignment is not available for receipts, thus guaranteeing that receipts cannot be duplicated. (The other limitation that the limited private type provides is that objects of this type may not be compared for equality.)

A *receipt* consists of a record of two components. The first component is the current status of the I/O request and is of type *rwstatus* initialized to *incomplete*. The other component is a pointer to a disposable semaphore. We use a pointer whose initial value is null in order to guarantee the proper use of receipts. Once the coordination of the request and completion has occurred the semaphore is used up (remember it was a one-use-only semaphore) and is discarded (i.e., the pointer is reset to null).

```
package DiscIOManager is
        type receipt is limited private;
        . . .
        receiptmisuse : exception;
private
        use Semaphores;
        type dsemaptr is access disposablesemaphore;
        type receiptrecord is record
                sema   : dsemaptr    : = null;
                stat   : rwstatus    : = incomplete;
        end record;
        type receipt is access receiptrecord;
end DiscIOManager;
```

Note that a receipt is actually implemented as a pointer which makes it possible for the requester and the disc manager to share the receipt.

The exception *receiptmisuse* is exported and is raised if a receipt is used improperly. In READ and WRITE it is raised when a receipt is passed whose *sema* field is not null and in WAIT when the receipt has not been initialized.

Operations for the Page Abstraction

There are six operations supplied by the DiscManager to operate on pages. The operations RESERVE and RELEASE are encapsulated in the DiscSpaceManager package. READ, WRITE, WAIT, and STATUS are encapsulated in the DiscIOManager package.

```
package DiscSpaceManager is
    procedure RESERVE (p : out page);
    procedure RELEASE (p : in page);
    outofpages : exception;
end DiscSpaceManager;

package DiscIOManager is
    . . .
    procedure READ    (p : in page; b : in out bufptr; r : in out receipt);
    procedure WRITE   (p : in page; b : in out bufptr; r : in out receipt);
    procedure WAIT    (r : in out receipt);
    function   STATUS (r : in receipt) return rwstatus;
    . . .
end DiscIOManager;
```

DiscManager Body and Separate Compilation

The body of the package DiscManager consists entirely of the two package bodies for the packages exported in the interface. As they are entirely without interactions or interdependencies, they can be developed independently. The separate compilation facilities enable the two implementations to be developed separately. The body contains two package stubs, indicated by the clause **is separate** (ARM 12.2, 10-6).

```
package body DiscManager is
    package body DiscSpaceManager is separate;
    package body DiscIOManager is separate;
end DiscManager;
```

The separately compiled subunit must specify the context, i.e., the library unit, of which it is a part. This context specification enables the compiler to provide the appropriate scope in which to compile the separate subunit. The scope includes all program units included in the with clause in the context library unit.

```
separate (DiscManager)
package body DiscSpaceManager is . . . end DiscSpaceManager ;
```

In addition, the context specification can include a with clause for the specific separate body. This may be done for documentation reasons or for dependencies that are endemic to that particular body. For example, the package LOW_LEVEL_IO is used only in the package DiscIOManager and not in any other part of the enclosing package. So, we could remove this package from the with clause of DiscManager and insert a with clause in the separate context specification.

```
with LOW_LEVEL_IO;
separate (DiscManager)
package body DiscIOManager is . . . end DiscIOManager;
```

Structure of the Body of DiscIOManager.

The package DiscIOManager provides the I/O operations. Internal to its body are two packages and several procedures that are used to support this interface. One package provides the scheduling mechanism, the other provides the interface for and the implementation of the actual disc handler. Package DiscScheduler provides two operations SCHEDULE and SERVICE to schedule a request and remove the proper request from the schedule, respectively. Package DiscHandler provides the data structure needed by the handler to expedite the request and coordinate it with the requester. The data type *dcb* (abbreviation for disc control block) contains the desired request, the disc address, a pointer to the data buffer, and a pointer to the receipt. Two internal procedures provide services needed by the READ and WRITE routines. The first is INITRECEIPT which initializes the receipt while the second, CONVERT, converts the page address to the internal disc address. Then come the exported I/O operations: READ, WRITE, WAIT and STATUS.

```
separate (DiscManager)
package body DiscIOManager is
        use DiscCharacteristics;

        package DiscHandler is
                type dcb is record
                        dreq   : discrequest;
                        addr   : discaddress;
                        bptr   : bufptr;
                        rcpt   : receipt;
                end record;
                type dcbptr is access dcb;
        end DiscHandler;

        package Discscheduler is
                procedure SCHEDULE   (d : in dcbptr);
                procedure SERVICE    (d : out dcbptr);
        end DiscScheduler;
```

procedure CONVERT (p : **in** page; d : **in out** dcbptr)
is . . . **end** CONVERT;

procedure INITRECEIPT (r : **in out** receipt; d : **in out** dcbptr)
is . . . **end** INITRECEIPT;

--   read, write, wait, status operations

package body DiscHandler **is separate**;
package body DiscScheduler **is separate**;

    end DiscIOManager;

Note that package DiscHandler is declared before DiscScheduler. This order must
be observed because the latter uses the former package in defining the scheduling
routines. For reason of convenience and ease of implementation, we separately
compile the bodies of the two internal packages.

Converting Pages to Disc Addresses

The page abstraction is mapped onto the disc in the following way. Half of the
pages reside on each platter. Within each platter, the pages start at track zero and
move inwards using both surfaces before moving to the next track. The sectors
are used in surface zero before moving to surface one. Since DiscCharacteristics
has been opened by a use clause at the beginning of the package body, we may
use its interface here. In particular, we use the disc constants.

procedure CONVERT(p : **in** page; d : **in out** dcbptr) **is**
begin
    d.addr.pl := INTEGER(p) / (INTEGER(page'LAST) / platters);
    d.addr.tr := INTEGER(p) **mod** tracks;
    d.addr.su := INTEGER(p) **mod** (sectors * surfaces) / sectors;
    d.addr.se := INTEGER(p) **mod** sectors;
end CONVERT;

Note first that the page object must first be converted to its base type INTEGER
and second that all division is integer division. The attribute LAST provides us
with the last value in the page abstraction and the expression page' LAST / platters
gives us the number of pages on each platter.

Initializing the Coordinating Receipt

The procedure INITRECEIPT checks to see that the receipt is not usable and has
not been misused. If the pointer to the receipt record is null, then the receipt has

not yet been used and a record is allocated. A pointer to a disposable semaphore indicates that some previous request has not been waited on and, hence, has been misused. Otherwise a semaphore is allocated and the status for the receipt is set to *incomplete*. The pointer to the receipt is passed to the *dcb*.

```
procedure INITRECEIPT(r : in out receipt; d : in out dcbptr) is
begin
        if r = null then r := new receipt end if;
        if r.sema = null
                then r.sema := new disposablesemaphore;
                else raise receiptmisuse;
        end if;
        r.stat := incomplete;
        d.rcpt := r;
end INITRECEIPT;
```

Note that we have not provided an initializing aggregate with the receipt allocation. This course has been taken for two reasons. First, no value can be given for the *sema* component because it is a task type that is treated as a limited private type and initial values cannot be given for limited private types in declarations and in allocations. Second, since we have to set the value *incomplete* for previously used receipts anyway, we chose to set all receipts regardless of length of use. Note also that we have not explicitly opened the interface of the package Semaphores but we have used one of its exported types. Since this package was used in the private part of the package specification for DiscManager, its interface is open throughout its entire package body.

Generic Subprograms and Allocation Aggregates

The implementation of the READ and WRITE routines is identical in all respects except the assignment of the I/O request to the dcb. This presents a prime case for a generic solution to their construction. Their implementation consists of creating a dcb, initializing the receipt to be shared by the handler and the requesting process, converting the requested page into a disc address and scheduling the request. The generic parameter is a value parameter, either READ or WRITE, of type discrequest.

```
generic iorequest : discrequest;
procedure RW(p : in page; b : in out bufptr; r : in out receipt) is
        d : dcbptr := new dcb(iorequest, (0,0,0,0), b, r);
begin
        INITRECEIPT(r, d);      --   set up the shared receipt
        CONVERT(p, d);          --   convert the page to a disc address
        SCHEDULE(d);--    schedule the request
end RW;
```

Note that the generic parameter is used in an *dcb* aggregate specification for the initializing allocation to the pointer to the *dcb*. There are four components in the record, the second component of which is itself a record. The aggregate is given in positional notation. Alternatively the aggregate specification could have used the named notation.

```
(
    dreq  = >  iorequest,
    addr  = >  (pl = > 0, tr = > 0, su = > 0, se = > 0)
    bptr  = >  b,
    rcpt  = >  r
)
```

The generic procedure is instantiated in the same manner as the generic packages have been instantiated in previous chapters.

```
procedure READ  is new RW(READ);
procedure WRITE is new RW(WRITE);
```

Note that the parameter list for READ and WRITE is not required. Only the name of the procedure is required. The actual parameter determines the actual semantics of the instantiation.

Access Exceptions

The predefined exception CONSTRAINT_ERROR may be raised in a number of different circumstances (ARM 11.7, 11-9) including the reference to a component of an accessed object when the access object itself has a null value instead of a pointer to accessible objects. This fact can be used to simplify the STATUS function. Instead of writing

```
function STATUS (r : in receipt) return rwstatus is
begin
        if r = null
                then raise receiptmisuse;
                else return r.stat;
        end if;
end STATUS;
```

we can use this exception and write

```
function STATUS (r : in receipt) return rwstatus is
begin
        return r.stat;
exception
        when CONSTRAINT_ERROR = > raise receiptmisuse;
end STATUS;
```

Note that the exception is handled rather than passed on as is. The exception CONSTRAINT_ERROR would be passed on to the caller if it were not handled. However, this exception has too wide an application and the user would have no frame of reference in which to interpret the exception because the structure of the receipt is unknown. For this reason we handle the predefined exception by reinterpreting it as an exception understandable to the user for this specific problem.

The same approach can be used for the WAIT routine. In fact it is doubly effective here because both the pointer to the *receiptrecord* object and the pointer to the semaphore object can be null. A program that does not exploit this feature might be written as follows.

```
procedure WAIT (r : in out receipt) is
begin
        if r = null or else r.sema = null
            then   raise receiptmisuse;
            else   P(r.sema);
                   r.sema := null;
        end if;
end WAIT;
```

Note that we used the short circuit **or else** operator because if in fact r = **null**, evaluation of r.sema = **null** would raise the CONSTRAINT_ERROR exception. Exploiting this exception yields

```
procedure WAIT (r : in out receipt) is
begin
        P(r.sema);             --  wait for completion of the request
        r.sema := null;        --  discard the used up semaphore
exception
        when CONSTRAINT_ERROR => raise receiptmisuse;
end WAIT;
```

Separate Compilation Revisited

With the separation of SpaceManager and DiscIOManager implementations, we illustrated the specification of the context for the body subunits. In the DiscIOManager body, there were two local packages whose implementations were separated as well. The question arises whether it is sufficient just to give the enclosing library unit, DiscManager in the separate clause, or whether the separate clause requires further refinement to enable the compiler to trace its lineage and its scope within the library unit. Ada requires the latter: the with clause must display the complete path name leading from a library unit to the closest surrounding scope of the separate unit. For example, if P is a library unit, Q is a separate unit in P and R is a separate unit in Q, the **separate** clauses of Q and R are

   separate (P) and **separate** (P.Q)

Thus, the disc scheduler package is prefixed with the clause

   separate (DiscManager.DiscIOManager).

Packaging a Task

The scheduler is implemented as a task that provides two entries INSERT and REMOVE which are renamed as the exported procedures SCHEDULE and SERVICE.

```
task Scheduler is
      entry INSERT   (d : in dcbptr);
      entry REMOVE (d : out dcbptr);
end Scheduler;


procedure SCHEDULE (d : in dcbptr)    renames Scheduler.INSERT;
procedure SERVICE    (d : out dcbptr)  renames Scheduler.REMOVE;
```

In preceding chapters we designed two different implementations of queues. Although we have not discussed dynamic queues which are built as lists of elements, we assume that a generic package for such queues exists and can be used for our Scheduler. The design of such a package would lead us too far from our subject matter. Since the Scheduler is defined in package DiscScheduler, its dependency on dynamic queues must be indicated in the with clause. The requirements for the specification of context leads to to the following with and separate clauses for the body of the scheduler:

```
with DynamicQueue;
separate (DiscManager.DiscIOManager)
package body DiscScheduler is
      . . .
end DiscScheduler;
```

We have localized this context to its innermost scope. One might consider whether it should also be included in the with clause of the library unit DiscManager as well. This is probably a good idea, because doing so provides good documentation of the library unit's dependencies. Specifying the local dependencies then refines these dependencies further.

The task body of the Scheduler accepts the calls on the entries REMOVE and INSERT. There is no need for an else clause in the select statement, because either one guard or the other will always evaluate to TRUE. When the queue is not empty, the first accept statement can be executed. When the queue is empty, the second accept statement can be executed. Note that priority is given to removing requests from the schedule.

```
task body Scheduler is
        package DiscQ is new DynamicQueue(dcbptr);
        use DiscQ;
begin
        loop
                select
                        when not EMPTY =>
                        accept REMOVE (d : out dcbptr) do
                                DEQUEUE(d);
                        end REMOVE;
                or
                        when REMOVE'COUNT = 0 or EMPTY =>
                        accept INSERT (d : in dcbptr) do
                                ENQUEUE(d);
                        end INSERT;
                end select;
        end loop;
end Scheduler;
```

Interrupts and Low Level I/O

The DiscHandler is implemented as a package whose body contains a task that provides the interrupt entry and associates this entry with the hardware-defined location for the disc interrupt. The task body contains three local procedures to position the read/write heads to the desired track, effect the actual transfer, and convert the device status to the exported status that hides certain internal problems.

```
with LOW_LEVEL_IO;
separate (DiscManager.DiscIOManager)
package body DiscHandler is
        use DiscCharacteristics, DiscScheduler, LOW_LEVEL_IO;

        task dh is
                entry DISCINTERRUPT;
                for DISCINTERRUPT use at discinterruptloc;
        end dh;

        task body dh is . . . end dh;

end DiscHandler;
```

The body of task *dh* interacts with the disc in two successive accept statements preceded by a SEND_CONTROL signal to the disc device and followed by a RECEIVE_CONTROL instruction to inspect the disc status. When the first accept statement is executed, the disc has found the page to be transferred and when the second accept statement is executed, the disc has terminated the tranfer. Task *dh* can then look at the disc status and detect whether or not errors occured.

```
. . .
SEND_CONTROL(disc, (seek, . . . ));
accept  DISCINTERRUPT;
RECEIVE_CONTROL(disc, . . . );
. . .
SEND_CONTROL(disc, (d.dreq, . . . ));
accept  DISCINTERRUPT;
RECEIVE_CONTROL(disc, . . . ));
. . .
```

The argument *d.dreq* in the SEND_CONTROL determines whether a page is read or written.

Hiding Selected Statuses

The disc status reported in the second parameter of RECEIVE_CONTROL indicates one of five possible states: transfer still going, transfer completed, read error, write error or seek error. Since *dh* waits for the disc interrupt, the*transfer still going* status will never be reported. Further, seek errors are of not interest to the user, who is interested only in knowing whether or not his read or write request was satisfied. Thus, where there is a read or write error reported by the disc unit, it will be passed on to the user. For other errors, the RETURNSTATUS routine will report them according to the request being performed. If it is a read request, the returned status will indicate a *readerror*, otherwise a *writerror*.

```
procedure RETURNSTATUS (d : in out dcbptr; s : in discstatus) is
begin
     case s of
          when done       => d.rcpt.stat := completed;
          when readerror  => d.rcpt.stat := readerror;
          when writerror  => d.rcpt.stat := writerror;
          when others     =>
               if d.dreq = read
                    then d.rcpt.stat := readerror;
                    else d.rcpt.stat := writerror;
               end if;
     end case;
end RETURNSTATUS;
```

Servicing Requests and Coordinating Completion

The operations have been specified that are needed to service the scheduled I/O requests. The handler itself is simply a loop that obtains a request from the scheduler, moves the head to the specified position, transfers the data if no problems occurred in the seek operation, converts the resulting operation's status, and signals through the shared receipt that the request has been completed.

```
        task body dh is
                d : dcbptr : = null;
                s : discstatus;
                --    returnstatus routine
        begin
                loop
                            SERVICE (d);           --   get an I/O request
                            <<SEEK>>;                   --   move head to the right track
                            if s = done then <<TRANSFER>>; end if;
                            RETURNSTATUS (d, s); --   determine status to return
                            v(d.rcpt.sema);       --   signal completion of IO request
                end loop;
        end dh;
```

Requestor and handler are synchronized through the disposable semaphore contained in the receipt. The requestor performs a WAIT operation at some time after the READ or WRITE request. The WAIT routine performs a P operation on the semaphore pointed to by the receipt. When the handler is done with a request, it signals this by the V operation which allows the requestor to proceed.

Exceptions during Task Communication

The management of disc space is provided by package DiscSpaceManager, which exports the procedures RESERVE and RELEASE. As we have often done in this solution, the underlying implementation of the package facilities consists of a task which is included in the package body of DiscSpaceManager.

```
        task SpaceManager is
                entry GETPAGE (p : out page);
                entry PUTPAGE (p : in page);
        end SpaceManager;
```

The implementation of RESERVE and RELEASE is included in the body of DiscSpaceManager with task SpaceManager. These procedures call the entries of SpaceManager and hide the existence of that task from the users of DiscSpaceManager. Since all the real work is done in GETPAGE and PUTPAGE, RESERVE and RELEASE consist of nothing more than calls to those entries.

```
procedure RESERVE (p : out page) is
begin
        SpaceManager.GETPAGE(p);
end RESERVE;

procedure RELEASE (p : in page) is
begin
        SpaceManager.PUTPAGE(p);
end RELEASE;
```

The implementation of GETPAGE and PUTPAGE is embedded in a select statement (in the body of task SpaceManager). Since we prefer getting pages back over allocating pages, we prefix GETPAGE with a guard that opens this alternative only if no requests for PUTPAGE are pending.

```
task body SpaceManager is
        . . .
begin
    loop
            . . .
        select
            when PUTPAGE'COUNT = 0  =>
            accept GETPAGE(p : out page) do  . . .  end GETPAGE;
        or
            accept PUTPAGE(p : in page) do  . . .  end PUTPAGE;
        end select;
            . . .
    end loop;
end SpaceManager;
```

The local declarations of the task body contain the objects that describe the the free and reserved pages. For the sake of simplicity, we implement the page status as a bit array, where the ith bit indicates whether or not the ith page is free.

```
task body SpaceManager is

        type availability is (free, inuse);
        bitmap : array (page) of availability  :=  (others => free);
        pragma PACK(bitmap);

begin
        . . .
end SpaceManager;
```

The bitmap is updated by GETPAGE and PUTPAGE. The former steps through the bitmap until it finds a free page, reserves it and returns the page it found. The latter sets the bit corresponding to the input page it receives to *free*. However, GETPAGE may not succeed in finding a page. In that case it must raise the exception *outofpages* which was included in the declarative part of DiscSpaceManager.

Some comments are in order on raising exceptions in an accept statement. If an exception is raised at the top level of an accept statement and not in an inner block of that statement, this exception is raised again in two places: in the task right after the accept statement and in the caller of the task where it called the particular entry. If one wants to avoid a TASKING_ERROR exception, it is strongly recommended that an exception handler be included in the task following the accept statement. In that case the effect is noticeable only in the environment of the entry call in the calling task. This environment or its surrounding scope also needs an exception handler for the exception raised in the called task. This is what one normally expects to provide anyway.

The select statement containing the accept statement for GETPAGE is embedded in a block in order to provide the scope within which to handle the exceptions raised in the accept body. The block is enclosed within a loop in order to keep the server process in continuous operation.

```
begin  -- body of package SpaceManager

    loop
        begin      --   block for handling raised exceptions
            select
                when PUTPAGE'COUNT = 0 =>
                accept GETPAGE (p : out page) do
                    for i in page loop
                        if bitmap(i) = free then
                            bitmap(i) := inuse;
                            p := i;
                            return;
                        end if;
                    end loop;
                    raise outofpages;
                end GETPAGE;
            or
                accept PUTPAGE (p : in page) do
                    bitmap(p) := free;
                end PUTPAGE;
            end select;
        exception
            when  outofpages => null;
        end; --   end block for fielding exceptions
    end loop;

end SpaceManager;
```

Note that the attribute COUNT is used to give priority to the entry PUTPAGE. As long as there are calls waiting on PUTPAGE, GETPAGE will not be enabled. The return statement provides the exit from the loop and termination of the rendezvous in the GETPAGE entry. Finishing the loop means that no free page was found.

Evaluation of the Ada Solution

Ada provides low level facilities which enable the systems programmer to write device handlers which interface directly with the devices and the processor's interrupt mechanism. The multitasking facilities provide a natural means of managing the various data structures required to implement the space management and request scheduling and a convenient way to coordinate cooperating processes. Separate compilation has been used extensively to break the program into manageable chunks that minimize the amount of program affected by changes. The abstract type facilities, and the information hiding abilities of package bodies have enabled us to hide implementation details and present only the desired logical interface to the user. The exception mechanism has been used to simplify the algorithms and move the processing of unusual conditions out of the main algorithm and into the exception handling portion of the unit. Further, the exception mechanism has been used to communicate status information between tasks.

15.4 The Complete Ada Program

package DiscCharacteristics **is**

```
        tracks      : constant INTEGER := 203;
        sectors     : constant INTEGER := 12;
        surfaces    : constant INTEGER := 2;
        platters    : constant INTEGER := 2;

        type discaddress is record
                pl  : INTEGER range 0 . . platters-1;
                tr  : INTEGER range 0 . . tracks-1;
                su  : INTEGER range 0 . . surfaces-1;
                se  : INTEGER range 0 . . sectors-1;
        end record;

        type discrequest is (seek, read, write);
        type discstatus is (busy, done, seekerror, readerror, writerror);

        sectorlength : constant INTEGER := 512; --    bytes
        type discbuffer is array (1 . . sectorlength) of byte;
        type discbufferptr is access discbuffer;

        type disccommand is record
                dreq    : discrequest;
                addr    : discaddress;
                bptr    : discbufferptr;
        end record;

        discinterruptloc : constant address :=  . . . ;

        pragma PACK(discbuffer);

end DiscCharacteristics;

with DiskCharacteristics;
package LOW_LEVEL_IO is
        type devicetype is ( . . ., disc, . . . );
        . . .
        use DiscCharacteristics;
        procedure SEND_CONTROL     (d : devicetype; c : in disccommand);
        procedure RECEIVE_CONTROL  (d : devicetype; s : in out discstatus);
        . . .
end LOW_LEVEL_IO;
```

```
package Semaphores is

        type disposablesemaphore is limited private;
        procedure P (s : in out disposablesemaphore);
        procedure V (s : in out disposablesemaphore);
        . . .
        pragma INLINE(P, V);
private

        task type disposablesemaphore is
                entry P;
                entry V;
        end disposablesemaphore;
        . . .
end Semaphores;



package body Semaphores is

        procedure P (s : in out disposablesemaphore) is begin s.P; end P;
        procedure V (s : in out disposablesemaphore) is begin s.V; end V;
        . . .
        task body disposablesemaphore is
        begin
                accept V;
                accept P;
        end disposablesemaphore;
        . . .
end Semaphores;
```

```
with DiscCharacteristics, LOW_LEVEL_IO, Semaphores;
package DiscManager is

    type page is private;
    pagelength : constant INTEGER := DiscCharacteristics.sectorlength;

    package DiscSpaceManager is
        procedure RESERVE (p : out page);
        procedure RELEASE (p : in page);
        outofpages : exception;
    end DiscSpaceManager;

    package DiscIOManager is

        type receipt is limited private;
        type rwstatus is (incomplete, complete, readerror, writerror);
        subtype buffer is DiscCharacteristics.discbuffer;
        subtype bufptr is DiscCharacteristics.discbufferptr;

        procedure READ    (p : in page; b : in out bufptr; r : in out receipt);
        procedure WRITE   (p : in page; b : in out bufptr; r : in out receipt);
        procedure WAIT    (r : in out receipt);
        function  STATUS (r : in receipt) return rwstatus;

        receiptmisuse : exception;

    private

        use Semaphores;
        type dsemaptr is access disposablesemaphore;

        type receiptrecord is record
            sema  : dsemaptr := null;
            stat  : rwstatus := incomplete;
        end record;
        type receipt is access receiptrecord;

    end DiscIOManager;

private

    use DiscCharacteristics;
    type page is new INTEGER range 1 . . platters*tracks*surfaces*sectors;

end DiscManager;

package body DiscManager is
        package body DiscSpaceManager is separate;
        package body DiscIOManager is separate;
end DiscManager;
```

```ada
separate (DiscManager)
package body DiscSpaceManager is

        task SpaceManager is
                entry GETPAGE (p : out page);
                entry PUTPAGE (p : in page);
        end SpaceManager;

        procedure RESERVE (p : out page) is
        begin
                SpaceManager.GETPAGE(p);      -- may raise outofpages
        end RESERVE;

        procedure RELEASE (p : in page) is
        begin
                SpaceManager.PUTPAGE(p);
        end RELEASE;

        Task body SpaceManager is

                type availability is (free, inuse);
                bitmap : array (page) of availability := (others => free);
                pragma PACK(bitmap);

        begin
            loop
                    begin
                        select
                            when PUTPAGE'COUNT = 0 =>
                            accept GETPAGE (p : out page) do
                                for i in page loop
                                        if bitmap(i) = free then
                                                bitmap(i) := inuse;
                                                p := i;
                                                return;
                                        end if;
                                end loop;
                                raise outofpages;
                            end GETPAGE;
                        or
                            accept PUTPAGE(p : in page) do
                                bitmap(p) := free;
                            end PUTPAGE;
                        end select;
                    exception
                        when  outofpages => null;
                    end;
                end loop;
        end SpaceManager;

end DiscSpaceManager;
```

```
separate (DiscManager)
package body DiscIOManager is

        use DiscCharacteristics;

        package DiscHandler is
                type dcb is record
                        dreq    : discrequest;
                        addr    : discaddress;
                        bptr    : bufptr;
                        rcpt    : receipt;
                end record;
                type dcbptr is access dcb;
        end DiscHandler;

        use DiscHandler;

        package DiscScheduler is
                procedure SCHEDULE(d : in dcbptr);
                procedure SERVICE  (d : out dcbptr);
        end DiscScheduler;

        procedure CONVERT (p : in page; d : in out dcbptr) is
        begin
                d.addr.pl  := INTEGER(p) / INTEGER(page'LAST / platters);
                d.addr.tr  := INTEGER(p) mod tracks;
                d.addr.su  := INTEGER(p) mod (sectors * surfaces) / sectors;
                d.addr.se  := INTEGER(p) mod sectors;
        end CONVERT;

        procedure INITRECEIPT(r : in out receipt; d : in out dcbptr) is
        begin
                if r = null then r := new receipt ; end if;
                if r.sema = null
                        then r.sema := new disposablesemaphore;
                        else raise receiptmisuse;
                end if;
                r.stat := incomplete;
                d.rcpt := r;
        end INITRECEIPT;
```

```ada
generic iorequest : discrequest;
procedure RW(p : in page; b : in out bufptr; r : in out receipt);

procedure RW(p : in page; b : in out bufptr; r : in out receipt) is
      d : dcbptr := new dcb (iorequest, (0, 0, 0, 0), b, r);
begin
      INITRECEIPT(r, d);
      CONVERT (p, d);
      DiscScheduler.SCHEDULE (d);
end RW;

procedure READ is new RW(READ);
procedure WRITE is new RW(WRITE);

procedure STATUS (r : in receipt) return rwstatus is
begin
      return r.stat;
exception
      when CONSTRAINT_ERROR => raise receiptmisuse;
end STATUS;

procedure WAIT (r : in out receipt) is
      use Semaphores;
begin
      P(r.sema);
      r.sema := null;
exception
      when CONSTRAINT_ERROR => raise receiptmisuse;
end WAIT;

package body DiscHandler is separate;
package body DiscScheduler is separate;

end DiscIOManager;
```

```
with DynamicQueue;
separate (DiscManager.DiscIOManager)
package body DiscScheduler is

        task Scheduler is
                entry INSERT     (d : in dcbptr);
                entry REMOVE  (d : out dcbptr);
        end Scheduler;

        procedure SCHEDULE  (d : in dcbptr)   renames Scheduler.INSERT;
        procedure SERVICE      (d : out dcbptr)  renames Scheduler.REMOVE;

        task body Scheduler is

                package DiscQ is new DynamicQueue (dcbptr);
                use DiscQ;

        begin
                loop
                        select
                                when not empty  = >
                                accept REMOVE (d : out dcbptr) do
                                        DEQUEUE(d);
                                end REMOVE;
                        or
                                when REMOVE'COUNT  = 0 or EMPTY  = >
                                accept INSERT (d : in dcbptr) do
                                        ENQUEUE (d);
                                end INSERT;
                        end select;
                end loop;
        end Scheduler;

end DiscScheduler;
```

```
with   LOW_LEVEL_IO, DiscCharacteristics, DiscScheduler;
use    LOW_LEVEL_IO, DiscCharacteristics, DiscScheduler;
separate (DiscManager.DiscIOManager)
package body DiscHandler is

     task dh is
          entry DISCINTERRUPT;
          for DISCINTERRUPT use at discinterruptloc;
     end dh;

     task body dh is

          d : dcbptr := null;
          s : discstatus;

          procedure RETURNSTATUS (d : in out dcbptr; s : in discstatus) is
          begin
               case s is
                    when done       => d.rcpt.stat := completed;
                    when readerror  => d.rcpt.stat := readerror;
                    when writerror  => d.rcpt.stat := writerror;
                    when others     =>
                         if d.dreq = read
                              then   d.rcpt.stat := readerror;
                              else   d.rcpt.stat := writerror;
                         end if;
               end case;
          end RETURNSTATUS;

     begin   -- task body of dh
          loop
               SERVICE(d);                    --  get an IO request

               -- SEEK (d, s)
               SEND_CONTROL(disc, (seek, d.addr, d.bptr));
               accept DISCINTERRUPT;
               RECEIVE_CONTROL(disc, s);

               if s = done then
                    -- TRANSFER (d, s)
                    SEND_CONTROL(disc, (d.dreq, d.addr, d.bptr));
                    accept DISCINTERRUPT;
                    RECEIVE_CONTROL(disc, s);
               end if;
               RETURNSTATUS (d, s);       --  determine the status to return
               V(d.rcpt.sema);            --  signal completion of request
          end loop;
     end dh;

end DiscHandler;
```

15.5 Reminders

1. Constants can be computed in Ada but not in Pascal.

2. Enumeration values must be distinct in Pascal within a scope. In Ada, enumeration values can be overloaded. Disambiguation can be accomplished using name qualification.

3. Pascal provides packed arrays. Ada provides a pragma to indicate to the compiler that the gaps between components in structured objects are to be minimized.

4. Pascal provides no means for synchronization or mutual exclusion. Ada on the other hand, provides the mechanisms to synchronize cooperating tasks and control exclusive access to data structures.

5. Unusual conditions must be reported by means of status variables in Pascal. Ada provides an exception mechanism that can be used to signal unusual conditions and to simplify an algorithm by removing the processing of these unusual conditions to exception handlers.

6. Access types in Ada automatically inherit an initial value null. In Pascal, the initial value is undefined.

7. Initialization of data structures is available in Ada at the time of declaration for static variables and at the time of allocation for dynamic variables.

8. Ada packages can be used to satisfy several design goals including encapsulation and information hiding.

9. Discrete types and subtypes have attributes that can be used in Ada in expressions. FIRST and LAST are among these and return the first and last values of the corresponding types and subtypes.

10. Interrupts can be associated with task entries by means of interrupt representations. An entry is associated with a particular system dependent interrupt location.

11. Ada provides a LOW_LEVEL_IO package which provides two operations, SEND_CONTROL and RECEIVE_CONTROL, to enable the programmer to interact with devices. The package is system dependent and may vary from system to system. The form, however, remains the same.

12. Private types in Ada provide data abstraction facilities. The implementation is entirely hidden from the user. The qualification limited further restricts the operations available for all abstraction.

13. Assignment, tests for equality and initial values in the allocations of dynamic variables are not allowed for limited private types.

14. The structure of private types is specified in the private part of the package specification.

15. Semaphores are easily implemented in Ada.

16. Subprograms can be specified to be compiled inline by using the pragma INLINE.

17. The context of library units must be specified by means of the with clause. All external library units used within the compiled unit must be specified in the with clause. Optimally a use clause may be given following the with clause.

18. Packages may be part of the visible part of a package.

19. Derived types provide a basic level of type abstraction. Some of the operations defined for the base type are inherited by the derived type. All of the values and literal identifiers are inherited by the derived type.

20. Type conversion is allowed between base and derived types by prefixing the object with the type name to be converted to and enclosing the object in parentheses. Conversion must follow the lineage of derivation.

21. Subtypes cannot be used as the implementation of private types.

22. Task types may be used as the implementation of private types.

23. Types cannot be renamed. However, subtypes provide a facility functionally equivalent to renaming.

24. Access violations produce the exception CONSTRAINT_ERROR.

25. Unhandled exceptions during task communication cause the TASKING_ERROR to be raised in the calling task at the point of call.

26. Package and subprogram bodies can be stubbed and separately compiled.

27. Separately compiled bodies must specify its context and lineage by means of with and separate clauses.

28. Generic procedures provide abstraction from nearly similar procedures. It is, however, not a macro facility.

29. The short circuit relational operators can be used to prevent exceptions from occurring during expression evaluation.

30. It is generally useful to package tasks and hide the actual tasking structure.

31. Tasks can be used effectively to manage data structures referenced and accessed by several tasks.

32. Entry calls are queued and the attribute COUNT reports the number of entry calls waiting to be serviced.

15.6 Problems

1. The reserve operation always begins the search for a free page at the beginning of the bitmap. On the average, 5000 entries would need to be examined if the disc utilization is high. Modify the DiscSpaceManager package so that the search will be more efficient.

2. No thought has been given to the problems normally encountered in "real" systems: e.g., crash and recovery. Modify the DiscSpaceManager package to save the current state of the bitmap on the disc and provide both cold and warm start routines. Cold start initializes available disc space to *free*; warm start restores the current state of the disc usage. How do these routines interact with DiscIOManager?

3. The first come, first serve (FCFS) scheduling policy works well if the demands on the disc are rather light. However, under heavy demands, characteristics such as seek time and rotational latency can be exploited to provide a more efficient disc scheduling algorithm. Write a shortest seek time first (SSTF) algorithm that minimizes the head movement between requests.

4. Sometimes disc operations fail. Intermittent failures can be successfully recovered from by some reasonable number of entries. Rewrite both the *seek* and *transfer* parts of task *dh* to attempt three times before admitting failure.

5. Intermittent failures may also occur at arbitrary times in the life of the disc. The handler should respond to these failure interrupts in order to take remedial action (or at least log the error). However, the task *dh* is either servicing a request-- in which case it will accept the interrupt-- or it is waiting on the queue for the entry SERVICE-- in which case it will not respond to any interrupt. Modify the relevant program segments s that *dh* will be able to respond to these interrupts. Assume there is a routine SYSTEM.LOG(s : string) that will log the string as an error message.

6. The current implementation supports only one disc unit. Rewrite as much of the package as is necessary to enable it to support two identical but independent disc systems.

Sixteen

Parallel Tasks

Topics: parallel tasks, task completion, the abort statement, nested accept statements, conditional accept statements, the POS attribute.

Issues: halting a task, abortion of tasks.

16.1 Problem Statement

A *table* is a data structure consisting of a number of data objects that have common attributes. (One can think of a table as an array of records.) Table entries each possess a unique key (a name for instance) identifying a particular entry. The problem considered in this chapter is to find the index of the table entry that matches the given key.

An effective way of searching for a table entry that matches the given key is by applying a *hashing* algorithm. A hashing function computes an index from the representation of the input key and uses this index as a starting point for the search through the table. In order to limit the extent of the problem and its solution, we assume that we know which keys are present in the table so that searching for a matching key will always be successful. We do not address the problem of how keys are entered into the table but focus entirely on a solution to the searching problem.

16.2 Problem Discussion

Let the keys be strings of a particular length, say four characters. The starting point of a search is determined by computing a value from the individual characters of the input key. We could, for instance, take the numeric representation of each character, multiply those numbers and take the result modulo the table size. Once this starting point has been determined, we can start the search.

A straightforward way to search the table is by a linear search. Beginning at the computed starting point, we check if the key is in that location. If so, the search is completed and the index of the current location is returned. If not, we move on to the next location and repeat the inspection. When the last location is reached without success, the search is continued at the beginning of the table.

This solution of a straightforward linear search is so trivial that it is hardly worth discussing its implementation. To make the solution more interesting, one might consider other hash coding techniques, such as quadratic or double hash, or one might introduce parallelism in the search. We to do the latter in order to illustrate some features of the tasking facilities of Ada that have not been covered in the preceding chapters. One might, of course, also combine the better hashing algorithms with parallel searching and achieve even better performance than with either one separately. We have chosen not to do that in this example in order to keep the algorithm simple enough so that the reader can concentrate on the parallel aspects of the solution.

The parallelism we propose is implemented by two independent tasks (or processes) that both perform a linear search. The first task starts at the starting point while the other task starts at the location next to the starting point (modulo the table size). Both tasks will traverse through the table in steps of two locations at a time going around once so that each task looks (at most) at half of the table and so that each location is visited (at most) by only one of the tasks. Suitable names for the tasks are EVEN and ODD. Their programs differ only in their starting point: the EVEN task starts at the hashed index and the ODD task starts at the hashed index + 1. Thus, if the starting point is given as an input parameter, there is no difference in their programs at all. Both tasks increment a local index that was initialized to the input parameter by two modulo the table size until the key is found or until the search reaches the starting point. Because we assume that we will search only for keys that are in the table, it is certain that one of the search tasks will succeed in finding the key. There is, of course, no point in having a task continue the search if the other one has already found the key. Thus, it is desirable to stop the task that is not going to be successful.

It should be observed that the parallel tasks will not exactly return to their respective starting points if the size of the table is an odd number. For example, if the result of the hash function is even, the EVEN task will start visiting the even indexed locations until it reaches the end. When it wraps around, it starts at location (*lasteven* + 2) **mod** *tsize*. But since *lasteven* = *tsize* -1 for odd table sizes, the EVEN task continues with location 1 and takes the odd numbered locations from this point onwards. To avoid this problem, we assume that the table size is chosen to be an even number. (The reason we wish to avoid this problem will be made clear below.)

If this strategy of stopping the task that will not find the key is adopted, there is actually no need to have it stop on its own account when it comes back to its starting point. Since it is certain that one of the tasks will find the key, the main program is will stop the other task when it receives the answer. Thus, a test for returning to the starting point need not be included in the search tasks.

In summary, the location of a given input key will be determined as follows. The main program first applies a hash function to the representation of the input key which results in a starting index for the parallel search. The program then activates the two parallel tasks EVEN and ODD with, respectively, the starting index and the location next to the starting index. The main program then waits until one of the tasks returns the desired index and, when it has received the answer, stops the task that is searching in vain.

16.3 An Ada Solution

The Table Package

The interface of the package TABLE provides the user with all the information that is needed to use the package. The user can enter keys into the table and lookup keys that already exist in the table. Notice that nothing is indicated about the parallel search or about the hashing strategy.

```
generic tsize : NATURAL := 354;    -- tsize must be even
package TABLE is

        type    key      is STRING(4);
        subtype tindex   is INTEGER range 0 . . (tsize - 1);

        function ENTER    (k : in key) return tindex;
        function LOOKUP  (k : in key) return tindex;

        toverflow : exception;

    end TABLE;
```

The package body of TABLE consists of the table object, three tasks TManager, ODD and EVEN, and three functions HASH, ENTER and LOOKUP. Note that the use of the keyword **others** is a standard way of initializing all elements of an array with the same value. The assigned expression is an aggregate of the proper size (ARM 4.3.2, 4-9). The parallel tasks ODD and EVEN have identical task bodies. For that reason, we first introduce a task type SearchTask and then declare ODD and EVEN as two distinct instantiations of that task type.

```
package body TABLE is

    blank    : constant key := (others => ' ');
    table    : array (tindex) of key := (others => blank);

    task      TManager   is  . . .  end TManager;
    task type SearchTask is  . . .  end SearchTask;

    ODD, EVEN : SearchTask;

    function HASH    ( . . . ) return tindex is . . . end HASH;
    function ENTER   ( . . . ) return tindex is . . . end ENTER;
    function LOOKUP  ( . . . ) return tindex is . . . end LOOKUP;

    task body TManager   is . . . end TManager;
    task body SearchTask is . . . end SearchTask;

end TABLE;
```

The Hash Function

The hashing algorithm treats each character as an integer, multiplies the individual components together, and then takes the result modulo *tsize*. Because a key object is a subtype of *string*, which is a subtype of type *array of character*, the individual characters are accessible as array elements. In order to convert the characters into integer numbers, we use the POS attribute defined for all discrete types (ARM 3.5.5, 3-16). The hash value is then computed by the expression:

character'POS(k(1)) * character'POS(k(2)) *
character'POS(k(3)) * character'POS(k(4)) **mod** tsize

where *k* is the key passed as input parameter to function HASH.

The Lookup Function

The function LOOKUP uses TManager to order the search requests in time and to activate the parallel search tasks. Its body is simply a call to the LOOKUP entry of task TManager and a return of the table index computed by TManager.LOOKUP.

TManager.LOOKUP(k, t); **return** t;

The Table Manager

The table manager, TManager, is implemented as a task for two reasons: to sequence the search requests and to synchronize the search tasks. TManager is designed with two entries: one called by the lookup function when a user requests the location of a key, and the other called by the parallel sc arch when it finds the designated key. The visible part of task TManager is

```
task TManager is
      entry LOOKUP (k : in key; t : out tindex);
      entry RESULT  (q : in tindex);
end TManager;
```

The body of TManager makes use of the feature of *nested* accept statements (ARM 9.5, 9-8) and consists mainly of an accept statement for entry LOOKUP. As part of processing the lookup entry, TManager waits until it receives the result from one of the parallel search tasks. Prior to waiting for the result, TManager must, of course, activate the parallel search tasks. These considerations lead to the following implementation of TManager.

```
task body TManager is
      start, cur : tindex;
begin
      loop
            accept LOOKUP (k : in key; t : out tindex) do
                  start := HASH (k);
                  ODD.SEARCH (k, (start + 1) mod tsize);
                  EVEN.SEARCH (k, start);
                  accept RESULT (q : in tindex) do
                        cur := q;
                  end RESULT;

                  <stop task that won't find key location>

                  t := cur;
            end LOOKUP;
      end loop;
end TManager;
```

Note that the accept statement for RESULT is included in the accept statement for LOOKUP. The effect is that the subprogram waits until one of the parallel search processes has found the key location in the table. Furthermore, the rendezvous continues until the result is found and the other task is halted. We will discuss the conditions for the rendezvous temrmination below.

Halting a Task

The ways in which a task is said to have *completed* its execution suggest a number of possible solutions to the problem of halting the task that is searching in vain. First, a task is said to have completed when it has finished the execution of its statement sequence. For the search task, this approach implies that some means of exiting the lookup loop must exist so that the loop terminates and the task finishes its execution in a normal manner. One way of determining termination is by using a global variable, *found*, shared by TManager and the two search tasks. When the one task has found the entry and passed the result to Tmanager, *found* is set to TRUE, and the other task takes note of the change and terminates its search. An obvious way to construct this is by the following loop control statement in the search task.

while not found **and** key / = table (index) **loop**

While this solution has the merit of simplicity, it requires built-in dependencies upon external facts and increases the overhead associated with the search.

A second way that a task is said to have completed is if an exception is raised that is not handled in the task. Tasks are governed by the same rules for exceptions as other scope units: the scope is terminated and a handler is invoked if one is defined. This might seem to be a tempting approach. However, exceptions are propagated between tasks only during a rendezvous. Since a rendezvous between Tmanager and a search task is planned only when the key has been found, this approach is not satisfactory.

The terminate alternative in a select statement is a third possible way for a task to complete its execution. If no calls for the entries of the select statement exist and there is a terminate alternative, the task may be terminated. This approach is of particular importance in determining when an enclosing scope can complete its execution (ARM 9.4, 9-6). The enclosing scope can complete its execution only if the dependent tasks have completed or are waiting in the terminate alternative. However, as it is extremely unlikely that the search will be implemented using a select statement, this approach is totally inappropriate.

Finally, a task completes its execution when it is abort ed (ARM 9.10, 9-18). Any task can abort any other task by naming it in the abort statement. The statement

abort ODD, EVEN;

aborts both of the search tasks. The advantage of this approach is that control for halting the task doomed to search in vain can be located in TManager and no knowledge of termination problems need be installed in the search tasks themselves.

Task Abort

There is one very important difference between these four alternative approaches. In the first approach (and in the second if the appropriate block structure is used to take care of exceptions), the search task can be structured so that it does not terminate but rather stops searching and returns to a state where it is ready for the next search. Unfortunately, in the third and fourth approaches, the tasks terminate and cannot be reactivated. Thus in choosing the fourth alternative, we must find a solution to this problem because we obviously want to do more than one search. Note that the initial placement of the declarations for ODD and EVEN in the sketch of the package body above is incorrect in the context of this problem.

One solution to the problem of task termination is to use an access type which denotes objects of the task type SearchTask. Then, at the beginning of each call to LOOKUP, two new search tasks are allocated to ODD and EVEN and then discarded at the completion of the LOOKUP procedure. The advantage of this approach is that new search tasks are available whenever needed and are discarded when no longer needed.

The same results can be obtained by a simpler means: by declaring ODD and EVEN as task objects local to the accept statement in TManager. In this way, the two tasks are created automatically when entry LOOKUP is elaborated and automatically destroyed when LOOKUP completes its execution. Unfortunately, in order to declare local objects in an accept body, we must use a block structure.

```
accept LOOKUP ( . . . ) do

        declare
                ODD, EVEN : SearchTask;
        begin
                . . .
        end;

    end LOOKUP;
```

Because of the rules governing task dependencies (ARM 9.4, 9-6), the execution of LOOKUP cannot complete until its two dependent search tasks complete. The simplest way of ensuring termination is to abort both tasks arbitrarily.

```
    abort ODD, EVEN;
```

However, this rather brute force solution can be refined to abort only the task that continues to search in vain for the desired key. (Of course, this assumes that the successful task will terminate normally.) By making the restriction concerning an even table size, we can determine from the resulting index which task was successful and which task is searching in vain.

```
        if (result - start) mod 2 = 0
            then    abort ODD;
            else    abort EVEN;
        end if;
```

The Search Tasks

The purpose of the search tasks is to accept a search request and traverse the table looking for a matching key. The visible part of the task type is as follows.

```
        task type SearchTask is

            entry SEARCH (k : in key; start : in tindex);

        end Searchtask;
```

The body of the task type consists of two sections: the accept statement to initialize the task for the search and the loop to do the actual search. Since the task must terminate either normally or be aborted deliberately, there is no enclosing loop (the task is a disposable object, not a continuous server).

```
        task body SearchTask is
            -- local declarations
        begin
            accept SEARCH . . . end SEARCH;

            loop . . . end loop;
                . . .
        end SearchTask;
```

Searching for a Matching Key

It is necessary for the accept body of entry SEARCH to complete as soon as possible in order that the Table Manager may continue and call other parallel search tasks. The actual search loop therefore should *not* be included in the accept body of search, because if that is done, the Table Manager must wait until the search is completed. (This has a disastrous effect if the Table Manager first calls the search task that is not going to find the matching key. The Table Manager would then permanently block itself !)

Instead, we program the accept body of the search task so that it limits its activity to accepting the input key and the starting point for the search. This makes it necessary to introduce another local variable, *clay*, which holds the input key after the accept body of search terminates.

```
task body SearchTask is
       clay        : key;
       locindex    : tindex;
begin
       accept SEARCH (k :in key; start : in tindex) do
              clay := k;
              locindex : = start;
       end SEARCH;
       . . .
end SearchTask;
```

The accept body is now very short so that the rendezvous with the Table Manager is limited to a minimal time interval. The actual search will take place after the accept statement has been executed.

```
while table (locindex) / = clay loop
       locindex : = (locindex + 2) mod tsize;
end loop;
TManager.RESULT (locindex);
```

The call on the entry RESULT by the search task transmits the result to the Table Manager and allows it to pass the result on to the lookup function that originally activated the Table Manager. Note that the search task will never reach this call of RESULT if it is searching in vain. In this case the search task loops indefinitely in the while statement. The only way to get the search task out of its infinite loop is by aborting the task once TManager has received the result from the other task.

16.4 The Complete Ada Program

```ada
generic    tsize : NATURAL := 354;    -- tsize is an even number
package   TABLE is

        subtype   key       is STRING(1 . . 4);
        subtype   tindex     is INTEGER range 0 . . (tsize - 1);

        function ENTER    (k : in key) return tindex;
        function LOOKUP   (k : in key) return tindex;

        toverflow : exception;

end TABLE;

package body TABLE is

        blank  : constant  key := (others => ' ');
        table  : array (0 . . (tsize - 1)) of key := (others => blank);

        task TManager is
             entry LOOKUP  (k : in key; t : out tindex);
             entry RESULT   (q : in tindex);
        end TManager;

        task type SearchTask is
             entry SEARCH  (k : in key; start : in tindex);
        end SearchTask;

        function HASH (k : in key) return tindex is
        begin
             return ( character'POS(k(1)) *
                      character'POS(k(2)) *
                      character'POS(k(3)) *
                      character'POS(k(4))) mod tsize;
        end HASH;

        function ENTER(k : in key) return tindex is  . . .  end ENTER;
```

```
        function LOOKUP (k : in key) return tindex is
              t : tindex;
        begin
              TManager.LOOKUP (k, t); return t;
        end LOOKUP;

        task body TManager is
              start, cur : tindex;
        begin
              loop
                      accept LOOKUP (k : in key; t : out tindex) do
                              declare
                                    ODD, EVEN : SearchTask;
                              begin
                                    start : = HASH (k);
                                    ODD.SEARCH (k, (start + 1) mod tsize);
                                    EVEN.SEARCH (k, start);
                                    accept RESULT (q : in tindex) do
                                            cur : = q;
                                    end RESULT;
                                    if (cur - start) mod 2 = 0
                                            then   abort ODD;
                                            else   abort EVEN;
                                    end if;-- correct iff size is even
                                    t : = cur;
                              end;
                      end LOOKUP;
              end loop;
        end TManager;

        task body SearchTask is
              clay : key;
              locindex : tindex;
        begin
              accept SEARCH (k : in key; start : in tindex) do
                      clay : = k;
                      locindex : = start;
              end SEARCH;
              while table(locindex) / = clay loop
                      locindex : = (locindex + 2) mod tsize;
              end loop;
              TManager.RESULT (locindex);
        end SearchTask;

end TABLE;
```

16.5 Reminders

1. Stopping a process in Ada is accomplished by shared variables, by exceptions, by a terminate alternative in a select statement, and by an abort statement. One of the disadvantages of the last two methods is that the affected task is killed and cannot be revived.

2. Array objects can be initialized in Ada by array aggregates. The aggregate must contain a value for each element of the array being assigned to. The keyword **others** makes the aggregate adapt to the size of the object being assigned to.

3. Accept bodies can be nested.

4. Previous chapters illustrated examples of task bodies where it did not matter whether task code was included in an accept statement or placed outside an accept statement. This chapter shows an example of a case in which it is mandatory that the task code (for the search task) be placed *outside* an accept statement.

5. If local objects are required in an accept statement body, a block must be embedded in the accept statement in order to declare them.

6. The POS attribute provides a means of converting an enumerated type into an integer.

16.6 Problems

1. The Ada programs for table lookup include a function for entering a new key into the table. Function ENTER takes a key as input parameter, searches for a table location that contains a blank, places the key in that location and returns the index of that location. If the table is full, the function reports an error condition. Extend the task TManager to implement this and fill in ENTER to use these facilities.

2. Suppose it is possible that someone applies function LOOKUP to a key that is not present in the table. In that case it may happen that the parallel search processes or tasks are both searching in vain. In Ada there would be a solution to this problem by rewriting the Table Manager so that it selects between accepting entry RESULT and a delay statement. If the result does not arrive by the time the delay is completed, the delay alternative is selected and any statements following the delay statement are executed. Solve the problem of absent keys in the manner indicated.

3. The restriction that the solutions are valid only if the table size is an even number should be eliminated. This can be done by redesigning the way

the table traversal index is incremented. It should be the case that, if the index starts tracing even numbered locations, it should continue to do so after wrapping around. The same should be true for the case in which the index starts tracing odd numbered locations. Rewrite the incrementation of the traversal index so that the describe restriction is lifted.

4. One possibility for creating search tasks was to use an access type that refers to search tasks. Rewrite the package to provide this implementation strategy. What would happen if instead of aborting the task, they were simply unreferenced: in other words, the access variables ceased to refer to them?

5. Several subprograms use a key as input parameter. This may cause some unnecessary copying. An alternative implementation introduces type *key* as an access type in Ada. Redesign the types that have to do with keys and rewrite the subprograms that use keys as input parameters.

6. The table lookup programs have been written using two parallel search tasks or processes. Redesign and rewrite the programs first for three parallel search tasks and then for N parallel search tasks, where N is a small constant whose value can be changed without having to change the programs. Is there a way to construct the programs so that N can be provided as a parameter to the entry LOOKUP?

A

A Scheduling Schema

In several of the chapters discussing concurrent solutions, the problem of scheduling has arisen and been dealt with in various ways. In most cases, a scheduler task was defined to act as the mediary between the various processes. In some special cases, scheduling was provided by exploiting the semantics and mechanisms of task intercommunication. In this appendix, we shall describe a scheme for a general scheduler that can be tailored to a given system.

A desirable approach would be to provide a generic package whose parameters determine the specific scheduling characteristics. However, this would require knowledge of internal implementation details which are hidden within the generic package and therefore is impossible. Instead, we describe a general approach, leaving certain details unspecified, that can be refined to provide the scheduling mechanism desired for a particular system. In addition, we provide a sample scheduler implementation.

A.1 A Scheduling Package

The package provides a particular view of the system: there are tasks that are consumers who make requests, and there are tasks that are producers who fulfill requests. In particular, there are an unknown number of producers whose services are contended for by the consumers. This class of interactions is by no means the only one, but does represent a large number of system configurations. However, other classes of interaction can be modeled in ways that are similar to this one.

The package provides the notion of priority scheduling of requests. The types of the requests and results are left unspecified because they are implementation dependent and of no interest to the general scheduling schema. (However, it may be quite useful to make the type *request* an enumerated type.)

431

```
type    request is . . . ;
type    result  is . . . ;
subtype priority is INTEGER range 1 . . maxpriority;
```

The constant *maxpriority* determines the highest priority.

The primary means of interaction and coordination between the scheduler and its clients (both the consumers and the producers) is the access type *signal*, which points to a priority request control block. The limited, private type *prcb* has one parameter which fixes the static priority of the *prcb* and is used by the scheduler to implement its particular priority scheduling policy.

```
type prcb (p : priority) is limited private;
type signal is access prcb;
```

Consumers submit requests to be serviced and eventually wait for the results. The type *signal* is used to coordinate the two operations. A SUBMITREQUEST operation requires a signal object that will be used later by WAITRESULT. The scheduler indicates that a waiting process is to be resumed by operating on that signal object after passing on the result. Misuse of the signal, e.g., waiting on a previously used signal that has not been used with SUBMITREQUEST prior to WAITRESULT, is indicated by the exception *signalmisuse*.

```
procedure SUBMITREQUEST  (s : in signal; r : in request);
procedure WAITRESULT     (s : in signal; r : out result);
```

Producers, on the other hand, indicate that they are ready to provide a service at a particular level of priority by the operation WAITREQUEST. When the scheduler determines that there is some request to be performed at that level of priority, the request is passed on to the server. The signal used in the WAITREQUEST operation is then used to coordinate the submission of the result in SUBMITRESULT. This latter operation is performed after the producer has been scheduled and has created the result for the specified request. Again, *signalmisuse* is raised if a signal is not used properly in SUBMITRESULT and WAITRESULT.

```
procedure WAITREQUEST   (s : in signal; r : out request);
procedure SUBMITRESULT  (s : in signal; r : in result);
```

The parameterized, limited private type *prcb* is implemented as a record which contains and active flag, the specified request, the result, a state specification and a semaphore task to provide the actual synchronization The exception *signalmisuse* is raised whenever the state is not correct for the particular operation.

```
type prcb (pri : priority) is record
        act  : boolean : = false; -- not currently in use
        req  : request;
        sem  : semaphore;
        res  : result;
end record;
```

The task Scheduler does the actual scheduling and dispatching, and is the heart of the package. It is also the part that is implementation dependent and, therefore, left unimplemented. The interface specifies three operations: REQUEST, SERVER, and RESULT. The entry REQUEST schedules the request specified in the *prcb* pointed to by the signal parameter. The entry SERVER schedules the server as a supplier for a any request. And, the entry RESULT schedules the return of the result submitted by the server.

```
task Scheduler is
        entry REQUEST (s : in signal);
        entry SERVER  (s : in signal);
        entry RESULT  (s : in signal);
end Scheduler;
```

The operator SUBMITREQUEST, which schedules the consumer, has several functions: it records the input request, sets the state to active (act := TRUE), and schedules the request, provided that the *prcb* is not currently in use. An access error (raised if *s* is null) is reinterpreted as the exception *signalmisuse*.

```
procedure SUBMITREQUEST (s :  signal; r : in request) is
begin
        if s.act then raise signalmisuse; end if;
        s.act   := true;
        s.req   := r;
        Schedule.REQUEST ( s );
exception
        when CONSTRAINT_ERROR  => raise signalmisuse;
end SUBMITREQUEST;
```

At some point after scheduling its request, the task issues the WAITRESULT operation. This operation simply issues a P on the signal's semaphore, and, upon completion of this operation, extracts the result from the referenced *prcb* and resets the state to inactive. A CONSTRAINT_ERROR, possible only if *s* is null, is reinterpreted as *signalmisuse*.

```
procedure WAITRESULT (s : in signal; r : out result) is
begin
        if not s.act then raise signalmisuse; end if;
        P (s.sem);
        r       := s.res;
        s.act   := false;
exception
        when CONSTRAINT_ERROR => raise signalmisuse;
end WAITRESULT;
```

The corresponding operations for the producers/servers are similar. The WAITREQUEST tells the scheduler that the producer is available to process a request at the specified level of priority. The operation submits the signal to the scheduler and waits on the semaphore component. Once the scheduler has signaled the waiting producer, the request is extracted from the signal and passed back to the producer and the state of the signal set to active. The same restrictions apply to the raising of the exception *signalmisuse*.

```
procedure WAITREQUEST (s : in signal; r : out result) is
begin
        if s.act then raise signalmisuse; end if;
        s.act := true;
        Scheduler.SERVER (s);
        P (s.sem);
        r := s.res;
exception
        when CONSTRAINT_ERROR => raise signalmisuse;
end WAITREQUEST;
```

Once the producer/server has determined the results for the request, it passes the results to the scheduler by means of the *prcb* referenced by the signal. Again, the exception CONSTRAINT_ERROR is reinterpreted as *signalmisuse*. Once the scheduler has accepted the results, the signal is reset to inactive.

```
procedure SUBMITRESULT (s : in signal; r : in result) is
begin
        if not s.act then raise signalmisuse; end if;
        s.res := r;
        Scheduler.RESULT (s);
        s.act := false;
exception
        when CONSTRAINT_ERROR => raise signalmisuse;
end SUBMITRESULT;
```

A.2 The Scheduler Program Text

package ScheduleManager **is**

       type   REQUEST **is** . . . ;
       type   RESULT   **is** . . . ;
       subtype priority   **is** INTEGER **range** 1 . . maxpriority;

       type prcb (pri : priority) **is limited private**;
       type signal **is access** prcb;

       procedure SUBMITREQUEST (s : **in** signal; r : **in** request);
       procedure WAITRESULT   (s : **in** signal; r : **out** result);
       procedure WAITREQUEST   (s : **in** signal; r : **out** request);
       procedure SUBMITRESULT   (s : **in** signal; r : **in** result);

       signalmisuse : **exception**;

private

       type prcb (pri : priority) **is**
          record
               act   : boolean := false; -- initialized to inactive
               req : request;
               sem : semaphore;
               res   : result;
          end record;

end ScheduleManager;

package body ScheduleManager **is**

       task Scheduler **is**
          entry REQUEST (s : **in** signal);
          entry SERVER   (s : **in** signal);
          entry RESULT   (s : **in** signal);
       end Scheduler;

       procedure SUBMITREQUEST (s : **in** signal; r : **in** request) **is**
       begin
          if s.act **then raise** signalmisuse; **end if**;
          s.act   := true;
          s.req   := r;
          Scheduler.REQUEST (s);
       exception
          when CONSTRAINT_ERROR => **raise** signalmisuse;
       end SUBMITREQUEST;

```
procedure WAITRESULT (s : in signal; r : out result) is
begin
        if not s.act then raise signalmisuse; endif;
        P (s.sem);
        r       := s.res;
        s.act   := false;
exception
        when CONSTRAINT_ERROR => raise signalmisuse;
end WAITRESULT;

procedure WAITREQUEST (s : in signal; r : out request) is
begin
        if s.act then raise signalmisuse; end if;
        s.act   := true;
        Scheduler.SERVER (s);
        P (s.sem);
        r       := s.req;
exception
        when CONSTRAINT_ERROR  => raise signalmisuse;
end WAITREQUEST;

procedure SUBMITRESULT (s : in signal; r : in result) is
begin
        if not s.act then raise signalmisuse; end if;
        s.res := r;
        Scheduler.RESULT (s);
        s.act := false;
exception
        when CONSTRAINT_ERROR => raise signalmisuse;
end SUBMITRESULT;

        task body Scheduler is separate;

end ScheduleManager;
```

A.3 A Sample Schedule Task Body

The scheduling policy that we will implement is as follows: requests will be scheduled in priority order and within priorities in first in, first out (FIFO) order. If a server is available for the request at the specified level of priority, the request will be passed to the activated producer. If no server is available at that level, the first producer at a lower level of priority will be activated for the request. If no server is available, then the request will remain queued until a server is available. Results will be passed to the waiting consumers as they are received by means of the signal which also serves to activate them.

Let us first assume that there exists a generic package that supplies a list as a private type along with sufficient operations to do what we wish: put values at the end of the list, remove values from the head of the list or the first occurrence within a list, iterate through the list, and remove the current element of the iteration from the list.

```
generic type element is private;
package ListManager is

    type list is private;

    -- iteration operations
    procedure STARTOFLIST        (l : in out list; e : out element);
    procedure NEXTINLIST         (l : in out list; e : out element);
    procedure REMOVECURRENT      (l : in out list; e : out element);
    -- insertion and removal
    procedure PUTATTAIL          (l : in out list; e : in element);
    procedure REMOVEFIRST        (l : in out list; e : in element);
    procedure REMOVEHEAD         (l : in out list; e : out element);
    . . .
    -- queries about lists
    function    EMPTY            (l : in list) return boolean;
    . . .

end ListManager;
```

We create three lists of signals: *reqlist* to create the schedule of requests; *servlist* to create the list of available servers; and *waitlist* to create the list of signals whose requests are being serviced and whose consumers are waiting for results.

```
package SignalList is new ListManager(signal);
use SignalList;

reqlist   : array (priority) of list;
servlist  : array (priority) of list;
waitlist  : array (request) of list;
```

The task Scheduler alternates between scheduling a request, server or result, and dispatching a server. The dispatching operation may be an empty one as, e.g., when no servers are available to be dispatched.

```
begin -- body of scheduler
     loop
          SCHEDULENEXT;
          DISPATCHNEXT;
     end loop;
end Scheduler;
```

The operation SCHEDULENEXT accepts indeterminately the entries REQUEST, SERVER and RESULT. A request is scheduled at the tail of the appropriate priority. A server is scheduled at the tail of the appropriate server list. A result causes a waiting request to be removed from the appropriate waitlist and dispatched immediately.

```
procedure SCHEDULENEXT is
     temps : signal;
begin                        -- Incorrect Ada
     select
          accept REQUEST (s : in signal) do
               PUTATTAIL (reqlist(s.pri), s);
          end REQUEST;
     or
          accept SERVER (s : in signal) do
               PUTATTAIL (servlist(s.pri), s);
          end SERVER;
     or
          accept RESULT (s : in signal) do
               REMOVEHEAD (waitlist(s.req), temps);
               temps.res := s.res;
               V(temps.sem);
          end RESULT;
     end select;
end SCHEDULENEXT;
```

The natural expression of this operation is in the form of the procedure above. The body of the scheduler is simple and clear with the two main actions appropriately abstracted. Unfortunately, Ada allows accept statements only in the actual body of a task and, hence, they cannot be encapsulated in a procedure, even if it local to the task. This represents a great loss in the power of computational abstraction within tasks. Therefore, instead of the above procedure, we must replace the procedure call in the body of the task with the select statement, and regretfully accept the loss of abstraction and its resulting clarity.

The operation DISPATCHNEXT loops through the request lists in priority order to determine if there is any server that can be dispatched. (Because of the inability to encapsulate SCHEDULENEXT, we shall decrease the abstraction on DISPATCHNEXT one level as well.)

```
-- DISPATCHNEXT
for i in reverse priority loop
        exit when DISPATCHREQ(i);
end loop;
```

Note that we have used the keyword reverse in the for statement. Because the highest number in the type *priority* is the highest priority, we want to process the array in reverse order.

The dispatching of requests (and thus servers) is more complicated. For a given request, it may be dispatched only if there is a server available for it. Therefore, we iterate through the *reqlist* to find the first request for which there is a server. Once a server is found, the request is moved to the wait list and the server is signalled to proceed with the specified request.

```
procedure DISPATCHREQ (p : in priority) returns boolean is
        tempreq, tempserv : signal;
begin
        if not EMPTY (reqlist(p)) then
                for i in reverse 1 . . p loop
                        if not EMPTY (servlist(i)) then
                                REMOVEHEAD (servlist(i), tempserv);
                                REMOVEHEAD (reqlist(p), tempreq);
                                PUTATTAIL (waitlist(tempreq.req), tempreq);
                                tempserv.req : = tempreq.req;
                                V (tempserv.sem);
                                return true;
                        end if;
                end loop;
        end if;
        return false;
end DISPATCHREQ;
```

A.4 Sample Task Body Program Text

generic type element **is** private;
package ListManager **is**

      type list **is private**;

      -- iteration operations
      procedure   STARTOFLIST   (l : **in out** list; e : **out** element);
      procedure   NEXTINLIST   (l : **in out** list; e : **out** element);
      procedure   REMOVECURRENT (l : **in out** list; e : **out** element);

      -- insertion and removal
      procedure   PUTATTAIL   (l : **in out** list; e : **in** element);
      procedure   REMOVEFIRST   (l : **in out** list; e : **in** element);
      procedure   REMOVEHEAD   (l : **in out** list; e : **out** element);
      . . .

      -- queries about lists
      function   EMPTY   (l : **in** list) **return** boolean;
      . . .

end ListManager;

with ListManager;
separate (ScheduleManager)
task body Scheduler **is**

      package SignalList **is new** ListManager(signal);
      use SignalList;

      reqlist   : **array** (priority) **of** list;
      servlist : **array** (priority) **of** list;
      waitlist : **array** (request) **of** list;

      temps   : signal;

```
        procedure DISPATCHREQ (p : in priority) returns boolean is
                tempreq, tempserv : signal;
        begin
                if not EMPTY (reqlist(p)) then
                        for i in reverse 1 . . p loop
                                if not EMPTY (servlist(i)) then
                                        REMOVEHEAD (servlist(i), tempserv);
                                        REMOVEHEAD (reqlist(p), tempreq);
                                        PUTATTAIL (waitlist(tempreq.req), tempreq);
                                        tempserv.req := tempreq.req;
                                        V(tempserv.sem);
                                        return true;
                                end if;
                        end loop;
                end if;
                return false;
        end DISPATCHREQ;

begin -- body of the task
        loop
        -- SCHEDULENEXT
                select
                        accept REQUEST (s : in signal) do
                                PUTATTAIL (reqlist(s.pri), s);
                        end REQUEST;
                or
                        accept SERVER (s : in signal) do
                                PUTATTAIL (servlist(s.pri), s);
                        end SERVER;
                or
                        accept RESULT (s : in signal) do
                                REMOVEHEAD (waitlist(s.req), temps);
                                temps.res := s.res;
                                V(temps.sem);
                        end RESULT;
                end select;

        -- DISPATCHNEXT
                for i in reverse priority loop
                        exit when DISPTACHREQ(i);
                end loop;
        end loop;
end Scheduler;
```

A.5 Problems

1. Change the sample Scheduler to schedule producers for specific requests rather than any request while ignoring the priority of the producer. Changes must be made to the interface as well as to the body of the scheduler.

2. Modify the sample Scheduler to try to provide results ahead of requests so that results can be satisfied immediately. Try to keep some small number of results always available.

3. The sample Scheduler is based on the static priority of the *prcb*. Modify the interface and the implementation to provide an additional notion of dynamic priority where the dynamic priority is initially that of the static priority but may be changed by a CHANGEPRIORITY operation once the request has been queued.

4. Problem 4 introduced the notion of a dynamic priority in addition to the static one. Chose one of the scheduler implementations and modify it to incorporate following internal dynamic priority policy: whenever a process is scheduled, increase the dynamic priority for the head of each lower priority queue. In this way, low priority processes eventually work their way to a high enough level of priority to be scheduled.

5. An alternative model of process scheduling is that of processes waiting on events. Modify the interface to reflect this model and provide the appropriate abstractions, and implement a policy that allows processes to wait on an event and enables them to specify their priority with respect to that event. Dispatch the highest priority process waiting in an event when the event occurs. A signaled event with no waiting processes has no effect, that is, events are remembered.

6. Change the signalling semantics in the previous problem so that all processes waiting on the signalled event are activated.

7. The sample solution assumed a predefined set of events as the basis for scheduling. It may be that the system is more dynamic than that: events may come and go depending upon the circumstances. Modify the interface and the implementation to allow the creation and destruction of events. The implementation of the type *event* should enable the creator to pass the request around to other processes. What strategy should be followed when a request is to be destroyed while processes are queued waiting to be serviced (remember the problems of raising exceptions between communicating tasks)?

B

Hints to Solutions

Chapter 1

Problem 1

Two directions are perpendicular if they differ by two. The text is derived from function OPPOSITE by replacing the number four by the number two.

Problem 2

The result statement in Pascal is

OPPOSITE := (dif = 4) **or** (dif = -4)

The return statement in Ada is

return dif = 4 **or** dif = -4;

The parentheses around the equalities are necessary in Pascal, but not in Ada.

Problem 3

If size = 1, none of the while statements are executed and the loop in the second Ada program immediately returns TRUE. The first Pascal program causes an array access error independent of size.

Problem 4

Using the same parameter and local names, the body of the Pascal procedure SUBTIME is

```
c := u.sec - v.sec;  b := u.min - v.min;  a := u.hr - v.hr;
if c >= 0 then w.sec := c
else begin b := b - 1; w.sec := 60 + c end;
```

```
if b >= 0 then w.min := b
else begin a := a - 1; w.min := 60 + b end;
if a >= 0 then w.hr := a else w.hr := 24 + a
```

The body of the Ada function starts out with exactly the same three subtraction assignments as the Pascal program, but it contains no assignments to a local *w*.

```
if c < 0 then b := b - 1; c := c + 60; end if;
if b < 0 then a := a - 1; b := b + 60; end if;
if a < 0 then a := a + 24; end if;
return (a, b, c);
```

Problem 5

We cannot introduce type NATURAL in Pascal, because the upperbound is the largest positive integer which depends on the particular machine on which you work. This number is expressible in Ada as INTEGER'LAST, but cannot be expressed in Pascal. Non-positive input is filtered out of the Pascal program by embedding the entire body in the then part of the statement

```
if N > 0 then <body> else ISPRIME := FALSE
```

Chapter 2

Problem 1

Local variable *weekdaynum* of integer range type cannot be replaced by a variable of type *weekday*, because Pascal does not have a standard function that corresponds to Ada's VAL attribute. It is not possible in Pascal to map an index into the corresponding value of an enumeration type. The Ada program is already written without a local variable of type *weekdaynum*.

Problem 2

The lowerbound can be moved to the year 1800, because this is the first exception of the leap year rule counting backwards from 1900. The upperbound cannot be moved beyond 2099. To make the algorithm general, one must add a term that takes into account that years that are a multiple of 100 are not leap years except for the ones that are divisible by 400. If the program takes 1 March of year zero as basis, the additional term is (y / 400 - y / 100).

Problem 3

A suitable type definition for dates is

```
type date is
        record m : month; d : day; y : year; end record;
```

Function *weekdayof* now maps an object of type *date* into a weekday. One cannot omit types *month*, *day* and *year*, because the fields may not be declared with anonymous types.

Type *weekday* could be replaced by an integer subtype representing the range 1 . . 7 or 0 . . 6. However, the numbers are far less expressive than the weekday names and the reader may have the wrong idea and do the mapping incorrectly. For instance, does number two represent Monday or Tuesday? That depends.

Problem 4

A type definition for Julian dates is

   type juldate **is record** d: daynum; y : year; **end record**;

where *daynum* is an integer subtype representing the range 1 . . 366. In a normal year, the day number of the first of each month is respectively

   1, 32, 60, 91, 121, 152, 182, 213, 244, 274, 305, 335.

These numbers can be stored in a constant array *firstnum* initialized in its declaration. The function that maps Julian dates into normal dates first checks whether the input concerns a leap year. This part can be written as

   (x.y **mod** 400 = 0) **or**
   (x.y **mod** 4 = 0 **and** x.y **mod** 100 /= 0).

If input *x* is a leap year, we wish to subtract one from x.d if x.d is greater than sixty, so that the daynumber corresponds to that of an ordinary year. Before doing that, one must check specifically for February 29. Since Ada treats input parameters read-only, we need a local variable *dn* to store the modified daynumber. Thus, in the case of a leapyear we write (assuming *dn* has been initialized to x.d)

   if dn = 60 **then return** (Feb, 29, x.y);
   elsif dn > 60 **then** dn := dn - 1;
   end if;

The remainder of the mapping can now be written as a case statement that distinguishes roughly between the four seasons:

   case dn / 91 **is**
       when 0 => . . .   -- winter
       when 1 => . . .   -- spring
       when 2 => . . .   -- summer ·
       when 3 => . . .   -- fall
   end case;

Let us look at one of the seasons, for example spring (dn / 91 = 1).

> **if** dn < firstnum (May) **then return** (Apr, dn - 90, x.y);
> **elsif** du < firstnum (Jun) **then return** (May, dn - 120, x.y):
> **end if**;

The solution can be polished slightly by subtracting one from all elements in array *firstnum* and using these elements in the return statements.

Problem 5

A suitable subtype declaration for the ordinal number *n* is

> **subtype** occurrence **is** INTEGER **range** 1 . . 5;

because a particular weekday cannot occur more than five times in one month. The first occurrence of a particular weekday is found by statements

> p := 1 + weekday 'POS(s) - weekday 'POS(weekdayof (m, 1, y)):
> **if** p < 0 **then** p := p + 7: **end if**;

The last statement corrects *p* in case the first statement assigns a negative number. Variable *p* must (unfortunately) not be declared of subtype *day* or the first statement may run into a range error. The nth occurrence is found by adding $(n - 1) * 7$ to variable *p*. The addition can be integrated with the last if statement into

> **if** p < 0 **then** p := p + 7*n: **else** p := p + 7*(n - 1);

The last occurrence can be found by increasing p by seven as long as the result is less than 32.

Chapter 3

Problem 1

After initializing all elements w(i) to zero, we write

> **for** j **in** 1 . . rowdim **loop** x := v(j);   -- Ada
>   **for** i **in** 1 . . coldim **loop** w(i) := w(i) + m(i, j)*x;
>   **end loop**;
> **end loop**;

This solution saves a little less than the one in the discussion, because w(i) is addressed twice in the assignment to w_i. In Pascal one may assign to the input matrix. Thus, we could first multiply all matrix elements with the proper vector component and then add the matrix elements:

> **for** j := 1 **to** rowdim **do**   {Pascal}
> **begin** x := v[j]; **for** j := 1 **to** coldim **do** m[i, j] := m[i, j]*x **end**

The output vector is constructed by adding the row elements. This solution requires no more space than the others, because in Pascal a value parameter is copied at every function call in any case. The solution may not be acceptable if the input matrix is passed by reference, because in that case the original matrix is modified. A similar solution in Ada uses more space, because input parameters in Ada are read-only. The solution requires therefore an additional local matrix of the same size as the input matrix.

Problem 2

In Pascal, the size of arrays is not computable. If a function takes an array parameter, it accepts arrays of a specific fixed size only. Thus, if u and v are n-dimensional vectors and x and y m-dimensional vectors, no INPROD function or procedure in Pascal can handle both. One needs to declare a function NINPROD and a function MINPROD, but one can compare their results, because those are both of type real.

Problem 3

A row is extracted from a matrix by the Ada function ROW:

```
function ROW(m : matrix; i: INTEGER) return vector is
      len : constant NATURAL := m 'LENGTH(2);
      v : vector(1 . . len);
begin
      for k in 1 . . len loop v(k) := m(i, k); end loop;
      return v;
end ROW;
```

One can write a similar function for extracting a column from a matrix. Matrix-vector multiplication can now be written as

```
for i in 1 . . coldim loop
      w(i) := INPROD(ROW(m, i), v);
end loop;
```

Problem 4

The vector addition, subtraction and scalar multiplication procedures use var parameters, but are not affected by the aliasing problem, because the elements of the input objects are used only once. Aliasing causes problems in the matrix multiplication procedures, because the elements of the input objects are used more than once in the computation. Take for instance MATVECMUL which writes out a vector. The easiest way to avoid the aliasing problem is to copy the input vector.

```
for k := 1 . . vecdim do locvec[k] := v[k];          {Pascal}
      . . .
 . . . w[i] := w[i] + M[i, j] *locvec[j]
```

In this version no problems arise if *w* and *v* are the same vectors.

Problem 5

The matrix and vector operations can be used without name qualification if we precede the package, in which the orthogonality test is included, by a use clause that lists MATMANAGEMENT and VECMANAGEMENT. Assuming function ROW is defined in package MATMANAGEMENT, the orthogonality test can be written as

```
function ORTHMAT(m : matrix) return BOOLEAN is
begin
    for i in 1 . . (coldim - 1) loop for j in (i + 1) . . coldim loop
        if INPROD(ROW(m,i), ROW(m,j)) /= 0 then return FALSE; end if;
    end loop; end loop;
        return TRUE;
end ORTHMAT;
```

If the package that includes function ORTHMAT is not in the scope of vector or matrix management, it should also be prefixed with a with clause that lists the vector and matrix packages.

Chapter 4

Problem 1

Two string indexes are required: one for the parameter *whole* and one for the parameter *part*. Use the attributes FIRST and LAST to define the two indices and to increment the substring index.

```
wi : POSITIVE range whole'FIRST . . whole'LAST;
pi : POSITIVE range part'FIRST . . part'LAST;
        . . .
if pi < part'LAST
        then   pi : = part'FIRST;
        else   pi : = pi + 1;
    end if;
```

Problem 2

Overload the concatenation operator "&" for *vstrings* and return a *vstring* aggregate.

```
return (a.len + b.len, a.str & b.str);
```

While the concatenation operation is clearly identical, the slice operation cannot be identical, because there is no way to overload the slicing operation. A function must be defined as follows.

> **function** slice (fst, lst : **in** POSITIVE; v : **in** vstring) **return** vstring;
> **begin**
> > **return** ((lst - fst) + 1, v.str(fst . . lst));
> **end**;

Replace the return statement that removes the substring with the following return statement.

> **return** slice (1, windowpos, whole) &
> > slice (windowpos + pat.len + 1, whole.len, whole);

Both operations are of general utility and should be exported.

Problem 3

The subtraction operation cannot be overloaded because the parameter and result profiles are identical. The suggested operation to overload is "/". An easy way to implement this operation is to use recursion: copy the implementation of "-" and replace the first return statement with the following statement,

> **return** vstring'(. . .) / part;

where the ellipses represent the aggregate currently being returned in *vstring* subtraction. The recursion will stop when no strings remain to be subtracted. Note the inefficiency that occurs: the search starts at the beginning of the new whole each time. An iterative version can be constructed that is more efficient: back up at most *part.len* - 1 characters and start searching again; however, a local copy of *whole* will have to be made. (Note that a similar strategy can be implemented recursively using *vstring* catenation and slicing).

Problem 4

Initialize *windowpos* to *whole.len* - *part.len*. Decrement *windowpos* instead of incrementing it and stop the loop when *windowpos* < 0.

Problem 5

In Pascal, the comparison must be done on a character by character basis. In Ada, the string comparison operator "<" can be used on either complete or sliced strings. Ada enables the program to be written in a more general and efficient manner.

Chapter 5

Problem 1

In Pascal parameters *a* and *b* can be used as initialized locals. We can write statements such as

> **if** a = 0 **then** a := b **else if** b = 0 **then** b := a;
> **if** b < 0 **then** b := -b; **if** a < 0 **then** a := -a

In Ada, input parameters are read-only. We need two local variables *p* and *b* and we can write

> **if** p = 0 **then return** q; **elsif** q = 0 **then return** p; **end if**;

The initializations assure that the GCD computation is now applied to two positive integers. An interesting way to compute the GCD in Ada without division is

> **loop**
>   **if** p = q **then return** p; **end if**;
>   **if** p > q **then** p := p - q; **else** q := q - p; **end if**;
> **end loop**;

Problem 2

Since type *pair* exported by package PAIRS is a private type, the record implementation of that type is not accessible outside package PAIRS. Since complex arithmetic is indeed defined outside of package PAIRS, the instantiation of

> **subtype** complex **is** COMPLBASICS.pairs;

does not give access to the representation either.

Problem 3

Package COMPL that derives type *complex* from type *numberpair* can use the automatically inherited functions for addition, subtraction and scalar multiplication, but must define its own versions of multiplication and division. These definitions do need the components of number pairs, but do not have access to those components if *numberpair* is a private type. In that case, we assume that package NUMBERPAIRS exports functions LEFT and RIGHT that have the obvious meaning. If we use for convenience the local variables

> ure : FLOAT := LEFT(numberpair(u));
> uim : FLOAT := RIGHT(numberpair(u));
> vre : FLOAT := LEFT(numberpair(v));
> vim : FLOAT := RIGHT(numberpair(v));

then the product is complex(ure*vre - uim*vim, ure*vim + vim*vre)

Problem 4

It is not necessary in Ada to store the components of the result in an output parameter or in a local variable. The result can be computed and returned in an aggregate. However, we lose the ability to compute the two greatest common divisors immediately before each component computation. Thus, the Ada program needs two local variables to store the two greatest common divisors before the component computations can take place. The addition programs need more local variables, because the gcd of the denominators is needed at the beginning (to avoid unnecessarily large products) and at the end (to compute the resulting denominator). This is true for both Pascal and Ada.

Problem 5

Type *complex* is elaborated in the private section as

type complex **is record** modu, arg : REAL; **end record**;

The body of package COMPL has access to the fields of complex variables. It defines, for example, a function that returns the real part:

function RE(u : complex) **return** REAL **is**
begin return u.modu*COSIN(u.arg); **end** RE;

The declaration of this function is included in the visible part of package COMPL. Addition of complex numbers results in a record with a *modu* field equal to

$$SQRT(p**2 + q**2 - 2*p*q*COSIN(r))$$
where p = u.modu, q = v.modu and r = u.arg - v.arg.

The *arg* field of an addition is the average of the input *args*. It is hardly useful to define this package COMPL as an instantiation of package PAIRS, because all functions would have to be redefined. To build a package for plane vectors as requested, one should define a generic package POLARITH which can be used to instantiate both COMPL and PLANEVECS. Package POLARITH defines a private type *polobj* which consists of a *modu* and *arg* field.

Problem 6

Function SCRAMBLE is defined in the body of PSWDS:

```
function SCRAMBLE(x : word) return word is
        subtype ch is CHARACTER;          -- rename
        y : word;
begin
        for i in 1 . . 10 loop
            y(i) := ch'VAL(ch'POS(x(i)) - 32 + i);
        end loop;          -- an example of a scramble expression
        return y;
end scramble;
```

The crucial statement in function CHECKPSWD is

> **return** p.val = SCRAMBLE(x);

A user cannot write a similar statement outside of package PSWDS, because the *val* field and function SCRAMBLE are accessible only in the body of PSWDS. Similar restrictions exist for the crucial statements in procedure SETPSWD:

> **if** p.init **then return**;
> **else** p.init := TRUE; p.val := scramble(x);
> **end if**;

Chapter 6

Problem 1

The headings of procedure TAB in Pascal and Ada are respectively

> **procedure** TAB(a, b : real; **function** F : real; n : integer);   {Pascal}
> **generic with function** F(x : REAL) **return** REAL;   -- Ada
> **procedure** TAB(a, b : REAL; n : POSITIVE);

Since the length of the subinterval is fixed, it can be stored in a local variable h (or a local constant in Ada). Its value is (b - a) / REAL(n) in Ada; in Pascal the conversion to real is not needed. Be sure to declare in Ada the generic procedure separate from its body. It is not allowed to define the procedure body immediately after the generic declaration. The body must be declared separately and its declaration must be preceded by the procedure heading without generic clause. Thus, the body declaration is

> **procedure** TAB(a, b : REAL; n : POSITIVE) **is**
>   h : **constant** REAL := (b-a) / REAL(n);
> **begin** . . . **end** TAB;

The function values are printed in a simple for statement with argument $x = h*REAL(i)$.

Problem 2

Area A(2n) is expressed in terms of area A(n) by the formula

> $A(2n) = 0.5*A(n) + h*ODD$,

where h is the length of the new interval (which is (b - a) / 2n) and ODD is the sum of the function values in the odd dividing points. This sum is computed by the statements

ODD := 0; newh := 0.5*h; c := newh + a;
for i **in** 0 . . n - 1 **loop** ODD := ODD + f(c + REAL(i)*h); **end loop**;

In Pascal, the input function f can be passed as a parameter to function TRAP, in Ada function TRAP is generic and takes f as a generic parameter.

Problem 3

The translation of the iterative Pascal program for Newton's Algorithm into Ada is

```
generic
    with function f(x : REAL) return REAL;
    with function g(x : REAL) return REAL;
function ZEROPOINT(a, b, eps : REAL);

function ZEROPOINT(a, b, eps : REAL) is
    fx, gx, x : REAL;
begin
    if f(a) = 0.0 or g(a) > g(b) then x := a else x := b; end if;
    loop
        fx := f(x); gx := g(x);
        if ABS(fx) < 0.5*eps then return x; end if;
        x := x - fx/gx;
    end loop;
end ZEROPOINT;
```

The translation of the recursive Ada program for Newton's Algorithm into Pascal is

```
function ZEROPOINT(function f,g : real; a, b, eps : real) : real;
    function NEWTON(x : real) : real;
        var fx;
    begin
        fx := f(x);
        if abs(fx) < eps then NEWTON := x
        else NEWTON := NEWTON(x - fx / g(x))
    end;
begin
    eps := 0.5*eps;
    if (f(a) = 0) or (g(a) > g(b)) then
        ZEROPOINT := NEWTON(a)
    else ZEROPOINT := NEWTON(b)
end;
```

Problem 4

Function PLUS that adds two character digits must take the carry of preceding additions into account. Since Ada does not allow output parameters in functions, variable *carry* must be a global variable (Ada does allow assignments to globals in functions). To make sure that the global variable is shared by no others than the

the subprograms for string addition, we write a package STRADD that hides variable *carry* in its body. The only function this package exports is string addition.

```
package body STRADD is
    subtype ch is CHARACTER;                    -- rename
    carry : NATURAL;
    function PLUS(u,v : ch) return ch is
        valu : NATURAL := carry;
    begin
        valu := valu + ch'POS(u) + ch'POS(v) - ch'POS('0');
        if val <= ch'POS('9') then carry := 0;
        else valu := valu - 10; carry := 1;
        end if;
        return ch'VAL(valu);
    end PLUS;

    function INTSTRADD(x, y : STRING) return STRING is
        xlen : constant NATURAL := x'LENGTH;
        ylen : constant NATURAL := y'LENGTH;
        zlen : constant NATURAL := MAX(xlen, ylen) + 1;
        xleneft : constant NATURAL := zlen - xlen;
        yleneft : constant NATURAL := zlen - ylen;
        z : STRING(1 . . zlen);
    begin carry := 0;
        for k in reverse 2 . . zlen loop
            if k <= xleneft then z(k) := PLUS('0', y(k));
            elsif k <= yleneft then z(k) := PLUS(x(k), '0');
            else z(k) := PLUS(x(k), y(k));
            end if;
        end loop;

        if carry = 1 then z(1) := '1'; return z;
        else return z(2 . . zlen);
        end if;
    end INTSTRADD;
```

Problem 5

If a real number is given in six decimals, its precision $x = 5*10^{-7}$ is denoted by $(5, 7)$, where the first number is the aberration and the second number the scale. The notation $x = (5, 7)$ expresses that the seventh decimal may be off by as much as five units. For the sake of simplicity we assume that the input numbers a and b are in the range $[1 . . 10]$ (which has no effect on the computation of the precision of the product) and that a and b have the same precision x. The result of $a \times b$ lies in between

Thus, the precision of the product is $(a+b) \times x$, ignoring higher powers of x. Since x is small compared to a and b, we are only interested in the most significant digit of x. Thus, the precision can be computed as follows.

```
type precision is record aber, scale : INTEGER; end record;
        . . .
function COMPREC(a, b : REAL; x : precision) return precision is
        xab, xsc : NATURAL;
begin        -- a, b in range 1 . . 10
        xab := INTEGER((a + b)*REAL(x.aber));
        xsc := x.scale;
        if xab > 100 then xsc := xsc - 1; xab := xab / 10; end if;
        if xab > 10 then xsc := xsc - 1; xab := (xab + 5) / 10; end if;
        if a*b >= 10.0 then xsc := xsc + 1; end if;
        return (xaber, xsc);
end COMPREC;
```

The correction in the last if statement is performed in order that the resulting precision is expressed relative to the normal form of the product in which the decimal point follows the first most significant digit. For example, let $a = 7.819$, $b = 3.146$ and $x = (5,5)$. The product is 24.598674 and its precision (5,5), because

$$10.965 \times (5,5) = (54.5,5) = (5,4).$$

Since the product is larger than ten, the scale is corrected from four to five. Thus, the resulting product should be rounded after the fourth decimal to 24.60.

Chapter 7

Problem 1

Array slicing provides an easy way to implement this version.

```
q.body (1 . . q.length - 1) := q.body (2 . . q.length);
```

Decrement the length after the slice assignment.

Problem 2

The Dequeue package should have the following interface.

```
generic size : POSITIVE;
        type element is private;
```

```
package Dequeue is
        procedure PUTATHEAD      ( ... );
        procedure PUTATTAIL      ( ... );
        procedure GETFROMHEAD  ( ... );
        procedure GETFROMTAIL  ( ... );
end Dequeue;
```

For stack and queue packages, instantiate Dequeue and rename operations
GETFROMHEAD for both, PUTATTAIL for queues and PUTATHEAD for stacks.

Problem 3

Because queues should not be assigned to, their type should be limited private.

```
generic type element is private;
package Q is
        type queue (size : POSITIVE) is limited private;
        procedure ENQ (e : in element; q : in out queue);
        procedure DEQ (e : out element; q : in out queue);
            . . .
private
        type queue is . . . ;
end Q;
```

Problem 4

In the Pascal implementation, the dequeue operation must be implemented as a
procedure since functions can return only scalar objects.   In the Ada
implementation, the size parameter for the open queue type should have a default
value. The instantiation should have the following form.

```
package QofQs is new Queue (openqueue);
```

The advantages of Ada over Pascal include the centralization of modifications, no
modifications for new instantiations, and greater safety.

Problem 5

As in Problem 4, the size parameter in the type definition should have a default
value. The INCREASE operation is implemented as follows.

```
procedure INCREASE ( q : in out queue; n : in POSITIVE) is
        newq : queue (q.size + n);
begin
        newq.len := q.len;
        newq.body(1 . . q.len) := q.body;
        q := newq;
end INCREASE;
```

A new queue with the specified increased size is declared as a local object and initialized to the current length and body of the queue. The new queue is then assigned to the parameter and returned. The inverse operation is implemented in a similar manner.

Two problems are encountered: the queue objects passed as parameters to INCREASE and DECREASE may be constrained, and the desired decreased queue size may be smaller than the actual queue. In the first case, the implementor can use the attribute CONSTRAINED to query whether or not the queue is constrained. In the second case, the desired decreased size can be checked against the current length.

Chapter 8

Problem 1

The FIND operation is quite similar to the INSERT and can be constructed from the latter by simply removing the insertion code and adding the appropriate code to cover the case when the label is not found. For the LIST operation, assume that a list package exists with a list type definition and a single operation APPEND for labels. The easiest way to implement LISTLABELS is recursively: if the current node is not a leaf, recurse down the left son; list the current node; and then recurse down the right son.

```
procedure LISTLABELS (b : in binarytree; l : in out list) is
begin
        if b.left /= null then
                LISTLABELS (b.left, l);
        end if;
        APPEND (b.label, l);
        if b.right /= null then
                LISTLABELS (b.right, l);
        end if;
end LISTLABELS;
```

Problem 2

The type *binarytree* is exported as a private type and the existing type definitions are moved to the private part of the package. The interface procedures require no changes to their specifications. However, the user no longer has access to the tree structure and you may want to provide a few additional navigations through the tree: ROOTNODE, LEFTSUBTREE and RIGHTSUBTREE. Status variables or exceptions may be needed because the private tree type does not have the value **null** to indicate an empty tree or a failed operation. Alternatively, a constant *emptytree* can be defined to supply this value. This constant is declared as a deferred constant.

Problem 3

The implementation is analogous to the FIND operation with the pruning operation implemented if the label has been found.   Pruning results when the pointer to the labeled node/subtree is copied into the output parameter and then set to null in the input tree. (here again, the tree parameter is the boundary case: if it has the desired label, the entire tree is effectively pruned.)

```
procedure PRUNE ( b : in out binarytree; l : in label;
                     s : out binarytree; ok : out BOOLEAN);
begin
        if b = null then
            ok : = false;
            return;
        elsif b.label = label then
            ok : = true;
            s := b; b := null;
            return;
        elsif b.label < label then
            PRUNE (b.left, l, s, ok);
        else PRUNE (b.right, l, s, ok);
        end if;
    end prune;
```

Problem 4

The easiest way to balance the tree is first to list the contents of the tree and then grow a new, balanced tree. Grow the new tree in a manner similar to doing a binary search: pick the middle element in the list as the root of the tree and then grow the left and right subtrees with the sublists to the left and right of the middle element. Assuming that all the required list operations exist, the tree growing operation is as follows.

```
procedure BUILDTREE (bt : in out binarytree; lt : in list) is
        mid : INTEGER; node : binarytree;
begin
        if EMPTY(lt) then return;
        mid : = LISTLENGTH(lt) / 2;
        insert (bt, LISTELEMENT(mid, lt), node);
        BUILDTREE (bt, SUBLIST(1, mid - 1, lt));
        BUILDTREE (bt, SUBLIST(mid + 1, LISTLENGTH(lt), lt);
    end BUILDTREE;
```

Problem 5

A generic n-array labeled tree is possible. Instead of having specifically named sons, construct the sons as an array of n trees. An auxiliary function is required in the generic specification to determine which of the n sons to traverse.

```
generic N : Positive;
        with function compare (lab1, lab2 : in vstring)
              return INTEGER range 1 . . N;
package NaryTree is
        . . .
end NaryTree;
```

Procedure INSERT can be implemented either recursively or iteratively. In the recursive version, the last elsif and else clauses are replaced by an else clause that determines which son to traverse (by calling COMPARE) and then recursively calls itself to traverse that son.

```
else   son := COMPARE (root.label, label);
       INSERT (root.branch(son), label, node);
```

Chapter 9

Problem 1

The operations can be implemented by overloading "<" and ">" and using the following formulae: a < b is defined to mean a <= b and a /= b; a > b is defined to mean a >= b and a /= b.

Problem 2

In the "+" operation, the for loop can be replaced by $s.e := s1.e$ **or** $s2.e;$. Analogously, the "*" operation's for loop is replaced by $s.e := s1.e$ **and** $s2.e;$.

Problem 3

The operation LISTSET takes a set as a parameter and returns a set literal. In order to construct the set literal with precisely the correct number of elements, an auxiliary counting operation needs to be defined that can be used in the local set literal object definition. The body of the function loops through the set and and if the element is present, inserts the element in the literal.

Problem 4

Assume that a generic list package exists that can be instantiated for integers. The following operations are needed: FIND, INSERT, REMOVE and LENGTH. The null set is merely an empty list; MAKESET merely copies the set elements from the literal into the set list; "+" finds the elements in the set and inserts them only if they are not in the list; "-" removes an element from the list; "*" constructs a set of elements in both lists--again using FIND. The boolean operations again are implemented using FIND.

Problem 5

Exceptions are needed to indicate illegal subset operations, specifically where elements are not in the subset range. The result of the addition of an element not in the subset should be undefined. The result of two conjoint (or overlapping) subsets is a new subset whose range is subset1.lb . . subset2.ub. If they are completely disjoint, that is subset1.ub + 1 < subset2.lb, the result of addition should be undefined. Set subtraction is defined if the two subsets overlap; element subtraction is defined only if the element is within the defined subset. Set multiplication can be construed as producing a new subset: the overlapping part, subset2.lb . . subset1.ub. The boolean operations should be undefined if the subset type is not included in the other, or the element is not in the subset type.

Chapter 10

Problem 1

There are two key changes. The first one is to make MONAD, DYAD and GENERATE functions that return a result lexeme instead of pushing it on the stack. The second is to make the while loop a recursive procedure with three out parameters: the operator lexeme, an operand lexeme, and a depth indicator (either 1 or 2) to indicate how many times the procedural stack has been popped. The body of the recursive procedure then mirrors the use of the stack: if an operator is encountered, return the operator and a depth indication of 1 (i.e., pop the stack); otherwise, recurse (i.e., push the lexeme on the stack). When control returns, one of three cases holds: the operator is monadic and the monad function is invoked; the operator is dyadic and the second lexeme has been popped (i.e., depth = 2) and the dyadic operation is invoked; or the depth is 1 and the stack must be popped once more, so the depth is set to 2 and the lexeme and operator are returned.

Problem 2

The indirect load operation is a monadic operation that requires a result lexeme as its operand. The result specifies the register that contains the address of the desired data. It seems to be a safe assumption that the address will always be in a register by the time the operator is encountered (e.g., R+b will have occurred). Extend the operators, and hence the operations, to include the monadic operator, *ind*. Given the assumption above, no change is needed in the MONAD procedure, but procedure GENERATE must be extended to include the indirect load in the result case. When the operation is *ind*, write the following aggregate.

(ind, load, REG, opnd.val)

Otherwise, do the existing write statement.

Problem 3

The driver and code generator are unaffected. Since assignment is treated as dyadic (e.g., a b : =), it is no different from any other dyadic operation as far as the driver is concerned. GENERATE doesn't really care what the opcode is as long as it is consistent with the class of the operand (i.e., so that it generates a legal instruction).

The dyadic operation, on the other hand, must be modified. The assignment operation, like subtraction and division is not commutative. Further, it is different from subtraction and division in that the left operand is the destination address and should not be a result lexeme, but rather a global or local identifier lexeme. The right operand, rather than the left, must be a result lexeme. A fairly clean solution is to swap the left and right operands before checking if the left operand is a result. Since we know the right (previously the left) operand is not a result, the left (previously the right) operand will be forced to a result lexeme if it is not aready one. For safety, the clause *opcode = store* can be added to the second if clause.

Further, conversion to real only makes sense in one case: when the right operand is integer and the left operand is real; converting the left operand makes no sense since it is the destination, not a value. However, one may safely assume that the parser will guarantee that the latter case will not occur.

Problem 4

The general structure of the message descriptor in Ada is as follows.

```
type msgdescriptor (mt : msgtype) is record
        sender : userid;
        id      : msgid;
        text    : textptr;
        case mt is
                when originator = > receiver : userid;
                when sender = > origid : msgid;
        end case;
end record;
```

The Pascal structure is analogous to the above.

The send operation needs to distinguish two cases: the first is when depositing the originating message -- the user id is retrieved from the originator variant; the second is when depositing the response -- the sender is used.

Problem 5

The Ada data structure is defined as follows.

      type persondescriptor;
      type person **is access** persondescriptor;
      type persondescriptor (s : sex) **is record**
            father : person;
            sibling : person;
            case s **is**
                  when male =>   wife : person;
                  when female =>   husband : person;
                                    oldest : person;
            end case;
      end record;

The Pascal structure is analogous to the above. The programs are straightforward. In recording the birth of a child, the operation requires a pointer to the father and an indication of the child's sex. The wife and siblings can be traced from the father. In counting the children, only the pointer to the person need be given, since the siblings can be traced through the mother by way of the father.

Chapter 11

Problem 1

In the first case, reversing the P operation can cause deadlock. A process gains access to the critical section (garded by *mutex*) and then waits for a slot. However, the critical section is now permanently blocked. In the second case, the order is immaterial because both operations release the semaphores and the synchronization and exclusion are correctly maintained by the P operations.

Problem 2

For the consumer, a Boolean flag indicates whether there is a message available or not in mailbox[i]. In the Pascal program associate a semaphore with each mailbox such that the producer does a P before putting a message in and the consumer does a V after he takes it out. Both set the Boolean flag appropriately. In the Ada program create a task for each mailbox that alternates between deposit and remove (an array of records, each of which contains a Boolean flag and a mailbox task).

Problem 3

The basic problem is: it is impossible to know in advance whether to accept either entry, i.e., whether the mailbox is full or empty. One inclination is to punt the issue and use exceptions when the box is full or empty and force the interface procedures to handle the problem. However, there is no clean way to implement a procedure that waits for resources.

A rather clean solution would be possible if the type definition did not allow unconstrained declarations, i.e., if there were not a default value for the type parameter. In the former case, the size would always remain the same and it could be copied into the task on its first entry call and remembered along with the current state of the mailbox.

Since no guard can be constructed that makes use of the parameter, no guard should be used. Instead, exploit the fact that a rendezvous lasts until the accept statement completes. This in effect can be used to provide the wait mechanism. If the mailbox is full, nest an accept statement for the RECEIVE entry within the SEND accept statement. Any further sends will wait on the entry and will not succeed until this call completes and that will occur only when a slot opens up because of the RECEIVE. Handle the RECEIVE accept statement in the same way if the mailbox is empty: nest a SEND accept statement.

Problem 4

Both programs should be simpler. In the Pascal case, only one semaphore is needed to control access to the mailbox. In Ada, only a loop with the DEPOSIT and REMOVE accept statements is needed.

Problem 5

In the Pascal program, only one semaphore is needed to control the critical section of depositing and removing the messages, since the two operations cannot proceed independently. Further, only a head pointer is needed in the data structure.

In Ada, the only simplification is in the data structure and its bookkeeping: only the head pointer is needed, *mesnum* is no longer needed because the head pointer provides the same function. The mailbox array should be indexed by 1 . . capacity so that no messages are present when head is equal to zero.

Chapter 12

Problem 1

Priority to readers can be established by having a guard in the STARTWRITE accept statement that disallows an entry call as long as there are any readers or outstanding entry calls on STARTREAD (i.e., STARTREAD'COUNT > 0).

Priority to writers can be established by putting an analogous guard on the STARTREAD accept statement.

Problem 2

Add two new entries STARTQUICKREAD and STOPQUICKREAD. No counts need to be maintained, as no consistency guarantees are made. Add the appropriate accept statements to the select statements. The problem now is to allow the quick reads during a write. Include the STOPWRITE accept statement in an internal select statement along with STARTQUICKREAD and STOPQUICKREAD. Construct the select statement in a loop such that the loop terminates as soon as the STOPWRITE entry call occurs.

The FCFS example cannot be modified easily because of the single entry point that stops on a write request.

Problem 3

As in Problem 2, add two new entries, STARTQUICKWRITE and STOPQUICKWRITE. A count should be kept, since the extensive write should still have exclusive access. Add the accept statements into the select statement and modify the STARTWRITE guard to wait until all readers and quick writers are done. Treat the STARTQUICKWRITE accept statement in the same way as STARTREAD.

The second example can be modified, since it does not try to gain access while writing, only during a reading cycle.

Problem 4

A task is needed to manage all the forks with an entry for each philosopher. The accept statement for each philosopher is guarded by the following.

> **when** rightfork(i) = available **and** leftfork(i) = available =>
> **accept** fork(i) **do** . . . ;

This solution provides central resource management and thus is not very useful for distributed systems.

Problem 5

The Host task provides a request-to-eat entry and a family of OBTAINFORKS entries. The requests to eat are logged in arrival time order. In the interest of maximizing concurrency, a philosopher's neighbors may be allowed to eat even though their requests were made later. However, no neighbor should be allowed to eat twice before the philosopher is allowed to eat. Once the forks are available, signal the waiting philosopher through the OBTAINFORKS entry for that philosopher.

> **accept** OBTAINFORKS(i);

The philosophers make their request and then call their OBTAINFORKS entry.

Chapter 13

Problem 1

Replace the variable *free* by *top*, replace *avail* and *availindex* by *freestack*. Initialization must occur at the beginning of the task body. Replace the current bookkeeping with the stack bookkeeping in each of the accept statement bodies.

Problem 2

Users send one of three requests to the ResourceManager: FANCYREQ, REQUEST or CONDREQ. The first represents a request for a fancy resource, the second for a resource of either kind and the third checks whether a resource is available and allocates one if this is so, or returns the null resource if none are available. The body of the ResourceManager contains the select statement:

```
select
    accept RELEASE(r : in resource) do . . . end RELEASE;
or
    when fancy > 0  = >
    accept FANCYREQ(r : out resource) do . . . decr(fancy);end FANCYREQ;
or
    when fancy > 0 or ordin > 0  = >
    accept REQUEST(r : out resource) do . . .
        if ISFANCY(r) then decr(fancy); else decr(ordin);end if;
    end REQUEST;
or
    accept CONDREQ(r : out resource) do . . .
        if ordin > 0 then . . . ; decr(ordin); else r : = nullres;end if;
end select;
```

The dots in the accept statements represent the actual resource selection and (de)allocation. The guards ensure that a fancy request is accepted only if fancy resources are available, while an ordinary request is accepted if there are resources available of either kind. The last accept statement is unguarded so that entry CONDREQ is always accepted, irrespective of the availability of resources. Users of CONDREQ are content to receive the null resource if no resources are free.

Since two select alternatives depend on fancy > 0, it is possible that one queue gets serviced more frequently than the other. This problem can be avoided by adding a priority indicator that points to the queue that was least recently served. The condition fancy > 0 is then extended respectively to

fancy > 0 **and** (prior **or** REQUEST'COUNT = 0)
fancy > 0 **and** (**not** prior **or** FANCYREQ'COUNT = 0)

For both queues the priority indicator is unimportant as long as the other queue is empty. But if the other queue is not empty, the priority indicator determines which of the two queues will be serviced. The priority indicator is set to FALSE in FANCYREQ (so as to give way to ordinary requests) and to TRUE in REQUEST (so as to give way to fancy requests).

Problem 3

Expand the implementation of the limited private type *resid* to include the time of allocation. The cost can then be computed on the basis of the length of use. The priority ought to be a factor in the usage, since the higher the priority, the better chance of gaining a resource. Thus, add the priority of the allocation to the *resid*. An alternative strategy might be to charge for priority only when contention arises and the priority managers must be used.

Chapter 14

Problem 11

See Chapter 11 for analogous implementation. Modular arithmetic will not work because the indices may not start at 0. More general problems occur if non - numeric indices, such as enumerated types, are used. The proper solution is to use the attributes FIRST and LAST and the discrete successor function SUCC within an if statement.

Problem 2

There is no longer a need for a task type nor for an initialization entry. Since the task will access all the interface buffers, no guard is suitable for the READ accept statement, and further, since no delay should be provided, no delay alternative, and, in fact, no select statement will be needed. However, two new parameters will be required: a keyboard identifier and a Boolean flag to indicate whether a character was available. The READKEYBOARD procedure must now be responsible for the wait if no character is available: incorporate the entry call and delay within a loop.

The basic problem in heavy traffic is the bottleneck caused by the centralization of access to the intermediate buffers.

Problem 3

The hardware handler should use a smaller time period. Intermediate buffering should be done using lists. Two problems must be considered. The first can have drastic results: completely out of list space. This would happen primarily if all keyboards suffered from the second problem: no consumption of the keyboard input. Some limit has to be put on keyboard input from a single keyboard that is sufficiently high so as to give the impression of unlimited input but not interfere with the other keyboards.

Problem 4

The data representation specification is analogous to the current implementation.

```
for inchar'SIZE use 8;
for status use record
        at mod 8;
        new    at 0*word range 0 . . 0;
        kbnr   at 0*word range 1 . . 4;
        err    at 0*word range 5 . . 5;
end record;
for inchar use at 8#77500#;
for status use at 8#77501#;
```

PROCESSCHAR must be changed to obtain a new character from the status and data buffers if there is one. The main loop of the device handler can still have a delay statement, but it should be quite a bit smaller to keep from losing data.

Chapter 15

Problem 1

Use an index variable local to the task that remembers the last position in the bitmap. Efficiency may be further increased if this index is set to the last page released (at least for one page reservation request).

Problem 2

Given the bitmap implementation that manages free and reserved space, several pages (sufficient to store the bitmap) must be reserved to contain the bitmap. Care should be taken that no one is allowed to deallocate the bitmap pages. Cold start initializes the bitmap and writes it to disc, while warm start reads it from disc and installs the disc copy into the bitmap. Since either warm start or cold start should be performed before allowing the allocation or deallocation of pages, no problems should occur with respect to the initial integrity of the bitmap. (Although you might want to protect yourself against random disc defects and their affect on the bitmap.)

Maintaining the consistency of the main memory and the disc copies can be a problem. If you write the bitmap after each change, a great deal of congestion can be created which only serves to increase the latency time between the change in memory and the change on the disc. Periodic checkpoints provide less congestion, but less safety as well.

Presumably, the space manager routines should interact with the I/O manager in the same manner as other system or user routines. However, since they are encapsulated within the same package, private arrangements between the two tasks can be made that might improve the efficiency of the checkpointing process.

Problem 3

Create two lists: the first represents requests that are before or on the current track; the second represents requests after the current track (i.e., 1 . . m, m + 1 . . n, where m is the current track). When a new request is to be scheduled, pick the closer of the two requests at the heads of each list. (Note: this can be implemented with one list and two pointers.) Some thought should be given to starvation - - that is, requests that never get serviced because they never are near enough to the current track. This problem is one of the main disadvantages of this policy.

Problem 4

A straightforward loop implementation.

Problem 5

There is no way that a task can wait on an accept statement and wait for an entry call to complete at the same time, that is, wait for the interrupt and wait for a request to be provided by the scheduler. However, the disc handler can wait on two entries at the same time. Provide a SERVICE procedure in the package DiscHandler and have it rename an additional entry SERVICE in task *dh*. Replace the current call to the scheduler service routine with a select statement that accepts both the service entry and the interrupt entry. Define an intermediary task that has no interface and which loops first calling the scheduler service routine and then passing the *dcb* on to the disc handler by calling its service routine.

Problem 6

Additional information is required in the package DiscCharacteristics: the number of discs. The number of pages calculation must reflect this fact. The conversion routine then maps the page onto the appropriate disc (pages 1 . . N are in the first disc, pages N + 1 . . . on the second disc, etc.). One further element is required in the disc address record: the disc number, 0 . . N - 1.

Chapter 16

Problem 1

Enclose the current accept statement and an accept statement for the new entry ENTER in a select statement. Within the accept statement, first hash the key and then look for an empty entry. When found, insert the new key.

Problem 2

```
select
        accept RESULT ( . . . ) do . . . end RESULT;
        if . . . -- abort the other task
or
        delay sometime;
        abort ODD, EVEN;
end select;
```

Problem 3

Before the search begins, record whether the starting index is odd or even. Replace the index increment statement by an if statement that checks for excession of the table size and restart at the appropriate beginning index value.

Problem 4

See the discussion earlier in the chapter for implementation details. The removing of the reference effectively deallocates the tasks and by implication, aborts them.

Problem 5

Straightforward implementation: the only thing that has to change is the type definition, if the access type denotes an array of characters, because the subscripting automatically dereferences the access type.

Problem 6

The lookup entry can be extended to include the parameter N which is then used as the upper index bound in an array of search tasks. In the search task, modify the increment statement to use N rather than 2. The easiest solution for stopping the tasks is to abort them all.

Appendix

Problem 1

The interface procedure WAITREQUEST must have the request as an in parameter instead of an out parameter. The list of servers, *servlist*, should be indexed by request rather than priority and the server listed according to the request it is willing to service. The strategy of the dispatching operation should reflect the change: schedule requests according to priority if possible; if no server is available for a request, check the next request. (Note that a new list operation is needed: REMOVE a particular element).

Problem 2

Change the dispatching program to signal producers before requests are made for resources. Associate a count with each type of request and attempt to keep that many results ahead of requests. The requirement to keep n results ahead will be sufficient to schedule the necessary producers. The dispatching of results must now change so that results are given out either when requested or when available. An extra list indexed by *request* is required to store the results.

Problem 3

Add the operation CHANGEPRIORITY to the interface so that it takes the *signal* as a parameter. If the request is still queued waiting to be serviced, remove it from the current priority list and put it a the end of the new priority list. Several policies are possible: the first, allow only a single change, that from the original priority to the new (in this case, the search for the request is limited to the priority list specified in the signal); second, allow an arbitrary number of changes (in this case, all the lists must be searched). If the request is currently being serviced, the operation has no effect.

Problem 4

In the dispatching routine, loop in reverse beginning at the next lower priority and remove the head of the list and put it at the tail of the next higher prioriy. An alternate implementation might put the lower priority request at the tail of the next higher, non - empty priority list.

Problem 5

Replace the type *request* by the type *event*. The interface operations simplify to two basic operations: WAIT and SIGNAL with events as parameters. A simplified version of the type *signal* can be used to implement the scheduling of the events (i.e., without the result field). In addition, the underlying implementation is simpler: only a wait list for each event is required with each list ordered by priority (assume that an INSERTAFTER operation exists in the list package). No dispatching routine is required since the effect of signalling the event will be immediate; the scheduling segment accepting event waits and signals is all that is required: the wait entry queues the process and the signal entry satisfies the head of the event list. Note that the use of the coordinating semaphore is needed only for the wait operation, and not for the signal operation.

Problem 6

Change the signal entry accept statement to signal all the processes queued on the wait list.

Problem 7

Provide a private type *event* (not a limited private type since the event must be copyable) and allocation/deallocation operations. The easiest way of implementing the event type is by means of a set of integers. The simplest is to have a predefined set, 1 . . n -- this implies an *outofevents* exception. However, the underlying implementation is simply an array of event wait lists indexed by the event. A more dynamic implementation allows any number of events and can best be implemented by a list of event wait lists. A flag in both cases can be used to determine whether a particular integer is available for allocation as an event.

Two strategies are possible concerning the deallocation of an event. First, do not allow the deallocation if the event has waiters. Second, deallocate the event but cause an exception to be raised in the wait operation. The latter requires a field in the intermediate *signal* type to indicate whether the event occurred or was deallocated so that the wait operation can provide the appropriate completion of operations.

INDEX

473